Luminos is the Open Access monograph publishing program from UC Press. Luminos provides a framework for preserving and reinvigorating monograph publishing for the future and increases the reach and visibility of important scholarly work. Titles published in the UC Press Luminos model are published with the same high standards for selection, peer review, production, and marketing as those in our traditional program. www.luminosoa.org

Multiculturalism in the British Commonwealth

Multiculturalism in the British Commonwealth

Comparative Perspectives on Theory and Practice

Edited by

Richard T. Ashcroft and Mark Bevir

UNIVERSITY OF CALIFORNIA PRESS

University of California Press, one of the most distinguished university presses in the United States, enriches lives around the world by advancing scholarship in the humanities, social sciences, and natural sciences. Its activities are supported by the UC Press Foundation and by philanthropic contributions from individuals and institutions. For more information, visit www.ucpress.edu.

University of California Press
Oakland, California

Suggested citation: Ashcroft, R. T. and Bevir, M. (eds.) *Multiculturalism in the British Commonwealth: Comparative Perspectives on Theory and Practice*. Oakland: University of California Press, 2019. DOI: https://doi.org/10.1525/luminos.73

Library of Congress Cataloging-in-Publication Data

Names: Ashcroft, Richard T., editor. | Bevir, Mark, editor.
Title: Multiculturalism in the British Commonwealth : comparative
    perspectives on theory and practice / edited by Richard T. Ashcroft and
    Mark Bevir.
Description: Oakland, California : University of California Press, [2019] |
    Includes bibliographical references and index. | This work is licensed
    under a Creative Commons [CC-BY-NC-ND] license. To view a copy of the
    license, visit: http://creativecommons.org/licenses . |
Identifiers: LCCN 2018045364 (print) | LCCN 2018048601 (ebook) | ISBN
    9780520971103 | ISBN 9780520299320 (pbk. : alk. paper)
Subjects: LCSH: Multiculturalism—Commonwealth countries—20th century.
Classification: LCC HM1271 (ebook) | LCC HM1271 .M84327 2017 (print) | DDC
    305.800971241/0905—dc23
LC record available at https://lccn.loc.gov/2018045364

27 26 25 24 23 22 21 20 19
10 9 8 7 6 5 4 3 2 1

When I read about clashes around the world—political clashes, economic clashes, cultural clashes—I am reminded that it is within our power to build a bridge to be crossed. Even if my neighbour doesn't understand my religion or my politics, he can understand my story. If he can understand my story, then he's never too far from me. It is always within my power to build a bridge. There is always a chance for reconciliation, a chance that one day he and I will sit around a table together and put an end to our history of clashes. And on this day, he will tell me his story and I will tell him mine.

—PAULO COEHLO

FIGURE 1. The Sackler Crossing, Royal Botanic Gardens, Kew, London. Copyright Chris Woodfield 2016.

This volume is dedicated to the memory of Chris Woodfield, who built bridges, and to his wife Jo, who walks on them still. With love and pride, Richard.

CONTENTS

PART III. MULTICULTURALISM IN THE "NEW" COMMONWEALTH

ACKNOWLEDGMENTS

Multiculturalism in the British Commonwealth: Comparative Perspectives on Theory and Practice derives from a conference held at the University of California, Berkeley, in 2014. The editors are grateful to the Mellon Foundation for their generous support of that conference. We would also like to thank Niels Hooper, Bradley Depew, and Archna Patel at the University of California Press for their help in bringing the project to a successful conclusion. Dr. Ashcroft would like to thank Rachel Bernhard and Mark Fisher for their insightful written comments on drafts of the editors' chapters, and for their ongoing support and encouragement. He would also like to thank Kristi Govella for her help copyediting the manuscript.

What is Postwar Multiculturalism in Theory and Practice?

Richard T. Ashcroft, University of California, Berkeley
Mark Bevir, University of California, Berkeley

Cultural diversity raises pressing issues for both political theory and practice. The remaking of the world since 1945 has increased demographic diversity within many states, and led to greater acknowledgment of the value of social heterogeneity. The heightened awareness of difference has contributed to pressure on traditional forms of liberal-democratic governance, which historically have operated within polities that are—or at least have assumed themselves to be—broadly culturally homogeneous. The term "multiculturalism" refers to the political, legal and philosophical strategies that emerged after World War II to accommodate this new-found social diversity. For much of this period, multiculturalism enjoyed a steady rise to prominence, but in recent years the growing consensus has been questioned by politicians and prominent social commentators. Whether this amounts to a "retreat" or "rebalancing" is still being debated, but it is clear that multiculturalism is being reevaluated. This volume adds to the existing empirical and normative literature by situating modern multiculturalism in its national, international, and historical contexts, bringing together practitioners from across the humanities and social sciences. It addresses questions vital for understanding contemporary debates: What is "multiculturalism," and why did it come about? What dilemmas has it posed for liberal-democratic governance? How have these been responded to in theory and practice, and are the different responses adequate? Are there alternative approaches to cultural diversity that have been overlooked?

We start this introductory chapter by sketching the different issues that may be characterized as "multicultural," noting how the scope of the term varies between different contexts and straddles theory and practice. We nevertheless provide a rough definition to help guide our analysis, and situate modern multiculturalism historically. We trace the connection between contemporary debates and the period of decolonization and globalization following World War II, which itself has its roots in the interrelated rise of nation, state, and empire in the early modern period. We demonstrate that the Commonwealth is a crucial context for studying multiculturalism, gathering together the key philosophical and empirical issues. We then show how this volume contributes to the literature by facilitating fruitful comparison across national, historical, and disciplinary boundaries. Finally, we set out the structure of the volume, and summarize the chapters that follow.

WHAT IS MULTICULTURALISM?

To call a society "multicultural" is to claim that it contains multiple cultural groups rather than just one. In the abstract, therefore, "multiculturalism" is simply the opposite of cultural homogeneity. In concrete terms, however, "multiculturalism" evokes a series of discourses regarding the appropriate way to respond to cultural and other forms of difference. These debates cover a wide variety of topics, including appropriate modes of dress, land rights, anti-racism, religious freedom, court procedure, immigration, language and educational policy, the scope of human rights, and even the basic structure and aims of the polis. The study of multiculturalism thus provides a meeting point for a variety of scholarly disciplines, including social science, law, history, anthropology, philosophy, and public policy. Discussion of multiculturalism is not limited to academia, however, but is also prominent in political and popular discourse.

In common use, the term "multiculturalism" can relate to a number of connected phenomena. For example, it may simply refer to the basic sociological fact of diversity, or alternatively to the challenges this diversity presents to our modes of thinking and governing. Sometimes it will directly invoke the policy or legal responses to these challenges, and some uses indicate normative approval of multicultural goals. Multiculturalism may be used as a catch-all term for the claims of marginalized groups, such as those who identify as LGBTQIA, people with disabilities, racial, ethnic and religious minorities, and women. A slightly different but overlapping usage refers to issues facing minority immigrants, and it is also frequently invoked in relation to minority national groups and indigenous peoples. Given the variegated nature of "multiculturalism," its meaning, application and value are inevitably contested, and subject to appropriation for different purposes in different contexts. This means we must guard against the temptation to reduce multiculturalism to a list of essential features that override its historicity.

Any simple definition of multiculturalism will therefore be potentially misleading, yet we must make some attempt to delineate the scope of our enquiry and enable comparison between the different cases.[1] The different multicultural debates bear a family resemblance to one another, and so it is possible to identify certain recurring situations which may usefully be labeled "multiculturalism."

For example, a common form of multiculturalism occurs where the practices of a previously dominant cultural group are challenged by the presence of a minority. Often members of the minority seek tolerance for behaviors that clash with majority norms, particularly if those norms have a disproportionate impact on their well-being. This may be accompanied by requests for exemptions from relevant legal provisions (e.g., regulations on animal slaughter), for reforms that facilitate the inclusion of the minority group (e.g., adapting rules on dress, language policies, or altering evidential procedure in courts), or for social policies aimed at promoting intra-societal understanding and inclusion (e.g., educational policy, reforming public symbols/holidays, or funding community activities).

Multiculturalism is not limited, however, to issues stemming from the interaction of minority and majority norms. It frequently engages broader issues in governance. For example, sometimes a minority will demand control of a practice, institution, or resource, such as the ability to conduct legal marriages, a separate religious court, or rights over land or language. Multiculturalism is thus also implicated in debates regarding fundamental aspects of the polis, including constitutional structures, national identity, immigration restrictions, basic rights, and forms of special political representation or self-rule. These questions can occur when there is no clear majority, but rather multiple groups co-exist within a polity. The precise scope of the term "multiculturalism" therefore varies across the different countries of the Commonwealth, but always involves the basic problem of how to manage deep-seated diversity, and consideration of the implications of this diversity for governance. Multiculturalism thus consistently challenges the validity of basic norms, and calls into question the political, economic and cultural processes through which they are expressed. Multiculturalism thereby inevitably poses societal dilemmas at the level of both theory and practice.

THEORY AND PRACTICE

There are several different senses of "theory" and "practice" relevant to this volume, the most salient of which relate to the understandings of multiculturalism in politics and academia.[2] In political practice, multiculturalism is largely construed in relation to postwar immigration. The central debate in this conceptualization is regarding the merits of assimilation versus integration, and how best to achieve the desired outcomes through adjustments in policy and law. This understanding of multiculturalism predominates worldwide in current political discourse and has been the subject of much recent public debate. Multiculturalism in academia is closely associated with political theory, where its scope is much broader than in political debates. In that literature, which is dominated by thinkers from Canada, Australia, and New Zealand, multiculturalism encompasses, not just immigrant integration, but also groups such as the Québécois and indigenous peoples and their claims for political autonomy or reparations.

Most uses of the term "multiculturalism" will draw on these understandings of its theory and practice, which continue to condition political and academic discourse even as they are subject to challenge. Yet there are other forms of theory and practice relevant to multiculturalism. For example, cultural diversity calls into question both standard methods of liberal-democratic governance, and the fundamental principles underlying them. Justifications of both liberalism and mass democracy are typically cast in terms of a moral universalism that presumes similarly situated individuals should be treated the same regardless of, inter alia, religion, race, sex, gender, culture, and sexual orientation. This traditional "difference-blind" approach has been called into question by multiculturalism, as have prominent formulations of doctrines such as political equality, state neutrality, and the rule of law. Increased cultural diversity highlights cleavages within liberal democracy masked by greater homogeneity, including those between individual rights and majority rule, positive and negative liberty, and between nation and state. These potentially destabilizing effects have been compounded by postwar immigration that threatened dearly held aspects of collective identities, including forms of national identity that many argue are necessary for liberal-democratic practice.[3] Multiculturalism therefore poses particularly acute problems for liberal democracies, highlighting tensions that straddle political philosophy and practice, between, for example, sameness and difference, public and private, local and central, individual and community, and particular and universal.

Furthermore, questions of theory and practice are not easily separated from each other even analytically. In broad terms, theory relates to how we understand the world, and practice to how we respond to the world by acting. Yet understanding and action inevitably feed into each other, and are therefore mutually constructing. Their interrelationship is especially clear in the case of multiculturalism, where theory and practice cut across each other *because* cultural diversity poses both pressing social questions and complex philosophical puzzles. In fact, multicultural adaptations to liberal-democratic governance are themselves attempts to mediate normative claims derived from abstract principles and the historical specificity of particular groups/issues. The challenges multiculturalism presents therefore vary in relation to the different political institutions, national histories, intellectual traditions, and forms of diversity present in each case. These contexts themselves alter how liberal democracy itself is understood in each country, feeding back into the ways practical problems and philosophical questions are tackled.

We propose that the interrelated nature of theory and practice is not, however, just a empirical feature of multiculturalism in postwar liberal democracies, but rather should be a basic philosophical presumption that informs how we approach its study. The editors share an underlying commitment to holism, which we have defended at length elsewhere.[4] Holism is grounded in the idea that we cannot approach facts or propositions in an isolated, atomistic way, as is typical in analytic philosophy or positivist social science. This means there are no entirely tautologous statements, pure facts, or self-evident truths, and so none of them can serve as unassailable foundations for our beliefs. Holism shows that our theories and observations—moral, political, and empirical—form an intertwined and mutually constructing set. Within these "webs of belief," our theories condition our observations and our experiences challenge our theories, which means there can be no points that are absolutely immune from revision. Instead, all knowledge arises within the contingent world view of particular individuals, who are in turn embedded in a nexus of traditions and practices constituted by the beliefs and actions of others. Abstract argument and empirical investigation are thus open-ended, and are undertaken by historically situated individuals against a background of overlapping influences. Holism therefore pushes us toward interpretivist forms of the human sciences and away from the logical positivism that still dominates modern social science research and government policy-making.[5] We should therefore privilege description and explanation, rather than prediction, and prefer certain types of empirical evidence over others. For example, holism indicates we should be wary of formal models that treat their data as atomized units of information to be processed, and focus instead on constructing continuous and coherent narratives. As holism commits us to the basic presumption that theory and practice constantly remake each other, it also implies that historical investigation and philosophical analysis are not separate activities, but rather must go hand in hand, and may productively inform each other.[6]

Proponents and critics of multiculturalism have, however, a common tendency to rely on unsubstantiated claims regarding the empirical consequences of multiculturalism, including the effects of multicultural political theory and political practice on each other.[7] Given the tangle of theoretical and practical issues raised by multiculturalism, it is unsurprising that the academic literature—in particular political theory—has fed into political and legal approaches to both immigrants and national minorities, and that theoretical understandings of multiculturalism have evolved in the light of political/legal practice as well as philosophical concerns.[8] Yet, while holism indicates that theory and practice are mutually constructing, it also suggests that this is a dynamic process that will take place in myriad different ways, constantly reshaping the beliefs and actions of particular actors. We must therefore be cautious of broad-brush claims regarding the *precise* effects of multicultural theory and practice, even as we acknowledge these effects must exist. Detailed historical study, including examining the relevant intellectual traditions and arguments, will be needed to recover these effects, and even then clear causation may be hard to establish. Any conclusions we draw regarding the theory and practice of multiculturalism are necessarily generalizations from concrete historical examples and must be applied with a suitable degree of caution.

Ultimately, therefore, holism foregrounds the importance of an integrated approach to studying multiculturalism. Particular beliefs, theories, or practices are neither plucked from the ether by pure reason nor revealed to consciousness by unmediated experience. They are only intelligible within an appropriately defined context, which must not only delineate the relevant concepts and modes of reasoning but should also foreground the dilemmas that have spurred a reevaluation—and potential reconstitution—of a set of beliefs and, through them, the broader theories and practices in which those beliefs are embedded. In order to understand multiculturalism in both its philosophical and empirical aspects, we must therefore situate it within its relevant historical, national, and intellectual contexts.

SITUATING POSTWAR MULTICULTURALISM

Although cultures have come into contact with each other throughout history, the problem of how to manage these interactions between and within states became especially prominent after 1945.[9] The parallel processes of decolonization and globalization set in motion the movement of both people and ideas on a vast scale, creating in many societies a substantive rise in cultural diversity and increased awareness of it. The related rise of human rights discourse, identity politics, and indigenous movements led to greater acknowledgement of the plight of minority groups, which in many societies prompted policies self-consciously addressing the challenges of cultural diversity. These policies started in the immediate aftermath of World War II, but became more prominent in the 1970s, when both Canada and Australia adopted official state multiculturalism. Many other liberal democracies adopted similar policy approaches in the following decades, with most public actors consistently endorsing multiculturalism in some form. The steady rise of multiculturalism was halted by the events of 9/11, which, as well as raising the specter of domestic terrorism, triggered the "war on terror" and the invasions of Afghanistan and Iraq. This has led some commentators to argue that multiculturalism is experiencing some form of crisis, adding fresh urgency to already volatile debates.[10]

Modern multiculturalism as a set of social realities and related series of discourses must therefore be situated primarily in the period from 1945 to the present day, which is the main focus of this volume. Its factual and philosophical roots go back much deeper, however, to the gradual, haphazard and contested rise of the nation and state as the dominant forms of social organization in the West. In the early modern period, the shift from smaller feudal and sacral communities to larger modern society gave rise to new forms of governance with which to manage the inevitable social upheaval.[11] As the modern liberal and bureaucratic state developed, it impinged on earlier forms of social organization, which inevitably provoked resistance, fueling conflict between the central and local. These tensions were exacerbated by the Reformation and the rapid socioeconomic changes driven by capitalism, with the rise of nationalism partly attributable to the dislocating effects of these. The modern nation-state thus evolved partly in order to manage greater social diversity, yet simultaneously facilitated forms of social and political cohesion operable on a far larger scale than in previous eras.

These developments coincided with the heyday of European imperialism, and both domestic and international policy during the nineteenth century were primarily narrated through developmental histories that valorized Enlightenment liberalism and rationalism.[12] Simple progressivist narratives became unsustainable in the twentieth century, however, when two world wars and a growing awareness of the realities of imperialism undercut assumptions regarding the superiority of the West. The postwar unraveling of imperialism therefore set the stage for contemporary multiculturalism by foregrounding hollow aspects of the West's self-understanding and causing a huge increase in its demographic diversity. Decolonization thus posed problems for liberalism and democracy at the level of both theory and practice, contributing directly to the series of postwar civic resettlements in both Europe and her former colonies. These reconstitutions of the state—and the self-understandings of the nation often conflated with it—resulted in the series of social dilemmas we refer to as "multiculturalism."

The British Commonwealth spans multiculturalism's relevant national, international, and historical contexts and therefore is vital for its study. The central sites of liberal-democratic governance are nations and states, which are both the fora within which the social world is remade and communities subject to that remaking. This means multiculturalism should be narrated in relation to national context, and the Commonwealth provides a rich array of cases to draw on. Given the direct connection of multiculturalism to imperialism, however, it cannot be understood purely as a domestic phenomenon. The intra- and international elements of multiculturalism are ineradicable, and thoughtful analysis requires an awareness of both. The Commonwealth foregrounds this dualism, forming a common context within which states have negotiated multiculturalism, and bringing about demographic, political, and cultural (including philosophical) connections between member countries. These connections have been forged primarily through Britain's imperial influence, but also through the "Old" Commonwealth's genesis of influential approaches to multiculturalism, and the "New" Commonwealth's role as a significant source of migrants to other member states.[13] The consistent movement of people, goods and ideas within the British Empire and Commonwealth has thus produced a degree of commonality across the member states, which aids our analysis. Utilizing it as a framework enables us to trace the different trajectories of multiculturalism, but also to find connected vantage points from which to compare these. For example, the Commonwealth provides a perspective from which to view both the nation-states and the cross-national movement central to multiculturalism. It also facilitates comparison across time and geographic locale, bridging the relevant short-, medium-, and long-term contexts. The Commonwealth and multiculturalism have grown alongside each other in the postwar period, and share roots in the earlier practices of imperialism and nation-state building that shaped modern liberal democracy. The rise and fall of empire is central to multiculturalism on both empirical and normative levels, which makes the Commonwealth a particularly useful framework for its study.

By cutting across disciplinary, temporal and geographical borders in one volume, *Multiculturalism in the British Commonwealth: Comparative Perspectives on Theory and Practice* highlights which aspects of multiculturalism are ubiquitous, and which are specific to particular localities. This volume thereby facilitates methodologically sound, intellectually fruitful comparison of the theory and practice of multiculturalism, enhancing previous scholarship. The literature is as variegated as multiculturalism itself, and so it is difficult to encapsulate it neatly or to identify clear gaps. Nevertheless, we can determine three main strands that this volume speaks to and enriches: political theory, specific case studies, and comparative work.

In the academy, multiculturalism is most closely associated with political theory, and has multiple strands which can be characterized in a variety of ways depending on one's purposes.[14] Nevertheless, it is possible to identify some features broadly accepted by advocates and opponents of multiculturalism alike. Most obviously, the agenda for the literature been shaped by the early work of the Canadian philosopher Will Kymlicka, which set out a liberal defense of multicultural rights grounded in the importance of culture for autonomous choice and self-respect.[15] The core debates revolve around the ability of liberalism to respond suitably to minority groups in both theory and practice, with Kymlicka's theory usually taken as the starting point.[16] The literature has been dominated by thinkers from the Old Commonwealth—especially Canada—which has likely contributed to a focus on concerns prominent in those countries. The political theory of multiculturalism is thus centered around appropriate policy approaches to, and the legal rights of, immigrant groups, minority nations such as the Québécois, and indigenous peoples. Most multicultural theorists utilize these categories of groups—albeit with varying levels of endorsement and rigidity—with the majority seeing them as entitled to different bundles of multicultural rights. Immigrant groups are usually only allocated "polyethnic" rights aimed at integrating them into the host society, whereas "national minorities" such the Québécois and indigenous groups are frequently seen as entitled to some form of political autonomy, with some theorists arguing that the latter also have a right to historical reparations.[17] There is therefore an overall tendency to separate groups and rights typologically, largely on the basis of the varying historical experiences of the relevant minorities and/or the putatively different role culture plays for the members of each. Whereas early multicultural theory tended to employ the universalist style of reasoning prevalent in post-Rawlsian liberal philosophy, subsequently there has been a shift toward more context-sensitive and politically oriented forms of theorizing.[18] This has led to qualification of the more robust normative claims associated with early philosophical multiculturalism, and a recent focus in Anglophone political theory on particular cases in their immediate historical circumstances. Nevertheless, most political theorists still utilize some form of the basic organizing typology of groups and rights drawn from the Old Commonwealth, and therefore the focus on immigrant groups and national minorities remains, as does the clear tendency of advocates of multiculturalism to limit claims to self-government to the latter.[19]

This volume makes an important contribution to the political theory literature in two main ways. Firstly, it highlights that the standard typology is tailored to historically specific situations and may have limited traction in contexts where not all of the groups are present. Also, by tracing the connections between the different forms of postwar multiculturalism, it demonstrates that even where all these groups are present, their precise interactions are conditioned by local factors, particularly their varying experiences of colonialism. In turn, this foregrounds problematic presumptions behind the ascription of different rights to different groups, particularly those grounded in functional accounts of the relationship between culture and liberal-democratic governance. For example, many prominent political theorists assume that "the nation" or "culture" plays a central—perhaps even necessary—role in governance.[20] Advocates of multicultural rights therefore tend to take for granted that there is a stable cultural "core" to the typical nation-state, which must be adjusted in response to minority claims, and critics often oppose multicultural rights on the grounds that they will erode common principles and values central to liberal democracy. Yet we will see that these sorts of assumptions have limited application in the New Commonwealth, and that the historical cases show the relationships between culture, nation, state, and governance to be both highly contingent and deeply conditioned by empire. This volume therefore complicates the typology of groups and rights that frames multiculturalism in political theory, foregrounding problematic assumptions behind it and forcing us to rethink central normative claims.

Secondly, this volume helps to mitigate a broader tension between universalist and contextualist approaches that poses risks for the study of multiculturalism. For example, abstract normative argument without an understanding of historical context falsely homogenizes real-world difference, yet methodological contextualism in turn has difficulty avoiding a relativism that loses normative purchase altogether. This volume considers multiculturalism without committing a priori to universalism or contextualism, and is therefore able to speak productively to both. Our case-by-case exploration of multiculturalism in its various historical, geographical, and temporal contexts militates against the homogenizing tendencies of universalist theory, but the overall volume highlights commonalities between the normative issues at play in different countries. It therefore provides material useful to both universalists and contextualists, while challenging extreme versions of either approach.

Another aspect of the multicultural literature is comprised of detailed investigations of individual countries, or specific cases within those countries.[21] This strand overlaps with some of the narrower contextualist case studies in political theory, but differs in that its primary focus is descriptive rather than normative. These case studies therefore tend to possess greater historical detail and depth than even the more empirically minded forms of political theory. Yet in doing so, they can lose sight of the international aspects of modern multiculturalism, or only assess these from a particular domestic perspective. This reduces the possibility of fruitful comparison across national contexts, and an empirical focus can mean that scant attention is paid to normative issues, which are inseparable from multiculturalism in both theory and practice. Even if descriptive accounts of the normative issues are provided, the lack of mechanisms for comparison and assessment make this literature less likely to address the core normative questions, or to do so in a context-specific way. Case studies thus run the risk of joining more radical contextualist political theory in focusing so tightly on particular circumstances that critical perspective is compromised.

As well as providing a series of detailed and insightful case studies of multiculturalism, the volume as a whole adds to the literature by retaining considerable historical depth without foregoing normative purchase. Using the Commonwealth to frame the array of cases covered in the different chapters ensures we do not lose sight of the fact that the different national contexts are connected by historical, international, and philosophical exchanges, which also influence the form multiculturalism takes within them. It ensures that the fundamental empirical and theoretical connections between multiculturalism, decolonization, and liberal-democratic governance are not hidden by the specific issues that occur in each country. This volume therefore facilitates comparison by highlighting the normative issues that reoccur across national contexts, while simultaneously throwing into relief their particular features.

The third aspect of the multiculturalism literature, and the one that this volume most obviously contributes to, is comparative in orientation. There are many excellent cross-national examinations of issues relevant to multiculturalism, embodying a vast array of methodologies, particular objects of study, and philosophical commitments. The comparative work on multiculturalism is therefore the most heterogeneous strand of the literature, and contains the greatest preponderance of self-consciously interdisciplinary work, making it difficult to summarize succinctly.[22] Some works focus on comparisons between countries within particular geographical areas or organizations, or nations grouped together on the basis that they raise similar issues or provide useful contrasts.[23] Other cross-national comparisons have focused on particular groups, such as indigenous peoples, or particular aspects of multicultural regimes, such as law, especially international or immigration law.[24] Yet others focus either on the broad outline of contemporary national policy regimes and discourses or on much more specific aspects of multicultural policies, including their social effects.[25]

The existing comparative work on multiculturalism is, of course, extremely valuable, but we hope to supplement it. Multiculturalism in all its aspects is part of a process of contestation in which individuals and communities remake their social structures and understandings—and thereby their individual and collective identities—through complex patterns of discourse and praxis. Politics, economics, and culture therefore interact in different ways in each context, constructing idiosyncratic forms of multiculturalism. Utilizing the Commonwealth as a framework brings out the subtleties of each country's response to cultural diversity, mitigating the risk of circumscribing our understanding of multiculturalism ahead of time through selecting a narrower metric of comparison. Placing contemporary multiculturalism against its historical backdrop also illustrates the ways in which long-term factors feed into current debates.[26] Examining the diverse historical sources of current legal and policy regimes mitigates the risk of reducing multiculturalism to current political and public understandings, thereby ignoring the thicker historical, cultural, and philosophical factors they draw on.

Overall, this volume speaks to and enriches all three main strands of the multicultural literature in ways that flow directly from our use of the Commonwealth as framework. Since the Commonwealth spans the relevant issues and time periods, we can approach multiculturalism in a holistic manner. Just as there is a family resemblance between the different issues that fall under "multiculturalism," there is also a family resemblance between the different countries in the Commonwealth that aids comparison across contexts and challenges assumptions prevalent in current debates. This volume will improve our understanding of any given national context, providing historical nuance that aids both comparison of contemporary policy debates and analysis of the normative issues, and we hope it will be a resource for scholars and students across various disciplines, sparking further scholarship.

STRUCTURE AND CONTENT

The volume is divided into three main sections, each dealing with a set of countries that raise distinctive but interrelated issues. The first section explores multiculturalism in the United Kingdom between 1945 and the present day. As the imperial metropole and subsequent head of the Commonwealth, Britain has been in a unique position to affect both the discourses and realties of multiculturalism, particularly in the immediate aftermath of World War II and the process of decolonization. This section will examine the political and legal trajectory of multiculturalism in the UK during this period, as well as analyzing historical and contemporary debates over Britishness and citizenship.

The second section looks at multiculturalism in the "Old" Commonwealth countries of Canada, Australia, and New Zealand.[27] These historically white-dominated settler colonies have a history that is dissimilar from most other parts of the former empire, and as "Greater Britain" their political, legal, economic, and cultural relationships with the UK were also substantively different. All three of these countries have had comparable processes of settlement, contact with indigenous peoples, and immigration, and are generally considered to be world leaders in official approaches to cultural diversity in the postwar era.

The third part of the book contains chapters on the "New" Commonwealth countries of India, Nigeria, Malaysia/Singapore, and Trinidad and Tobago. These countries, although culturally and politically disparate, are all marked by histories of internal religious and ethnic diversity, and their experiences of both colonization and independence differ substantially from the Old Commonwealth. There are a number of commonalities and connections between them, which sharpens our understanding of multiculturalism, throwing into relief experiences elsewhere.

PART I: BRITISH MULTICULTURALISM

In chapter 2, the volume editors take a long-term view of multiculturalism in Britain, charting its political and legal trajectory from World War II to the present day. We argue that the radical changes undergone in Britain since 1945 must be traced back to the process of decolonization, which forced a reassessment of Britain's place in the world. A cross-party attempt to secure the Commonwealth as a distinct British sphere of influence led directly to legal reforms that sparked an unanticipated influx of nonwhite immigration. This resulted in an idiosyncratic "regime" of multiculturalism, comprised of tough external immigration controls and a generous internal regime of race-relations legislation, welfare rights, and pluralist accommodations for minority cultural groups. The bifurcated approach remained broadly stable from 1962 on, but there has been a strong rhetorical and weaker policy shift in recent years. Our narrative demonstrates that multiculturalism in Britain is closely associated with debates over immigration, race, citizenship, and national identity, and we argue that the interaction of these debates were a significant cause of the Brexit vote and renewed calls for Scottish independence. We conclude that the framing of multiculturalism in Britain as solely relating to immigrant integration is therefore inadequate, since it hides deeper connections between multiculturalism, basic constitutional issues, and a British national identity struggling to define itself after empire.

In chapter 3, Nasar Meer and Tariq Modood explore controversies over multiculturalism in contemporary Britain, arguing that recent political rejections of it have not been reflected in a wholesale change of policy, and that it is helpful to think of British multiculturalism as undergoing a rebalancing, rather than retreat. They argue that the fluid nature of British multiculturalism means that it can be co-opted by different actors for a variety of purposes. They identify three main strands in contemporary British multiculturalism: a "cohesion" strand that emphasizes assimilation to majority norms; a secular and anti-essentialist account that focuses on "lifestyle" and behavioral identities; and a "political" multiculturalism, prominent since the 1990s, that incorporates the priorities of both of the above but also stresses the inclusion of ethno-religious minority groups. It is this latter form of multiculturalism that has been subject to rhetorical criticism and policy rebalancing, but even here they find that British politicians of all stripes define "Britishness" through a simultaneous appeal to political-institutional history and cultural diversity.

PART II: THE "OLD" COMMONWEALTH

In chapter 4, Avigail Eisenberg examines the most prominent example of state multiculturalism in the world, that of Canada. She argues that multiculturalism in Canadian politics usually only refers to the issues surrounding the protection and integration of nonwhite immigrants and not the separate cases of Quebec and indigenous peoples. Despite the separation of these groups into different "silos," they still interact with each other through political and legal contests in ways that undercut the aims of Canadian multiculturalism. Firstly, the constitutional entrenchment of multiculturalism has politicized it by overriding the more local measures of the 1970s, which has prompted Quebec to allege anti-democratic overreach by the federal government. Secondly, multicultural policy is operationalized through a legal mechanism of "reasonable accommodation," which assumes that majority practices are a norm from which deviation must be justified. Thirdly, collective rights of groups have been subject to a "distinctive culture test" colored by the above, which renders legal remedies superficial and ignores deeper concerns over identity, recognition, and colonialism. Eisenberg concludes that the Canadian multicultural provisions and the normative ideals that underlie them have therefore been politicized and distorted, and instead of fulfilling principles of cultural equality and democratic inclusion, current arrangements rather aim at accommodating difference without disturbing the status quo.

In chapter 5, Geoffrey Brahm Levey shows that Australian multiculturalism has a distinctive architecture. He argues that Australian state multiculturalism is best understood as an expression of a broader "liberal nationalist" approach to national identity, citizenship, and cultural diversity that emerged as part of a reassessment of Australian identity. He sees three animating propositions in Australian multiculturalism as it relates to this question of national identity. Firstly, Anglo-Australian identity and culture were formative in establishing Australia's institutions and "way of life," and should be duly acknowledged. Secondly, national identity will inevitably change over time with the changing composition of Australian society. Thirdly, it must be ensured that all Australians, including those not of the majority culture, enjoy the same rights and opportunities. Levey concludes that Australian multiculturalism is a policy framework that seeks to check the cultural-nationalist aspects of the core culture from overreaching and violating its liberal-democratic aspects. This feature of Australian multiculturalism is not well grasped by the political class or the general public, and therefore those who cite Australia as further evidence of a worldwide trend toward liberal universalism, or a purely civic conception of the nation, fundamentally misread the Australian case.

In chapter 6, Katherine Smits shows that New Zealand is both bicultural and multicultural. The term "multiculturalism" was first introduced in New Zealand in the 1970s to refer to settler-Maori relations, but it is now assumed to apply to the diversity resulting from non-British immigration. She argues that cultural pluralism in New Zealand is shaped by the interactions between shifting and competing discourses regarding multi- and biculturalism, indigenous peoples and civic values. New Zealand's national identity historically contains a strong commitment to social justice, but this was challenged by the neoliberalism of the mid-1980s. The related "rebranding" of New Zealand was aimed partly at encouraging foreign investment, but it also attempted to co-opt Maori communal values to mitigate the internal effects of welfare cuts. Public resistance was articulated through liberal nationalism cast in social justice terms, and by the Maori, who made calls for self-government under the Treaty of Waitangi and emerging international norms. New Zealand's multiculturalism is therefore framed by the values and discourses of the various political, economic, and nationalist projects of state and nonstate actors. Yet it is also developed and invoked in order to support them, becoming a form of governmentality sustained by languages of value.

PART III: THE "NEW" COMMONWEALTH

In chapter 7, Rochana Bajpai details the "multicultural" elements in the Indian Constitution of 1950 that predate similar policies in Western democracies. These have given rise to an extensive regime of group rights that ranges across many policy areas and levels of government. Bajpai puts forward three key theses regarding the constitutional settlement and Indian multiculturalism more broadly. Firstly, rejection of colonial forms of devolved governance and the convergence of the interests of liberals and nationalists during constitution-making led to the emergence of a multicultural framework that was significantly "limited" in several respects. Secondly, India's constitutional compromise on multiculturalism suffers from a deficit in terms of normative justification, eliding the distinction between rights for members of groups, and rights for groups. Thirdly, although there has been a gradual expansion of multicultural policies, because of the normative deficit these are seen as discretionary concessions motivated by electoral considerations rather than matters of justice, which in turn plays into the rhetorical strategies of the Hindu Right. Bajpai concludes that multiculturalism in India therefore needs to recover resources from a range of alternative traditions to justify multiculturalism, and to complement the recent discursive shift back toward communitarian secularism, group rights, fair equality of opportunity, and more radical participatory democracy.

In chapter 8, Farah Godrej analyzes what appears to be an ambivalence about the notion of secularism in Gandhi's thought, which she argues is due to two different conceptions of religion. The first sees religion as a practice-based seeking after truth through reflection on one's own conscience, in the light of one's own religious traditions. This view relies on the Jainist metaphysic of *anekantavada,* which sees divine truth as something that can only ever be partially understood by a human mind situated in particular circumstances. The second view understands religion as claiming absolute doctrinal truth, which is the view of religion implicit in the metaphysics of the Abrahamic religions and at work in colonial missionary practices. Godrej argues that Gandhi thought the first "private" understanding of religion could nevertheless usefully inform a public political practice of engagement with other views, but that the second form of religion should be strictly separated from politics because of its tendency to facilitate competition and ideological entrenchment. This reconstruction of Gandhi's views shows him to have been prophetic regarding the debates around religion and secularism in modern India, which are arguably driven by a Western understanding of secularism that is anathema in the Indian context historically, politically, and on a deeper metaphysical level.

In chapter 9, Wale Adebanwi traces the history of cultural diversity in Nigeria, showing how it is intimately connected to colonial forms of rule and the influence of these on constitutional negotiations around independence. He argues that the federalism adopted at independence based on the existing administrative regions was problematic, since it institutionalized an unstable tripartite balance of power, encouraging the regions to become loci of loyalty competing with the nation itself, while simultaneously glossing over the existence of more than three hundred underlying minority groups. This led to civil war and (eventually) a more radical but more stable form of devolved government that better reflects Nigeria's vast diversity. Adebanwi concludes that the compromised form of federalism adopted at independence was largely the result of British practices of rule that constructed, not just the country itself, but also the problematic discourses through which the indigenous groups understood one another. This created an overall understanding of multiculturalism as a "menace," as well as a broader suspicion of polycentric government. This narrative is symptomatic of broader issues in postcolonial Africa, where failure adequately to manage multicultural difference has frequently led to overt or covert centralization, dictatorship, and the silencing of minorities.

In chapter 10, Daniel Goh examines the twin cases of Malaysia and Singapore. Against conventional explanations privileging nationalism, Goh argues that the key influence in each was state-building related to capitalist development, which responded to the contradictions of colonial and postcolonial racial formation. Given the racialized character of the division of labor inherited from Britain, each side pushed for a political multiracialism that suited its economic approach. This meant the state builders eventually fell out, because Singapore looked toward transforming itself into an industrial hub, while Kuala Lumpur privileged agrarian and natural resource capitalist development. Patronage multiracialism aligned with economic policy favoring the *bumiputera* ("son of the soil" in the Malay language) was institutionalized in Malaysia, whereas corporatist multiracialism abetting statist capital accumulation was pursued in Singapore. Goh argues that by the 1980s and 1990s the contradictions of postcolonial racial formation were surfacing in both states, which led to the adoption of new forms of multiculturalism supposedly more suited to an era of globalization. In the era of global financial crises, however, the old multiracialisms remain institutionally dominant over the new forms of multiculturalism. Goh concludes that although Malaysia and Singapore developed their political institutions and economies divergently and on different multiracial premises, the evolution of their forms of multiculturalism have been "arrested" by underlying political and economic contradictions.

In chapter 11, Viranjini Munasinghe examines the case of Trinidad and Tobago, concentrating on the approach to cultural diversity on the politically dominant, and more populous and diverse, island of Trinidad.[28] She argues that the absence of a clear symbolic core to the nation—whether homogeneous settler, or indigenous—shapes Trinidadian multiculturalism. This multiculturalism is marked by a struggle where ethnic groups battle for the nation against the background of a rigid colonial racial hierarchy of Europeans as masters, Africans as slaves, and East Indians as indentured laborers. The legacy of this colonial racialization, combined with national imperatives to indigenize and mediate diversity, subsequently fixed African ancestry as the ideological culture-history referent. This made Afro-Creoles the legitimate inheritors of both nation and state, a cultural hegemony that, ironically, draws sustenance from homogenizing national narratives that invest only some groups with "native" privilege. Munasinghe concludes that more recent Indo-Trinidadian charges of state bias in sponsorship of Afro-Trinidadian culture have been possible only because homogenizing national narratives of creolization did not (or could not) establish an uncontestable new purity. In Trinidad, the dialectical play between homogenizing and cosmopolitan narratives and metaphors, founded on colonial race hierarchies, continues to resist consolidation of either African or Indian ancestry as the nation's symbolic core.

CONCLUSIONS

Multiculturalism is comprised of a series of overlapping issues and discourses, with the precise nature of what is at stake varying from country to country. This fluidity makes identifying common themes and questions difficult. As editors, we therefore decided to let the authors speak for themselves before drawing the different threads together in a concluding chapter. There we provide a philosophically inflected comparison of the different historical examples of multiculturalism that accounts for the variety across the Commonwealth, yet also draws out the deeper connections between its different forms. We argue that the dominant forms of multiculturalism in theory and practice are unduly narrow, leading to an unhelpful siloing of "multicultural" issues, groups, and rights. Ultimately, we conclude that achieving a fruitful, holistic multiculturalism requires modes of governance that are far more polycentric and pluralist than present ones.

"Multiculturalism" as we have narrated it here is part of the wider story of the development of the modern state through liberal-democratic governance, domestic nation- and state-building, and the rise and fall of imperialism. Britain is of course central to this story. As the leading imperial power, the first country to industrialize, and the progenitor of much modern liberal theory and practice, Britain has had a unique role—for good or ill—in forming the modern world. This role has helped to forge indelible connections between otherwise radically different countries, and the collapse of the British Empire after 1945 prompted a fundamental remaking of those nations and states. The postwar British Commonwealth is therefore vital for understanding the evolution of modern multiculturalism, and the dilemmas it poses for the theory and practice of contemporary liberal democracy.

NOTES

1. For another discussion of the scope of multiculturalism, see Jacob T. Levy, *The Multiculturalism of Fear* (Oxford: Oxford University Press, 2000), chap. 5. We share his view that in such accounts "[u]sefulness, not truth, is the goal" (p. 125). Imposing a rigid typology of multicultural groups of rights is unhelpful.

2. For a differing account of the relationship between the theory and practice of multiculturalism, see Will Kymlicka, "The Essentialist Critique of Multiculturalism: Theories, Policies, Ethos," in Varun Uberoi and Tariq Modood, eds., *Multiculturalism Rethought: Interpretations, Dilemmas, New Directions* (Edinburgh: Edinburgh University Press, 2015), 209–49. Kymlicka's organizing vocabulary in "The Essentialist Critique" is different from ours, revolving around the distinction between philosophical approaches, actual policies, and real-world outcomes. By multicultural "policy," he means government responses to the full range of issues/groups covered by the political theory of multiculturalism. By "practice," he generally means the social outcomes of those policies, although he alleges his critics blur the distinction between the results of government policies and the philosophical justifications behind them (ibid., 225–29). In contrast, we use "policy" or "political practice" to mean government attempts to integrate minority immigrants, and the accompanying public debates. We distinguish multicultural policy/practice in this sense from the broader scope of the term "multiculturalism" in political theory. Nevertheless, our commitment to philosophical holism means that at some points we use "practice" as a more general contrast to "theory" in order to distinguish theoretical "webs of belief" from the social practices in which they are instantiated. Some of Kymlicka's arguments in "The Essentialist Critique" against the thinkers he calls "post-multiculturalist" turn on something like this broader distinction, although we believe our defense of polycentricity is not caught by these. In any event, the different uses of the terms are either specified or (we hope) clear from the context.

3. There is a clear historical correlation between the rise of liberal democracy and the development of the modern nation-state, and long-standing theoretical connections traceable to, inter alia, J. S. Mill (see "Of Nationality as Connected with Representative Government" in Mill, *Considerations on Representative Government* [London: Parker, Son, & Bourn, 1861]). Many scholars have subsequently argued that some version of the cultural nation plays a key role in the functioning of modern governance, e.g., Benedict Anderson, Ernest Gellner, and David Miller.

4. See Richard T. Ashcroft and Mark Bevir, "Liberal Democracy, Nationalism and Culture: Multiculturalism and Scottish Independence," *Critical Review of International Social and Political Philosophy*

21, no. 1 (2018): 65–86; Richard Ashcroft and Mark Bevir, "Pluralism, National Identity and Citizenship: Britain after Brexit," *Political Quarterly* 87 (2016): 355–59; and Mark Bevir, *The Logic of the History of Ideas* (Cambridge: Cambridge University Press, 1999).

5. See Mark Bevir, *A Theory of Governance* (Berkeley: University of California Press, 2013).

6. For instance, holism suggests that the application of existing theoretical frameworks is necessary for ordering and analyzing historical data, even if these frameworks must remain open to revision in the light of new information. Nevertheless, while we know that theory and practice continually remake each other, the ways in which they do so are not always apparent. Historical investigation may help to foreground these processes, thereby illuminating the dilemmas that have spurred reconstitution of beliefs, the traditions those beliefs draw on, and the practices through which they are expressed. Philosophical analysis of the normative issues raised by practical examples may thereby highlight over-looked similarities between different concrete cases, suggesting a change in how we approach these in practice. Inversely, a comparative historical examination may help to clarify the normative issues at stake, thereby problematizing existing philosophical frameworks and pointing to the value of a new set of philosophical questions and political arrangements.

7. These claims can be regarding the results of specific polices, laws, and discourses, or the broader social consequences of cultural diversity. We therefore agree with Kymlicka that clear evidence of the effects of multicultural policies in liberal democracies is "not easy to locate", and is both "tentative" and "preliminary" (Kymlicka, "Essentialist Critique," 216–17). It is notable, however, that Kymlicka attempts to assess the effects of multiculturalism on substate national minorities, indigenous peoples, and immigrant groups separately. We argue that this sort of typological separation of multicultural groups and rights is unstable philosophically and ineffective in political practice, which indicates that assessment of the real-world effects of multiculturalism should also be holistic, requiring both historical and philosophical investigation.

8. The influence of practice on theory can be seen in Kymlicka's later work (e.g., *Multicultural Odysseys: Navigating the New International Politics of Diversity* [Oxford: Oxford University Press, 2007], and "Essentialist Critique"), which is more empirical and comparative than his earlier more philosophical work (see his *Liberalism, Community, and Culture* [Oxford: Oxford University Press, 1989], and *Multicultural Citizenship: A Liberal Theory of Minority Rights* [Oxford: Oxford University Press, 1995]).

9. For a series of "histories" of the multicultural debate see "Introduction" and "Part I: Trajectories" of Anthony Simon Laden and David Owen, eds., *Multiculturalism and Political Theory* (Cambridge: Cambridge University Press, 2007). These histories emphasize different aspects of the debates, but are broadly compatible with each other and our account. While the connection to decolonization is widely acknowledged, we differ by foregrounding the ways in which the intersection of liberal, colonial, and multicultural governance conditioned the various forms of postwar multiculturalism, and in our suggested response of polycentricity and pluralism.

10. See Christian Joppke, "The Retreat of Multiculturalism in the Liberal State: Theory and Policy," *British Journal of Sociology* 55 (2004): 237–57.

11. Benedict Anderson, Ernest Gellner, Michel Foucault, Karl Polanyi, and Max Weber, all argue for this in their different ways.

12. See *Historicism and the Human Sciences in Victorian Britain,* ed. Mark Bevir (Cambridge: Cambridge University Press, 2017).

13. For convenience we use "United Kingdom" and "Britain" interchangeably, i.e., including Northern Ireland in both. We use "Old" and "New" Commonwealth to distinguish the white-settler colonies of Canada, Australia, and New Zealand from other colonies in the Empire that were never intended to be permanently settled by the British, and whose relationship to Great Britain was marked by more nakedly extractive practices. These terms have functioned historically as thinly veiled proxies for race, and their use is more common in Britain than elsewhere, but even though this volume problematizes them, we find the distinction helpful as shorthand. For the reasons given in n. 27 below, we do not generally include South Africa and Zimbabwe in the Old Commonwealth.

14. Different theorists conceptualize the debates according to their particular concerns, but many of these accounts are complementary rather than competing. For instance, multiculturalism is both a debate *within* liberalism between strands of universalism and contextualism, and a debate *between* liberalism and its communitarian, republican, and postcolonial critics. Multiculturalism is often associated with the identarian "politics of difference," yet this can be cast in terms of both "positional" and "cultural" difference, as it is by Iris Marion Young (see her "Structural Injustice and the Politics of Difference," in Laden and Owen, eds., *Multiculturalism and Political Theory*, 60–88). Nevertheless, it seems generally accepted that the early association of multicultural political theory with the claims of minority groups that were not overtly cultural (e.g., women or those with disabilities) later shifted to a focus on issues relating to immigrants and national minorities. The "politics of difference" is closely related to the "politics of recognition," which is broken down by Charles Taylor into the "politics of equal dignity" and the "politics of difference" (Charles Taylor, "The Politics of Recognition," in Amy Gutmann, ed., *Multiculturalism: Examining the Politics of Recognition* [Princeton, NJ: Princeton University Press, 1994]). In turn, multiculturalism as the "politics of recognition" is often contrasted—albeit controversially—with the "politics of redistribution" more closely associated with liberal egalitarian and social democratic theory (see Nancy Fraser's "From Redistribution to Recognition? Dilemmas of Justice in a 'Post-Socialist' Age," *New Left Review* 1, no. 12, July–August 1995, and Brian Barry's *Culture and Equality* [Malden, MA: Polity Press, 2001]). Feminist theory arguably cuts across all of these debates, with different theorists falling on different sides of the various divides. For useful introductions to, and summaries of, the political theory literature along these lines see Laden and Owen, eds., *Multiculturalism and Political Theory*; Sarah Song, *Justice, Gender and the Politics of Multiculturalism* (Cambridge: Cambridge University Press, 2007); and Song, "Multiculturalism," in *The Stanford Encyclopedia of Philosophy*, ed. Edward N. Zalta, accessed November 19, 2018, https://plato.stanford.edu/archives/spr2017/entries/multiculturalism.

15. See Kymlicka, *Liberalism, Community, and Culture* and *Multicultural Citizenship*.

16. See Laden and Owen, eds., *Multiculturalism and Political Theory*, 7. Prominent respondents to Kymlicka include Charles Taylor, Iris Marion Young, Susan Moller Okin, Brian Barry, Chandran Kukathas, Bhikhu Parekh, James Tully, Roger Scruton, Jacob T. Levy, Seyla Benhabib, Kwame Anthony Appiah, Jeremy Waldron, and Sarah Song.

17. See James Tully, *Strange Multiplicity: Constitutionalism in the Age of Diversity* (Cambridge: Cambridge University Press, 1995), and Glen Sean Coulthard, *Red Skin, White Masks: Rejecting the Colonial Politics of Recognition* (Minneapolis: University of Minnesota Press, 2014).

18. "Context-sensitive" covers a broad range of theoretical approaches, ranging from utilizing historical examples to illustrate abstract points to more radical approaches that use historical context to generate normativity itself. For a fuller discussion, see Jacob T. Levy, "Contextualism, Constitutionalism, and *Modus Vivendi* Approaches," in Owen and Laden, eds., *Multiculturalism and Political Theory*, 173–97. By "politically oriented" we mean approaches that prioritize actual political processes, in particular democratic deliberation, in determining outcomes. For a helpful discussion, see Anthony Simon Laden, "Negotiation, Deliberation, and the Claims of politics," in Owen and Laden, eds., *Multiculturalism and Political Theory*, 198–217. For a fuller account of the effect of the contextual turn on multicultural political theory, see Song "Multiculturalism," and for an example of work that is sensitive to both contextual and political strands without being conditioned by them, see her *Justice, Gender and the Politics of Multiculturalism*.

19. The separation of groups and rights is central to Kymlicka's theory of multiculturalism as set out in his early work, and his influence over liberal multiculturalism and the wider debate has ensured that his typology is ubiquitous in the literature. Some version of it also seems to be implicit in other defenses of multiculturalism, such as Charles Taylor's politics of recognition, which draws on Herderian accounts of culture and defends the right to cultural survival in perpetuity. Taylor's views on Quebec clearly suppose that minority national groups have rights to some form of self-government that immigrant groups do not: see the report he co-authored with Gérard Bouchard, *Report of the Commission*

on Accommodation Practices Related to Cultural Difference (Quebec: Government of Quebec, 2008). Postcolonial theorists such as Tully and Coulthard, who are critical of mainstream multiculturalism in theory and practice, also nevertheless advocate self-rule for indigenous groups historically subject to colonization, albeit that this does not turn squarely on the role of culture. Admittedly, some actors in the debate do not fall neatly into the typology as we have articulated it. For example, Iris Marion Young is broadly sympathetic to a multicultural politics of difference, yet rejects the usual multiculturalist focus on ethno-religious groups and the distribution of rights, instead focusing her critique on underlying structures of social power and domination. Alternative accounts of freedom from domination draw on civic republicanism and thereby emphasize the quality of social and political relations within and across groups, opening spaces for accommodations based on culture, as well as some group self-government that is not. Critics of Kymlicka such as Brian Barry, Susan Moller Okin, and Roger Scruton reject most "multicultural" rights on principle, including robust political autonomy for minority groups. Chandran Kukathas takes the opposite view, granting self-rule to any group or association that desires it, albeit not directly on the basis of culture (see Kukathas, *The Liberal Archipelago: A Theory of Diversity and Freedom* [Oxford: Oxford University Press, 2003]). The later Kymlicka does move away from a strict application of his typology towards a greater emphasis on international discourses and more context-sensitive forms of multiculturalism. We will discuss this shift in more detail in the concluding chapter to this volume, but for now it suffices to note that much of the later Kymlicka's work is comparative and empirical rather than political theory per se, and so the norm in theoretical accounts of multiculturalism is still to focus on immigrants, national minorities, and indigenous peoples as separate groups, and only seriously to contemplate substantive self-rule for the latter two.

20. Kymlicka's and Charles Taylor's multiculturalism has clear links to cultural nationalism (see notes 3 and 4 above), as do recent debates about "muscular liberalism" and national identity in the UK and elsewhere.

21. See Celeste Lipow MacLeod, *Multiethnic Australia: Its History and its Future* (Jefferson, NC: MacFarland, 2006); Alain G. Gagnon and Raffaele Iacovino, *Federalism, Citizenship and Quebec: Debating Multinationalism* (Toronto: University of Toronto Press, 2007); Alan C. Cairns, *First Nations and the Canadian State: In Search of Coexistence* (Kingston, Ont.: Institute of Intergovernmental Relations, Queen's University, 2005); Andrew Sharp, *Justice and the Māori: Māori Claims in New Zealand Political Argument in the 1980s* (Oxford: Oxford University Press, 1990); and Paul M. Sniderman and Louk Hagendoorn, *When Ways of Life Collide: Multiculturalism and Its Discontents in the Netherlands* (Princeton, NJ: Princeton University Press, 2009).

22. See Michael A. Burayidi, ed., *Multiculturalism in a Cross-National Perspective* (Lanham, MD: University Press of America, 1996); Fethi Mansouri, ed., *Cultural, Religious and Political Contestations: The Multicultural Challenge* (Cham, Zug, Switzerland: Springer, 2015); and Fethi Mansouri and Boulou Ébanda de B'béri, eds., *Global Perspectives on the Politics of Multiculturalism in the 21st Century: A Case Study Analysis* (London: Routledge, 2014).

23. See Ofra Bengio and Gabriel Ben-Dor, eds., *Minorities and the State in the Arab World* (Boulder, CO: Lynne Reiner, 1999); Maya Shatzmiller, ed., *Nationalism and Minority Identities in Islamic Societies* (Montreal and Kingston, Ont.: McGill–Queen's University Press 2005); Will Kymlicka and Baogang He, eds., *Multiculturalism in Asia* (Oxford: Oxford University Press, 2005); and Irene Bloemraad, *Becoming a Citizen: Incorporating Immigrants and Refugees in the United States and Canada* (Berkeley: University of California Press, 2006).

24. See James Crawford, *The Rights of Peoples* (Oxford: Clarendon Press, 1988); Samuel L. Myers and Bruce P. Corrie, eds., *Racial and Ethnic Economic Inequality: An International Perspective* (New York: Peter Lang, 2006); Paul Havemann, *Indigenous Peoples' Rights in Australia, Canada & New Zealand* (Oxford: Oxford University Press, 1999); Keith Banting and Will Kymlicka, eds., *Multiculturalism and the Welfare State: Recognition and Redistribution in Contemporary Democracies* (Oxford: Oxford University Press, 2006); Will Kymlicka, *Multicultural Odysseys* (Oxford: Oxford University Press, 2007), Rachel Sieder, ed., *Multiculturalism in Latin America: Indigenous Rights, Diversity and Democracy* (New

York: Palgrave Macmillan, 2002); and Christian Joppke, *Immigration and the Nation State: The United States, Germany, and Great Britain* (New York: Oxford University Press, 1999).

25. For the broader comparative work on policy, law, and governance, see e.g., Crawford Young, *Ethnic Diversity and Public Policy: A Comparative Inquiry* (New York: Macmillan, 1998); and Augie Fleras, *The Politics of Multiculturalism: Multicultural Governance in Comparative Perspective* (New York: Palgrave Macmillan, 2009). For a sample of the vast array of detailed work in the social sciences, see, e.g., Matthew Wright and Irene Bloemraad, "Is There a Trade-off between Multiculturalism and Socio-Political Integration? Policy Regimes and Immigrant Incorporation in Comparative Perspective," *Perspectives on Politics* 10, no. 1 (2012); John Sides and Jack Citrin, "European Opinion about Immigration: The Role of Identities, Interests and Information," *British Journal of Political Science* 37 (2007): 477–504; and Steven Weldon, "The Institutional Context of Tolerance for Ethnic Minorities: A Comparative, Multilevel Analysis of Western Europe," *American Journal of Political Science* 50, no. 2 (2006): 331–49.

26. Arguably *Multiculturalism in Asia* by Kymlicka and He is a work in a similar vein.

27. South Africa and Zimbabwe (formerly Rhodesia) can be considered part of the Old Commonwealth, and were by British elites in the first half of the twentieth century. We have not, however, considered them in this volume, for two main reasons. Firstly, their histories of institutionalized racial apartheid were not aimed at integrating immigrants or granting genuine self-rule to minorities, but rather attempts to control and oppress a majority racial "group." They are therefore part of the broader story of decolonization but do not sit easily within a discussion of genuine attempts at accommodating cultural (or other) diversity (see Kymlicka in *Liberalism, Community, and Culture,* chap. 13). Secondly, both of these countries left the Commonwealth in the 1960s, although they later rejoined (and in Zimbabwe's case, left again). Their forms of governance were therefore deeply isolationist for a long period of the twentieth century and had very little overlap with the policies of bi- and multiculturalism developed in Canada, Australia, and New Zealand.

28. Since it is almost entirely populated by people of African descent, the island of Tobago (which has a population of around 60,000, compared to Trinidad's 1.3 million) is much less ethnically diverse than Trinidad, and political/economic power is therefore overwhelmingly Trinidadian, as are the dominant narratives of nationhood. We follow Viranjini Munasinghe in using "Trinidad," "Indo-Trinidadian," and "Afro-Trinidadian," common shorthand that makes sense especially in a discussion of multiculturalism.

PART I

British Multiculturalism

2

——

British Multiculturalism after Empire

Immigration, Nationality, and Citizenship

Richard T. Ashcroft, University of California at Berkeley

Mark Bevir, University of California at Berkeley

The United Kingdom of Great Britain and Northern Ireland is composed of several nations, and therefore has always been culturally diverse. Yet "multiculturalism" did not arise as a distinct phenomenon in Britain until after 1945, when the country was transformed by the end of Empire.[1] This chapter provides an overview of this modern British multiculturalism.[2] It supplements the existing literature by situating recent developments within the overall trajectory of postwar British multiculturalism and politics, highlighting connections to broader national debates and contextualizing the other chapters in this volume.[3]

Our goal is therefore primarily descriptive rather than normative, so here we will largely ignore the philosophical literature. Instead we focus on the relevant UK policy and law, outlining the central features of this framework.[4] We trace the development of this distinctive multicultural "regime" and identify aspects of the postwar political landscape that influenced it. There are several ways of delineating British politics during this period, but the three most important traditions for understanding the evolution of British multiculturalism are social democracy, conservatism, and what we call British exceptionalism, a Whiggish view of the world that valorizes the evolution and exportation of British political institutions, values, and ideas.[5] The first two have dominated national politics via the two major parties, yet operate partly against the background of the last. Our central thesis is that the interactions between actors situated within these three traditions have conditioned the particular form multiculturalism has taken in the UK, entangling it in wider debates over immigration, nationality, and citizenship.

The central dilemma facing postwar Britain was how to understand its role in the world, and the idea of Britishness itself, in a nonimperial context. Britain responded to this challenge by undertaking a radical overhaul of its law relating to nationality and citizenship. As well as creating the modern welfare state, an expansive redefinition of British nationality was passed in 1948 with little fanfare, in the main because a widespread belief in British exceptionalism combined with prominent strands of conservative and social democratic thinking to ensure cross-party support. The British Nationality Act 1948 was intended to secure Britain's place at the head of a robust Commonwealth of Nations, but instead led to an unexpectedly large influx of nonwhite migrants. The speed and scale of this immigration challenged British national identity, and put pressure on the new welfare state. Ultimately, this postwar reconstitution of the British polity gave rise to a distinctive form of "British multiculturalism," which combined tough immigration controls with an internal regime of citizenship rights, race-relations legislation, and pluralistic accommodations for minorities. This framework of law and policy has persisted in its broad outlines from the mid-1960s until the present, but since the turn of the millennium there has been a reaction against some aspects of it. The recent shift is more pronounced in rhetoric than policy, however, and therefore British multiculturalism may be better understood as undergoing a "rebalancing" rather than a "retreat." Whatever the correct characterization, we suggest that Brexit and renewed calls for Scottish independence are entangled with current disagreements over multiculturalism. Understanding these connections in turn highlights that multiculturalism raises fundamental questions regarding the structure and purpose of the British polity.

For the sake of clarity, we have split our narrative into five sections: the period of open borders between 1945 and 1962; the emergence of the distinctive British approach to multiculturalism between 1962 and 1979; the persistence of this "regime" under pressure from the Conservative Party governments of 1979–97; the developments under New Labour and the subsequent Conservative governments from 1997 to 2016; and finally, the connections to the recent referendum on EU membership and renewed calls for Scottish independence.

1945–1962: THE PERIOD OF OPEN BORDERS

The British state was created in 1707, and Linda Colley has argued forcefully that a distinctive understanding of "Britishness" was first forged through the struggle against France and the period of empire-building that followed.[6] Historians still debate the precise impact of imperialism on British domestic culture, but we believe it is clear that the Empire was a fundamental part of British national identity from at least the mid-Victorian period up until the mid-twentieth century.[7] Decolonization after 1945 therefore threatened both Britain's international standing and its sense of self. In response, postwar governments tried to position Britain at the head of a Commonwealth sphere of influence that would allow key aspects of British identity and influence to be preserved, albeit in a slightly diminished form.

The importance of spreading its forms of governance has been a long-standing theme in British public discourse, and a key justification of the Empire was that—unlike other European forms of imperialism—it would ultimately prepare its colonies to rule themselves.[8] Shifting from an overt "Whig imperialism" to a more egalitarian "Commonwealthism," was therefore a natural response to the problem posed by decolonization, and a continuation of British exceptionalism rather than a rejection of it. As Randall Hansen demonstrates in his measured and detailed analysis, this Commonwealth vision had bipartisan influence in the immediate postwar period, when the question was not whether, but how, to achieve it.[9]

The Attlee government's solution was to redefine British nationality in 1948 in such a way as to simultaneously reaffirm and transform the relation of Britain to her colonies. Until the British Nationality Act 1948, there was no legal definition of citizenship in UK law, which revolved around the concept of subjecthood.[10] Subjecthood was granted automatically to everyone born within the British Empire and Commonwealth, nominally giving recipients all the privileges attached to the status of British subject equally.[11] One of these privileges, albeit one that had previously existed primarily as a convention, was the right to migrate to Britain. Ireland had already rejected the unilateral ascription of British subjecthood to its citizens, but the immediate trigger for reform was the Canadian Citizenship Act of 1946, which defined Canadian citizenship for the first time and made British subjecthood for Canadians dependent on that citizenship, rather than being a direct grant from the British Crown. This change meant there was now the potential for conflict between subjecthood dependent on domestic citizenship and the universal British version.[12]

The 1948 British Nationality Act attempted to reconstitute common subjecthood status throughout the Commonwealth and Empire by creating a new citizenship in UK law, and making all grants of British subjecthood dependent on some form of citizenship, whether in Britain or elsewhere. The two most important categories of citizens under the Act were "Citizens of the United Kingdom and Colonies" (CUKCs) and "Citizens of Independent Commonwealth Countries" (CICCs). These two categories covered the vast majority of British subjects, with the former receiving subjecthood directly from the UK and the latter via their domestic citizenship. Both had broadly the same rights in relation to the UK, including the right to live and work there, to vote, and even to stand for Parliament.[13] The crucial legal effect of the British Nationality Act 1948 for our purposes was twofold. First, it gave *statutory* form to a right to immigrate to the UK previously possessed only as a convention (and even then unevenly), granting this right to the vast majority of those in the Empire/Commonwealth.[14] Secondly, it linked this right to a new form of citizenship conferred by the UK on almost everyone in the Empire who was not a citizen of an independent country.

Part of the motivation for these reforms was that the right to migrate to the UK was considered a clear—but largely symbolic—way of reasserting Britain's status as the "mother country," and thereby its commitment to the freedom and equality of both its individual subjects and the nations in the Empire and Commonwealth. Astonishingly, there is little indication that any of the politicians involved thought that this right would be utilized on a mass scale, instead presuming that prewar patterns of migration, which largely consisted in a flow from Britain to the "Old" Commonwealth, with a small number in return, would continue as before.[15] Nevertheless, the 1948 Act opened the UK to the possibility of legally protected mass immigration from the predominantly nonwhite countries of the "New" Commonwealth. Contrary to popular belief, however, active recruitment from these countries was limited to a few employers; the Attlee government looked primarily to continental Europe to meet postwar labor shortages. In fact, the Labour government and its Conservative successor sought to discourage further New Commonwealth immigration by "informal" means, pressuring the Jamaican, Indian, and other governments to put administrative roadblocks in the way of potential immigrants.[16] It is equally clear, however, that this was conducted as private government-to-government business, because any attempt to distinguish between Old and New Commonwealth immigrants would have been seen as racist, undermining the rhetoric of British Exceptionalism that justified the UK's role as the head of a multi-racial Commonwealth. This would have had potentially devastating effects on foreign relations and Britain's conception of itself in the postwar world.

The commitment to the Commonwealth informed by British exceptionalism aligned with elements of the other two traditions. Anti-racism and the creation of a citizenship that provided a full range of civil, political and socioeconomic rights were central parts of Labour's postwar project. This meant that social democrats—and some liberal conservatives—could not as a matter of principle countenance race-based immigration restrictions and usually assumed that the new "Marshallian" citizenship would effectively assimilate new migrants into Britain.[17] In addition, there was a powerful group in the Conservative Party—and some in Labour—who saw a special connection between Britain and the anglophone Old Commonwealth. Many Conservatives may have wanted to restrict nonwhite immigration, but when faced with a choice between restricting all Commonwealth immigration or none, they opted to reject any restrictions at all in order to keep the door open to those in "Greater Britain."[18]

Given this confluence of interests, further legal reform restricting New Commonwealth immigration was impossible during this period, with the Colonial Office effectively exercising an institutional veto.[19] Despite racially tinged public and political pressure, this impasse remained in place until the late 1950s, when a variety of factors removed the impediments to immigration reform. Once social democratic and conservative actors were no longer politically restrained by the goal of securing Commonwealth relations, anti-immigrant public opinion produced further legislation on immigration and nationality.[20] Out of this arose a distinctive British form of multiculturalism.[21]

1962–1979: THE BIRTH OF "BRITISH MULTICULTURALISM"

By the 1960s, it had become clear that Britain would not be able to secure the Commonwealth as distinct sphere of influence, which diminished the immediate political influence of British exceptionalism. The resulting shift in focus onto Europe and the United States paved the way for immigration reform, and a compromise between the two main parties and traditions in terms of how to deal with cultural diversity.[22] The result was a bifurcated legal framework of multiculturalism, which consisted, on the one hand, of tough external immigration controls parsed in increasingly racialized terms, and, on the other, of a strong internal race-relations regime of broad citizenship rights that rejected "assimilation" in favor of "integration." This dichotomous approach defined multiculturalism as a political issue in the British context.

As the Commonwealth ideal faded in the late 1950s and early 1960s, the influence of the Colonial Office declined markedly, allowing the Ministry of Labour to push for immigration restrictions.[23] Pressure for reform increased after race riots in Notting Hill and Nottingham in 1958 highlighted growing public resistance to nonwhite immigration.[24] Conservative and Labour backbenchers began to question the assumption that the flow of immigrants could effectively be assimilated by granting citizenship rights.[25] Informal measures could no longer stem the tide, and rumors of impending controls resulted in a spike of immigrants arriving from the New Commonwealth during 1961.[26] All of this led Harold Macmillan's government to pass the Commonwealth Immigrants Act 1962.[27]

In legal terms, the difficulty facing the Conservative Party under Macmillan was how to restrict the immigration of individuals who were all British subjects, and many of whom were British citizens. Although it would have been possible to simply exclude individuals from independent Commonwealth countries such as Canada and India (i.e., CICCs), that would still have allowed large-scale immigration by CUKCs from countries that were not yet independent, since their citizenship status was the same as that of those born in the UK. The government could have created a specifically British citizenship distinct from citizenship in the colonies, but it was reluctant to offend the inhabitants of the remaining colonies by unilaterally changing their citizenship status. In any event, any attempt to do so would have involved a lengthy period of legal and political wrangling and was therefore unattractive.[28] Instead, the Conservatives opted to keep the basic structure of the British Nationality Act 1948 in place, but to amend it so as to limit the right of entry to: (i) those born in the UK; and (ii) those CUKCs whose passports were issued under the authority of London rather than by a colonial administration.[29] These restrictions on entry were coupled with a nominally race-blind work-voucher scheme that prioritized skilled workers and capped immigration for each category at a certain limit.[30]

The overall effect of the 1962 reforms was to make almost all CICCs and those CUKCs born and living in the colonies subject to immigration control, which meant you could possess the primary citizenship status of a CUKC without having a right even to enter Britain, let alone live there. The Bill passed despite opposition from the Labour Party, which nevertheless did nothing to overturn the Act after it returned to power in 1964, when the focus shifted to what form of immigration control there should be, and how to deal with those that had already arrived. Yet once the initial taboo against any form of immigration control had been breached by the Commonwealth Immigrants Act 1962, growing hostility to nonwhite immigration made further legislation inevitable.[31] There was another Act in 1968 in response to the Kenyan crisis, which shamefully abandoned the Asians in Kenya to their fate by unilaterally revoking their right of entry as CUKCs after the fact, thereby denuding their citizenship of any meaningful protections.[32] More legislation followed in 1971, restricting immigration even further.[33] The Immigration Act 1971 employed criteria that turned even more decisively on race, such as the notorious "patriality" requirement, which allowed most white descendants of British colonists into the UK but effectively barred nonwhites.[34] Nevertheless, it must be understood that none of this could do much to stem the tide of family reunifications, despite gradual tightening of the rules for determining cases of secondary immigration from this period on.[35]

The correlate of this tightening of external immigration controls in racialized terms was the imposition of an increasingly potent internal race-relations regime over the same period, with acts passed by Labour in 1965, 1968 and 1976.[36] The 1965 Race Relations Act outlawed discrimination in public places and incitement to racial hatred, and set up the Race Relations Board. The 1968 Act extended nondiscrimination to the key areas of housing and employment and created the Community Relations Commission. The 1976 Act amalgamated the two previous bodies into the (now defunct) Commission for Racial Equality, and introduced the idea of indirect discrimination.[37] Measures were put in place at the local level too, with the establishment of Community Relations Councils and Racial Equality Councils. These reforms, although arguably inspired by the universalist aspects of the social democratic tradition, were nevertheless accompanied by a conscious shift in the mid-1960s away from "assimilation" to "integration."[38] In a famous statement in May 1966, Labour Home Secretary Roy Jenkins clearly articulated a racially diverse conception of Britishness that did not require assimilation into the dominant anglophone culture, saying: "Integration is perhaps rather a loose word. I do not regard it as meaning the loss, by immigrants, of their own national characteristics and culture. I do not think that we need in this country a 'melting pot,' which will turn everybody out in a common mould, as one of a series of carbon copies of someone's misplaced vision of the stereotyped Englishman. . . . I define integration, therefore, not as a flattening process of assimilation but as equal opportunity, accompanied by cultural diversity, in an atmosphere of mutual tolerance."[39]

This shift meant that "Britain turned against the idea of assimilating her immigrants earlier than any other country in the Western world," instituting a series of exceptions from general laws for ethnic, racial, and religious minorities.[40] These accommodations were accompanied by a high degree of funding and activism engaged with the needs of minority communities. The price of *external* immigration control extracted by the predominantly anti-racist social democratic tradition and the more liberal wing of the Conservative Party was therefore a generous *internal* multicultural regime. This cross-party consensus emerged around the time of the Labour government's White Paper on immigration in 1965 and can be attributed to the interaction of aspects of the traditions with the historical circumstances and the goals of political actors.[41]

The Conservative Party was willing to accept this compromise, since its leadership struggled over this period to restrain overtly racialized interpretations of conservatism. The dominant "One Nation" conservatism exemplified by Harold Macmillan pursued social welfare through pragmatic paternalist policies; it did not seek to reverse the basic thrust of the welfare state, yet still clung to a conception of the country that drew on British exceptionalism.[42] Its organic conception of community and nation in historical (but not directly racial) terms was, however, challenged by the scale and speed of New Commonwealth immigration. Some Conservatives, such as Enoch Powell and Cyril Osborne, put up increasingly strident opposition to nonwhite immigrants on the grounds they could not be effectively assimilated. In doing so, these Conservatives blurred the line between cultural and ethnic/racial difference, tying arguments over immigration to issues surrounding race, which in turn colored debates over citizenship, Britishness, and multiculturalism. The majority of the Conservative Party leadership were avowedly anti-racist, but as concern about Commonwealth relations became less influential, they struggled to restrain the more prejudiced elements of their party. The Conservative leadership was therefore willing to maintain a bipartisan consensus to keep immigration out of front bench politics as much as possible, even though it might present them with something of an electoral advantage in the short term.[43]

There was also something of an uneasy balance within the social democratic tradition and the Labour Party that helped bring about the bifurcated approach to multiculturalism. During this period, social democracy was predominantly marked by an optimistic progressivism aimed at enhancing welfare through a combination of state action and community organization, primarily in the form of legal rights ascribed to all citizens equally by central government. Nevertheless, there was also strand of social democratic pluralism that sought the decentralization of political power and a diversity of free associations that would allow a more open, flexible form of community.[44] Within the Labour Party, this meant that strong anti-racist and anti-imperialist elements had to be balanced against the suspicion of the working class and the Trades Union Congress (TUC) that large-scale immigration could lead to unemployment, and would damage the power of collective bargaining and hence standards of living.[45] There were numerous examples of racial prejudice on the shop floor, but nevertheless the TUC was officially anti-racist, and the influence of that principle on the social democratic movement as a whole was so strong that Labour took a more consistently pro-immigrant line than the Conservatives. The combination of the universalist parts of the tradition with the more pluralist strand thus arguably led to the toleration and preservation of differences within a framework of broad citizenship rights.

The different strands of social democracy and conservatism in British politics ensured that the price of restrictive immigration reform was a strong internal race-relations regime and a notable degree of internal cultural pluralism. This consensus represented a balance both between the two main traditions and parties, and elements within them. Nevertheless, the racial overtones of public discourse and the subsequent immigration reforms are impossible to ignore. Part of the problem, as Christian Joppke argues, was that the expansive definition of citizenship introduced in 1948 could not be used itself as the sole criterion for restricting immigration.[46] In the face of public resistance to the influx of people from the New Commonwealth, immigration restrictions had to be recast to operate on proxies of birth and ancestry, which in the British legal and political context effectively meant race. The ultimate legacy, therefore, of the cross-party influence of British exceptionalism in the years immediately after World War II was twofold. Firstly, it triggered reforms that intertwined race, immigration, nationality, and citizenship in law and politics. Secondly, it helped create a distinctive British approach to multiculturalism comprised of tough external immigration controls and an internal race-relations regime of broad citizenship rights and pluralist accommodations.[47]

1979–1997: AN UNEASY STATUS QUO

Given Prime Minister Margaret Thatcher's dominance of the political landscape in these years, and her deserved reputation for anti-immigration rhetoric, radical policies, and political confrontation, one might expect her control of central government to have led to significant changes in the approach to multiculturalism. In fact, the existing bifurcated regime was broadly maintained in policy terms, although support for it was no longer entirely bipartisan.

In terms of immigration and nationality law, the British Nationality Act of 1981, which finally overturned the legal regime created by the 1948 Act, was a significant piece of legislation, but it was not as radical a departure from the practices of the preceding two decades as is often claimed.[48] The 1981 Act repealed the 1948 Act, "all but abolished the status of British subject," and finally put in place a clear definition of British citizenship, which corresponded directly to the right to live in Britain.[49] The remaining CUKCs were split into two different categories, but neither of these received the right to enter the UK. The controversial terminology of "patriality" was done away with, but its effects were largely preserved by a shift away from a pure *jus soli* that gave British nationality to almost anyone born on UK soil to include elements of a *jus sanguinis* approach, making British citizenship dependent on having a parent who is a UK citizen or "settled" in Britain.[50] Crucially, it would seem that the criteria for immigrating to the UK under the British Nationality Act 1981 were much the same as under the Immigration Act 1971, and a version of the status quo was thus preserved in immigration law.[51] Nevertheless, Thatcher's anti-immigration rhetoric embodied a cultural nationalism with racialized undertones, as demonstrated by her infamous appearance on World in Action in the run-up to the 1979 election. It must also be noted that many of the secondary immigration rules were significantly tightened from this point on in ways that seemed to target nonwhite immigration.[52]

The other arm of British multiculturalism also remained broadly in place, despite more direct attacks on it by the Thatcher governments.[53] Thatcher's brand of neoliberal "conservatism" was still committed to universal citizenship rights, albeit shorn of the welfarist elements, and so she had no reason to attack the difference-blind aspects of the race-relations regime, leaving this part of the bipartisan consensus largely intact. Elements of the "integration not assimilation" approach also survived during this period, since Thatcher governments passed many accommodations for minorities that extended Labour Party policies of the 1970s.[54] Surprisingly, Thatcher's attack on the welfare state as a whole failed to undermine the basic thrust of the multicultural regime, even if it weakened it in some respects. In part, this was because implementation of much of the relevant welfare provision was in the purview of local governments dominated by the Labour Party. For instance, local authorities were charged under section 71 of the Race Relations Act 1976 with eliminating unlawful discrimination and promoting equal opportunity, and were permitted under the Act to advertise jobs in specialist presses in order to encourage more applications from minorities. In some cases this morphed into de facto affirmative action hiring policies and thus increased diversity. The correction of "indirect discrimination" also allowed more interventionist policies, and section 35 permitted the provision of services targeted directly at the special needs of minority groups, a trend that increased after the Scarman Report on the Brixton riots of 1981. Anti-racism and multiculturalism became core parts of teacher training and the curricula designed predominantly at the local level, much of which was inspired by the pluralist rhetoric of Lord Swann's 1985 Report on Education.

The perceived excesses of some local government, most notably in Liverpool and London, were utilized by central government in the 1980s as a reason to reduce local funding and power. Yet even afterwards local authorities had substantial funds under their control, and significant welfare responsibilities for community services, housing, and education. During this period social democracy in Britain was therefore expressed through a more activist anti-racism and valorization of difference, and the Labour Party became closely associated with a commitment to multiculturalism.[55] Overall, British multiculturalism became "entrenched" during this period at the local level, and so the distinctive bifurcated approach arising out of the postimperial experience remained largely intact. In the face of neoliberalism, however, the compromise between social democracy and conservatism—and the strands of universalism and pluralism within them—transitioned into an uneasy balance between more homogeneous parties and different levels of government.

1997–2016: RENEWAL, RETREAT, REBALANCING

New Labour's form of social democracy had important consequences for British multiculturalism. Its leading practitioners hailed primarily from the Fabian strand of social democracy, which traditionally placed great faith in a liberal democracy informed by social science.[56] This inheritance meant their reinterpretation of the tradition was heavily impacted by modern social science research and techniques, which affected how they conceived of and responded to political issues, including multiculturalism. The two most influential strands of social science on New Labour were new institutionalism and communitarianism.[57] Whereas Thatcher promoted markets, competition, and the "hollowing out" of the state, New Labour drew on new institutionalism to defend the use of broader "networks" of governance, consultation, and private/public partnerships within a context of "joined up government."[58] Whereas Thatcher declared, "there is no such thing as society," New Labour drew on a communitarianism that valorized shared values and an "active citizenship" comprised of both rights and duties. And whereas Thatcher attacked the economic "dependency" engendered by the welfare state, New Labour drew on both new institutional and communitarian conceptions of social capital in order to reduce exclusion.

New Labour impacted multiculturalism in a variety of ways, marrying a pluralist idea of local governance—including devolution—that emphasized difference to a revitalized sense of citizenship, trust, and obligation to the community.[59] It also reasserted the value of the welfare state, extended the scope of the race-relations regime and hate speech laws,[60] and consolidated UK anti-discrimination law.[61] There was a relaxation of the position on nonwhite immigration through the dropping of the controversial "primary purpose" immigration rule, which had previously been used to limit the right of British citizens (predominantly of South Asian ethnicity) to bring their spouses to the UK.[62] Overall, therefore, New Labour initially reinvigorated the bifurcated framework, with the publication of the report by the Commission on the Future of Multi-Ethnic Britain in 2000 perhaps being the "high-water mark" of postwar British multiculturalism.

British multiculturalism was put under strain, however, by events in the early 2000s. Race riots in the north of England in 2001 were the initial trigger for a reevaluation of multicultural policy, a process accelerated by the events of 9/11, the wars in Afghanistan and Iraq, and the London bombings of July 2005. The government responded with a more strident emphasis on the need for immigrant and minority communities to assimilate British values and traditions, with similar views articulated by the nongovernment Left in David Goodhart's famous series of articles in *Demos* and *Prospect*.[63] This shift can be seen in numerous statements by figures such as Communities Secretary Ruth Kelly,[64] the various reports on the 2001 riots,[65] David Blunkett's introduction to the 2002 White Paper *Secure Borders, Safe Haven*,[66] the introduction of "ideological" criteria for community group funding,[67] and in the fact and form of the new nationality test and citizenship ceremonies.[68] These changes were accompanied by a tightening of immigration and asylum law and draconian anti-terrorism legislation. Security measures were also linked explicitly to assimilationalist policies which often muddled together counterterrorism work with community relations.[69] British Muslims became particular objects of public and governmental suspicion, which exacerbated criticism of multicultural policies from both majority and minority groups.

Policies and rhetoric in this vein have been continued by the governments of David Cameron and Theresa May. Both Cameron and May are self-described "One Nation" conservatives, construing national identity in terms of a shared and cohesive set of values.[70] Prime Minister Cameron famously declared in 2011 that the "state doctrine of multiculturalism" had failed, explicitly citing it as a cause of domestic terrorism because of its putative role in "weakening our collective identity," advocating instead the need for a "muscular liberalism" that asserts "British values."[71] This rhetoric was strengthened after the 2015 election, when he introduced anti-extremism legislation and adopted further immigration restrictions, commenting: "For too long, we have been a passively tolerant society, saying to our citizens: as long as you obey the law, we will leave you alone. It's often meant we have stood neutral between different values. And that's helped foster a narrative of extremism and grievance. . . . This Government will conclusively turn the page on this failed approach. As the party of one nation, we will govern as one nation, and bring our country together. That means actively promoting certain values."[72] Brexit has meant that the stance on immigration has hardened further under the May governments, as has the accompanying rhetoric regarding social cohesion and shared values.[73]

British multiculturalism therefore initially underwent a revival during this period. That has been followed by something of a backlash, however, which draws on elements in all three of the main political traditions we have identified. New Labour relied on both new institutionalism and communitarianism, thereby simultaneously affirming difference and social cohesion, and advocating both local community governance and efficient public administration. New Labour's version of social democracy therefore initially led to a renewal of British multiculturalism, but its disparate commitments have come under pressure from events since 2001, and the Labour Party has responded by reemphasizing the centralizing and homogenizing aspects of its tradition at the expense of the pluralistic ones.[74] This shift toward social cohesion and shared values has been followed by Conservative politicians in recent years, who have drawn on long-standing parts of their own tradition in doing so, including an emphasis on institutions and values that have evolved historically. The result has been an overall tendency in British political discourse since the millennium to juxtapose "multiculturalism" and liberal nationalism, and to advocate more robust forms of the latter. The dominant articulation of the national community in current British public discourse is therefore in terms of political and moral values, which are frequently couched in the language of British exceptionalism. The appeal to "unique" British values and practices is, however, usually accompanied by an emphasis on anti-racism and the culturally diverse nature of modern Britain. It is therefore plausible to argue, as Meer and Modood do in this volume, that recent events should not be understood as a full-scale retreat from the postwar approach of "integration not assimilation," but rather as a "rebalancing" of Britain's distinctive bifurcated approach to multiculturalism in the light of current concerns.

It is noteworthy, however, that in articulating their liberal nationalisms for the new millennium, the leaderships of both major parties have often utilized language reminiscent of the form of British exceptionalism popular after World War II.[75] The imagery of Empire was invoked even more directly by the campaign to leave the EU, which explicitly framed Brexit as an opportunity to rekindle Britain's globe-straddling past.[76] It was perhaps inevitable that the May governments have sought to sell Brexit to the public in similar terms, yet they have been accused—not unfairly—of expressing their liberal nationalism in ways that play on the ethno-culturalism that marred the referendum.[77] In so doing, they have arguably echoed problematic aspects of the conservative tradition (and the Conservative Party) that were prominent during the birth of British multiculturalism in the 1960s. These recent articulations of national identity are unpopular with some aspects of the social democratic Left, which has a deep-seated commitment to anti-racism, multiculturalism, and difference. The lukewarm opposition to Brexit of the current Labour Party leader, Jeremy Corbyn—largely driven by traditional social democratic fear of the effect of highly mobile foreign labor competing with British workers—has, however, hampered resistance to the overall trend toward homogenizing forms of nationalism.

2016 ON: BREXIT AND BEYOND

Our narrative has taken us from 1945 to the present day, demonstrating that for much of this period the basic form and understanding of British multiculturalism has remained broadly stable. This consistency is to some extent the result of the path-dependency created by the postwar immigration, nationality, and citizenship reforms, themselves partly inspired by British exceptionalism. We suggest that it is also because the underlying policy regime has been able to balance aspects within and across social democracy and conservatism—and the two main political parties through which they are expressed—over time. We end, however, by complicating our story. We analyze Brexit and renewed calls for Scottish independence, illustrating the ways in which both issues are at least partly rooted in debates over multiculturalism. This not only enriches our understanding of British multiculturalism, but also suggests that its proper scope reaches beyond current discursive boundaries to include basic constitutional issues.

Brexit was driven by conflicting evaluations of multiculturalism, national identity, and the worth of multiple citizenships.[78] Resistance to immigrant multiculturalism was a substantial factor in the Leave vote. Immigration, multiculturalism, race, and security were frequently conflated in public discourse during the campaign, most succinctly in the UK Independence Party's notorious "Breaking Point" poster depicting a massed column of mostly nonwhite, young male migrants in southeastern Europe. This played into the narrative that multiculturalism has damaged social cohesion, making Brexit part of a broader contest over national identity. The emotive nature of nationalism complicated the debate, with immigrant multiculturalism—and thereby the EU—seen by some Leave voters as undermining what it means to be British. Differences in the national identities that underlie "Britishness" complicated matters even further. A significant sense of Englishness correlates more strongly with Euroscepticism than Scottish, Welsh, and Northern Irish identities do, and this may be linked to divergent views as to whether—and which—national identity is threatened by immigration and multiculturalism.[79] In addition, many UK voters identify as European as well as British, adding a further layer to the conflict between plural identities.

The various national identities in contemporary Britain are in turn entangled with the multiple citizenships at play. Most referendum voters possessed both European and British citizenship, with many Leave voters feeling that the former has undermined aspects of the latter. This is partly because the economic impact of the freedom of movement conferred by EU citizenship has likely varied—at least in the short term—across different demographics and geographical areas in the UK. This has strengthened the perception that the welfare state is under threat, even if it seems likely that any such problems in reality have more to do with austerity than immigration. The erosion of the economic elements of British citizenship central to the multicultural regime—and the postwar national settlement more broadly—are therefore also part of Brexit. Political aspects of different citizenships were also in conflict, and many who voted Leave were concerned about a loss of British political sovereignty to the EU and a lack of institutional accountability. The high-handed dismissal of these very real concerns by the Remain campaign, and the EU itself, was unhelpful.

Yet a lack of democratic responsiveness is arguably a problem within the UK itself, with the 62 percent of voters in Scotland who wanted to remain in the EU being overridden by those in England and Wales.[80] Proponents of Scottish independence therefore paint Scotland as different from other parts of the UK in its embrace of both multiculturalism and immigration.[81] These purported differences partly underpin the SNP's claim that Scotland suffers a "democratic deficit" within the UK that was mitigated by devolution, but has been exacerbated by Brexit.[82] Although this argument is couched in democratic language, we have argued elsewhere that it implicitly relies on the claim that the *cultural* nation is a necessary condition of successful liberal-democratic politics.[83] This claim connects Scottish independence to the political theory of multiculturalism, most notably Will Kymlicka's defense of political autonomy for "national minorities" based on the role culture plays in meaningful choice and self-respect.[84] Whether or not this "cultural nationalism" is ultimately persuasive—which we strongly doubt—our analysis makes it clear that recent claims of Scottish independence are not just closely connected to multiculturalism and Brexit in a causal sense, but also on a deeper theoretical level.

CONCLUSIONS

Our narrative suggests that the roots of our current political confusion can be uncovered through understanding the trajectory of multiculturalism in postwar Britain, which arose as a response to the destabilizing of British power and national identity by decolonization. This chapter has argued that modern British multiculturalism is the direct consequence of the failed postwar attempt to construct a geopolitically relevant Commonwealth of Nations, itself inspired by a widespread belief in British exceptionalism. The result has been a distinctive bifurcated form of multiculturalism, comprised of tough external immigration controls coupled with an internal regime made up of citizenship rights, race-relations legislation, and pluralistic accommodations for minorities. A broad consensus in favor of this distinctive type of multiculturalism was maintained from the mid-1960s until the early 2000s. In recent years, however, there has been something of a shift toward more assimilative forms of liberal nationalism, frequently articulated through the rhetoric of British exceptionalism.

Multiculturalism in modern Britain as a demographic fact and policy framework is thus primarily the result of nonwhite immigration after 1945. The overall effect of the postwar transformation of Britain has been to ensure that debates over multiculturalism, citizenship, and national identity are entangled with one another. The connection between multiculturalism and postwar immigration is widely acknowledged by public actors, as is the ineluctable role of race. Yet the broader effects of the postwar legal and political reforms on multiculturalism in the UK are often ignored. Framing "British multiculturalism" in terms of integrating nonwhite immigrants obscures the deeper challenges to national identity and liberal-democratic governance posed by decolonization. The British nation and state are deeply connected to empire, which continues to cast a shadow over contemporary debates even as we try to move beyond its legacy. This is illustrated by the inability of political actors of both Left and Right successfully to articulate a vision of modern Britain without drawing on some form of British exceptionalism, directly invoking imperial imagery, or lapsing into ethnically tinged nationalism. This suggests that Britain has not yet negotiated the dilemmas posed by the dissolution of the Empire, nor forged a stable identity without it.[85]

Both Brexit and Scottish independence are best understood as part of these ongoing and interrelated contests in Britain over multiculturalism, national identity, and citizenship. We suggest that the failure in current political discourse to appreciate the interrelated nature of these issues has several problematic consequences. Firstly, it facilitates the divisive, racially charged rhetoric that allows multiculturalism-as-immigration to become an empty signifier for all of contemporary Britain's social ills. Secondly, it has hampered the ability of the different factions within the two major parties to agree on the cause, scope, and import of Brexit, contributing to a lack of clear political alternatives. Thirdly, it hides the connection between multiculturalism and broader questions of governance, reducing the possibility of addressing all the relevant issues in a holistic manner. And lastly, it glosses over the historical claims, normative values, and accounts of the nation that implicitly inform contemporary public discourse, but which may not stand up to public or intellectual scrutiny when foregrounded.

Multiculturalism in Britain should be understood as raising questions regarding its basic constitutional structure, and even the purpose of Britain as a polity. Recent events may therefore call for more than simply "rebalancing" the existing legal framework. British multiculturalism may not be amenable to top-down policy solutions; rather, it may require restructuring our modes of governance, and perhaps the United Kingdom itself, from the ground up.

NOTES

1. We follow Harry Goulbourne in seeing the postwar changes as a "sufficient condition" for calling Britain a multicultural country. See his *Race Relations in Britain Since 1945* (London: Macmillan, 1998), 26. For a longer-term view, see Panikos Panayi, *An Immigration History of Great Britain: Multicultural Racism since 1800* (New York: Pearson Longman, 2010), 280ff. See also Rieko Karatani, *Defining British Citizenship: Empire, Commonwealth, and Modern Britain* (London: Frank Cass, 2003), who emphasizes the importance of decolonization but also traces the links between the postwar reforms and earlier imperial practices.

2. For convenience we use the terms "United Kingdom" and "Britain" interchangeably, including Northern Ireland in the latter. We use "Old" and "New" Commonwealth to distinguish the white-settler colonies of Canada, Australia and New Zealand from other colonies in the Empire which were never intended to be permanently settled by the British, and whose relationship to Great Britain was marked by more nakedly extractive practices.

3. See Randall Hansen, *Citizenship and Immigration* (Oxford: Oxford University Press, 2000), to whom we are indebted for much of the basic thrust and structure of our narrative. We also rely on Christian Joppke, *Immigration and the Nation-State: The United States, Germany, and Great Britain* (Oxford: Oxford University Press, 1999), and Karatani, *Defining British Citizenship.*

4. Our focus is therefore narrower than much of the literature in sociology, cultural studies, and history, which usually looks at multiculturalism as a broader social phenomenon, or explores the role of the Empire in national identity through detailed examination of particular aspects of British society and culture. In order to provide an overview within the space available, we have focused on the bare legal and political bones, which still provide a clear sense of the nature and development of British multiculturalism, and how it relates to postimperial dilemmas in national identity and governance.

5. We have not included new liberalism and its associated political parties in our narrative, as during this period it was either indistinct from social democracy and the Labour Party on the relevant issues or politically marginalized. The traditions we utilize here to help understand British multiculturalism are aggregate concepts we delineate according to our purposes, which means they are justified by their descriptive and explanatory traction across the entire postwar period. Not only do the interactions between the various forms of social democracy, conservatism, and British exceptionalism provide a plausible account of the birth of British multiculturalism just after World War II, they continue to explain features of its development right up until the present day, including the recent "rebalancing," Brexit, and renewed calls for Scottish independence. As aggregate concepts, the traditions also help to explain general features of British national identity, which is itself necessarily an abstraction from the intentional states of individuals. See Richard T. Ashcroft and Mark Bevir, "Liberal Democracy, Nationalism and Culture: Multiculturalism and Scottish Independence," in *Critical Review of International Social and Political Philosophy* 21, no. 1 (2018): 65–86. And see Mark Bevir, *The Logic of the History of Ideas* (Cambridge: Cambridge University Press, 1999) for a full account of our postfoundational methodology.

6. See Linda Colley, *Britons: Forging the Nation, 1707–1837* (Bath: Bath Press, 1992).

7. As well as in Colley's *Forging the Nation,* the centrality of empire to British national identity is argued convincingly by John MacKenzie, "Empire and Metropolitan Cultures," in Andrew Porter, ed., *The Oxford History of the British Empire:* vol. 3 (Oxford: Oxford University Press, 1999), 270–93, and throughout Catherine Hall's work (see, e.g., her "British Cultural Identities and the Legacy of the Empire," in David Morley and Kevin Robins, eds., *British Cultural Studies: Geography, Nationality and Identity* (Oxford: Oxford University Press, 2001, 27–39). We consider the centrality of the empire to British national identity and culture to be incontrovertible, even if there may be legitimate disagreement about the precise form of this influence over time. For a selection of essays which broadly support the editors' view see Morley and Robins, eds., *British Cultural Studies*; Stuart James Ward, ed., *British Culture and the End of Empire* (Bath: Manchester University Press, 2001); Sarah Stockwell, ed., *The British Empire: Themes and Perspectives* (Oxford: Blackwell, 2008); Helen Brocklehurst and Robert Philips, eds., *History, Nationhood and the Question of Britain* (New York: Palgrave Macmillan, 2004); and Antoinette Burton, ed., *After the Imperial Turn: Thinking with and through the Nation* (Durham, NC: Duke University Press, 2003). For the opposite view, see Bernard Porter, *Absent-Minded Imperialists: Empire, Society and Culture in Britain* (Oxford: Oxford University Press, 2006), and P. J. Marshall, "No Fatal Impact? The Elusive History of Imperial Britain," *Times Literary Supplement*, March 12, 1993, 8–10.

8. "The British nation was defined by its imperial task: it was this that raised the British above other nations" (Hall, "British Cultural Identities," 37).

9. Attlee and Churchill both subscribed to the Commonwealth vision, and its centrality is a commonplace. See Hansen, *Citizenship and Immigration*; Joppke, *Immigration and the Nation-State*; James Hampshire, *Citizenship and Belonging* (New York: Palgrave Macmillan, 2005); Paul B. Rich, *Race and Empire in British Politics* (Cambridge: Cambridge University Press, 1996); Ian R. G. Spencer, *British Immigration Policy since 1939: The Making of Multiracial Britain* (New York: Routledge, 1997); Ward, "Introduction" in Ward, *British Culture,* 7–8; and Karatani, *Defining British Citizenship.*

10. Hereafter "BNA 1948."

11. There were some minor exceptions, such as the children of foreign diplomats. For an excellent discussion of the development of British law in relation to subjecthood, nationality, and immigration

before the twentieth century, see Karatani, *Defining British Citizenship,* starting on p. 40 with *Calvin's Case* (1608). The ascription of subjecthood had been complicated historically by some colonies having their own naturalization laws, which also conferred the status of British subject, albeit solely within their own territory, as opposed to the direct, automatic, and universal grant of British subjecthood from the Crown. The granting of British subjecthood was systematized and rendered uniform by the creation of the "common code" around World War I, but even then local autonomy over immigration legislation meant that the Dominions were able to exclude some British subjects (primarily nonwhites) from entering their territory and, through legislation and administrative measures, create their own nationality and something like their own de facto "citizenship." Thus the "universal" rights of British subjects were restricted in practice if not in theory. Nevertheless, the common status of British subject was seen as playing an important role in binding Britain and the Empire and Commonwealth together. See Karatani, ibid., 76–90, and Hansen, *Citizenship and Immigration,* 36–39.

12. See the Irish Nationality and Citizenship Act of 1935. Ireland was considered an anomalous case, however. Canadian nationality had been previously defined as separate from British in the Canadian Nationals Act 1921, but this was done in such a way that it was not a departure from the common code. See Karatani, *Defining British Citizenship,* chaps. 2 and 3, and Hansen, *Citizenship and Immigration,* 42.

13. Spencer, *British Immigration Policy since 1939,* 54–55.

14. Karatani, *Defining British Citizenship,* 76–90, and above.

15. Karatani, *Defining British Citizenship,* 116; Hansen, *Citizenship and Immigration,* 49–55; Spencer, *British Immigration Policy since 1939,* 55; and Joppke, *Immigration and the Nation-State,* 107.

16. Hansen, *Citizenship and Immigration,* 6–10, 59; Hampshire, *Citizenship and Belonging,* 20–24; and Spencer, *British Immigration Policy since 1939,* chaps. 1–3; Panayi, *Immigration History of Great Britain,* 60–61; Karatani, *Defining British Citizenship,* 127–28;

17. The term "Marshallian citizenship" derives from the definition provided by the British sociologist T. H Marshall (1893–1981). See also Joppke, *Immigration and the Nation-State,* 223–24; Hansen, *Citizenship and Immigration,* 88; and Rich, *Race and Empire in British Politics,* 152, 180, 201.

18. Joppke, *Immigration and the Nation-State,* 102, 223ff.; Karatani, *Defining British Citizenship,* 128–29; and Hansen, *Citizenship and Immigration,* 63–64.

19. Hansen, *Citizenship and Immigration,* 63–64, 73–78, and Spencer, *British Immigration Policy since 1939,* 66ff.

20. While we do not deny that the ultimate immigration regime and subsequent legislation warrant charges of racism, we follow Hansen and Joppke in seeing elite political opinion as responding to public racism rather than, as is supposed by some historians, driving and constructing it (for the opposite view, see Kathleen Paul, *Whitewashing Britain: Race and Citizenship in the Postwar Era* [Ithaca, NY: Cornell University Press, 1997]). We take this view for several reasons. Firstly, as political scientists our presumption is that ceteris paribus in democratic systems, politicians follow public opinion rather than determine it, and even when British political elites are out of step with public opinion on social issues, they tend to be more "progressive" rather than less so. We do not claim that postwar British political elites were free of racism—far from it—but as Hansen points out in *Citizenship and Immigration,* 245ff., it seems unlikely that the prevalence of casual public racism and incidents of racial violence were the result of a concerted campaign by Westminster and Whitehall rather than deep-rooted attitudes in the populace. Secondly, Paul's explanation seems to take cross-cutting racism to be the dominant motivation for politicians of all parties and persuasions in relation to immigration. As our sketches of social democracy, conservativism, and British exceptionalism make clear, however, there are different strands of each tradition, and the traditions vary in both content and prominence over time. It is more intuitively plausible that the motivations of the relevant political actors varied according to the particular aspects they drew on from their own traditions, and that the overall political and legal outcome was a result of the interaction of these differences, rather than a single factor that cut across all of them. This accords more closely with Hansen's analysis and seems particularly likely given the prominence

of anti-racism in the social democratic tradition and the plurality of interrelated issues involved (race, citizenship, nationality, imperialism, international relations). Thirdly, this approach fits with our overall methodological commitments, which draw on postfoundational modes of analysis, as discussed above. For example, our postfoundationalism leads us to presume the sincerity of the statements of historical actors regarding their motivations in the absence of strong evidence to the contrary, and we find Hansen's account of the primary sources convincing in this regard.

21. Although Karatani argues convincingly for a "continuity" between British imperial citizenship and immigration policies before and after World War II, her narrative does not fundamentally conflict with ours, because she also makes it clear that: (a) up until 1962, immigration restrictions did not apply to British subjects desiring to move to Britain precisely because of imperial concerns and the subsequent attempt to secure Britain's place at the head of a multicultural Commonwealth; and (b) it was the series of immigration reforms from 1962 on that were the primary legal mechanism for constructing who "belonged" to Britain, and hence postimperial "Britishness."

22. See Stuart James Ward, "A Matter of Preference: The EEC and the Erosion of the 'Old Commonwealth' Relationship," in Alex May, ed., *Britain, the Commonwealth and Europe* (New York: Palgrave Macmillan, 2001), 156–80, for an account of the weakening of the Commonwealth ideal. It was further damaged by the exit from the Commonwealth of South Africa and Rhodesia. The Suez Crisis in 1956 had also been a significant blow to Britain's international prestige and sense of itself as a great power, pushing it closer to the United States.

23. Hansen, *Citizenship and Immigration,* 80–87, 93ff., and Hampshire, *Citizenship and Belonging,* 22–24.

24. Spencer, *British Immigration Policy Since 1939,* 87, 99ff., and Karatani, *Defining British Citizenship,* 128.

25. Karatani, *Defining British Citizenship,* 131–32; Hansen, *Citizenship and Immigration,* 80–87, 120; Spencer, *British Immigration Policy since 1939,* 63–65; Joppke, *Immigration and the Nation-State,* 104; and Goulbourne, *Race Relations in Britain since 1945,* 56ff.

26. Hansen, *Citizenship and Immigration,* 97–100, and Spencer, *British Immigration Policy since 1939,* 121.

27. Hereafter CIA 1962.

28. Hansen, *Citizenship and Immigration,* 101, and Karatani, *Defining British Citizenship,* 128–129.

29. Hansen, *Citizenship and Immigration,* 109–110.

30. Spencer, *British Immigration Policy Since 1939,* 122, and Karatani, *Defining British Citizenship,* 130ff., show the primary aim of the work voucher scheme was not to control immigration per se, but to reduce or even eliminate nonwhite immigration from the New Commonwealth.

31. Prime Minister Edward Heath's acceptance of large numbers of Asians from Uganda in similar circumstances in 1972 should not be seen as a reassertion of the Commonwealth ideal, given his clear Eurocentrism and the fact that those taken in from Uganda by the UK—28,000 out of 50,000, with the rest being taken by other countries at the UK's request—were admitted as refugees, not citizens, even if they were eventually naturalized.

32. The CIA 1962 had been grafted onto the BNA 1948 in such a way that many Asians in Kenya who were excluded from Kenyan citizenship after independence were CUKCs with passports issued under the authority of London, and therefore had a right to immigrate to the UK. The basic effect of the CIA 1968 was to restrict the right of entry of entry into Britain to those CUKCs born in the UK or who had at least one parent or grandparent born there, which left the door ajar for some primary immigration from the white Old Commonwealth but little else. See Hansen, *Citizenship and Immigration,* 169ff., and Spencer, *British Immigration Policy since 1939,* 140ff.

33. Joppke, *Immigration and the Nation-State,* chap. 4. The only government defeat was on new immigration rules in 1972, but that was tied politically to EU accession and was swiftly reversed in any event. See Hansen, *Citizenship and Immigration,* 201–2.

34. J. M. Evans, "Immigration Act 1971," *Modern Law Review* 35, no. 5 (1972): 508–24.

35. Joppke, *Immigration and the Nation-State*, chap. 4, 114ff., and Hansen, *Citizenship and Immigration*, chap. 10.

36. All abbreviated to "RRA [Year]" hereafter.

37. See Panayi, *Immigration History of Great Britain*, 268ff., for a useful summary of these Acts and their main provisions. Also Joppke, *Immigration and the Nation-State*, chap. 7, and Goulbourne, *Race Relations in Britain since 1945*, 100ff.

38. These Acts were all passed by a Labour Party government, yet did not establish an overt framework of affirmative action, and the Rose Report of 1969, intended to be the counterpart to Gunnar Myrdal's influential *An American Dilemma: The Negro Problem and Modern Democracy* (New York: Harper & Brothers, 1944), explicitly referred to the universalist idiom of Marshallian citizenship (see T. H. Marshall, *Citizenship and Social Class* [Cambridge: Cambridge University Press, 1950], and Adrian Favell, *Philosophies of Integration: Immigration and the Idea of Citizenship in France and Britain* [London: Macmillan, 1998], 98–99). Karatani (*Defining British Citizenship*, 176n93) points out that Prime Minister James Callaghan explicitly linked the CIA 1968 to the upcoming Race Relations Act 1968 in an attempt to diffuse accusations of racism.

39. Roy Jenkins, *Essays and Speeches* (London: Collins, 1967), 267.

40. See Joppke, *Immigration and the Nation-State*, 223–33, for a useful discussion.

41. See Karatani, *Defining British Citizenship*, 177n99; Hansen, *Citizenship and Immigration*, 150; Joppke, *Immigration and the Nation-State*, 223; and Panayi, *Immigration History of Great Britain*, 269, for details of this "consensus" and the 1965 White Paper.

42. For useful accounts of these long-standing aspects of the Conservative tradition, see Julia Stapleton, *Public Intellectuals and Public Identities in Britain since 1850* (Manchester: Manchester University Press, 2001), and Robert Leach, *British Political Ideologies* (London: Prentice Hall, 1996).

43. See Hansen, *Citizenship and Immigration*, 88, 119–120; Joppke, *Immigration and the Nation-State*, 104; and Spencer, *British Immigration Policy since 1939*, 126ff.

44. An example of this strand of socialist thinking can be found in G. D. H. Cole. See Marc Stears, "Guild Socialism," in *Modern Pluralism: Anglo-American Debates since 1880*, ed. Mark Bevir, 40–59 (Cambridge: Cambridge University Press, 2012).

45. On the TUC position and practice in general, see Hansen, *Citizenship and Immigration*, 130–31, and Goulbourne, *Race Relations in Britain since 1945*, 85.

46. See Joppke, *Immigration and the Nation-State*, chap. 4.

47. Hansen argues convincingly in *Citizenship and Immigration* that the 1948 reforms (and thus postimperial concerns) are primarily responsible for the trajectory of the various legal reforms that followed and thus, in our parlance, for the structure of British multiculturalism. Karatani's argument does not fundamentally conflict with this claim.

48. Hereafter "BNA 1981." See Karatani, *Defining British Citizenship*, 182–85.

49. See Hansen, *Citizenship and Immigration*, 213–14; Goulbourne, *Race Relations in Britain since 1945*, 54; and Hampshire, *Citizenship and Belonging*, 42–43.

50. Broadly, a permanent resident, see Hampshire, *Citizenship and Belonging*, 43. Karatani *Defining British Citizenship*, chap. 3, also shows how elements of *jus sanguinis* had been present in previous regimes, particularly the rules introduced around the time of World War I.

51. Karatani, *Defining British Citizenship*, 179ff., Hansen, *Citizenship and Immigration*, 207ff., and Spencer, *British Immigration Policy since 1939*, 147.

52. E.g., through the primary purpose rule. See also Joppke, *Immigration and the Nation-State*, 114ff., and Spencer, *British Immigration Policy since 1939*, 147ff., especially regarding the Immigration Act 1988.

53. See Favell, *Philosophies of Integration*, chap. 4, 233. Favell's account is slightly different from ours, although this seems mainly in emphasis. For instance, he stresses the way the bifurcated British

approach to multiculturalism can be cast as a public order issue in the UK, and argues that the Marshallian idiom is as much a justificatory myth as a driving political motivation. He does agree that British multiculturalism is the result of a pragmatic compromise, which traditionally balances pluralist and centralist elements, and that these pluralist elements are under threat (see chap. 7 generally and 233–34 and 252–53).

54. E.g., §11 of the Employment Act 1989.

55. See Joppke, *Immigration and the Nation-State,* chap. 7; and J. A. Chandler, *Explaining Local Government: Local Government in Britain since 1800* (Manchester: Manchester University Press 2007), chaps. 9–12; and Nasar Meer, *Citizenship, Identity and the Politics of Multiculturalism: The Rise of Muslim Consciousness* (New York: Palgrave Macmillan, 2010), 24–25.

56. We refer here not simply to prominent Labour Party members such as Tony Blair, Gordon Brown, and Peter Mandelson, but also to academics and private sector researchers, such as those working at Demos, the Foreign Policy Centre, and the Institute for Public Policy Research.

57. See Mark Bevir, *New Labour: A Critique* (London: Routledge, 2005) for a fuller account of this argument. The New Times project of the late 1980s and 1990s, spearheaded by Stuart Hall, has "retrospectively been heralded as New Labour's intellectual compass" by some; see Pathik Pathak, *The Future of Multicultural Britain: Confronting the Progressive Dilemma* (Edinburgh: Edinburgh University Press, 2008), 98ff. Nevertheless, arguably the version absorbed into New Labour, was filtered through the formal social science of new institutionalism, and therefore differed importantly from Stuart Hall's more radical democratic vision of it, as evidenced by his subsequent rejection of New Labour.

58. The phrase "hollowing out" is from R. A. W. Rhodes. See Rhodes, "The Hollowing Out of the State: The Changing Nature of the Public Service in Britain," *Political Quarterly* 65, no. 2 (1994): 138–51.

59. Ben Pitcher, *The Politics of Multiculturalism: Race and Racism in Contemporary Britain* (New York: Palgrave Macmillan, 2009), 79–80, and Pathak, *Future of Multicultural Britain,* 107ff.

60. The Race Relations (Amendment) Act 2000 and the Racial and Religious Hatred Act 2006.

61. The Equality Act 2010 and its precursor the Equality Act 2006.

62. Pathak, *Future of Multicultural Britain,* 11, and Joppke, *Immigration and the Nation-State,* chap. 4.

63. David Goodhart, "Too Diverse?" *Prospect* 95, February 2004; "National Anxieties," *Prospect* 123, June 2006; and David Goodhart, *Progressive Nationalism: Citizenship and the Left* (London: Demos, 2006), 22.

64. Quoted in Meer, *Citizenship, Identity and the Politics of Multiculturalism,* 24.

65. Pathak, *Future of Multicultural Britain,* 40ff.

66. United Kingdom, Home Office, *Secure Borders, Safe Haven* (London: Home Office, 2002).

67. For a discussion of these reports, see Pitcher, *Politics of Multiculturalism,* 100–101.

68. See ibid., 67ff. For a more positive view of these, see chapter 2 by Meer and Modood in this volume. These tests were in part designed by Bernard Crick and came into force in 2005; they were revamped by the Cameron government in 2013 to include British "values" and "history." See Home Office, *Life in the United Kingdom: A Guide for New Residents,* 3rd ed. (London: Home Office, 2013).

69. See Meer, *Citizenship, Identity and the Politics of Multiculturalism,* 22–23, and chapter 2 by Meer and Modood in this volume.

70. "Theresa May Vows to Be 'one nation' Prime Minister," BBC News, July 13, 2016.

71. David Cameron, transcript, "Speech on Radicalisation and Islamic Extremism," *New Statesman,* February 5, 2011, accessed November 29, 2018, http://goo.gl/Z7gmbT.

72. Quoted in Peter Dominiczak and Rosa Prince, "David Cameron to Fast-Track Tough Anti-Terror Laws," *Daily Telegraph,* May 13, 2015, accessed November 29, 2018, http://goo.gl/76TmcY. Cameron's governments introduced a cap on non-EU immigration, tightened student visa rules, passed legislation making it harder for migrants to receive welfare benefits and free health care, and introduced more legislation primarily targeting illegal immigration. See, e.g., the Immigration Act 2014.

73. See "Shared Values Unite UK People, Says PM in Easter Message," BBC News, April 16, 2017.

74. In his keynote speech at the 2012 Labour Party conference the then Labour leader Ed Miliband took the extraordinary step of claiming the label "One Nation" for Labour.

75. See Pitcher, *Politics of Multiculturalism*.

76. This trope was ubiquitous in the referendum campaign. See Nigel Farage's exhortation to reconnect with "our kith and kin in the Commonwealth" in his "Why You Should Vote for Brexit This Thursday," *Independent,* June 20, 2016. See also Mike Finn, "Dunkirk, Bond and All That: The Brexit Myth of British Exceptionalism," August 23, 2016, accessed November 29, 2018, http://blogs.lse.ac.uk/brexit/2016/08/23/dunkirk-bond-and-all-that-the-brexit-myth-of-british-exceptionalism, and Shaj Mathew, "Brexit Exposes Britain's Massive Inferiority Complex," *New Republic,* June 22, 2016, for discussion and further links.

77. See, e.g., Amber Rudd's speech at the Conservative Party conference on October 4, 2016, accessed November 29, 2018, https://blogs.spectator.co.uk/2016/10/full-text-amber-rudds-conference-speech, and the subsequent accusations of racism and ethno-nationalism that it provoked: Shane Croucher, "British Jobs for British Workers: How a Far-Right Meme Went Mainstream," *International Business Times,* October 6, 2016, and Harry Cockburn, "Amber Rudd Speech Likened to Hitler's *Mein Kampf,*" *Independent,* October 5, 2016.

78. Richard Ashcroft and Mark Bevir, "Pluralism, National Identity and Citizenship: Britain after Brexit," *Political Quarterly* 87 (2016): 355–59.

79. Ibid., 355–56 and n. 4.

80. Lord Ashcroft, "How the United Kingdom Voted on Thursday . . . and Why," June 24, 2016, accessed November 29, 2018, http://lordashcroftpolls.com/2016/06/how-the-united-kingdom-voted-and-why.

81. *Scotland's Future* (Edinburgh: Scottish Government, 2013), 271.

82. "Alex Salmond: We Must Leave UK but Maintain Our Other Unions," *Herald,* July 12, 2013.

83. Ashcroft and Bevir, "Liberal Democracy, Nationalism and Culture."

84. Will Kymlicka, *Liberalism, Community, and Culture* (Oxford: Oxford University Press, 1989), and *Multicultural Citizenship* (Oxford: Clarendon Press, 1995).

85. For an influential and insightful discussion, see David Marquand, "After Whig Imperialism: Can There Be a New British Identity?" *Journal of Ethnic and Migration Studies* 21, no. 2 (1995): 183–93.

3

Accentuating Multicultural Britishness

An Open or Closed Activity?

Nasar Meer, University of Edinburgh
Tariq Modood, University of Bristol

In this chapter, we explore some of the political discourse around contemporary debates about Britishness and the alleged "retreat" of multiculturalism. Although new discourses of Britishness have accompanied new policies prioritizing types of unity, neither of these have completely overridden the recognition of "difference" and anti-discrimination that previously comprised multiculturalism at both the local and national levels. On the contrary, although a sense of plural Britishness owes something to the UK's multinational character, it undeniably also reflects the political integration and contestations of postwar Commonwealth migrants and their descendants. While the story of Commonwealth nonwhite immigration to Britain is one of incremental immigration controls, it is also a story about anti-racism and multiculturalism guiding the redefinition of what it means to be a "British" citizen.

Some years ago we argued that contemporary revisions of British multiculturalism could be understood as evidence of a "civic re-balancing."[1] That reading was in marked contrast to an emerging thesis, proposed by a number of commentators, which pointed to a "post-multicultural" era, or at least contained the view that we were witnessing a "retreat" of multiculturalism.[2] We agreed (and still do) that the *term* had become politically damaged, but we concluded that the policies and discourses that make up the strands of British multiculturalism remained in place, even though they have been contested and joined by others. We sought to show that there are a number of intellectual and political developments (sometimes competing, sometimes complementary) that have been shaping British multiculturalism over the medium to long term, in which current changes need to be located and interpreted. One implication being that it is a mistake to view British multiculturalism as a completed or closed project, not least because the identities it seeks to take account of are dynamic, even when they are coherent, and a *political* multiculturalism would thus always need to be open to renewal—as indeed it has been.

Our argument was that it is short-sighted to view the elevation of previously perhaps underemphasized features of national identity as an abandonment of British multiculturalism. Such developments need no more lead to the abandonment of British multiculturalism than would lead to the abandonment of other public policy approaches concerned with promoting equality of access, participation, and public recognition, such as gender mainstreaming and the disability rights agenda. On the contrary, in the case of a multiculturalism sensitive to ethnic, racial, and religious differences, the pursuit of an inclusive national identity appeared to reconcile itself to what had earlier been promoted (perhaps to the disappointment and frustration of critics of multiculturalism). For example, even as he and other Conservatives spoke derisively of multiculturalism, the leading right-wing Cabinet Minister Michael Gove MP also stated "Britishness is about a mongrel identity."[3] Similarly, Pauline Neville-Jones, a figure regarded as on the right of the Conservative Party, led a review group that argued: "We need to rebuild Britishness in ways which . . . allow us to understand the contributions which all traditions, whether primarily ethnic or national, have made and are making to our collective identity."[4] Indeed, a Leverhulme project that interviewed cabinet ministers and shadow cabinet ministers in 2007/08 did not find a uniformity of views on this matter but instead considerable cross-party agreement that British national identity had to be opened up to include minorities, and that politicians and the state had a role to play in this process.[5]

Even while emphasizing that integration was something that had to be worked on, politicians of all hues made glowing references to the opening ceremony of the 2012 London Olympics and the success of Team GB, including the Somalia-born Mo Farah and the mixed race Jessica Ennis. Indeed, the opening ceremony of the Olympic Games in London in July 2012 was an excellent expression of a multicultural Britishness that New Labour tried to articulate without ever quite succeeding. Its positive reception in the British media—including the same papers that had lambasted the Commission on Multi-Ethnic Britain (CMEB) some years earlier—shows how far we have advanced.[6] An Australian political theorist opined that the Britain displayed at the Olympics meant that many countries were now "looking to Britain as an example of a dynamic multicultural society united by a generous patriotism."[7] The left-wing journalist Yasmin Alibhai-Brown, a member of the CMEB, who returned her MBE as a protest against the Iraq War, wrote: "These two weeks have been a watershed of true significance. There has been a visceral reaction among black and Asian Britons to what we have seen. For some, it has been perhaps the first time they have really felt a part of this country. For others, the promise of tolerance and integration has come true."[8]

Since the publication of "The Multicultural State We're In" in 2009, which covered the period since the mid-1960s in broad terms and the New Labour governments in detail, public policy developments have continued apace. There has not yet, however, been much peer-reviewed analysis of the Conservative-Liberal coalition (2010–15) or the subsequent Conservative majority government (2015–).[9] In this chapter, we thus begin by reminding ourselves of the core features of British multiculturalism as we have understood it, before turning to the present government's strategy, which is deemed by some to be forging a new path. Current multicultural strategy is allied (indeed twinned) with significant changes in both immigration/settlement policies and approaches to anti-terrorism; the former are widely touted as being more restrictive and perhaps even leading to something like a British guest worker model, and the latter identifies "integration" as one of the primary objectives of counter-radicalism.[10]

We should not, however, ignore the potential significance of centrifugal tendencies for questions of "integration" in Britain that have become increasingly prominent since the publication of our 2009 article. These include the galvanized movement for the "break up of Britain" evident in the 45 percent of the electorate that voted in favor of Scottish independence; the potential fracturing of the European project and the prospect of splintering states therein (or formal tiering of membership); and the rise of popular English nationalisms, whether in relatively benign, though ultraconservative, forms like the English Democrats, or more menacing articulations of the Far Right that explicitly trade on an anti-Muslim rather than an anti-minority platform such as the English Defence League.[11]

CONTEXTUALIZING THE TERRAIN

While multiculturalism in Britain had for some time been perceived as creaking under the weight of "culturally unreasonable or theologically alien [Muslim] demands," there was a noticeable increase in governmental and non-right-wing criticism of multiculturalism after urban riots in the north of England in 2001.[12] By 2004, a swathe of publications and institutions of the center and/or liberal left—including *Prospect,* the *Observer,* the *Guardian,* the Commission for Racial Equality (CRE), Open Democracy, Channel 4, and the British Council—had held seminars or produced special publications with titles like "Is Multiculturalism Dead?" With a chorus of commentators declaring that multiculturalism had been killed by the London bombings of 7/7,[13] it is therefore not surprising that it is commonplace to characterize British multiculturalism as being "in retreat."[14]

In querying the validity of this assessment, we distinguish at the outset between those seeking to point to a normative or descriptive tendency and others who have made little attempt to disguise their political motives in rejecting Britain's multiculturalism. In the latter camp, we could include, on the center left, the influential commentator David Goodhart, who evidently sympathizes with the position of those he perhaps unfairly calls "Burkeans" that "we feel more comfortable with, and are readier to share with and sacrifice for, those with whom we have shared histories and similar values. To put it bluntly—most of us prefer our own kind."[15] We could also include Trevor Phillips, previously chair of the Commission for Racial Equality (CRE) and its successor, the Equality and Human Rights Commission (EHRC), who stated that Britain should "kill off multiculturalism," because it "suggests separateness."[16] While in opposition David Cameron characterized British multiculturalism as a "barrier" that divided British society,[17] and subsequently as Prime Minister argued that "the doctrine of "state of multiculturalism" has encouraged culturally different people to live apart from one another and apart from the mainstream."[18] Perhaps seeking to stake out a British *Leitkultur* (lead culture), Cameron also complained that multiculturalism led to the minimization of Christianity as a guiding public ethos, allowing "segregated communities to behave in ways that run completely counter to our values and has not contained that extremism but allowed it to grow and prosper."[19]

While a much stronger and vitriolic critique is not unusual from a center right in Britain that has historically lamented and contested governmental interventions recognizing the diversity of minority populations,[20] opposition to the recognition and support of minority cultural practices in Britain has undoubtedly had a qualitatively greater impact since it was joined by "the pluralistic center-left [and] articulated by people who previously rejected polarizing models of race and class and were sympathetic to the 'rainbow,' coalitional politics of identity."[21]

One outcome for the British approach is that the inclusion of ethnic minorities is now increasingly premised upon greater degrees of qualification. This was epitomized by the introduction of citizenship tests, the swearing of oaths during citizenship ceremonies and language proficiency requirements for new migrants, as well as repeated calls for an unambiguous disavowal of "radicalism" or "extremism" from Muslims in particular. Writing in the *British Journal of Sociology* in 2004, Christian Joppke interpreted these changes as evidence of a "retreat" from multiculturalism and a "turn to civic integration" that is "most visible in Britain and The Netherlands, the two societies in Europe . . . that had so far been most committed to official multiculturalism."[22] Our argument was that Joppke assumes that "civic integration" and "multiculturalism" constitute a dichotomy or a zero-sum equation, and thus ignores the extent to which they could just as plausibly be synthesized in a potential outgrowth of one another. For if it is the case that Britain is engaged in a "retreat" from multiculturalism, heralding a victory for liberal or republican universalism, would it not follow that, as Keith Banting and Will Kymlicka point out, it must "have rejected the claims of substate national groups and indigenous peoples *as well as* immigrants. After all, the claims of national groups and indigenous peoples typically involve a much more dramatic insertion of ethnocultural diversity into the public sphere, and more dramatic degrees of differentiated citizenship [emphasis in original]."[23]

Since this does not appear to be the case in Britain at least, with quite the opposite in fact seeming to be true, one explanation of the "widely divergent assessments of the short history and potential future of multiculturalism" pertains to the meaning and usage of the term itself. Indeed, this "highly contested and chameleon-like neologism whose colours change to suit the complexion of local conditions" seems to have a "chameleon" quality that is adopted differently in support of different projects.[24] For example, while some intellectuals, commentators, and politicians of differing persuasions have in recent years united in their rejection of post-immigration multiculturalism—our concern here—their critiques have simultaneously revealed the diverging ways in which multiculturalism in Britain has been conceived.

This chapter argues that there are *at least* three discernible contemporary positions: (1) an integration and social cohesion perspective that seeks to include minorities through a process of greater assimilation to majority norms and customs; (2) an alternative, explicitly secular "multiculture" or "conviviality" approach that welcomes the "fact" of difference, and stresses lifestyle- and consumption-based behavioral identities that are anti-essentialist in orientation, and which invalidate "group" identities; and (3) a political multiculturalism that can to some extent incorporate the priorities of either or both of these positions, while also inclusive of "groupings," not least subjectively conceived ethno-religious minority groupings.[25]

Of these three positions, it appears that the latter had been taking a cumulative and progressive institutional form since the early 1990s, mainly by developing certain racial equality discourses and policies beyond their starting points in a response to minority ethnic and religious assertiveness.[26] This has taken legal form in, for example, the outlawing of religious discrimination and the incitement to religious hatred, and an educational form in the inclusion in England of some non-Christian, non-Jewish faith schools within public sector maintained by local authorities.[27] It is *this* multiculturalism that has been the principal target of recent critiques from across the political spectrum. We argue, however, that rather than having been defeated, the fate of this peculiarly British multiculturalism currently remains undecided and might equally be characterized as subject to a "re-balancing" rather than a wholesale "retreat." One way to begin to explore the plausibility of this argument is to look at the most robust, coherent public policy advocacy of multiculturalism that Britain has known.

THE MULTICULTURAL MOMENT?

In the course of ushering in an era "after multiculturalism," Yasmin Alibhai-Brown has argued that "all societies and communities need to take stock periodically to assess whether existing cultural and political edifices are keeping up with the people and the evolving habitat."[28] Just such an exercise was the production of a report on *The Future of Multi-Ethnic Britain* by the Commission on the Future of

Multi-Ethnic Britain (CMEB). This report, sponsored by the Runnymede Trust and chaired by the political philosopher Bhikhu Parekh,[29] made over 140 policy recommendations to help Britain take advantage of "its rich diversity" and realize its full potential as "a confident and vibrant multicultural society."[30] It strongly endorsed both the possibility *and* desirability of forging a meta-membership of "Britishness" under which diversity could be sustained. To this end, its recommendations not only sought to prevent discrimination or overcome its effects, but simultaneously championed an approach that could move *beyond* conceptions of formal equality by recognizing the substantive elements of "real differences of experience, background and perception."[31] For example, the CMEB advocated a systematic type of ethnic monitoring that would "go beyond racism and culture blind strategies" and could be implemented across public institutions in order to promote an awareness of cultural diversity in general, and unwitting discrimination in particular.[32] This "multicultural moment" following the Stephen Lawrence Inquiry was when the New Labour government declared its commitment to creating a country where "every colour is a good colour," "everyone is treated according to their needs and rights," and "racial diversity is celebrated."[33] As then Prime Minister Tony Blair insisted:

"This nation has been formed by a particularly rich complex of experiences….. How can we separate out the Celtic, the Roman, the Saxon, the Norman, the Huguenot, the Jewish, the Asian and the Caribbean and all the other nations [*sic*] that have come and settled here? Why should we want to? It is precisely this rich mix that has made all of us what we are today."[34]

This was not only a time of reflection on the presence of institutional racism alongside Britain's ethnic diversity, however, but a period in which the policy recognition of Britain's historical multinational diversity was being concretized by devolution in Scotland, Wales, and Northern Ireland. It was not unreasonable, then, that post-migrant ethnic minorities too were seeking recognition of particularities arising from previously demeaned identities; not as self-governance, but through an endorsement of the pluralizing of the mainstream with their own distinctive differences derived from ethnicity, religion, or culture. This high-water mark of British multiculturalism was in truth the consequence the cumulative political movement following the migrations of the parents and grandparents of many of Britain's post-immigrant ethnic minorities, who had exercised their Commonwealth citizenship by moving to its metropole from South Asia, the Caribbean, and elsewhere. The CMEB recommended that the government formally declare Britain "a multicultural society," hoping that this would invalidate the social and political inequalities derived from minority cultural differences.[35]

That the report was subject to an unrelenting critique from the Right, not least in the national media, has been well documented elsewhere.[36] What is worth noting here, however, is the extent to which it also incurred the wrath of some prominent liberals who considered its approach a grave contravention of universalistic principles, not least those recommendations that promoted diversity as a means to facilitate equality.[37] Lord Anthony Lester, one of the founders of the Runnymede Trust and a key architect of Britain's race-equality legislation, said of the report that "much of the more theoretical sections is written entirely from the perspective of victims, with little to challenge attitudes and practices prevalent among some minorities and their leaders that are difficult to reconcile with the ideals of a liberal-democratic society based upon the rule of law."[38] Such a view minimizes, however, both a key problem identified by the CMEB—the role of differences that serve as an obstacle to political equality in the public sphere—and substantive elements of the British approach that has intertwined, albeit inconsistently, agendas relating to equality and diversity.[39]

A MOVE TO NATIONAL COHESION

One of the components of diversity that we have in mind has developed a prominence over a longer duration and increasingly in the shadow of a policy trajectory concerning naturalization and civic unity. For example, the 1997-98 government-sponsored inquiry into citizenship education chaired by Sir Bernard Crick explicitly avoided the relationship between citizenship and nationality: "We're not dealing with nationality, we're dealing with a skill, a knowledge, an attitude for citizenship," Crick insisted.[40] This understanding of citizenship as mainly about delivering the knowledge and skills to pupils so as to promote active participation has shifted significantly over time.[41] Whereas citizenship and nationality were clearly distinguished by the original Qualification Curriculum Advisory Commission (QCA), they were explicitly juxtaposed in the domain of naturalization following Crick's "migration" from the Department of Education to the Home Office after the 1998 report.[42]

The Home Office Advisory Group, also chaired by Crick, was set up by Home Secretary David Blunkett to develop proposals for language and citizenship education for immigrants applying for naturalization as British citizens. The Advisory Group's report, published in September 2003, demonstrates the ways in which the "failed integration hypothesis" of the various community cohesion reports/strategies has informed the citizenship strategies for "new" migrants to the United Kingdom.[43] For example, the Nationality, Immigration and Asylum Act (2002) explicitly introduced a test for residents seeking British citizenship (implemented in 2005), and those immigrants applying for "indefinite leave to remain" in the UK (effectively implemented since April 2, 2007). Applicants must show "a sufficient knowledge of English, Welsh or Scottish Gaelic" and also "a sufficient knowledge about life in the United Kingdom" through passing the test.[44]. If applicants do not have sufficient knowledge of English, they should attend English for Speakers of Other Languages (ESOL) and citizenship classes. Some categories can get free tuition, but in principle applicants have to pay for the classes, and also for the test itself.

Overall, the focus of David Blunkett's citizenship strategy was less on the deliberative quality of identities, forged (and modified) in interaction with others, than on a rather more "practical" intervention, in which basic skills (English language proficiency and a superficial "knowledge of life in the UK") become the means whereby civic responsibilities can be taken up. The ability to speak English thus formed the bedrock of the dialogic, participatory, and active citizenship elements advocated by Blunkett's citizenship/integration discourse. The provision of English-language training for new and established migrants was described in the *Strength in Diversity* consultation document as a means of providing "practical support" that would "overcome the barriers to integration" that might face those newly arrived in Britain.

This relationship between English-language skills and the idea of a culture of active citizenship resurfaced as being central to the findings of the Commission on Integration and Community Cohesion (CICC) in both its interim statement and final report published in 2007.[47] In the latter, English-language proficiency is linked with enhancing participation in civic culture in new and established migrant groups. The emphasis on English-language proficiency and increasing participation and dialogue between communities found in the Cantle-Blunkett civic assimilationist discourse (and to a certain extent in the CICC's recommendations) is, however, relegated to the category of "taken for granted skills" new migrants are expected to possess. As Prime Minister Gordon Brown wanted more from immigrants than just the ability to speak English and to have knowledge of "life in the UK," he wants would-be citizens to "become British" at a deeper level.[48]

It is telling, however, that the government insisted that "it would be unfair for migrants to have to answer questions on British history that many British people would have difficulties with." Home Office explanatory documents stress that the tests aim at "integration," but without this meaning "complete assimilation."[45] What this illustrates are the strong emphases on the experience of living in Britain rather an attempt to define Britishness per se. A critical interpretation of these initiatives is offered by Derek McGhee who is worth quoting at length:

> The "integration" of "new" migrant communities in asylum and immigration policy, as well as the desegregation of "established" migrant communities in community cohesion discourses, were to be achieved through a common policy solution: the establishment of an inclusive sense of common citizenship. In turn, in asylum and immigration policy, the emphasis in the process of attaining British citizenship began to have a distinct "community cohesion" flavor, especially in its emphasis on the "new citizenship pedagogy," namely, on building the capacity in "new citizens" for effective engagement and "active citizenship." This was to be achieved by transforming naturalization from a bureaucratic process into "an act of commitment to Britain and an important step in the process of achieving integration into

our society." The acquisition of the English language and knowledge of "British life" were presented as key to successful integration of "new" migrants, as, without them, according to the Home Office, migrant communities were ill-equipped to take an active role in society.[46]

It is difficult not to recognize this as a particularly critical reading, however, given the kinds of measures introduced and the extent to which they retain strong commitments to anti-discrimination and the recognition of difference within them. For example, in the Home Office's *Strength in Diversity,* the government maintains that: "Civil renewal is at the heart of the Government's vision of life in our 21st century communities. It aims to reconnect citizens with the public realm by empowering them to influence the development of solutions to problems affecting them. It is vital that barriers to participation— from lack of confidence and capacity to express one's views to prejudices which lead to exclusion—are tackled so that the aspiration for wider engagement can be translated into reality."[49]

This perhaps also illustrates two further continuities. The first concerns the utilization of notions of social capital within stipulations of civic renewal, as elaborated at the beginning, and the second is what has been termed the "Janus face" of British race-relations traditions (progressive to insiders but regressive to outsiders). This is perhaps symbolically illustrated by how "Britain as a diverse society" is one of the six areas upon which applicants seeking citizenship are tested. Yet it is also worth noting how on several occasions government ministers at the time maintained that "this is not a test of someone's ability to be British or a test of their Britishness. It is a test of their preparedness to become citizens."[50] The key point is that while scholars took the rhetorical failure/demise of multiculturalism at face value, when it required empirical rebuttal.[51]

IMMIGRATION, INTEGRATION, AND SECURITY

In "The Multicultural State We're In" (2009), we surveyed a number of further public policy documents and developments in public policy and concluded that what had been taking place in Britain could accurately be called a "retreat" of multiculturalism. Rather, the emergent multiculturalism of the 1990s that was attempting to accommodate Muslim communities has been simultaneously subjected to at least two critiques. One emphasizes commonality, cohesion, and integration; the other was alive to fluidity, multiplicity, and hybridity, especially in relation to expressive culture, entertainment, and consumption. Each critique was a reaction against ethno-religious communitarianism, but neither emphasized what is not usually present in some form in most accounts of multiculturalism. Hence, we argued that "it is better to see these newly asserted emphases and the interaction between these three positions, as a re-balancing of multiculturalism rather than its erasure."[52] But this should not be taken to mean that we underestimate the implications of competing developments.

The Immigration, Asylum and Nationality Act 2006 was the basis for the post-Blair migration and integration strategy of Prime Minister Gordon Brown and Home Secretary Jacqui Smith from 2008 on. In particular, Brown elaborated how becoming a British citizen should not just be a matter of the applicants' choice, but ought to reflect a contract whereby they accept the responsibilities of *becoming* British and thus "earn" the right to citizenship.[53] To support this, a status of "probationary citizenship" was created as a pathway between temporary immigration status and either naturalization or the right to abode. Crucially, the length of this period could be reduced by two years in cases where applicants demonstrated that they were contributing to the community through "active citizenship." This could be achieved through "formal volunteering" or "civic activism." The idea of taking this further and developing a points-based system of citizenship was put forward in 2009. This included the prospect of "deducting points or applying penalties for not integrating into the British way of life, for criminal or anti-social behaviour, or in circumstances where an active disregard for UK values is demonstrated."[54]

An overview of the new selectivity under the managed migration points system provided by McGhee points to the consolidation into five "tiers" of the more than eighty existing work and study routes to permission to remain:

- Tier 1: Highly skilled workers (e.g., scientists or entrepreneurs)
- Tier 2: Skilled workers with a job offer (e.g., nurses, teachers, engineers)
- Tier 3: Low-skilled workers filling specific temporary labor shortages (e.g., construction workers for a particular project)
- Tier 4: Students;
- Tier 5: Youth mobility and temporary workers (e.g., working holidaymakers or musicians coming to play a concert)[55]

The Conservative-Liberal coalition government narrowed these tiers further, mainly by eliminating Tier 3.[56] The most controversial change, taking away the right to remain in Britain for more than five years from most Tier 2 migrant workers earning less than £35,000 a year, did not come into effect until April 2016.[57] This last reform may perhaps be taken perhaps as evidence of an emerging guest-worker type of approach for new migrants, although Brexit will certainly complicate matters still further.

A notable trend during the period we were initially exploring was the tendency for slippage between integration and security agendas. Whereas this was initially *implicit,* it is now a much more explicit coupling. Indeed, the striking development, and one that could not have been anticipated by proponents of multiculturalism in the 1990s, is how the assemblage of citizenship strategies has been reorganized to give a central role to counterterrorism strategies. This has not happened overnight with the present government, and indeed owes some provenance to the previous administration and the way in which following the London bombings, and several aborted bombings in a similar "leaderless Jihad," the Labour government (1997–2010) created seven working groups comprising representatives of Muslim communities under the rubric of "Preventing Extremism Together" (PET, or "Prevent").[58] These were clustered as follows: (1) engaging with young people; (2) providing a full range of education services in the UK that meet the needs of the Muslim community; (3) engaging with Muslim women; (4) supporting regional and local initiatives and community actions; (5) imam training and accreditation and the role of mosques as a resource for the whole community; (6) security—Islamophobia, protecting Muslims from extremism, and community confidence in policing; and (7) tackling extremism and radicalization.

Initiated by the Home Office, this would later fall under the remit of the subsequently created Department for Communities and Local Government (DCLG). These working groups devised a series of proposals to develop "practical means" of tackling violent extremism. Sixty-four recommendations were put forward in a report published in November 2005, which especially emphasized three recommendations that would serve as central planks in the unfolding of government strategies concerned with preventing violent extremism.

These included, firstly, the development of a "scholars' roadshow" coordinated by British Muslim organizations to facilitate "influential mainstream" Muslim thinkers to address audiences of young British Muslims. The rationale being that these speakers would distil effective arguments against extremist justification for terrorism in denouncing it as un-Islamic, so as to "counter the ideological and theological underpinnings of the terrorist narrative."[59] A second proposal focused on the creation of Muslim forums against extremism and Islamophobia. These could be led by key individuals and brought together members of local Muslim communities, law enforcement, and public service agencies to discuss how to tackle extremism and Islamophobia in their area. The third and perhaps most substantive recommendation, in terms of proposed structural capacity building within British Muslim communities, promoted the formation of a Mosques and Imams National Advisory Board (MINAB). To this end, a steering group of Muslim leaders undertook an extensive national consultation on matters such as the accreditation of imams, better governance of mosques, and interfaith activity. Alongside this professional development program or "upskilling" of imams and mosque officials, recommendations were also made for a national campaign and coalition to increase the visibility of Muslim women, and specifically to empower and equip them in the course of becoming "active citizens."

While Prevent inevitably included some security-related work, it was criticized for a variety of reasons, "ranging from targeting the wrong people to stigmatizing Muslim communities by treating them all as potential terrorists."[60] Two recurring issues were that: firstly, intelligence agencies were using the softer cohesion aspects of Prevent "to spy and illicitly collect intelligence, which has dramatically harmed the programme as a whole";[61] and secondly, that Prevent was oriented to address wider social policy within Muslim communities which implied that this policy was only valuable because it contributed to counterterrorism (something illustrated by the fact that funding was directly linked to the size of the Muslim population in a local authority, not on the basis of known risk).

It is unsurprising that a strategy premised upon entering, and to some extent reformulating, the life worlds of British Muslim communities has been the subject of critical debate in the study of ethnic relations more broadly.[62] That this objective was intended could be gleaned from the fact that immediately after the London bombing, the Home Office signaled that it would establish a Commission on Integration and Cohesion (COIC) "to advise on how, consistent with their own religion and culture, there is better integration of those parts of the community inadequately integrated."[63]

The previous government had sought to advance Prevent through a variety of local community partnerships and across statutory bodies, as well as voluntary agencies and community groups "with police forces, local authorities and their partners working closely together to oversee and deliver the project."[64] To foster these outcomes the Prevent-related funding of around £45 million to foster these outcomes for the period from 2008–9 to 2010–11 was distributed via local authorities. The Prevent strategy thus signaled some diffusion of formal responsibilities for policy implementation and service delivery in a way that some see as indicative of broader developments in "governance" practices whereby "responsibility and accountability for a wide range of social issues is increasingly focused towards local levels, while at the same time centralized control in terms of resources and target-setting is maintained."[65]

While it is not immediately apparent in the earlier quotation, the incorporation of faith-based groups from the non-profit "third sector" is potentially party to novel approaches to engaging with religious minorities through the practices and models of representation, stakeholders, and advocacy in the consultative arena; perhaps as a development of what has been termed a multicultural "municipal drift."[66] The extent of this shift is not the central focus here, other than in elaborating the manner in which the Prevent agenda, in constituting part of the broad counterterrorism strategy, appears to be simultaneously subject to at least two broader prevailing dynamics, comprising firstly "the implementation of anti-terrorist laws that can be used disproportionately against Muslims leading to the potential for their increased surveillance and control and thereby serving to reduce Muslims' trust of state institutions, while [secondly] at the same time pursuing approaches that acknowledge, and stress the importance of, the involvement of British . . . Muslim communities in helping to combat extremism."[67]

Spalek and Imoual frame these dynamics relationally in terms of "harder" and "softer" strategies of engagement, whereby the former may be understood as consisting of various means of surveillance, policing, intelligence gathering, and so on.[68] The latter, meanwhile, would include the development of dialogue, participation, and community feedback between Muslim communities, state agencies, and voluntary organizations in a way that may serve to increase trust in "the battle for hearts and minds." For example, the Prevent strategy also emphasized long-established equality traditions historically orientated towards ethnic and racial minorities and sought to extend them to Muslims: "The Prevent strategy requires a specific response, but we must also make the most of the links with wider community work to reduce inequalities, tackle racism and other forms of extremism (e.g. extreme far right), build cohesion and empower communities. . . . Likewise, it is recognised that the arguments of violent extremists, which rely on creating a 'them' and an 'us,' are less likely to find traction in cohesive communities."[69]

This built upon recognition of Muslim religious difference in government policies and legislation that has been manifested in other ways, including measures against religious discrimination as set out in the Equality Acts of 2006 and 2010. The tensions, then, surround the extent to which the prevailing British citizenship being extended to Muslims through social and community-cohesion measures is twinned, or placed within the same register as, counterterrorism strategies that import or rely upon certain securitized "hard" aspects of this dimension of state-Muslim engagement. The risk has always been that "active citizenship" for Muslims is to some extent framed in terms of demonstrable counterterrorism activities in a way that assumes that Muslim communities in general are the "locus. . . of extremism."[70] Arguably, this risk is now being actively stated as a policy ambition, as the concern is expressed within the Prevent strategy that insufficient attention has been paid to whether Muslim organizations comprehensively subscribe to mainstream British values.

As then Home Secretary Theresa May stated in her foreword to the second iteration of the Prevent strategy: "We will respond to the ideological challenge of terrorism and the threat from those who promote it. In doing so, we must be clear: the ideology of extremism and terrorism is the problem; legitimate religious belief emphatically is not. But we will not work with extremist organizations that oppose our values of universal human rights, equality before the law, democracy and full participation in our society. If organizations do not accept these fundamental values, we will not work with them and we will not fund them."[72] As such, while it is not quite the case that, as Liz Fekete has suggested, public policy engaging with Muslims amounts to being "tough on mosques, tough on the causes of mosques," it has become common to find statements such as that made by the former Communities Secretary Ruth Kelly, that Muslim organizations must take "a proactive leadership role in tackling extremism and defending our shared values."[71]

The new Prevent strategy thus takes a much more interventionist line regarding the constellation of British Muslim politics, forthrightly insisting that the government will not fund organizations "that hold extremist views or support terrorist-related activity of any kind."[73] Much here hinges on the word "extremist," and mainstream organizations easily fall foul of this threshold by, for example, taking oppositional positions on foreign policy or towards the state of Israel. The current integration strategy of Department for Communities and Local Government thus explicitly asserts the previously implicit view that Prevent is "distinct from but linked to integration, tackling non-violent extremism where it creates an environment conducive to terrorism and popularises ideas which are espoused by terrorist groups."[74] A parallel effort was the Conservative-Liberal coalition's three-year "Near Neighbours" strategy, a program to "bring people together in diverse communities, helping them build relationships and collaborate to improve the local community they live in," which was run by the Church Urban Fund, a Church of England charity set up in 1987, and initially focused on Birmingham, Bradford, Leicester and East London.[75] Nevertheless, the Prevent agenda remains the British government's most significant investment in Muslim civil society organizations.

CONCLUSIONS

While new policies, complementing anti-discrimination strategies and recognition of "difference," albeit with an emphasis on commonalities, have been introduced in the twenty-first century at both local and national levels, this has not eliminated multiculturalism. It is most striking that when senior British politicians seek to define Britishness, they simultaneously appeal to a political-institutional history (monarchs, rule of law, parliamentary democracy, etc.) and to cultural diversity.[76] Although this sense of plural Britishness owes something to the UK's multinational character, it undeniably also reflects the political integration of postwar Commonwealth migrants and their descendants. In general, the story of Commonwealth nonwhite immigration to Britain is one of immigration controls, but also of redefining what it means to be "British" through anti-racism and multiculturalism.

NOTES

1. See Nasar Meer and Tariq Modood, "The Multicultural State We're In: Muslims, 'Multiculture' and the 'Civic Re-Balancing' of British Multiculturalism," *Political Studies* 57, no. 3 (2009): 473–97. In retrospect, it might have been more appropriate to term what we were describing a "civic thickening," which does not imply that we have had too much of one rather than the other. In addition to the original piece, see how this argument was taken up by Daniel Faas, *Negotiating Political Identities: Multiethnic Schools and Youth in Europe* (Farnham, Surrey, UK: Ashgate, 2010); Dan Rodriguez-Garcia, "Beyond Assimilation and Multiculturalism: A Critical Review of the Debate on Managing Diversity," *Journal of International Migration and Integration* 11, no. 3 (2010): 251–71; Fethi Mansouri and Juliet Pietsch, "Local Governance and the Challenge of Religious Pluralism in Liberal Democracies: An

Australian Perspective," *Journal of Intercultural Studies* 32 (2011): 279–92; and Peter Kivisto, "We Really Are All Multiculturalists Now," *Sociological Quarterly* 53, no. 1 (2012): 1–24.

2. Christian Joppke, "The Retreat of Multiculturalism in the Liberal State: Theory and Policy," *British Journal of Sociology* 55, no. 2 (2004): 237–57.

3. Michael Gove, "What Do Britons Have in Common?" (paper presented at Quilliam Foundation Conference, April 23, 2009); Gove, "1688 and All That," in *Being British: The Search for the Values That Bind the Nation,* ed. Matthew d'Ancona and Gordon Brown, 197–207 (Edinburgh: Mainstream, 2009); and Gove, "All Pupils Will Learn Our Island Story" (speech, October 5, 2010).

4. Pauline Neville-Jones, *An Unquiet World: Submission to the Shadow Cabinet* (London: National and International Security Policy Group, 2007), 23. Accessed November 30, 2018, http://image.guardian. co.uk/sys-files/Politics/documents/2007/07/26/securityreport.pdf..

5. Varun Uberoi and Tariq Modood. "Inclusive Britishness: A Multiculturalist Advance," *Political Studies* 61, no. 1 (2013): 23–41.

6. Sunder Katwala, "An Island Story: Boyle's Olympic Opening Was Irresistibly British," *Open Democracy,* July 31, 2012, and Commission on the Future of Multi-Ethnic Britain, *The Future of Multi-Ethnic Britain: The Parekh Report* (London: Profile Books, 2000).

7. Thinethavone Soutphommasane, "Labour Can Make the Most of a Britain Alive with Olympic Spirit," *Observer,* August 19, 2012.

8. Yasmin Alibhai-Brown, "Mo's Joyful Embrace of Britishness and Why These Games Mark a Truly Historic Watershed," *Independent,* August 12, 2012.

9. Paul Thomas, *Youth, Multiculturalism and Community Cohesion* (New York: Palgrave Macmillan, 2011).

10. Alan Travis, "Skilled Migrants to Lose Right to Settle in UK," *Guardian,* February 29, 2012.

11. Chris Allen, "Opposing Islamification or Promoting Islamophobia? Understanding the English Defence League," *Patterns of Prejudice* 45, no. 4 (2011).

12. Modood, *Multiculturalism,* 100.

13. Examples include William Pfaff's (2005) certainty that "these British bombers are a consequence of a misguided and catastrophic pursuit of multiculturalism"; Gilles Kepel's (2005) observation that the bombers "were the children of Britain's own multicultural society," and that the bombings have "smashed" the implicit social consensus that produced multiculturalism "to smithereens," alongside Martin Wolf's (2005) conclusion that multiculturalism's departure from the core political values that must underpin Britain's community "is dangerous because it destroys political community . . . [and] demeaning because it devalues citizenship. In this sense, at least, multiculturalism must be discarded as nonsense." See Pfaff, "A Monster of Our Own Making," *Observer,* August 20, 2005; Kepel, "Europe's Answer to Londonistan," *Open Democracy,* August 24, 2005; and Wolf, "When Multiculturalism Is a Nonsense," *Financial Times,* August 31, 2005. These views have also been elaborated in Andrew Anthony, *The Fallout: How a Guilty Liberal Lost His Innocence* (London: Jonathan Cape, 2007); Nick Cohen, *What's Left? How Liberals Lost Their Way* (London: HarperPerennial, 2007); Michael Gove, *Celsius 7/7* (London: Weidenfeld & Nicolson, 2006); and Melanie Phillips, *Londonistan: How Britain Created a Terror State Within* (London: Gibson Square Books, 2006). This suggests a large degree of convergence between commentators of the "Left" and "Right" on the topic of multiculturalism.

14. Bryan Appleyard, "Eureka," *Sunday Times,* December 17, 2006; Joppke, "Retreat of Multiculturalism"; Kepel, "Europe's Answer to Londonistan"; and Rod Liddle, "How Islam Killed Multiculturalism," *Spectator,* May 1, 2004.

15. David Goodhart, *The British Dream: Successes and Failures of Post-war Immigration* (London: Atlantic Books, 2014), and Goodhart, "Too Diverse?" *Prospect,* February 20, 2004.

16. Quoted in Tom Baldwin, "I Want an Integrated Society With a Difference," interview with Trevor Phillips, *Times,* April 3, 2004.

17. David Cameron, speech, Handsworth Mosque, Birmingham, January 30, 2007.

18. David Cameron, speech, Munich Security Conference, February 5, 2011, accessed November 30, 2018, www.number10.gov.uk/news/speeches-andtranscripts/2011/02/pms-speech-at-munich-security-conference-60293.

19. Quoted in Riazat Butt, "Cameron Calls for Return to Christian values as King James Bible turns 400," *Guardian*, December, 16, 2011.

20. See Tariq Modood, "Remaking Multiculturalism after 7/7," *Open Democracy*, September 29, 2005. The Center Right objects particularly to public provisions for minority cultural practices, on the grounds that these deviate from a core "majority" national identity to which minorities are required to assimilate. A good example of this view can be found in the *Salisbury Review*, a conservative magazine that was founded in 1982 with the influential conservative philosopher Roger Scruton as its editor. The role it played in the Honeyford affair—a controversy regarding multicultural education—provides an excellent case study of the main political argumentation contained within this position. See J. Mark Halstead, *Education, Justice and Cultural Diversity: An Examination of the Honeyford Affair, 1984–85* (London: Falmer Press, 1988).

21. Madeleine Bunting, "It Takes More than Tea and Biscuits to Overcome Indifference and Fear," *Guardian*, February 27, 2006, goes on to say that "the old alliance with the centre-left is fraying to breaking point; old allies in the battles against racism have jumped sides."

22. Joppke, "Retreat of Multiculturalism," 253. However, Christian Joppke, "Immigration and the Identity of Citizenship: The Paradox of Universalism," *Citizenship Studies* 12, no. 6 (2008): 537, withdrew this claim.

23. Keith Banting and Will Kymlicka, eds., *Multiculturalism and the Welfare State Recognition and Redistribution in Contemporary Democracies* (Oxford: Oxford University Press, 2007), 7.

24. David Pearson, of Victoria University in New Zealand, quoted in Peter Kivisto and Thomas Faist, *Citizenship: Discourse, Theory, and Transnational Prospects* (London: Blackwell, 2007), 35, a similar point is made by Katherine Smith, "Research, Policy and Funding: Academic Treadmills and the Squeeze on Intellectual Spaces," *British Journal Of Sociology* 61, no. 1 (2010): 176–95.

25. Some of the material in this chapter was published in N. Meer and T. Modood, "The Multicultural State We Are In: Muslims, 'Multiculture' and the 'Civic Re-balancing' of British Multiculturalism," *Political Studies* 57, no. 3 (2009): 473–97. The authors thank the publishers of the journal, Wiley-Blackwell, for permission to republish it.

26. Tariq Modood, *Multicultural Politics: Racism, Ethnicity and Muslims in Britain* (Edinburgh: Edinburgh University Press, 2005).

27. Tariq Modood, *Multicultural Politics: Racism, Ethnicity and Muslims in Britain* (Edinburgh: Edinburgh University Press, 2005).

28. Yasmin Alibhai-Brown, "After Multiculturalism," *Political Quarterly* 72, no. 1 (2001), 47.

29. Commission on the Future of Multi-Ethnic Britain, *Future of Multi-Ethnic Britain*. Interest disclosure: Modood was involved in this report.

30. Ibid., viii.

31. Ibid., 296.

32. Ibid., 297.

33. United Kingdom, Home Office, *Statement of Intent: Changes to Tier 1, Tier 2 and Tier 5 of the Points Based System; Overseas Domestic Workers; and Visitors* (London: Home Office, 2012).

34. Tony Blair, "Tony Blair's on Britain Speech," *Guardian*, March 28, 2000.

35. Commission on the Future of Multi-Ethnic Britain, *Future of Multi-Ethnic Britain*, 296.

36. Eugene McLaughlin and Sarah Neal, "Misrepresenting the Multicultural Nation, the Policy-Making Process, News Media Management and the Parekh Report," *Policy Studies* 25, no. 3 (2004): 155–74.

37. See Brian Barry, *Culture and Equality: An Egalitarian Critique of Multiculturalism* (Malden, MA: Polity Press, 2001).

38. Anthony Lester, "Nailing the Lie and Promoting Equality—The Jim Rose Lecture" (speech, Runnymede Trust, October 15, 2003).

39. Of course, feminists have long critiqued the ensuing power imbalances contained within the public/private sphere distinction. While one of the earliest, extended, critiques may be found in the work of Carole Pateman (1970), the late Iris Marion Young is probably the best-known advocate of consolidating the critique of the public/private sphere distinction by incorporating a multitude of minorities that are potentially oppressed by an unreconstructed public sphere. This led her to argue that "a democratic public sphere should provide mechanisms for the effective recognition and representation of the distinct voices and perspectives of those of its constituent groups that are oppressed or disadvantaged" (Young, *Justice and the Politics of Difference* [Princeton, NJ: Princeton University Press, 1990], 165).

40. Interview with Sir Bernard Crick, June 2002 quoted in Dina Kiwan, "Citizenship Education at the Cross-Roads: Four Models of Citizenship and Their Implications for Ethnic and Religious Diversity," *Oxford Review of Education* 34, no. 1 (2008): 39–58.

41. Ibid., 62.

42. Qualifications and Curriculum Authority, *Education for Citizenship and the Teaching of Democracy in Schools: Report of the Advisory Group on Citizenship,* ed. Bernard R. Crick et al. (London: Qualifications and Curriculum Authority, 1998).

43. United Kingdom, Home Office, *Life in the United Kingdom: A Journey to Citizenship* (London: Home Office, 2004).

44. Ibid., 11.

45. Ibid., 14.

46. Derek McGhee "The Paths to Citizenship: A Critical Examination of Immigration Policy in Britain since 2001," *Patterns of Prejudice* 43, no. 1 (2009): 48.

47. United Kingdom, Commission on Integration & Cohesion, *Our Shared Future: Themes, Messages and Challenges: A Final Analysis of the Key Themes from the Commission on Integration and Cohesion Consultation* (London: Home Office, 2007).

48. Ibid., 50–51.

49. United Kingdom, Home Office, *Strength in Diversity: Towards a Community Cohesion and Race Equality Strategy* (London: Home Office, 2004).

50. Quoted in Kiwan, "Citizenship Education at the Cross-Roads," 69.

51. See Meer and Modood, "Multicultural State We're In"; Uberoi and Modood. "Inclusive Britishness"; Peter Taylor-Gooby and Edmunde Waite, "Toward a More Pragmatic Multiculturalism? How the UK Policy Community Sees the Future of Ethnic Diversity Policies," *Governance* 27, no. 2 (2014): 267–89; Anthony Heath and Neli Demireva, "Has Multiculturalism Failed in Britain?" *Ethnic and Racial Studies* 37, no. 1 (2014): 161–80.

52. Meer and Modood, "Multicultural State We're In," 490.

53. Gordon Brown, "Managed Migration and Earned Citizenship," speech, Camden Centre, London, February 20, 2008, www.astrid-online.it/static/upload/protected/RDON/RDON-BROWN-Managed-Migration-and-Earned-Citizenship-20_02_08.pdf, accessed February 17, 2019.

54. Tufyal Choudhury, "Evolving Models of Multiculturalism in the United Kingdom," in *Interculturalism: Europe and Its Muslims in Search of Sound Societal Models,* ed. Michael Emerson (Brussels: Centre for European Policy Studies, 2011), 124.

55. McGhee, "Paths to Citizenship," 52.

56. Travis, "Skilled Migrants to Lose."

57. Ibid. and Damian Green, "Making Immigration Work," speech, the Policy Exchange, February 2, 2012, accessed November 30, 2018, www.homeoffice.gov.uk/media-centre/speeches/making-immigration-work.

58. Marc Sageman, *Leaderless Jihad: Terror Networks in the 21st Century* (Philadelphia: University of Pennsylvania Press, 2008).

59. Foreign and Commonwealth Office, "EIWG Fact Sheet," www.fco.gov.uk/servlet/Front?pagename = OpenMarket/Xcelerate/ShowPage&c = Page&cid = 153388310360. The "Radical Middle

Way" project was also supported by the Home Office (see http://impacteurope.eu/partners/radical-middle-way).

60. Jamie Bartlett and Jonathan Birdwell, *From Suspects to Citizens: Preventing Violent Extremism in the Big Society* (London: Demos, 2010), 8.

61. Ibid.

62. Basia Spalek and Alia Imoual, "Muslim Communities and Counter-Terror Responses: 'Hard' Approaches to Community Engagement in the UK and Australia," *Journal of Muslim Minority Affairs* 27, no. 2 (2007): 185–202; Robert Lambert, "Empowering Salafis and Islamists Against Al-Qaeda: A London Counter-Terrorism Case Study," *PS: Political Science & Politics* 41, no. 1 (2008), 31–35; and Derek McGhee, *The End of Multiculturalism? Terrorism, Integration & Human Rights* (Maidenhead, England: Open University Press & McGraw-Hill Education, 2008).

63. Outlined by Tony Blair himself. See the prime minister's press conference, August 5, 2005.

64. United Kingdom, Home Office, Office for Security & Counter-Terrorism, *Preventing Violent Extremism: A Strategy for Delivery* (London: Home Office, 2008), 9.

65. Spalek and Imoual, "Muslim Communities and Counter-Terror Responses," 188.

66. See Daniel DeHanas, Therese O'Toole, Tariq Modood, and Nasar Meer, Taking Part: *Muslim Participation in Contemporary Governance,* www.bristol.ac.uk/medialibrary/sites/ethnicity/migrated/documents/mpcgreport.pdf, accessed February 17, 2019; and Meer and Modood, "Multicultural State We're In."

67. Spalek and Imoual, "Muslim Communities and Counter-Terror Responses," 191.

68. Ibid.

69. United Kingdom, Home Office, Office for Security & Counter-Terrorism, *Preventing Violent Extremism,* 6–7.

70. Spalek and Imoual, "Muslim Communities and Counter-Terror Responses," 194.

71. Liz Fekete, "Anti-Muslim Racism and the European Security State," *Race and Class* 46, no. 1 (2004): 25, and speech by Communities Secretary Ruth Kelly to Muslims on Working Together to Tackle Extremism, Local Government House, London, October 11, 2006.

72. United Kingdom, Home Office, *Prevent Strategy* (London: Home Office, 2011), 1.

73. Ibid., 35.

74. United Kingdom, Department for Communities and Local Government, *Creating the Conditions for Integration* (London: Home Office, 2012), 16–17.

75. See United Kingdom, Ministry of Housing, Communities & Local Government, press release, "Multi-faith Communities to Benefit from New £3 Million Grant," February 27, 2014. Accessed November 30, 2018, https://www.gov.uk/government/news/multi-faith-communities-to-benefit-from-new-3-million-grant.

76. Uberoi and Modood. "Inclusive Britishness."

PART II

Multiculturalism in the "Old" Commonwealth

4

───────

Multiculturalism in a Context
of Minority Nationalism and
Indigenous Rights

The Canadian Case[1]

Avigail Eisenberg, University of Victoria

Canada has long been considered a world leader at promoting the values of multiculturalism. In part, this is because Canada is a remarkably diverse society with diversity reflected in its state institutions and, in part, this is because some of the leading normative theorists of multiculturalism have written with the Canadian experience in mind.[2] Canada is globally admired for its success at recognizing and protecting diversity in its laws and Constitution, and at integrating new immigrants as well as long-standing minorities into mainstream life. Yet, despite these successes, some minorities in Canada continue to experience racism, higher rates of poverty and unemployment, and lower rates of educational attainment than the dominant French and English groups.[3] Also, Canada's multicultural policy is not popular amongst the Québécois and Indigenous peoples[4] because, in some respects, the policy has been implemented at the expense of their legal and political status.[5]

The very idea that multiculturalism threatens the status of Quebec and Indigenous peoples is ironic given that the success of multiculturalism in Canada is often explained in terms of Canada's antecedent legal, linguistic, and cultural pluralism. Canada was founded through a set of treaty relations between European settlers and Indigenous people, and through agreements between English and French colonies, both of which inform its Constitution.[6] It would be ironic if multiculturalism turned out to pose a threat to forms of diversity that are often considered foundational to the policy's success.

The claim is also surprising since Canadian multiculturalism was never intended to protect the cultures of Indigenous peoples or French Canada. Multicultural policies aim to recognize and celebrate cultural diversity, to protect minorities

67

from discrimination, and to facilitate minority integration into the public culture. In contrast, Quebec and Indigenous peoples seek to secure and, in some cases, expand their jurisdictional authority over a territory and over areas of life important to their communities. These jurisdictional claims sometimes include, but cannot be reduced to, protecting their cultural values and practices. Both groups are considered founding peoples with constitutional status that supersedes the cultural and religious protections targeted by multiculturalism. This difference—between founding peoples and cultural minorities—is reflected in Canada's federal division of powers, which guarantees Quebec legislative supremacy over numerous areas of public life in which the protection of cultural and linguistic distinctiveness is especially important (such as educational policy). It is also reflected in the constitutional protection of Aboriginal rights,[7] which separates and shields these rights from others that are guaranteed in the document.[8] As Kymlicka observes, the policies governing Canadian diversity regarding ethnic minorities, Quebec, and Indigenous peoples have different origins, are embodied in different legislation, refer to different parts of the constitution, are administered by different government departments, and are guided by different concepts and principles; "each forms its own discrete silo, and there is very little interaction between them."[9] Yet despite attempts to separate these different kinds of protections, they can become entangled and, on occasion, attempts by courts and policy-makers to manage cultural diversity generate a hornet's nest of political controversy amongst these groups.

In this chapter I examine three key features of Canadian multiculturalism in practice and explain why they are perceived as threatening to either Quebec or Indigenous peoples. These three features—constitutional recognition, reasonable accommodation and cultural rights—comprise the leading approaches by which the normative ideals of multiculturalism are translated into laws and policies in Canada. As a normative ideal, multiculturalism is sensitive to the ways in which possessing a minority identity can be a source of disadvantage and disrespect, and as a form of liberal justice is committed to rectifying them.[10] Whereas the multicultural ideal can be attained in different ways, the three features I examine here are central to the Canadian approach and, I argue, have sometimes politicized and distorted relations amongst Canada's founding peoples and cultural minorities.

THE POLITICS OF CONSTITUTIONALLY PROTECTING MULTICULTURALISM IN CANADA

Over the past forty years, over forty nation-states have entrenched cultural or Indigenous rights in their constitutions.[11] In 1982, when Canada added the Charter of Rights and Freedoms to its constitution, it included a section (§27) that states: "This Charter shall be interpreted in a manner consistent with the preservation and enhancement of the multicultural heritage of Canadians." This was initially viewed as a statement of national values rather than a justiciable means of protecting cultural diversity, but when combined with other Charter rights, it has successfully strengthened the identity of Canada as a multicultural society and enhanced the protection of minority rights. At the same time, the constitutional protection of multiculturalism has met with strong resistance in Quebec. To understand why this is the case, it is worth briefly considering how minority rights were protected before 1982, and the impact on Quebec of constitutionally entrenching these rights.

Legislative Protections for Multiculturalism

Minority rights are protected through hundreds of policies and regulations passed by all levels of government in Canada, which advance the aims of cultural equality and integration in relation to immigration and settlement, education, housing, zoning, employment, arbitration, translation, policing, recreation, security, and other areas of public life. Some of these policies were initially passed in the 1970s and 1980s in response to federal and provincial human rights acts and the Multiculturalism Act (1988), all of which remain central sources of multicultural values today.[12] The Multiculturalism Act established four political commitments to guide federal legislators in policy-making: (1) to provide funding for programs aimed at the cultural maintenance of ethno-cultural groups; (2) to remove cultural barriers to full participation in Canadian society; (3) to encourage cultural interchange; and (4) to support official language acquisition by immigrants. Throughout the 1980s and 1990s, these aims, together with a generous infrastructure of legislators and bureaucrats, led to numerous initiatives and policy changes that together changed the symbolic order of Canada. In the words of one critic, until that time, Canada had been fixated "on Anglo-conformity . . . and, to a lesser extent, cultural dualism."[13]

Even before the Multiculturalism Act was passed, minority rights were protected by provincial human rights acts, which were passed province-by-province after World War II to help realize Canada's commitments as a signatory of the UN Universal Declaration of Human Rights.[14] Starting with Ontario in 1948 and ending with Quebec in 1976, the provinces passed nonidentical acts that protected provincial residents against discrimination on numerous grounds (e.g., gender, age, ethnicity, race, religion, political affiliation) and in numerous areas of life (e.g., in relation to employers, landlords, insurers, schools, on billboards and signs, in restaurants and other businesses). The acts are nonidentical in the sense that some offer broader protections in more contexts than others do. The acts are also statutory rather than constitutional, which means they can be altered by an act of the provincial legislature rather than requiring a constitutional amendment. As creations of provincial governments, they are controlled by provincially designed processes and by tribunals that are appointed and funded by provincial governments.[15] Provinces each have a good deal of control over the content of the acts and how aggressively they are enforced.

Whereas most of the human rights acts were passed before multiculturalism was on the agenda, the acts provide some of the most important protections for minorities in the public sphere. Unlike constitutional rights, which ensure that law is consistent with guaranteed rights, human rights acts protect individuals from discrimination in the context of everyday life. They play a crucial role in facilitating cultural integration in the workplace, consumer interaction, rental accommodation, and other areas of public life where people are most likely to experience discrimination in ways that marginalize them from the mainstream and deny them equal access to opportunities and resources.

These two important sources of multiculturalism—the Multiculturalism Act and provincial human rights acts—remain key to the protection and management of social diversity in Canada, but both have lost considerable symbolic power compared to what they had in the past. The global backlash against multiculturalism has been felt in Canada as well.[16] Today, fewer bureaucrats work directly on initiatives connected to the Multiculturalism Act, and the cabinet no longer includes a minister of multiculturalism, as once was the case. The Multicultural Directorate has lost some of its funding and the high profile it had twenty years ago.[17] In many respects, multiculturalism is no longer presented as a priority of the federal government, except rhetorically, where it is sometimes used to project an image of Canada intended to attract skilled immigrant labor and expand Canada's economic opportunities on the global market.[18] In short, even though some of the infrastructure inspired by multiculturalism remains in place, the resources committed to it, and the political resolve of nationally elected governments to advance the values and ideals of multiculturalism, have diminished.

Provincial human rights acts have also lost much of their symbolic power and legal status, mainly due to the constitutional entrenchment of the Charter of Rights and Freedoms. The Charter contains powerful guarantees of equality rights (s15), religious freedom, and freedom of conscience (s2a), which have been used in hundreds of cases to strike down law and shape government policy affecting cultural and religious minorities. Once the Charter came into force, the protection of rights, including minority rights, was increasingly overseen by courts, which have the power to require all federal and provincial law to conform to provisions guaranteed in the Charter. This includes provincial human rights acts, which are a form of provincial law. So, whereas before 1982, the protection of minority rights was generally the responsibility of provincial governments, after entrenchment, rights protection became a judicial responsibility, with the Supreme Court of Canada in Ottawa being the court of final appeal. Provincial human rights acts continue to address claims of discrimination in everyday life, but these acts are symbolically and legally subordinate to the Charter. Similarly, the jurisdictional authority of provincial governments over the protection of nondiscrimination rights for minorities is now also subordinate to the Charter.[19]

Quebec and the Charter

This transfer of power from provincial governments to a national court system was especially problematic in Quebec because in 1982 it refused to endorse the amended Constitution as all other provinces had done. To date, Quebec has still not agreed to the constitutional package, even though the Constitution is legally binding on the province. In negotiations leading up to entrenchment, many Quebecers suspected that the constitutional amendments were part of a strategy orchestrated by the central government to weaken Quebec nationalism by enhancing the power of federal institutions, such as the Supreme Court of Canada, to establish and protect the rights of citizenship. And they were not far wrong in their suspicions. The Charter has proven to be a powerful source of "citizenization" and is symbolically and legally crucial to the integration of Canadians, including new immigrants.[20]

Today, some thirty years after this conflict, these tensions remain unabated. For instance, in 2013, the then-Quebec government proposed to pass legislation, which it called the *Chartre des Valuers*, that would prohibit provincial government employees and teachers from wearing religious symbols such as crosses, kippahs, hijabs, niqabs and turbans, to work. The legislation, which failed to pass following the electoral defeat of the government that proposed it, would have changed the terms by which religious minorities had access to the public sphere and employment within the province.[21] The broad consensus amongst legal commentators was that the *Chartre* would not survive a constitutional challenge and was "plainly" unconstitutional.[22] But, in the context, this was hardly a redeeming fact. The controversy served to underline a message, which was helpful to Quebec nationalists at the time, that the management of social diversity in the province had been transferred from the province to the federal courts.

The politics of minority nationalism combined with constitutional entrenchment has politicized the protection of minority rights in Quebec. With every court decision, Quebecers are reminded that judges, not legislators, decide how the aims and ideals of multiculturalism are translated into public policy, and that the Charter's protections are imposed by the central state on a national minority without its consent.[23] As a result, objections to decisions of the Supreme Court of Canada are often expressed in Quebec also as concerns about democracy—that the decisions of an unelected and anglophone-dominated court overrule the decisions of local legislators who are accountable to the people of Quebec and more sensitive to their values. Even though Quebec courts also interpret the Charter and often decide cases in a manner consistent with Supreme Court of Canada rulings, the constitutional tensions between Quebec and Canada have enabled Quebec nationalists to frame Canadian multiculturalism and its protection in the Charter as an imposition by the central state on a national minority.[24]

A good illustration of this framing is found in *Multani v. Commission scolaire Marguerite-Bourgeoys,* a case about a Sikh boy who wanted to wear his kirpan to school in Montreal.[25] The conflict initially involved a disagreement between a parent's association and the district school board but was eventually appealed to the Supreme Court of Canada, which decided in favor of Multani on the basis of Charter protections for religious freedom (s2a) and multiculturalism (s27). The Court emphasized that accommodating Multani helps to realize multicultural values by demonstrating "the importance that our society attaches to protecting freedom of religion and to showing respect for its minorities."[26] The decision led to widespread debate in Quebec about minority rights and to a government-commissioned report, written by two prominent scholars—Gérard Bouchard and Charles Taylor—on minority accommodation in Quebec. Perhaps as a way of assuaging minority nationalist sentiment, Bouchard and Taylor characterize the conflict as a challenge to "local decision making." They argue that to encourage citizens to manage their own differences, to avoid congesting the courts, and to respect Quebec's distinctive integration model, conflicts about cultural diversity in Quebec are better resolved through a "citizen route" rather than a "legal route."[27]

The *Multani* controversy may well illuminate a distinctive "intercultural" approach to integration and social diversity in Quebec. Quebec claims that its interculturalist approach places more emphasis than multiculturalism on the integration of ethnic minorities into the distinct culture of the dominant group.[28] That Quebec should favor such an approach is hardly surprising given that the French majority in the province is, itself, culturally and linguistically vulnerable and insecure as well.[29] But, at the same time, and despite some understandable divergence between Quebec and Canada about multicultural policy, there can be no doubt that debates about minority rights in Quebec are politicized and distorted by ongoing nationalist opposition to the entrenchment of the Charter and the expansion of the Supreme Court's authority. The controversy about *Multani* was driven by a politically motivated rejection by Quebec nationalists of Ottawa-based decision-making (i.e., the Supreme Court of Canada's ruling). It provided some political elites in Quebec with an opportunity to exaggerate the distinctiveness of Quebec's approach to managing cultural diversity in order to enhance the electoral appeal of Quebec nationalist politics. On this more political and strategic view, the conflict over the kirpan in Montreal did not occur because Quebecers reject the values and principles of multiculturalism, but because this high-profile court case was decided outside Quebec by constitutional provisions to which Quebec had never consented.

The Risks of Reasonable Accommodation

In addition to constitutional entrenchment, a second feature of Canadian multiculturalism that politicizes the protection of minority rights is reasonable accommodation. Reasonable accommodation is the legal standard used to translate the values of cultural equality and nondiscrimination into practical reforms in workplaces and public institutions so that they are more fully accessible to minorities.

Over the years, the reasonable accommodation standard has become closely tied to the public philosophy of Canadian multiculturalism. The standard was introduced into Canadian law in the mid-1980s in cases about religious discrimination in the workplace. Employers were required by the court to adapt workplace rules in order to "accommodate" the religious commitments of their employees within the limits of what is "reasonable" and short of undue hardship. As one legal scholar explains the principle, "facially neutral rules that have adverse effects on the basis of creed or religion are a violation of the right to religious equality unless the employer has taken reasonable steps, up to the point of undue hardship, to accommodate religious observance."[30] Since then, the principle has been used outside the employment context, first in 2006, in the case of *Multani,* discussed above. The court decided that the accommodation of Multani's kirpan was "reasonable" because it could be managed with minimal risk to school safety.[31] In 2007, the Bouchard-Taylor Commission was mandated to explore whether practices of "reasonable accommodation" in Quebec conform to Quebec's core values.[32]

In all these contexts, the principal aim of reasonable accommodation is the same, namely, to ensure that individuals are treated equally and in a manner that is sensitive to their differences, including differences related to their cultural and religious identities. As Bouchard and Taylor explain, an appropriate measure of fairness and equality ensures that all people have equal access to the public sphere, including to employment, housing, and public services, in full light of their differences.[33] Where rules disadvantage some groups without that being intended, the solution is to adjust the rule to accommodate the difference. The aim of reasonable accommodation is to mitigate the discriminatory effects of rules and workplace practices by making provision for an exception to the rule or a specific adaptation of it.

Despite the commitment to equality that animates the standard, some critics argue that, in practice, reasonable accommodation is far too protective of the status quo and has been used too often to shield unjust workplace practices. This is because the standard, at least in the context of employment cases, requires minorities to be accommodated only to the degree that doing so is "reasonable" and does not cause the employer undue hardship.[34] This means that the more fundamental a rule is to workplace practice, the less likely it is that accommodation will appear to be reasonable, even if the rule will cause minorities, people with disabilities, or women to be treated unfairly. The chief justice of Canada's Supreme Court, Beverly McLachlin, recognized this in a ruling relating to the exclusion of women as firefighters through fitness standards for recruits that favored men. Reasonable accommodation, she argued, prevents the court from transforming standards despite their discriminatory and exclusionary effects: "The right to be free from discrimination is reduced to a question of whether the 'mainstream' can afford to confer proper treatment on those adversely affected, within the confines of its existing formal standard. If it cannot, the edifice of systemic discrimination receives the law's approval. This cannot be right."[35] On her view, the alleged hardship of reforming status quo practices can be a poor test of whether accommodation is unfair and instead may indicate only the degree to which the dominant group's position of power is written into the way that social institutions work.[36]

Instead of enhancing equality, the framework of reasonable accommodation can preserve and protect dominant norms and practices that disadvantage less powerful groups. It thereby offers a conservative translation of the normative ideals of multiculturalism, and one that favors reforms consistent with protecting the status quo. Using this standard, multiculturalism will appear to favor inclusivity as long as being inclusive is consistent with mainstream norms and practices. Beyond these limits, minority accommodation could appear "unreasonable."

In addition to these conservative tendencies, a second drawback of reasonable accommodation is the adversarial incentive encouraged by the standard. Because accommodation depends on whether it is "reasonable" or not, the standard incentivizes managers, employers, landlords and other respondents who wish to resist minority accommodation to articulate reasons why, in the case of their business, accommodation is "unreasonable" and will cause them undue hardship. For instance, employers can avoid accommodating minorities only if they provide convincing evidence to show that accommodation will significantly compromise their profits, unduly restrict their productivity, or undermine workplace standards (as in the case of fitness tests and firefighting) to an unreasonable degree. These kinds of arguments were made in *Multani*, where the school board tried, unsuccessfully, to convince the court that allowing Multani to wear his kirpan would compromise the safety of other children and thereby undermine a central purpose of school, which to provide a safe environment in which children can learn.[37] In these and many other cases, the standard creates an incentive for respondents to define the status quo as intrinsically tied to practices that cannot change without jeopardizing the very enterprise at issue.

Unsurprisingly, a similar adversarial incentive can motivate state actors in disputes about whether minority rights ought to be protected. In order to resist accommodating minorities, political actors have an incentive to articulate ways in which accommodation will unduly burden public values. Recent debates in Quebec again offer a good illustration. The Quebec government defended its proposed *Charte des Valeurs,* which would have prohibited religious dress and ostentatious religious symbols, on the grounds that religious dress in the public sphere undermined Quebec's identity and core public values, which reject religion in the public sphere. At the same time, it defended, as important features of Quebec's historical *patrimoine culturel,* a crucifix that hangs in the main chamber of Quebec's National Assembly, and the illuminated cross that overlooks Montreal from the top of Mont Royal. These seemingly contradictory positions on the religious symbols of minorities and the majority can be reconciled only if one believes that minority accommodation must be consistent with the majority's existing cultural preferences.

As these conflicts show, reasonable accommodation can work in conservative ways. It can reduce cultural equality to a project that, at best, inserts minorities into the public culture only insofar as doing so does not upset the dominant group's position of power. Its adversarial incentive can lead dominant groups to raise the stakes in a dispute by claiming that their identity or core values will be threatened if they have to accommodate minority practices. These tendencies, along with the ongoing dispute in Canada about constitutional entrenchment, point to some of the deeply political features of Canadian-Quebec debates about minority rights, and to two ways in which multiculturalism becomes entangled in the politics of minority nationalism.

THE PROTECTION OF CULTURAL RIGHTS

We now turn to what is often recognized as the central feature of multicultural-ism, the protection of cultural rights. These rights are integral to the central aim of multiculturalism, which is to acknowledge that people's attachment to features of their identities can be a legitimate basis for the recognition and protection of their cultural practices and beliefs. The recognition and protection of cultural identity have been linked to broader principles of justice, equality, human rights, and democratic citizenship.[38] Over the past thirty years, a leading task of scholars and policy-makers who work on issues related to multiculturalism has been to distinguish between cultural claims that advance these important values and those that do not. As a result of these efforts, the success of states in protecting human rights and democratic citizenship is partly measured today in terms of how well they protect minority cultures.

The Canadian experience suggests, however, that the state's protection of cul-tural rights is no substitute for the fair treatment of minorities, and this is per-haps nowhere more evident than in cases about protecting the cultural rights of Indigenous peoples. As previously mentioned, in Canada, Aboriginal rights are legally distinct from rights protected by multiculturalism, and Indigenous peoples are recognized as possessing unique status as "First Nations," rather than as the ethnic minorities whose interests multiculturalism is meant to address. Yet the limitations of protecting cultural rights are similar for both groups.

In the case of Indigenous peoples, since the 1990s, one of the leading approaches taken by the courts to Indigenous rights in Canada, has been to recognize dis-tinctive and integral cultural practices as Aboriginal rights. On the face of it, this kind of recognition is desirable and is certainly an improvement on previous approaches adopted by the state. Until the 1970s and 1980s, the Canadian state used Indigenous cultural differences as a justification for denying Indigenous peoples rights to jurisdictional authority on their ancestral territories, the right to vote, the right to educate their children in traditional practices, and even the right to basic civil liberties.[39] Against a historical background in which Indigenous culture was denigrated, the possibility of having it recognized, constitutionally protected, and socially respected through state-mandated guarantees appears attractive.

Yet despite some significant improvements over the past thirty years in the treatment of Indigenous peoples, cultural rights have not fulfilled their initial promise. Beginning in the 1970s, Indigenous peoples advanced legal claims for rights and resources, some of which were based on arguments about the need to recognize and protect features of their cultural identity. Eventually, in the 1990s, the courts became receptive to the cultural aspect of these claims, but simultaneously imposed guidelines, in the form of a "distinctive culture test," to distinguish claims that would receive protection from those that would not. The test requires Indigenous claimants to submit evidence to show that the cultural practice they are seeking to protect (e.g., to hunt, fish, or trade in particular customary ways) is "distinctive and integral" to their culture, a "defining characteristic" of their culture, and that their community has adhered to the practice since before contact with European settlers.[40]

No such legal test is applied to the rights claims of cultural and religious minorities in Canada, but these disputes about cultural rights share a feature with Indigenous claims. In most of these cases, the court assesses and interprets the cultural practice at issue before deciding whether it should be legally protected. For instance, in cases about wearing kirpans, kippahs, or veils, or practicing polygamy, judges often assess how important the practice is to the individual or group in order to determine the extent to which claimants will suffer disadvantage in the absence of cultural protection. Such assessments are characteristic of cases involving religious practices, despite the deeply personal nature of religious practices. For instance, in *R. v. N.S., 2012 SCC 72*, a Muslim woman refused to remove her niqab, which covered her face as she gave evidence against those she accuses of sexually assaulting her.[41] Judges resolved the conflicts in two stages; firstly by determining how important the niqab is to the woman who wears it, which requires scrutinizing features of the practice, the woman's religious beliefs, and her personal behavior; secondly, only once the judges have determined what is at stake for this woman do they weigh the importance of the niqab in this context against the importance of the rule in criminal cases that accusers face those they accuse when giving testimony. Such assessments of cultural or religious values can be hazardous. Judges, as cultural outsiders, will sometimes misinterpret minority practices and, as several studies show, stereotype and essentialize minority cultures in the course of their rulings.[42] But in addition to this problem, such assessments are likely to be experienced as highly intrusive by minorities, and may lead them to become more insular and resistant to outsider influence in general.

In the case of Indigenous claimants, these problems are intensified by the historical backdrop of colonialism. Through the distinctive culture test, the Canadian court places itself in a position of deciding whether Indigenous cultural practices are sufficiently central and integral to a community's culture to merit legal protection. The distorting effects of requiring Indigenous claimants to justify their cultural practices are many, but three are sufficient to explain the problem: first, requiring a cultural practice to be justified in this manner encourages communities to self-essentialize by reducing complex practices to a set of pre-defined scripts that claimants believe will be easily understood by judges; second, insofar as cultural practices are more likely to be protected if they have historical continuity and are widespread, such justifications discourage communities from revealing internal disagreement about how important practices are or how long they've been considered important; and, third, such justifications may create incentives for communities to marginalize members who do not participate in the practice or do not understand it. In at least these three ways, legal tests to establish cultural rights are likely not only to distort the claims of Indigenous peoples but also to distort Indigenous cultures.[43]

While these are important concerns, little evidence exists that Indigenous communities have become more culturally static or homogeneous as a result of how the state now protects cultural rights. Instead, the main consequence of the "distinctive culture test" is to dissuade claimants from seeking legal protection from Canadian courts for their cultural practices. Both the intrusiveness of evidence gathering and the distorting effect of legal argumentation mean that cultural rights are difficult to secure. In addition, cultural rights cases also risk damaging relations amongst community members. For Indigenous peoples, the costs of cultural rights may outweigh the benefits, as all such cases involve asking the court of the colonizing state to decide what counts as central and integral to an Indigenous culture. For this reason alone, a more attractive option for these communities is to look for ways other than state-protected rights to protect their culture and ways of life.

As the distinctive culture test illustrates, cultural rights are no panacea for cultural injustice. In some cases, actual cultural rights—that is, those that are recognized and protected by courts or tribunals—provide only a semblance of cultural recognition and respect. Indigenous peoples in Canada cannot successfully defend their claims for cultural protection through processes that depend on Canadian courts assessing their cultures and deciding what gets protected.[44] In fact, this strategy tends to breed a damaging cynicism. The Canadian state advertises its recognition and protection of Indigenous cultures while neglecting to address the basics of human well-being—pollution, poverty, and child suicide—in Indigenous communities. Cultural rights appear impotent, or worse, a handmaiden of neoliberalism and a cover for neocolonial policies. Modest claims for cultural protection become the focus of attention and debate, while the consequences of colonial dispossession and coercive assimilation are ignored. Ironically, in an age and place where culture has been acknowledged as an important source of respect and empowerment, Indigenous peoples in Canada are less likely to frame their claims in terms of culture and less likely to argue for cultural rights today than they have been in the past.

CONCLUSIONS

Canada is often portrayed as a "multicultural success story" in light of its numerous policies and programs that successfully manage a highly diverse population guided by the normative ideals of multiculturalism. But understanding multiculturalism in relation to multinationalism and against a background of colonialism, reveals several shortcomings and risks of multiculturalism in Canada, some of which may have resonance elsewhere.

First, the constitutional protection of multiculturalism has entangled minority rights in the politics of minority nationalism. The lesson to be learned in this case is that, if local control of social diversity matters, as it does in many multinational states, the decisions of national courts about minority rights will become politicized and are easily portrayed, whether opportunistically or not, as an imposition of the dominant majority on the minority, and thereby a threat to the local values of the national minority.

Second, reasonable accommodation can have the effect of encouraging a conservative status quo to be even more conservative and unyielding to the protection of minority rights. It can shield dominant norms from serious interrogation about their fairness and inclusivity. In this vein, today we see anxious governments that are quick to emphasize social integration as the sovereign value of multiculturalism, despite social circumstances—such as racism and anti-Muslim sentiment—that erect impenetrable barriers to the integration of minorities. The adversarial incentive contained within reasonable accommodation can motivate opponents of minority rights to exaggerate the significance to them of practices or rules that they might be required to change. Measures to ease the integration of minority rights into mainstream life thereby become politicized, and the national identity of dominant groups takes on heightened significance.

Finally, cultural rights are no substitute for cultural fairness. Even though today Canadians are more likely to respect Indigenous customs and ties to territory than they did fifty or a hundred years ago, the protection of Indigenous cultural rights by the Canadian state has not translated into cultural security for Indigenous peoples. Instead, cultural security has more effectively been enhanced by measures that recognize Indigenous jurisdictional authority over territory and features of community life. This suggests that, of the many different approaches that can be taken to protecting Indigenous rights, the legal protection of cultural rights may not be the best approach. It may also suggest, in the case of ethno-cultural minorities that stand to benefit from multiculturalism, that what matters more than the approach adopted is the political will to ensure that the approach leads to just outcomes. As in the case of constitutional protection and reasonable accommodation, cultural rights are impotent or even damaging in the absence of a political and societal commitment to the normative ideals of multiculturalism, in particular, the ideal that an appropriate measure of fairness and equality requires all people to have equal access to the public sphere in full light of their differences.

NOTES

1. The author would like to thank Didier Zuniga for his research assistance.

2. In particular, Will Kymlicka, Charles Taylor, and James Tully.

3. See, e.g., Yasmeen Abu-Laban and Christina Gabriel, *Selling Diversity: Immigration, Multiculturalism, Employment Equity, and Globalization* (Toronto: University of Toronto Press, 2002); Himani Bannerji, *The Dark Side of Nation: Essays on Multiculturalism, Nationalism and Gender* (Toronto: Canadian Scholars' Press, 2000); and Neil Bissoondath, *Selling Illusions: The Cult of Multiculturalism in Canada* (Toronto: Penguin, 1994).

4. In this chapter, the term "Aboriginal" is used when discussing constitutional relations in Canada because this is the term used in Canada's Constitution. Otherwise, the term "Indigenous" is used. "Indigenous" is generally understood to include a broader set of peoples, some of whom may not be constitutionally recognized as Aboriginal people.

5. For discussion of Quebec's attempts since 1982 to distinguish its approach to diversity from Canadian multiculturalism, see Will Kymlicka, "Ethnocultural Diversity in a Liberal State: Making Sense of the Canadian Model(s)," in *Belonging? Diversity, Recognition and Shared Citizenship in Canada,* ed. Keith Banting, Thomas Courchene, and F. Leslie Seidle (Montreal: Institute for Research in Public Policy, 2007); Marie McAndrew, "Quebec's Interculturalism Policy: An Alternative Vision," ibid.; Daniel Salée, "The Quebec State and the Management of Ethnocultural Diversity: Perspectives on an Ambiguous Record," ibid., 112–17; and Gérard Bouchard, "What Is Interculturalism?" *McGill Law Journal* 56, no. 2 (2011): 435–68, who notes that, for political reasons, "all Quebec governments (federalist or not) have rejected multiculturalism since its adoption by the federal government in 1971" (462). Whereas Quebec's concerns about multiculturalism have been debated and discussed widely in the scholarship, relatively little attention has been paid to the tensions between Canadian multiculturalism and the status of Indigenous people. For one exception, see David Macdonald, "Aboriginal Peoples and Multicultural Reform in Canada: Prospects for a New Binational Society," *Canadian Journal of Sociology* 39, no. 1 (2014): 72–75.

6. See, e.g., Will Kymlicka, *Finding Our Way: Rethinking Ethnocultural Relations in Canada* (Oxford: Oxford University Press, 1998), and Jeremy Webber, *Reimagining Canada: Language, Culture, Community, and the Canadian Constitution* (Montreal and Kingston, ON: McGill–Queen's University Press, 1994).

7. Aboriginal rights are entrenched in §35 of the Constitution which reads: "(1) The existing aboriginal and treaty rights of the aboriginal peoples of Canada are hereby recognized and affirmed. (2) In this Act, 'Aboriginal Peoples of Canada' includes the Indian, Inuit and Métis peoples of Canada. (3) For greater certainty, in subsection (1) "treaty rights" includes rights that now exist by way of land claims agreements or may be so acquired. (4) Notwithstanding any other provision of this Act, the aboriginal and treaty rights referred to in subsection (1) are guaranteed equally to male and female persons."

8. In addition to being entrenched in a separate part of the document, §25 of the Constitution Act (1982) states: "The guarantee in this Charter of certain rights and freedoms shall not be construed as to abrogate or derogate from any aboriginal, treaty or other rights or freedoms that pertain to the aboriginal peoples of Canada."

9. Kymlicka, "Ethnocultural Diversity in a Liberal State," 39–40.

10. This definition of multiculturalism is drawn from Will Kymlicka, *Multicultural Citizenship: A Liberal Theory of Minority Rights* (Oxford: Clarendon Press, 1995), chap. 5. In *Multicultural Citizenship,* Kymlicka builds into his normative account of multiculturalism distinctions between the claims of national minorities and ethnic groups and his account of "multicultural citizenship" distinguishes between three kinds of group-differentiated rights: self-government rights, polyethnic rights, and special representation rights (ibid., 26–33). Whereas these distinctions, and his subsequent work on applying multicultural ideals to Canadian institutions, help move his account from the purely theoretical and abstract level, to a more sociological level, they are not designed to bridge all the gaps between theory and practice nor to identify, as my account is intended to do, the ways in which institutional

practices can distort and limit the very multicultural ideals that they are meant to advance. For an account that focuses on respect, esteem, and the damage caused by misrecognition, see, too, Charles Taylor, "The Politics of Recognition," in *Multiculturalism: Examining the Politics of Recognition*, ed. Amy Gutmann (Princeton, NJ: Princeton University Press, 1994).

11. Explicit mention of "identity," cultural rights or "indigenous identity" can be found in the constitutions of Argentina, Belize, Bolivia, Brazil, Bulgaria, Croatia, Ecuador, Guatemala, Kosovo, Mexico, Nicaragua, Panama, Paraguay, Peru, Poland, Romania, Slovakia, Slovenia, and Venezuela, as well as in statutes passed by regions in Italy, Spain (Catalonia), and Germany (the *Lander*). See Ilena Ruggiu, *Il guidice antropologo: Costituzione e tecniche di composizione dei conflitti multiculturali* (Milan: Franco Angeli, 2012), 219–33.

12. See Carl James, ed., *Possibilities and Limitations: Multicultural Policies and Programs in Canada* (Halifax, NS: Fernwood, 2005).

13. Abu-Laban and Gabriel, *Selling Diversity,* 109.

14. In addition, the federal government passed the Canadian Human Rights Act in 1977. It protects individuals against discrimination in federally regulated activities.

15. The funding for provincial processes is notoriously dependent on the sympathy of the elected government at the time for public oversight of private business practices in relation to discrimination claims. See R. Brian Howe and David Johnson, *Restraining Equality: Human Rights Commissions in Canada* (Toronto: University of Toronto Press, 2000).

16. See Keith Banting and Will Kymlicka, "Canadian Multiculturalism: Global Anxieties and Local Debates," *British Journal of Canadian Studies* 23, no. 1 (2010): 43–72.

17. Starting in 1996, the Ministry for Multiculturalism and Citizenship was renamed the Ministry of Canadian Heritage and then subsumed into the Ministry of Citizenship and Immigration (CIC) where the administration of the Multiculturalism Program became a lesser concern. The 2012 *Evaluation of the Multiculturalism Program* concludes that the program's goals are not well integrated into the CIC mandate and that the program needs better support from the CIC (Citizenship and Immigration Canada 2012). The report also notes that it is difficult to assess whether the program is receiving adequate funding given the diffusion of responsibilities for different aspects of it. It concludes that the approval process for proposals associated with the program lacks transparency and is inefficient.

18. Abu-Laban and Gabriel, *Selling Diversity.*

19. See, e.g., *Vriend v. Alberta, 1 SCR 493* (1998), in which the Alberta Human Rights Act was found unconstitutional for failing to protect individuals against discrimination on the basis of sexual orientation.

20. As one of Canada's leading constitutional scholar put it, citizens who became "Charter Canadians" after 1982 were wedded to their newly entrenched rights and hostile to attempts by political elites to revise the constitution further. See Alan Cairns, *Charter versus Federalism: The Dilemmas of Constitutional Reform* (Montreal and Kingston, ON: McGill–Queen's University Press, 1992).

21. Assemblée nationale du Québec/National Assembly of Quebec, 40th Legislature, 1st session, Bill no. 60, "Charter affirming the values of State secularism and religious neutrality and of equality between women and men, and providing a framework for accommodation requests," accessed November 18, 2018, www.assnat.qc.ca/en/travaux-parlementaires/projets-loi/projet-loi-60-40-1.html (§§38–43).

22. Tsvi Kahana quoted in Sean Fine, "Is Quebec's Secular Charter Constitutional? Nine Legal Experts Weigh In," *Globe and Mail,* September 14, 2013.

23. The subordination of provincial legislative autonomy to the national Charter was at the heart of Prime Minister Pierre Trudeau's political strategy in the 1980s to combat the centrifugal drift of Canadian federalism. In Trudeau's view, Canadian federalism was being pulled apart by both Quebec nationalism and the economic power of western Canada's oil-rich provinces. The effect of this drift in Quebec has proven to be lasting.

24. See esp. Bouchard, "What is Interculturalism?" 462.

25. *Multani v. Commission scolaire Marguerite-Bourgeoys, 2006 SCC 6, 1 S.C.R. 256* (2006).

26. Ibid.

27. See Gérard Bouchard and Charles Taylor, *Report of the Commission on Accommodation Practices Related to Cultural Difference* (Quebec: Government of Quebec, 2008), 19.

28. The differences between multiculturalism and interculturalism have been subject to several commentaries. For the Canadian debates, see Bouchard, "What Is Interculturalism?"; McAndrew, "Quebec's Interculturalism Policy"; Salée, "Quebec State"; and Daniel Weinstock, "Interculturalism and Multiculturalism in Canada: Situating the Debate," in *Liberal Multiculturalism and the Fair Terms of Integration,* ed. Peter J. Balint and Sophie Guérard de Latour (New York: Palgrave Macmillan, 2013). For a broader view that considers European debates, see Nasar Meer and Tariq Modood, "How Does Interculturalism Contrast with Multiculturalism?" *Journal of Intercultural Studies* 33, no. 2 (2012): 175–96.

29. Drawing on Bouchard's work, Weinstock concludes that "multiculturalism and interculturalism basically agree on the normative principles concerning the fair terms of integration," but disagree on the facts to which the principle must apply ("Interculturalism and Multiculturalism in Canada," 97–98). They differ, according to Weinstock, primarily because interculturalism aims at integrating minorities by changing their cultures and identities beyond what is required for linguistic integration, to include such things as "taking into account the Quebec nation"; integrating in accordance with the "moral contract" linking all Quebecers; and emphasizing the "creation of a common public culture, based on shared values, history and respect for both minority and majority groups" (ibid., 103). These kinds of requirements, Weinstock argues, are not part of Canadian multiculturalism and, in his view they are "fraught with peril," a fact illustrated by the attempts of the Canadian government to use constitutional reform to reshape Quebec values in order to enhance Quebec's integration into Canada (ibid., 106).

30. Bryce Ryder, "The Canadian Conception of Equal Religious Citizenship," in *Law and Religious Pluralism in Canada,* ed. Richard Moon (Vancouver: University of British Columbia Press, 2008), 90.

31. *Multani v. Commission scolaire Marguerite-Bourgeoys,* ¶8.

32. Bouchard and Taylor, *Report of the Commission,* 33.

33. Ibid., 161. Bouchard and Taylor use the phrase "concerted adjustment" to describe "reasonable accommodation." The principle at stake remains the same—that fairness sometimes requires the revision of public rules and values in order to include minorities who adhere to different practices and beliefs. However, "concerted adjustment" implies that, in Quebec, these changes are a two-way street, thereby "concerted," and require minorities to adapt to the public culture of Quebec.

34. Shelagh Day and Gwen Brodsky, "The Duty to Accommodate: Who Will Benefit?" *Canadian Bar Review* 75, no. 3 (1996): 439.

35. *British Columbia (Public Service Employee Relations Commission) v BCGEU, 3 SCR 3, 176* (1999) at 42. The ideals spelled out by McLachlin in this decision have recently been reiterated by the Court in *Moore v BC (Education) SCC 61 at para 61 and 62* (2012).

36. A similar argument is made about the construction of "merit" in workplace settings by Iris Young, *Justice and the Politics of Difference* (Princeton, NJ: Princeton University Press, 1990), 200–206.

37. *Multani v. Commission scolaire Marguerite-Bourgeoys,* ¶¶44 and 48.

38. See Kwame Anthony Appiah, *The Ethics of Identity* (Princeton, NJ: Princeton University Press, 2005); Amy Gutmann, *Identity and Democracy* (Princeton, NJ: Princeton University Press, 2003); Kymlicka, *Multicultural Citizenship;* Charles Taylor, *Multiculturalism and the "Politics of Recognition"* (Princeton, NJ: Princeton University Press, 1994); and James Tully, *Strange Multiplicity: Constitutionalism in the Age of Diversity* (Cambridge: Cambridge University Press, 1995).

39. Patrick Macklem, *Indigenous Difference and the Constitution of Canada* (Toronto: University of Toronto Press, 2001), 56.

40. See, e.g., *R. v. Van der Peet, [1996] 2 S.C.R. 507,* Summary, accessed November 18, 2018, https://scc-csc.lexum.com/scc-csc/scc-csc/en/item/1407/index.do.

41. *R. v. N.S., 2012 SCC 72, [2012] 3 S.C.R. 726,* accessed November 18, 2018, https://scc-csc.lexum.com/scc-csc/scc-csc/en/item/12779/index.do.

42. On the problem of essentialism in relation to legal decisions about cultural minorities, see Pascale Fournier, "The Ghettoization of Difference in Canada: 'Rape by Culture' or the Danger of a Cultural Defense in Criminal Law Trials," *Manitoba Law Journal* 26 (2002), 81–113; Anne Phillips, *Multiculturalism without Culture* (Princeton, NJ: Princeton University Press, 2007); and Alison Dundes Renteln, *The Cultural Defense* (Oxford: Oxford University Press, 2004). For a broader exploration of issues regarding "minorities within minorities" see Avigail Eisenberg and Jeff Spinner-Halev eds., *Minorities within Minorities: Equality, Rights and Diversity* (Cambridge: Cambridge University Press, 2001).

43. See Russell Barsh and James Youngblood Henderson, "The Supreme Court's Van der Peet Trilogy: Naïve Imperialism and the Robes of Sand," *McGill Law Review* 42, no. 4 (2002): 993–1009; John Borrows, "Frozen Rights in Canada: Constitutional Interpretation and the Trickster," *American Indian Law Review* 22, no. 1 (1997–98): 37–64; and Gordon Christie, "Aboriginal Rights, Aboriginal Culture and Protection," *Osgoode Hall Law Journal* 36, no. 3 (1998): 447–84.

44. For a discussion of different ways in which culture is defined and interpreted by judicial bodies domestically and internationally, see Avigail Eisenberg, "Domestic and International Norms for Assessing Indigenous Identity," in *Identity Politics in the Public Realm,* ed. Avigail Eisenberg and Will Kymlicka (Vancouver: University of British Columbia Press, 2011).

5

____

Australia's "Liberal Nationalist" Multiculturalism

Geoffrey Brahm Levey, University of New South Wales

Australia doubled its population through immigration in the space of fifty years following World War II, a feat otherwise achieved only by countries with much smaller populations, such as Israel and Luxembourg. The Australian population numbered 7.6 million in 1947, including some 87,000 Aboriginal and Torres Strait Islander people. The rest were mostly the descendants of people from Great Britain and Ireland. Three-quarters of the overseas born—then about 10 percent of the total population—came from the British Isles. By June 2013, Australia's population had reached 23.13 million. The overseas born now amounted to 27.6 percent of the estimated resident Australian population and another 20 percent had at least one parent born overseas.[1] As of the 2011 census, the United Kingdom accounted for only about one-fifth of the overseas born, while another fifth came from five Asian countries: China, India, Vietnam, Philippines, and Malaysia.[2] For some years, Australia has been even more immigrant-rich than the other major "immigrant democracies," the United States (13.1 percent foreign-born ca. 2013) and Canada (20 percent). And it well surpasses the former imperial powers of Europe, now grappling with immigration, including Britain (12.3 percent), France (12 percent), and the Netherlands (11.6 percent).[3]

Accompanying this demographic transformation has been an equally profound shift in Australia's policy response to cultural diversity. After trying policies of racial exclusion and cultural assimilation, Australia has fashioned a distinctive "liberal nationalist" architecture that governs its approach to citizenship, cultural diversity, and national identity. Its adoption of state multiculturalism in the 1970s, following Canada, is an integral piece of this political architecture. How Australia understands and practices multiculturalism—what it emphasizes, discounts, and ignores—distinguishes its approach to negotiating cultural diversity.

Australian multiculturalism was first and foremost a repudiation of previous Australian responses to human diversity. I will begin then with some brief comments on the pre-multiculturalism era before turning to the development of Australian multiculturalism and its career in recent years.

THE PRE-MULTICULTURALISM ERA: 1901–1972

From federation of the six British colonies in 1901 until at least the 1940s, Australia defined itself as an ethnic nation. The newly established Commonwealth of Australia passed the Immigration Restriction Act (1901), known as the "White Australia" policy, as its first order of business. Australian democracy was to be reserved for those of the "British race."[4] Those not of British descent were deemed unassimilable and were to be excluded from Australian society; this applied as much to Aborigines inside Australia as to would-be immigrants outside it.[5]

Australia's initial response to diversity was thus one of intolerance and exclusion, grounded in a particular ethno-nationalism, that is, a construction of national identity based on a shared descent and culture.[6] Some claim that the White Australia policy was egalitarian in that it sought to avoid replicating the United States' experience of racial divisions and a labor underclass.[7] Be that as it may, the policy appealed to a form of racial determinism and exclusion.

Officially abolished in 1973, the White Australia policy effectively began to unravel in the 1940s under pressure to populate Australia and grow the economy. As too few British immigrants could be found, the definition of acceptability was broadened first to allow northern Europeans entry and then southern Europeans, who didn't look very "white" at all.[8] In 1945, a federal Department of Immigration was established and charged with formulating a national assimilation policy.[9] Where previously the reigning ethno-nationalist assumption was that race determines culture, henceforth and increasingly Australia entertained the notion that Anglo-conformity could be achieved through assimilation.[10] This cultural-nationalist formula—which required cultural conformity but no longer the "right" ethnic heritage—grew to ascendancy in the 1950s and early 1960s.

Nevertheless, some began to question the assimilationist approach in the 1950s. Sociologists working with immigrant groups reported that assimilation policies and expectations were undermining migrant absorption.[11] Increasing numbers of migrants were returning to their home countries. By 1964, the Department of Immigration changed tack by casting its migrant programs in terms of "integration" instead of "assimilation."[12] By 1968, the department further capitulated after realizing that full assimilation was an unlikely outcome, regardless of the terminology used. At this point, "integration" signified a new policy direction and was not simply a more palatable term.[13] The insistence that migrants abandon their original language, culture, and identity was replaced by an emphasis on simply settling and servicing migrants as they are.

THE ADOPTION OF MULTICULTURALISM: 1973–1999

The 1970s saw Australia grappling with local and international developments that precipitated a profound rethinking. A reformist Labor government led by Gough Whitlam was elected in 1972 after decades of conservative rule. It officially buried the White Australia policy in 1973, signed international human rights protocols and introduced anti-discrimination institutions and law. At the same time, Britain's receding imperial ambitions and switch to the European community in 1973 forced Australia and Australians to reassess their sense of self.[14] The Australian state and Anglo-Australian identity were pried apart. While Anglo-Australian culture and institutions remained dominant, the state was no longer coterminous with this particular identity.[15]

Australian multiculturalism emerges out of this reconfiguration. Al Grassby, immigration minister in the Whitlam government, alluded to the concept in a landmark policy speech titled "A Multi-cultural Society for the Future."[16] Similarly, Prime Minister Whitlam referred to Australia as a "multicultural nation" on the passing of the Racial Discrimination Act 1975, which, he said, "wrote it firmly into the legislation that Australia is in reality a multicultural nation, in which the linguistic and cultural heritage of the Aboriginal people and of peoples from all parts of the world can find an honoured place."[17]

Australian policymakers imported the idea of "multiculturalism" as a public policy for managing cultural diversity from Canada, where it had been officially introduced a few years earlier. But where Canada introduced multiculturalism strategically in a context of long established minorities, bilingualism and a restive Quebec, Australian multiculturalism began as a pragmatic effort to settle and support recent migrants, many from non-English-speaking backgrounds, or so-called "NESBs."[18] In the 1980s, the multiculturalism project was reframed as addressing "all Australians" rather than only migrants and "ethnics," and centered on the themes of social cohesion, cultural identity, and equality of opportunity and access.[19] Nevertheless, multicultural affairs continued to be administered by the Department of Immigration until 2011.

In 1989, the first national multiculturalism policy statement—*National Agenda for a Multicultural Australia,*[20] overseen by the Hawke Labor Party government—identified four main planks: the right of all Australians to maintain their cultural identities within the law; the right of all Australians to equal opportunities without fear of group-based discrimination; the economic and national benefits of a culturally diverse society; and respect for core Australian values and institutions—reciprocity, tolerance, and equality (including of the sexes), freedom of speech and religion, the rule of law, the Constitution, parliamentary democracy, and English as the national language.

There have been four subsequent national policy statements. *A New Agenda for Multicultural Australia* and *Multicultural Australia: United in Diversity* were both developed during the term of the conservative Howard government.[21] *The People of Australia* was issued by the minority Gillard Labor government.[22] The Turnbull coalition government launched the current policy, *Multicultural Australia: United, Strong, Successful,* in March 2017.[23] With the exception of the last policy, these documents have offered refinements in presentation and emphasis while largely retaining the key principles of the 1989 policy. I will come to the current policy below. Here, it is worth highlighting some of the evolution in the preceding policies.

The *National Agenda,* the first national multicultural policy, presented a citizenship-cum-social justice model of multiculturalism. A decade later the *New Agenda* put greater stress on national identity, social cohesion, and community harmony.[24] It announced that the policy would henceforth be called "Australian multiculturalism" to underscore how "our implementation of multiculturalism has been uniquely Australian."[25] Australians' citizenship obligations (as against rights) were now foregrounded as the first plank of the policy. The *National Agenda* had stressed the defining importance of Australia's British heritage. The *New Agenda* also acknowledges that "Australian culture includes . . . our British and Irish heritage," along with Indigenous Australians and home-grown customs.[26] However, it adds a dimension in speaking of "our evolving national character and identity," a curious addition given the Howard government's conservatism. The Gillard government's multicultural policy went further by not even mentioning Australia's British or European heritage and instead promoting the country's long-standing diversity: "Australia's multicultural composition is at the heart of our national identity and is intrinsic to our history and character."[27]

Australian multiculturalism formally applies also to Aboriginal and Torres Strait Islander peoples. At the same time, it recognizes their "special status," and that "it is appropriate that their distinct needs and rights be reaffirmed and accorded separate consideration."[28] Unfortunately, this recognition has seen little efficacious policy to date. A recent example, and among the most egregious, is the Turnbull government's summary rejection of *The Uluru Statement from the Heart,* the outcome of a national process of deliberation on suitable constitutional recognition for and by Indigenous Australians, in which they called for the "establishment of a First Nations Voice enshrined in the Constitution."[29] In any case, these initiatives have little to do with multicultural policy. For their own part, many Aboriginal leaders have rejected their inclusion under "multiculturalism," believing that this compromises Aborigines' special status and weakens their claims based on their particular historical experience.[30]

The federal provisions on multiculturalism have their counterparts in each of the Australian states and territories and often in local governments as well. The states of New South Wales and Victoria and the Australian Capital Territory have each enshrined their multicultural principles and approaches to cultural diversity in legislation, while the other states and the Northern Territory have followed the federal governmental model and opted for policy statements or charters.[31] During the Howard, Rudd, Abbott and Turnbull governments, it has been state and local governments that have often maintained the momentum behind Australian multiculturalism.

Some argue that Australian multiculturalism began as a sensible effort to improve the absorption of migrants only to morph into a quest to redefine Australian national identity.[32] The criticism overlooks how the reforms of the 1970s inevitably implied some change in Australia's self-understanding and identity. "Anglo-Australia" could no longer define the country exclusively in its own image and interests once it had committed to a nondiscriminatory immigration program, an increasingly cultural diverse population, and the principle of nondiscrimination in Australian law and policy. Moreover, while the Howard and Gillard governments' multicultural policies may have referred to Australia's evolving and multicultural national identity, Australian multiculturalism has neither in policy nor in practice repudiated the established institutions and culture. The Australian Multicultural Advisory Council (AMAC), a government-appointed body, illustrated the point in its report to the Rudd government. While today's "Australia is very different to the Australia of the mid-20th century," it wrote, "much is unchanged: our political and legal institutions; our democracy; our liking for freedom, fairness and order; our language and the way we speak it; our love of the beach, the bush and sport."[33]

Looking back over the history of Australian multicultural policy and practice, one may discern three animating propositions in relation to national identity. First, Australia's British heritage and established institutions should be duly acknowledged as an essential part of its foundation. Second, Australian national identity will inevitably change over time with the changing composition of Australian society. Third, in the meantime, between a foundational past and an open future, the task is to ensure that all Australians, whatever their cultural heritage, enjoy the same rights and opportunities. This set of propositions conforms to what some political theorists call "liberal nationalism," a view that recognizes the inevitability in practice of a dominant culture and the legitimacy of some *limited* institutional privileging of it.[34] The first feature arguably distinguishes Australian multiculturalism from its federal Canadian counterpart where the Anglo cultural inheritance is formally denied. The second feature arguably distinguishes Australian multiculturalism from Quebec's policy of interculturalism and the policies of many European countries, where the dominance of the foundational culture tends to be considered indelible.[35] The third feature is common to most liberal versions of multiculturalism in seeking to check the power and privileging of the dominant cultural majority at the expense of other citizens.

Australia's is therefore a decidedly liberal and pragmatic version of multiculturalism.[36] However, even among liberal multiculturalisms, it is modest. Just how modest can be gleaned from Joseph Raz's typology of liberal responses to diversity.[37] Historically, the first liberal response to diversity was *toleration*. Here, minorities are left to live as they please as long as they do not interfere with the dominant culture. After toleration, Raz says, came *nondiscrimination,* which protects the individual rights and liberties of all citizens by outlawing discrimination on the basis of race, religion, ethnicity, and other group characteristics. In this it seeks to ensure that the common citizenship rights of liberalism are truly common. The most recent liberal response to diversity is *affirmative multiculturalism,* which rejects the individualistic focus of the nondiscrimination model, recognizes the value of cultural diversity, and actively assists groups to maintain their distinct cultures within the larger society.

Despite its name, Australian multiculturalism is overwhelmingly concerned with nondiscrimination and the protection of common citizenship rights—Raz's second-stage issues. The policy makes it plain that diversity is always subject to Australian political values and institutions, that English is the national language, and that all rights and entitlements under the policy attach to individuals and not to groups. Some Australian provisions arguably do fit Raz's profile of affirmative multiculturalism, for example, the multicultural Special Broadcasting Service (SBS), grants-in-aid to community groups, and interpreter services and multilingual government materials. However, these measures are also integrationist in purpose and effect. They are the opposite of the "separationist" multiculturalism and sanctioning of "parallel lives" of concern in Britain and elsewhere. Interpreter and translator services, for example, allow the effective administration of the business of government and enable migrants from non-English-speaking backgrounds to access resources and participate in civic affairs. SBS is a "public good" resource that all Australians can access and enjoy. The grants-in-aid programs—which were always modest, and were mostly abandoned by Howard in the 2000s—were based on the belief that having some diversity in the community enriches the lives of all Australians, and not just those of the grantees.

Although the term "liberal nationalism" scarcely figures in Australian political discourse, Australians have lived according to this basic architecture since the 1970s. It has not, however, gone uncontested. The most politically significant challenge comes from old-time Anglo-Australian conformity. This kind of cultural-nationalist sentiment remains strong in certain quarters.

The other broad oppositional camp includes a variety of civic nationalists, postnationalists, and cosmopolitans. It rejects the liberal nationalist assumption that Anglo-Australian culture has a certain foundational status and contends that such notions only stymie multiculturalism proper. Some of these critics argue for abandoning the notion of national identity altogether, contending that shared political values and a civic compact are sufficient for national cohesion.[38] Others argue that multiculturalism, cultural diversity, or a multicultural cosmopolitanism should be the basis of a new Australian national identity, though what this would amount to is unclear.[39] A more nuanced civic nationalist position agrees that civic or liberal-democratic values should be the basis of Australian national identity, but argues they should be expressed in a nationalist idiom by invoking episodes in Australian life that best exemplify them in action.[40]

The civic-cum-postnationalist positions in Australia are mostly confined to academic discourse and bookshops. An exception was the Australian Citizenship Council, an independent body established to advise the government on Australian citizenship matters. It recommended that a "civic compact" setting out the ground rules by which Australians live should replace the notion of a national identity.[41] Tellingly, the proposal went nowhere. That a citizenship body should make such a recommendation is also unsurprising. The formal acquisition of citizenship is arguably the one institutional domain where civic nationalist assumptions, or something like them, prevail.[42] To become an Australian citizen, one must accept Australian political values and institutions and pledge fidelity to the country and its people. The process does not require that one look, dress, or speak in a way that might be identified as "typically Australian." In this, Australia follows the pattern and, indeed, the achievement of modern liberal citizenship in separating formal political membership from expressions of the national culture.

Cultural conservatives have criticized Australia's "procedural" citizenship as too cold and sterile and call for it to be reinfused with warm national-cultural content and sentiment.[43] In contrast, many on the left find the liberal model of citizenship so compelling that they wish to extend its civic regime into every aspect of Australian governance and national life. Both inclinations conflate what Australia's liberal nationalist framework seeks—rightly, in my view—to separate.

RETREAT AND RESURGENCE: THE 2000S

Since the mid-1990s and especially in the wake of the 2001 World Trade Center attacks and the rise of militant Islam, there has been much talk of a retreat from multiculturalism or a "differentialist turn" in public policy in many countries.[44] Australia witnessed the same trend. In the late 1990s, a populist clamor against immigration and multiculturalism erupted, led by Pauline Hanson, a provincial fish-and-chip shop owner, who won a seat in the national parliament and went on to found her "One Nation" political party. In its first years One Nation won significant electoral support, especially in Hanson's home state of Queensland. Hanson and her party eventually fizzled out of political existence until her election to the Australian Senate almost two decades later in 2016.

As Hanson's political resurrection indicates, coolness to cultural difference remains strong among Australians. Public opinion research consistently finds that a majority of Australians agree with the proposition that migrants should adopt the way of life of the country rather than maintain their distinct customs and traditions.[45] At the same time, polls over many years show that between 60 and 70 percent of Australians support multiculturalism.[46] The apparent inconsistency suggests that "multiculturalism" is popularly associated with immigration, rather than viewed as a public policy that supports and accommodates cultural difference.

As noted, the Howard government updated its multiculturalism policy in 2003. In some ways, given the fraught times and John Howard's own antipathy to multiculturalism as a divisive doctrine, the very fact the policy was re-endorsed at all suggests how accepted some notion of multiculturalism had become to Australians. Howard came to office fiercely opposed to multiculturalism. In his first years as prime minister, he conspicuously avoided even saying the word, notwithstanding his government having a multiculturalism policy.[47] He rarely missed a beat in promoting Anglo-Australia as the core of Australian national identity, which migrants were expected to embrace.[48] In 1999, for example, he sought to have the legendary Australian tradition of "mateship" enshrined in the preamble to the Australian Constitution by referendum (the Senate blocked his proposal). Concerned about social cohesion in the wake of international and some local controversies involving Muslims, Howard introduced a raft of policies that promoted traditional Christian values.[49] The 2003 policy update *Multicultural Australia: United in Diversity* was a mere five pages long and suggested a government going through the motions. There was a palpable sense that it was only a matter of time before the Howard government recanted on multiculturalism.

That time came in late 2006. Following the Netherland's reassessment of multiculturalism, Britain's decision to introduce a new citizenship test, and general concerns about the integration of Muslims in Europe, the Howard government flagged its intention to drop the word "multiculturalism" from governmental use.[50] In January 2007, the Department of Immigration and Multicultural Affairs became the Department of Immigration and Citizenship. The residency eligibility period for acquiring citizenship was extended from two to four years, and a citizenship test (covering English-language proficiency, history and values) was introduced for those seeking to become Australian citizens.[51] Controversially, the citizenship test included questions on Australian cricket heroes and other cultural icons along with questions on Australian political institutions.

Prime Minister Kevin Rudd's Labor Party government, elected to office in November 2007, showed little interest in issues of cultural diversity and generally retained its predecessor's purge of the word "multiculturalism." Its "social inclusion" policy was framed exclusively in terms of socioeconomic disadvantage and ignored the situation of cultural minorities. In 2008, Rudd convened a "2020 Summit" at the national parliament, inviting a thousand of Australia's "best and brightest" to share their ideas about the nation's future. Notwithstanding some thirty years of official multiculturalism, the event was held on the first days of the Jewish festival of Passover, leaving many of the Jewish Australians invited unable to attend.[52] Such examples show that although liberal nationalist multiculturalism may be the predominant or default position in contemporary Australian politics, a strong current of Anglo-Australian indifference, if not outright resistance, to accommodating diversity persists.

Still, the progressive retreat from multiculturalism in the decade to 2010, when Rudd was deposed as Labor leader and prime minister, was not a return to the rank assimilationism of old. Howard's citizenship test sought English-language proficiency and knowledge of the Australian way of life, but it did not try to discourage migrants and their children from speaking foreign tongues as well, as was the case in the pre-multicultural era and as some conservative commentators still demand today.[53] Also, the Rudd government revised the citizenship test in 2010, removing Howard's national-cultural tropes and instead emphasizing Australia's political institutions and values (thus returning citizenship acquisition to the terms of civic nationalism). The retreat from "multiculturalism" during this period seemed to be more about messaging than the underlying policies. Talk of "multiculturalism," it was thought, was encouraging "separatism" and the impression that "anything goes." Substituting the language of "citizenship" and "integration" and emphasizing "core Australian values" were intended to arrest these perceived trends.[54]

The "retreat from multiculturalism," such as it was, seemed destined to continue on Julia Gillard's watch after she replaced Rudd as prime minister in 2010. During the subsequent election campaign, Gillard rejected high levels of immigration, spoke of the "preciousness" of the Australian way of life, and, on assuming office, removed "multicultural affairs" even from the title of the parliamentary secretary assisting the minister for immigration and citizenship. She pivoted, however, after the precipitous collapse of Labor Party support in the election, which left her leading a minority Labor government with the aid of independents and minor parties. As an ex-Labor politician put it, "We abandoned multicultural Australia and they abandoned us."[55] Earlier in the year, AMAC had recommended that multiculturalism be retained and reinvigorated with new programs. Gillard's minority government acted on these recommendations in February 2011, launching a new and affirmative multiculturalism policy. This move stood in stark contrast to the international scene. Days earlier, British Prime Minister David Cameron and French President Nicolas Sarkozy had each publicly condemned multiculturalism.[56] German Chancellor Angela Merkel had similarly denounced "multicultural society" as a failed experiment some months earlier.[57]

In announcing Australia's new cultural diversity policy, Immigration and Citizenship Minister Chris Bowen rebutted European criticisms of multiculturalism in the Australian context. The "genius of Australian multiculturalism," as Bowen called it, lay in three factors.[58] First, Australian multicultural policy had always insisted on "respect for traditional Australian values." These mainly liberal-democratic values—including the freedom of the individual, equality between the sexes, tolerance, the rule of law, and parliamentary democracy, but also English as the national language—always prevail if ever there is a clash with minority cultural practices. David Cameron had portrayed British-style multiculturalism as allowing communities to live largely "separate lives" devoid of shared values, and advocated "muscular liberalism" as the antidote.[59] Bowen argued that Australian multiculturalism just is "a matter of liberalism." As he elaborated: "If Australia is to be free and equal, then it will be multicultural. But, if it is to be multicultural, Australia must remain free and equal."[60] Indeed, Bowen argued that Australia was more successful than even Canada in this regard. While in Canada "debates about language and the ongoing make-up of the nation continue," Australia enjoys a greater "national consensus on our values" and the "geographic integrity of our nation" is settled.[61]

Second, Australian multiculturalism succeeds, Bowen argued, because it is a "citizenship-based" model. Unlike the European situation of guest workers being blocked from full integration, Australia encourages migrants to become citizens and accords full rights and benefits to all those who take the pledge of commitment as a citizen. Finally, Australian multiculturalism has enjoyed bipartisan support over the years. Both Labor and Liberal governments have helped develop and guide multiculturalism policy, so each party has had a stake in the policy's success.

Bowen's cited factors for the success of Australian multiculturalism are valid. I would add a few others. Australia's highly selective, skill-based immigration policy doubtless helps in moderating the challenges of social integration compared to many European countries.[62] Also, the architecture of the policy itself contributes to the successful record. As noted above, the Australian policy combines liberal principles—the rights to cultural identity (liberty) and nondiscrimination (equality)—with the public benefits of a culturally diverse society competing in a global economy (public goods). It also pragmatically negotiates the delicate issue of national identity, neither equating multiculturalism with a new definition of that identity (as in federal Canada) nor seeking to protect the historic identity from cultural diversity policy in perpetuity (as does Quebec with its interculturalism policy).

There are also significant weaknesses and tensions in Australian multiculturalism that went unremarked in Bowen's speech. One is the lack of attention given to "inclusion" (or "fraternity" in its classic tricolor formulation) as a principle and a social practice in its own right. Also, the acceptance of Anglo-Australian culture and institutions as foundational obviously is in some tension with the acceptance that Australian national identity and culture will inevitably change over time with a culturally diverse society. The tension is managed in that the expectation is that such changes will occur "organically" over generations rather than through social engineering or legislative imposition. Moreover, even as an intergenerational process, the vision is not entirely open-ended. As noted, Australian multiculturalism insists on respect for the country's liberal-democratic and parliamentary institutions. To this extent, the "British inheritance" will continue to enjoy precedence whatever other changes may eventuate to reflect and accommodate Australia's cultural diversity.

OLD AND NEW CHALLENGES: THE ABBOTT AND TURNBULL GOVERNMENTS

A Liberal and National Party coalition led by Tony Abbott was elected to office in September 2013. Its position on multiculturalism appeared fraught and confused. As a minister in Howard's government, Abbott—an arch monarchist and avowed Catholic—had presented a "conservative case" for multiculturalism. "By accepting difference," he wrote, "multiculturalism strives to avoid confrontation. By stressing respect, it aims to foster the kind of dialogue that diminishes the potential for conflict."[63] He rejected attempts to prevent Muslim women from wearing headscarves and the "spurious obstacles" placed in the way of building mosques and establishing Muslim schools. Later, as opposition leader, Abbott confided that he had changed his mind about multiculturalism when running Australians for Constitutional Monarchy and found that Indigenous people and migrants were among "the strongest supporters of the Crown in our constitution" as "part of embracing Australia." He endorsed multiculturalism because it ultimately was no threat to the traditional Australian way of life, saying: "The policy of multiculturalism, which all sides of politics support, expresses our willingness as a nation to let migrants assimilate in their own way and at their own pace, because of our confidence in the gravitational pull of the Australian way of life."[64]

As prime minister, Abbott lost some of his previous enthusiasm for multiculturalism even as a conservative strategy. He reprised the Howard government's removal of multicultural affairs from ministerial responsibility, downgrading the portfolio to a parliamentary secretary assisting the minister for social services. Also scratched were the National Anti-Racism Strategy and grants programs. The new parliamentary secretary for multicultural Affairs, Senator Concetta Fierravanti-Wells—herself the daughter of Italian migrants—promoted multiculturalism as a form of assimilation, explaining: "We become Australians and we assimilate at different paces. It's a process, really."[65] Reflecting the conflicting inclinations within the government, Fierravanti-Wells' Department of Social Services (then home to Multicultural Affairs) was meanwhile promoting an architectonic vision of multiculturalism. On its web page, it advocated a "Better Australia" in which "changes to organisations and structures . . . will result in a lasting capacity to respond to cultural diversity without the need for on-going external or additional support."[66]

Abbott's and Fierravanti-Wells' support for multiculturalism sprang from a similar cultural nationalist outlook, the belief that the core culture and institutions of the country should remain proudly Anglo-Australian in character. Another challenge to multiculturalism soon emerged, however, from a different political quarter. The attorney-general, Senator George Brandis, announced his intention to repeal the Racial Discrimination Act's anti-vilification provisions—which had been added in 1995—in the name of free speech. Section 18C of the RDA renders unlawful acts that "offend, insult, humiliate or intimidate" persons on the basis of their race, color or national or ethnic origin. Section 18D provides exemptions for such conduct where it is done reasonably and in good faith in artistic, scientific, academic, or journalistic pursuits in the public interest. Brandis stated that he wanted to "re-centre [the] debate so that when people talk about rights, they talk about the great liberal-democratic rights of freedom of expression, freedom of association, freedom of worship and freedom of the press."[67]

The catalyst was a 2011 federal court decision that found the conservative columnist Andrew Bolt to have breached the race-hate laws in two published articles in which he had questioned the identity and motives of light-skinned Indigenous people. Abbott denounced the decision and pledged to reform the RDA if elected to govern. However, where Abbott's interest included protecting an ally in the media, Brandis is well known as a moderate in his party and for his civil libertarianism. He is also a long-standing supporter of multiculturalism in Australia.

The proposed changes to the RDA sparked a public outcry. Brandis responded by appointing an outspoken free-market libertarian, Tim Wilson, as human rights commissioner at the Australian Human Rights Commission in December 2013. Wilson had once called for the abolition of the Commission as an illegitimate use of state authority. Dubbed the "freedom commissioner" by Brandis, his role was to balance the perceived social justice focus of the other commissioners and to prosecute the case for free speech as the most fundamental and cherished of all liberties. Wilson assumed the role with zeal, denouncing the protections against nondiscrimination and of equal opportunity as dangerous "positive liberties", which further antagonized community groups. Ethnic and religious leaders from the Greek, Arabic, Chinese, Indigenous, Jewish, and other communities mobilized against the changes and cooperated as never before. In March 2014, after protracted public debate and community representations, the government circulated a draft of its proposed changes to the RDA for comment and announced that it would hold a review on the matter. In August 2014, it was revealed that more than 76 percent of the 4,100 submissions to the review inquiry opposed the draft amendments.[68] Days later, Abbott announced that his government would no longer pursue changes to the RDA, saying, "Leadership is about preserving national unity on the essentials and that is why I have taken this position."[69]

The episode reveals much about Australian liberal democracy and its version of multiculturalism. First, in challenging the state regulation of citizen relations at all, the classical libertarian position of Wilson and his former employer, the Institute of Public Affairs, was unlikely to resonate much in Australia, which some have called a "Benthamite society."[70] From its inception, Australians have looked to government to solve every imaginable problem, including bad weather. Australians' nondeferential attitude to authority and tradition is oft noted—and conventionally traced to their convict origins—but they do not instinctively fear government intervention.

Second, the attorney-general's more moderate, civil libertarian stance also faced a "perception" difficulty. His insistence on the need to "balance" freedom of speech and protection against the incitement to racial hatred is precisely what the RDA's racial vilification provisions had been designed to achieve. Although the language of "offend" and "insult" could legitimately be questioned as overbroad and subjective, the tribunals and the courts have never interpreted them in isolation, such that someone merely taking offense or feeling insulted could seek relief under the Act. An action must meet a number of stringent tests before it can be considered unlawful, including falling outside of the "public interest" exemptions. Until the Bolt case, the balance struck by sections 18C and 18D of the RDA was widely thought to have worked well, a period of some sixteen years. The 2011 Bolt decision was certainly controversial, but even it did not turn on his targets simply being offended or insulted.[71] Critics of the provisions cite their "chilling effect" on speech; meanwhile, Bolt reminds Australians every day of how *unsilenced* he is by continuing to write provocative newspaper columns, and now with his own commentary television program.

Third, and most important, for ethnic minorities the anti-vilification provisions have immense symbolic as well as practical significance. As noted, Australian multiculturalism has mainly been about nondiscrimination and *common* citizenship rights. After decades of racial exclusion and then cultural assimilationism, the switch to "multiculturalism" signaled an attempt to better realize Australia's own long-proclaimed commitment to liberal-democratic values. No longer was it judged acceptable to deny people entry on the basis of their skin color or ethnic or national origin, or to exclude them from offices and opportunities on the basis of such group characteristics. All citizens are deemed entitled to full and equal participation in the society. Australian multiculturalism does not emphasize minority cultural maintenance. Neither has it sought to frame the nation as "a community of communities" (as in Britain).[72] Rather, it has been preoccupied with trying to create a society in which *individuals* from diverse backgrounds are able to enjoy the *same* liberties and opportunities. Mostly, this effort has focused on combatting direct, invidious discrimination and promoting "tolerance" and "community harmony." Reforms designed to alleviate *indirect* discrimination, where institutions inadvertently adversely impact particular groups, have been piecemeal, at best.

Other measures associated with liberal multiculturalism, such as symbolic recognition, public subsidization of minority activities, and the public celebration of diversity, are minimal in Australia. There are no dedicated seats for ethnic group representation in the national and state parliaments. And, as the example of the 2020 Summit (discussed above) illustrates, multicultural Australia is still not much attuned to accommodating difference. Indeed, Australian multiculturalism has been slow to recognize inclusion as a worthy principle in its own right. "Inclusion" or "inclusiveness" appear in the 1989, 1999 and 2003 national multicultural policies either as a corollary of equality and access and equity concerns or else as bringing all Australians, not just migrants or "ethnics," under the umbrella of multicultural policy.[73] The 2011 national policy recognizes that "inclusion" involves not only formal rights and entitlements but also how people are "looked upon" and whether they are made to feel they belong. The second principle of the policy states that the "Australian Government is committed to a just, *inclusive* and socially cohesive society." It elaborates: "Australia's multicultural policy aligns with the Government's Social Inclusion Agenda where Australians of all backgrounds *feel valued* and can participate in our society."[74] These sentiments were a step forward, but they were scarcely supported in policy or even in public rhetoric.

Ethnic minorities' sense of acceptance and belonging in multicultural Australia is thus still largely tied to the legal protections against discrimination. The anti-vilification provisions of the RDA are considered to be a vital extension of the principle of nondiscrimination and a public sign of their societal acceptance. This is why they mobilized so concertedly against the proposed repeal of the federal provisions despite still being protected by anti-discrimination laws and multi-culturalism policies at the state level. For them, at stake was the message that a dilution of the federal protections would send about their standing in modern Australia. It would throw into question whether they still retained, in Whitlam's 1975 phrase, "an honoured place."

The campaign for reform of the RDA may have been waged on (civil) libertarian principles, but the fear was that watering down the anti-vilification provisions would reopen the door to ethnic and cultural-nationalist prejudice. When the attorney-general stood in the Australian Senate and defended his reforms, saying, "People do have a right to be bigots, you know," he painted a vivid picture of the kind of Australia that minorities and seemingly the public at large thought had been left behind long ago.[75]

Against this background, the Turnbull coalition government's multicultural policy represents something of a watershed.[76] Malcolm Turnbull became prime minister after defeating Abbott in a party leadership challenge in 2015. His Liberal-National coalition then retained government by a single seat in the 2016 federal election. Many people thought Turnbull—a small-*l* liberal and progressive on many social issues throughout his life— had joined the wrong party. On several issues, he swung to the right to secure the party leadership and to appease the conservatives in the coalition. However, the Turnbull multicultural policy reflects a personal and philosophical outlook that only partly and incidentally converges with the preferences of his conservative colleagues.

The 2017 policy, *Multicultural Australia: United, Strong, Successful,* marks a significant departure from the previous national multicultural policies in a number of respects. It is the first multicultural policy statement to eschew the word "multiculturalism." Its guiding principles are stated in the abstract, disconnected from the specific circumstances of cultural minorities. So, for example, instead of affirming a right to cultural respect and cultural freedom, as in past policies, it opts for a general statement of respect and of freedom, including religious freedom. Instead of affirming principles of access and equity, nondiscrimination, or social justice for cultural minorities as before, it opts for a general endorsement of "equality." Racism or racial hatred is condemned four times in the policy, discrimination but twice. The 2017 policy puts the onus on citizens and "new Australians" to integrate into the existing institutions. Compared with its predecessors, the current policy says little about what steps government and public institutions will take to assist in the integration process and help accommodate cultural minorities. The 2017 policy reprises the reference to "our British and Irish heritage" made in the 1989 and 1999 multicultural policies but omitted from the 2003 and 2011 policies. However, the policy also breaks new ground in the degree to which it affirms the importance of "inclusion" and a sense of "belonging." These words or variations thereof are stressed some eleven times.

The Turnbull government's multicultural policy thus performs a kind of inversion. Previous multicultural policies emphasized the import of the liberal-democratic values of liberty and equality for cultural minorities while ignoring inclusion or belonging as an important value in its own right. The 2017 policy more than fills the latter gap, only to strip away the importance of the values of liberty and equality as fair terms of accommodation for cultural minorities. As mentioned, there are both personal and philosophical factors behind these changes.

Throughout his political career, Turnbull had avoided using the word "multiculturalism." His stock reference was rather to Australia being "the most successful multicultural society in the world." The phrasing has the advantage of avoiding what is, in sections of his party, a controversial term and state policy, but it also conveys, I think, his genuine belief in Australia as a welcoming country for people of all backgrounds. Turnbull himself practiced that welcome and openness. When addressing community groups, for example, he typically included a sentence or two in the community language. Turnbull's reluctance to say the "M-word" is thus very different from Howard's cultural nationalism. Yet his government's multicultural policy ditches core principles of Australian multiculturalism in a way that Howard's never did. The Howard government's retreat from multiculturalism conforms to what some scholars have called "post-multiculturalism"[77] or a "civic rebalancing"[78] during the first decade of the twenty-first century. Multicultural policies were continued in substance, if not always in name, but with greater focus on national identity, social cohesion, and the obligations of citizenship.

As I have suggested elsewhere, the 2017 multicultural policy marks a new kind of "post-multiculturalism."[79] The driving conviction is that multiculturalism in Australia has succeeded in doing its job such that it is no longer needed. Thus, on this account, "multicultural" policy should be mainstreamed. As the Liberal Party's then shadow immigration minister Scott Morrison put it in an Australia Day address in London: "For the past four decades . . . [t]he primary focus of multiculturalism has been to build an appreciation of ethnic and cultural diversity to combat intolerance and discrimination that was denying Australians the opportunity to fully participate in Australian life. It has had success in this regard."[80]

The imperative now, Morrison contended, is to ensure that cultural minorities are not themselves frustrating the social and economic participation of their members and to focus on what Australians share rather than play to their differences. Morrison calls this a "post-multiculturalism approach" in which the "remedies are . . . more likely to fall within the domain of more mainstream social and economic portfolio policy areas."

In August 2018, Australia's recent tradition of changing party leaders and prime ministers mid-term continued. Turnbull was challenged for the Liberal Party leadership by disgruntled conservatives in the party with the unintended result that Morrison, who had not challenged Turnbull, became leader and prime minister. Since Morrison virtually wrote the rationale for the 2017 multicultural policy, we can expect little change on this front until the next election, due in 2019. Soon after becoming prime minister, Morrison declared that he had no interest in the so-called culture wars surrounding Australian identity, further underscoring his remove from the cultural nationalism of Abbott and Howard.[81]

CONCLUSIONS

Australian multiculturalism is an expression of a broader liberal nationalist approach to national identity, citizenship and cultural diversity that emerged after decades of ethnic nationalist (racial exclusion) and then cultural nationalist (assimilation) politics. In the liberal nationalist approach, Anglo-Australian institutions and culture are credited with a certain foundational status, but their privileging is seriously limited and equal citizenship rights and opportunities are extended to cultural minorities. In this sense, Australian multiculturalism is a policy framework that seeks to check the cultural-nationalist aspects of the core culture from overreaching and violating its liberal-democratic side.

This feature of Australian multiculturalism is not well grasped by the political class or the general public. Many on the left cling to the notion that multiculturalism is a free-standing political philosophy that celebrates diversity. Cultural conservatives tend, however, to view it as a "politically correct" assault on (Anglo-)Australian culture and identity rather than as an attempt to honor liberal-democratic values that are also part of the "British inheritance." Meanwhile, ordinary Australians' endorsement of "multiculturalism" can similarly refer to widely differing notions. Some have in mind an unhurried process of assimilation to the traditional Australian way of life. Others mean a nondiscriminatory immigration policy and a generally tolerant attitude to cultural diversity, but without government policy affirming cultural difference. And yet others mean the kinds of principles and programs found in official multicultural policy or even more extensive forms of cultural recognition.

Support for multiculturalism at the national level has waxed and waned, often depending on the predilections of the prime minister and government of the day. Genuine bipartisan support characterized the initial period spanning the 1970s and early 1980s. That bipartisanship frayed somewhat when the Liberals were in opposition from 1982 to 1996. The Howard government lent multiculturalism nominal support until 2007, when it shelved the policy in name at least, a development effectively continued by the Rudd Labor government (which ironically restored bipartisanship). The Gillard minority Labor government reinvigorated multiculturalism policy and programs between 2011 and 2013. But this enthusiasm evaporated under the Abbott coalition government, in office until September 2015. The Turnbull government inaugurated a new "post-multiculturalism" multicultural policy in 2017, predicated on the assumption that Australian multiculturalism had done its assigned job and is no longer needed.

Both in terms of official policy and how it has operated in practice, Australian multiculturalism is more about "making room" for cultural minorities than "making over" the country, at least in the short term. Those who cite Australia as evidence of a worldwide trend towards liberal universalism accompanied by a purely civic conception of the nation, fundamentally misread the Australian case.[82] The turn to multiculturalism has undoubtedly helped to open up public space and opportunities for minorities compared to "old Australia." It is equally clear that minorities continue to be underrepresented in many Australian institutions and most leadership positions, and that the current mainstreaming approach is, at best, premature.[83] The coalition government and the Liberal Party both suffer from a serious, chronic underrepresentation of women, of any cultural background, within their ranks. Meanwhile, cultural nationalists remain a genuine political force and will continue to press their case for Anglo-Australian precedence given the opportunity. To date, the liberal nationalist architecture that Australia has developed since the 1970s has weathered such challenges and resentment. Even the current "post-multiculturalism" policy is based on the success of Australian multiculturalism rather than its repudiation as a policy approach.

Looking ahead, the key question is what the Labor Party will do in this area should it be elected to government, as presently seems likely. Key advocates of multiculturalism in the Gillard government, such as Chris Bowen, remain senior figures in the opposition. Australia's liberal nationalist multiculturalism may prove more resilient than the recent, ill-founded attempt to declare it obsolete.

NOTES

1. Australia, Bureau of Statistics, *Australian Demographic Statistics,* Cat. No. 3101.0 (June 2013).

2. Australia, Bureau of Statistics, *Cultural Diversity in Australia,* Cat. No. 2071.0 (June, 2012–13).

3. Organisation for Economic Co-operation and Development, "Foreign-Born and Foreign Populations," in *OECD Factbook* (2016); id., *International Migration Outlook 2016 France* (2016).

4. Gwenda Tavan, *The Long, Slow Death of White Australia* (Melbourne: Scribe, 2005) and Sean Brawley, "Mrs. O'Keefe and the Battle for White Australia," *Memento*, no. 33 (Winter 2007): 6–8, accessed February 21, 2019, www.naa.gov.au/naaresources/publications/memento/pdf/memento33.pdf.

5. Cultural assimilation policies of sorts could be claimed in regard to some Aboriginal groups before the 1940s, though these were typically predicated on biological assimilation, such as the need to "breed out the color." See Anthony Moran, "White Australia, Settler Nationalism and Aboriginal Assimilation," *Australian Journal of Politics and History* 51 (2005), 168–93.

6. For the classic statement distinguishing "ethnic" and "civic" forms of nationalism, see Hans Kohn, *The Idea of Nationalism: A Study in Its Origins and Background* (New York: Macmillan, 1944).

7. Robert Birrell, *A Nation of Our Own: Citizenship and Nation-Building in Federation Australia* (Melbourne: Longman, 1995); Keith Windschuttle, *The White Australia Policy* (Melbourne: Scribe, 2004).

8. Douglas Cole, "'The Crimson Thread of Kinship': Ethnic Ideas in Australia 1870–1914," *Historical Studies* 14 (1971): 511–25.

9. Ann-Mari Jordens, *Alien to Citizen: Settling Migrants in Australia, 1945–1975* (Sydney: Allen & Unwin, 1997).

10. Anna Haebich, *Spinning the Dream: Assimilation in Australia, 1950–1970* (North Freemantle, Western Australia: Freemantle Press, 2008).

11. Mark Lopez, *The Origins of Multiculturalism in Australian Politics, 1945–1975* (Melbourne: Melbourne University Press, 2000), 54–55.

12. Jordens, *Alien to Citizen*, 17.

13. Jerzy Zubrzycki, "The Evolution of the Policy of Multiculturalism in Australia," *Global Cultural Diversity Conference Proceedings* (Canberra: Department of Immigration and Citizenship, 1995).

14. James Curran and Stuart Ward, *The Unknown Nation: Australia after Empire* (Melbourne: Melbourne University Publishing, 2010).

15. Alastair Davidson, *From Subject to Citizen: Australian Citizen in the Twentieth Century* (Cambridge: Cambridge University Press, 1997).

16. A. J. Grassby, *A Multi-cultural Society for the Future* (Canberra: Australian Government Publishing Service, 1973).

17. Gough Whitlam, "Speech at the Launch of the Office of the Commissioner for Community Relations" (1975).

18. Frank Galbally, chairman, *Migrant Services and Programs* (Canberra: Australian Government Publishing Service, 1978); Australia, Ethnic Affairs Council, *Australia as a Multicultural Society* (Canberra: Australian Government Publishing Service, 1978).

19. Australia, Council on Population and Ethnic Affairs, *Multiculturalism for All Australians* (Canberra: Australian Government Publishing Service, 1982).

20. Australia, Office of Multicultural Affairs, *National Agenda for a Multicultural Australia* (Canberra: Australian Government Publishing Service, 1989).

21. Australia, Department of Immigration and Multicultural Affairs, *A New Agenda for Multicultural Australia* (Canberra: Australian Government Publishing Service, 1999); Department of Immigration and Multicultural and Indigenous Affairs, *Multicultural Australia, United in Diversity. Updating the 1999 New Agenda for Multicultural Australia: Strategic Directions for 2003–2006* (Canberra: Australian Government Publishing Service, 2003).

22. Australia, Department of Immigration and Citizenship, *The People of Australia: Australia's Multicultural Policy* (Canberra: Department of Immigration and Citizenship, 2011).

23. Australia, Department of Social Services, *Multicultural Australia: United, Strong, Successful* (Canberra: Department of Social Services, 2017).

24. Stephen Castles et al., *Mistaken Identity: Multiculturalism and the Demise of Nationalism in Australia* (Sydney: Pluto Press, 2001), 809–811.

25. Australia, National Multicultural Advisory Council, *Australian Multiculturalism for a New Century* (Canberra: Australian Government Publishing Service, 1999), 3.

26. Ibid., 7.

27. Australia, Department of Immigration and Citizenship, *People of Australia,* 2.

28. Australia, Office of Multicultural Affairs, *National Agenda for a Multicultural Agenda,* 49; Department of Immigration and Multicultural Affairs, *New Agenda for Multicultural Australia,* 7.

29. Daniel McKay (2017), *Uluru Statement: A Quick Guide,* Research Paper Series, 2016–17, Law and Bills Digest Section (Canberra: Parliamentary Library), http://parlinfo.aph.gov.au/parlInfo/download/library/prspub/5345708/upload_binary/5345708.pdf, accessed February 21, 2019.

30. Stephen Castles, "Multiculturalism in Australia," in *The Australian People,* ed. James Jupp (Cambridge: Cambridge University Press, 2001), 809; Evelyn Scott, "The Importance of Reconciliation for Multiculturalism" (speech, Logan Diggers Club, October 7, 2000), *Indigenous Law Resources,* www.austlii.edu.au/au/other/IndigLRes/car/2000/0710.html, accessed February 21, 2019.

31. E.g., the New South Wales *Community Relations Commission and Principles of Multiculturalism Act 2000; Multicultural Queensland—Making a World of Difference* (2005), and the Western Australia *Charter of Multiculturalism* (2004).

32. Brian Galligan and Winsome Roberts, *Australian Citizenship* (Melbourne: Melbourne University Press, 2004).

33. Australia, Multicultural Advisory Council, *The People of Australia: The Australian Multicultural Advisor Council's Statement on Cultural Diversity and Recommendations to Government* (Canberra: Australian Multicultural Advisor Council, 2010), 11.

34. See, e.g., Yael Tamir, *Liberal Nationalism* (Princeton, NJ: Princeton University Press, 1993); Will Kymlicka, *Multicultural Citizenship: A Liberal Theory of Minority Rights* (Oxford: Clarendon Press, 1995); and David Miller, *On Nationality* (Oxford: Clarendon Press, 1995).

35. Gérard Bouchard, "What Is Interculturalism?" *McGill Law Journal* 56, no. 2 (2011): 435–68; Charles Taylor, "Interculturalism or Multiculturalism?" *Philosophy and Social Criticism* 38 (2012): 413–23; and Geoffrey Brahm Levey, "Diversity, Duality and Time," in *Multiculturalism and Interculturalism: Debating the Dividing Lines,* ed. Nasar Meer, Tariq Modood, and Ricard Zapata-Barrero (Edinburgh: Edinburgh University Press, 2016), 201–24.

36. James Jupp, "A Pragmatic Solution to a Novel Situation: Australian Multiculturalism," in *Political Theory and Australian Multiculturalism,* ed. Geoffrey Bahm Levey (New York: Berghahn Books, 2008), 225–41.

37. Joseph Raz, *Ethics in the Public Domain: Essays in the Morality of Law and Politics* (Oxford: Clarendon Press, 1994).

38. See, e.g., Stephen Castles et al., *Mistaken Identity;* Donald Horne, *The Avenue of the Fair Go: A Group Tour of Australian Political Thought* (Sydney: Harper Collins, 1997); Ghassan Hage, *White Nation: Fantasies of White Supremacy in a Multicultural Society* (Sydney: Pluto Press, 1998); and Mary Kalantzis, "Multicultural Citizenship," in *Rethinking Australian Citizenship,* ed. Wayne Johnson and John Kane (Cambridge: Cambridge University Press, 2000).

39. See, e.g., Mark Latham, "A Big Country: Australia's National Identity," (speech, Sydney, April 20, 2004); Catriona Elder, *Being Australian: Narratives of National Identity* (Sydney: Allen & Unwin, 2007); and Anthony Moran, *The Public Life of Australian Multiculturalism: Building a Diverse Nation* (Cham, Switzerland: Palgrave Macmillan, 2017).

40. Tim Soutphommasane, *Reclaiming Patriotism* (Cambridge: Cambridge University Press, 2009).

41. Australia, Citizenship Council, *Australian Citizenship for a New Century* (Canberra: Australian Government Publishing Service, 2000).

42. Geoffrey Brahm Levey, "Liberal Nationalism and the Australian Citizenship Tests," *Citizenship Studies* 18 (2014): 175–89.

43. Katharine Betts and Robert Birrell, "Making Australian Citizenship Mean More," *People and Place* 15 (2007): 45–61.

44. Rogers Brubaker, "The Return of Assimilation? Changing Perspectives on Immigration and Its Sequels in France, Germany, and the United States," *Ethnic and Racial Studies* 24 (2001): 531–48; Christian Joppke, "The Retreat of Multiculturalism in the Liberal State: Theory and Policy," *British Journal of Sociology* 55 (2004): 237–57.

45. Andrew Markus, "Attitudes to Multiculturalism and Cultural Diversity," in *Multiculturalism and Integration: A Harmonious Relationship,* ed. James Jupp and Michael Clyne (Canberra: ANU Press, 2011).

46. Murray Goot and Ian Watson, "Immigration, Multiculturalism, and National Identity," in *Australian Social Attitudes: The First Report,* ed. Shaun Wilson et al. (Sydney: UNSW Press, 2005); "Most Still Enjoy a Culture Cocktail," *Australian,* December 22, 2005; and "Galaxy Poll Shows Most Australians Think Multiculturalism Works Well," News Limited Network, January 24, 2013.

47. Paul Kelly, "The Curse of the M-word," *Weekend Australian,* August 30–31, 1997.

48. Carol Johnson, "Howard's Values and Australian Identity," *Australian Journal of Political Science* 2 (2007): 195–210; and John Tate, "John Howard's 'Nation' and Citizenship Test: Multiculturalism, Citizenship, and Identity," *Australian Journal of Politics and History* 55 (2009): 97–120.

49. Marion Maddox, "Secularism and Religious Politics: An Australian Exception?" (paper presented at *Secularism and Beyond: Comparative Perspectives,* University of Copenhagen, May 29–June 1, 2007).

50. Andrew Robb, "The Importance of a Shared National Identity" (speech, Transformations Conference, Australian National University, Canberra, November 27, 2006).

51. Farida Fozdar and Brian Spittles, "The Australian Citizenship Test: Process and Rhetoric," *Australian Journal of Politics and History* 55 (2009): 496–512.

52. "Jews Silenced at Canberra Talkfest," *Australian Jewish News,* March 6, 2008.

53. E.g., Andrew Bolt, "The Foreign Invasion," *Daily Telegraph* (Sydney), August 2, 2018.

54. Robb, "Importance of a Shared National Identity."

55. Morris Lemma quoted in Paul Kelly, "Weighed Down by the M-word," *Australian,* February 23, 2011.

56. "State Multiculturalism Has Failed, Says David Cameron," BBC News, February 5, 2011; "Sarkozy Joins Allies Burying Multiculturalism," Reuters, February 11, 2011.

57. "Merkel Says German Multicultural Society Has Failed," BBC News, October 17, 2010.

58. Chris Bowen, "The Genius of Australian Multiculturalism" (speech, Sydney Institute, February 11, 2011).

59. "State Multiculturalism Has Failed, Says David Cameron,"

60. Bowen, "Genius of Australian Multiculturalism."

61. Ibid.

62. Oliver Marc Hartwich, *Selection, Migration and Integration: Why Multiculturalism Works in Australia (and Fails in Europe)* (St. Leonards, NSW, Australia: Centre for Independent Studies, 2011).

63. Tony Abbott, "A Conservative Case for Multiculturalism," *Quadrant* 50 (2006): 40–43.

64. Tony Abbott, "Vote of Thanks at the Inaugural Australian Multicultural Council Lecture" (speech, Parliament House, Canberra, September 19, 2012).

65. "Query over Future of Multiculturalism," SBS News, December 3, 2013.

66. Australia, Department of Social Services "Settlement and Multicultural Affairs: A Better Australia" (2014; web page discontinued but on file).

67. Jessica Wright, "George Brandis to Repeal 'Bolt laws' on Racial Discrimination," *Sydney Morning Herald,* November 8, 2013.

68. Heath Aston, "Few Back Change to Race Laws," *Sydney Morning Herald,* August 1, 2014.

69. Heath Aston, "Tony Abbott Dumps Controversial Changes to 18C Racial Discrimination Laws," *Sydney Morning Herald,* August 5, 2014.

70. Hugh Collins, "Political Ideology in Australia: The Distinctiveness of a Benthamite Society," *Dædalus* 114, no. 1, *Australia: Terra Incognita?* (Winter 1985): 147–69.

71. *Eatock v. Bolt* (2011), FCA 1103 (September 28).

72. Commission on the Future of Multi-Ethnic Britain, *The Future of Multi-Ethnic Britain: The Parekh Report* (London: Profile Books, 2000).

73. Geoffrey Brahm Levey, "Inclusion: A Missing Principle in Australian Multiculturalism," in *Liberal Multiculturalism and the Fair Terms of Integration,* ed. Peter Balint and Sophie Guérard de Latour (New York: Palgrave Macmillan, 2013).

74. Australia, Department of Immigration and Citizenship, *People of Australia* (emphasis added).

75. Aston, "Few Back Change to Race Laws."

76. Australia, Department of Social Services, *Multicultural Australia.*

77. Will Kymlicka, "The Rise and Fall of Multiculturalism? New Debates on Inclusion and Accommodation in Diverse Societies," *International Social Science Journal* 61 (2010): 97–112.

78. Nasar Meer and Tariq Modood, "The Multicultural State We're In: Muslims, 'Multiculture' and the 'Civic Re-Balancing' of British Multiculturalism," *Political Studies* 57, no. 3 (2009): 473–97.

79. Geoffrey Brahm Levey, "The Turnbull Government's Multicultural Policy: Towards a New Post-Multiculturalism" (unpublished paper, UNSW, Sydney, 2018).

80. Scott Morrison, "Australia—The Land of Our Adoption" (address to the Menzies Centre for Australian Studies, King's College, London, January 24, 2013).

81. David Crowe, "Scott Morrison Vows to Change Laws on Religious Freedom but Won't Be a 'culture warrior' PM," *Sydney Morning Herald,* September 7, 2018.

82. See, e.g., Christian Joppke, *Citizenship and Immigration* (Cambridge: Polity Press, 2010).

83. See, e.g., Australia, Human Rights Commission, *Leading for Change: A Blueprint for Cultural Diversity and Inclusive Leadership Revisited* (Sydney: AHRC, 2018).

6

Multiculturalism, Biculturalism, and National Identity in Aotearoa/New Zealand

Katherine Smits

In February 1840, New Zealand's newly arrived first governor, William Hobson, concluded a ceremony at which a treaty was signed between the British Crown and some Maori chiefs at Waitangi on New Zealand's North Island, with the words: "He iwi tahi tatou"—We are one people now. Hobson's optimistic claim (armed conflict between Maori and the British broke out a few years later) is still cited today to invoke national unity in New Zealand. Ironically, it set the stage for a public debate about cultural difference and national identity that has dominated the country's politics throughout its short post-settlement history. For most of that period, cultural difference was taken to refer to Maori and the British, or Pakeha, but over the past twenty-five years, the claims and discourse of diversity have broadened to encompass a wide range of polyethnic communities created as a result of liberalized immigration policies in the mid-1980s.

Multiculturalism can of course refer to the demographic realities of diversity, or to a set of governmental programs designed to protect, preserve, and promote minority cultures, or to the normative arguments for recognition that underlie these. The demographic facts of cultural and ethnic pluralism in New Zealand, which encompasses both indigenous and polyethnic groups, have particular implications for normative arguments and policies. In this chapter I focus on both normative claims and state-sponsored and public discourses around cultural diversity. The terminology is particular in New Zealand: although the term "multiculturalism" referred to settler-Maori relations when first introduced to public debate in the 1970s, it is now assumed to refer to polyethnic diversity resulting from non-British immigration. It thus usually excludes attitudes and policies relating to indigenous Maori.[1] The latter are considered part of "biculturalism," a policy position developed in the 1990s and still effectively pursued, although the term is much less frequently used. In terms of demographics, New Zealand is both bicultural and multicultural, but unlike Australia and Canada, it has no specific legislation addressing multiculturalism, nor have governments of any stripe developed dedicated umbrella policies to cover polyethnic diversity. There are, as we shall see, particular policies in the area of state services that refer to minority ethno-cultural groups, often providing special status for Pacific Islander peoples, and grouping them together with indigenous Maori.

This chapter will explore bicultural as well as multicultural claims and arguments, positioning indigenous and polyethnic recognition and rights claims in the context of a matrix of political and historical frames, and examining the way in which multiculturalism is shaped by, and shapes the normative and ideological discourses around political value and meaning that prevail in New Zealand. A consistent theme will be the relationship between cultural pluralism and other state policy projects: political, economic, and nationalist. Multiculturalism is framed by the values and discourses of these projects, but is also developed and invoked in order to support them. In this latter sense, multiculturalism may be understood as a form of governmentality, sustained by a language of value.[2] I rely in this aspect of my analysis (though I do not spell out its theoretical foundations) on a loosely Foucauldian governmentality approach, in which the conduct and attitudes of citizens are shaped by discourses and practices supported by the state in order to maintain its legitimacy.[3] Those discourses and practices reflect the distinctive and complex historical, social, economic, and global matrix in which New Zealand is located. I argue that multiculturalism as a set of normative claims and policy positions is intelligible only in the context that shapes it, and in which it shapes political action and meaning.

Multiculturalism in New Zealand is framed by the country's specific historical circumstances, as well as its current position in global politics and the world economy, and by the terms of its available public discourses. New Zealand is a settler society with a relatively recent colonial history, dating from the early nineteenth century. Colonization brought into contact the indigenous Maori and settler British, who came mainly via the Australian colonies, with their own recent and bloody history of the colonial destruction of indigenous peoples. Although there were some early non-British migrants, such as Chinese and Dalmatians, who migrated to work in the gold and gum industries, the first substantial influx of non-British migrants was the arrival in the 1950s of Pacific Islander (Pasifika) unskilled workers on temporary work visas, many of whom stayed.[4] Broader ethnic diversity dates only from the mid-1980s—not coincidentally, a period of intense modernization in New Zealand's socioeconomic history. Compression in terms of the pace of cultural diversification and social change, and the consequent emergence of cultural anxieties around political and economic, as well as cultural change, are key factors shaping public discourse about multiculturalism. Maori-settler relations are of course another, and polyethnic multiculturalism is very much shaped in the bicultural or bi-national context of indigenous claims.[5] The status of Pasifika peoples as immigrants who are often grouped with Maori for service provision, is another key framing factor.

Both multiculturalism and biculturalism are shaped by shifting and sometimes competing discourses around civic values and national identity, in the context of broader state economic and regulatory policy. The values of egalitarianism, social justice, and state support for communities are historically key parts of New Zealand's national identity dating back to the 1930s. Despite the devaluing of these elements of national discourse by neoliberal governments since the mid-1980s, social justice is still invoked to justify affirmative action and service delivery to and equal rights for minorities. This is one of several paradoxes around multiculturalism and neoliberalism: the liberalization and acceleration of immigration to New Zealand was part of a raft of modernizing policies starting in the 1980s, and the cultural diversity this policy shift has produced has been appropriated for the construction of a national identity or "brand" that can be marketed abroad. At the same time however, polyethnic cultural diversity has exacerbated public anxieties about withdrawal of governmental support to communities and rapid changes in traditional (white) New Zealand cultural values. The relationship between the neoliberal state and indigenous biculturalism is similarly complex. The revival of Maori political claims, particularly to ownership of resources and culture, has accelerated in response to increased cultural diversity, as Maori have sought to distinguish their status from that of polyethnic groups. At the same time, in order to reinforce its legitimacy, the state invokes traditional Maori culture not only to promote trade and tourism, but also to provide a language of belonging and community membership that is otherwise absent from neoliberal discourse.

These framing factors allow us to analyze multiculturalism in New Zealand in the context of its domestic history and politics. In turn, this facilitates comparisons with other settler societies, particularly Australia, with which New Zealand shares many aspects of national identity but against which it also tends to define itself globally. Multicultural policy is also, of course, influenced by international discourses around cultural diversity, in particular the emergence of an international norm of indigeneity over the past few decades.[6]

ETHNIC DIVERSITY AND IMMIGRATION POLICY

For most of New Zealand's post-European settlement history, the overwhelming majority of its immigrants have been British, and despite changed migration patterns, this persists, although the gap between British and non-British immigrant numbers has substantially decreased. In 2015–16, 9 percent of all approvals for residence were granted to UK citizens (a steady decline from 26 percent a decade earlier), compared to 18 percent and 16 percent for arrivals from China and India respectively.[7] Unlike Australia, New Zealand had no official "White New Zealand" policy, but government policies persisting well into the twentieth century aimed to encourage British and discourage Chinese immigrants.[8] The 1881 Chinese Immigration Act imposed a poll tax on Chinese immigrants, and the 1899 Immigration Restriction Act restricted South Asian immigration. It is only in the past two decades that a change in the European/non-European proportions of the population has developed. In the most recent census (2013), 74 percent of New Zealanders identified as European, 14.9 percent as Maori, 11.8 percent as Asian (predominantly Indian and Chinese, followed by Korean, Filipino, and Japanese), 7.4 percent as Pacific Islander (mainly Samoan, but also Cook Islander and Tongan), and 1.2 percent as Middle Eastern, Latin American, or African. The population of Asian New Zealanders has almost doubled from the 2001 Census, while the population of other groups has increased more steadily.[9] The proportion of Asian New Zealanders is expected to rise to 15.8 percent in 2026, up from 9.7 percent in 2006, while the proportion of European (mainly British) New Zealanders is projected to fall to 69.5 percent in 2026, down from 76.8 percent in 2006.[10] As New Zealand's population rises, its ethnic diversity broadens: between 1996 and 2006, the number of North East Asians who immigrated increased 55 percent; sub-Saharan Africans by 71 percent; South and Central Asians by 66 percent; and Middle Easterners and North Africans by 56 percent. The number of New Zealand residents who originated from the UK or Ireland increased by 9 percent. The proportion of Pasifika New Zealanders has increased, but as a result of this population's high birthrate, rather than immigration. A high birthrate also fueled an increase of almost 40 percent in Maori New Zealanders between 1991 and 2013.[11]

Increased ethnic diversity is accompanied, not surprisingly, by other forms of cultural diversity. In terms of religion, the 2013 Census showed that 49 percent of New Zealanders identified as Christians, down from 55 percent in the 2006 Census. There was a corresponding increase in the number of New Zealanders identifying with non-Christian religions, particularly Sikhs, Hindus, and Muslims, and this is attributable to increased Asian immigration. In overall numbers, a little over 1 percent of New Zealanders identify as Muslim, and a little over 2 percent identify as Hindu. While the percentages are small, the rate of change is fast: the proportion of New Zealanders identifying with non-Christian religions tripled between 2001 and 2013, from 2 percent to 6 percent. In terms of languages, the number of people who could speak two languages rose by from 15.8 percent in 2001 to 18.6 percent in 2013.[12]

The sharp increase in ethnic diversity in New Zealand is the result of legislative change in the mid-1980s, part of a raft of modernizing laws and policies and an economic shift to neoliberalism introduced by Prime Minister David Lange's Labour government. The Immigration Act passed in 1987 ended explicit preference for British, European, and North American (white) immigrants and introduced a system whereby skills, and then points, were assessed irrespective of race or country of origin. The new legislation aimed at a less discriminatory, more deliberately internationalist migration policy, targeting work skills needed to fuel national economic growth. This was in line with a new neoliberal policy emphasis on growth and on competitiveness in the international economy. The legislation was preceded by a review of immigration that described New Zealand as an immigrant society, dating from the earliest Maori arrivals.[13] This signaled a shift in conceptions of national identity, normalizing polyethnic diversity as a fundamental aspect of modern New Zealand identity. Diverse immigration to New Zealand has increased rapidly since then, which makes for an interesting comparison with Australia. There, European immigration diversified from the early 1950s, broadening out to Asian and Middle Eastern countries of origin in the 1970s. In New Zealand, public debates and anxieties about immigration generally have arisen at the same time as racist concerns and moral panics about non-European and nonwhite immigration.

Until recently, the accepted policy towards immigrants across the political spectrum was assimilation, with no state recognition of polyethnic cultures. In 1999, Augie Fleras and Paul Spoonley commented that cultural pluralism in New Zealand was cast not as a social good, but as a constraining factor or a potential problem to be managed.[14] From around the turn of the twenty-first century, successive left- and right-of-center governments have endorsed cultural and ethnic diversity as a social good for New Zealand. For example, the Ministry of Social Development, under the recent center-right National Party government reported that increased diversity can be a good thing for a society and its economy.[15] This reflects to some extent the "sari, samosa and steelband" version of multiculturalism, which emphasizes the color and celebration of local cultures rather than reducing substantive inequalities.[16] But state agencies and ministries also explicitly address the needs of diverse populations in areas such as social service provision, health, and education, in accordance with prevailing values of social justice in New Zealand. Integration, rather than assimilation is emphasized; state agencies promote the recognition of and dialogue across cultural communities. The Human Rights Commission now lists as a key goal the promotion of "harmonious relations between diverse groups," and part of the brief of the Race Relations Commissioner is to pursue this. The promotion of diversity and intercultural dialogue was a key policy area for the Labour government of 1999–2008; the "Connecting Diverse Communities" project, introduced in 2007, aimed at "improving connections with cultural identity," addressing discrimination and strengthening intercultural relationships.[17] There is little difference currently between the two major parties on this issue: in recent national elections both have actively courted Asian votes, elevating Chinese and Indian New Zealanders to prominent positions on the PR party list (New Zealand uses a mixed-member proportional system of election to its unicameral parliament.) In government, the National Party has continued to promote ethnic and religious inclusiveness, typically invoking the economic advantages of diversity.

This shift to integration policies in New Zealand has coincided with a shift in the opposite direction, toward explicit rejection of multiculturalism in Britain, Europe, and Australia.[18] In part this reflects New Zealand's relatively small Muslim population—anxieties in the post 9/11 period about fundamentalist Islam in ethnic communities were much more muted here than in other countries (as I discuss below). But it also reflects the role that discourse about cultural difference plays in New Zealand. Recognition of indigenous Maori cultural claims and aspirations has meant that assimilation into a dominant culture cannot be advocated with the same degree of public legitimacy in New Zealand as it can in other countries. But if the bicultural context lends some protection to the recognition of polyethnic diversity, it also limits it: no government has introduced an umbrella policy of multiculturalism or legislation on the issue, and biculturalism remains the dominant discourse of diversity.

THE BICULTURAL CONTEXT

Crucial to understanding both state policy and public responses to ethnic diversity in New Zealand is the central relationship between the dominant white Pakeha society and the Maori. The liberalization of immigration in the 1980s followed a decade of renewed Maori political mobilization, and a new consciousness of indigenous identity as the grounding for sovereignty claims. This took place, of course, in the context of the global emergence of indigenous political movements in settler states. Because the relationship between Maori and polyethnic claims in New Zealand has such an influence on attitudes to multiculturalism in New Zealand, it's important to establish the distinction between them. While both kinds of groups argue for official recognition of cultural identity and practices, indigenous communities crucially argue for some degree of autonomy, self-governance, and self-determination. In theoretical thinking about this in democracies, we can stake out two key positions: liberalism's argument based on individual autonomy, as set out by Will Kymlicka, and the argument for indigenous sovereignty based on the illegality of imperial conquest—associated with James Tully, among others.

Kymlicka argues that the difference between polyethnic and indigenous (and minority national) communities is that only the latter constitute societal cultures—that is, they form the entire and self-enclosed context in which the social identities, systems of meaning and value, and life plans of individual members are shaped.[19] In order for members of such communities to exercise their autonomy, their societal cultures, their contexts for autonomy must be protected and preserved. Indigenous communities and national minorities constitute societal cultures, Kymlicka argues, because their members never chose—historically or currently—any form of incorporation or integration. Polyethnic groups constituted through immigration are by contrast only partial communities; their members have chosen to affiliate to the larger societal culture. Their cultural identities and practices still merit recognition and protection, but only so that those members can be included and integrated as autonomous members of the broader societal culture. Here we can draw also on Charles Taylor: public recognition of cultural membership is an essential aspect of individual members' sense of personal worth and value.[20] This focus on integration as recognition and inclusion is reflected in the public policies toward polyethnic groups argued for and implemented in New Zealand. As the Ministry of Social Development's Social Report of 2016 comments: "Cultural identity is important for people's sense of self and how they relate to others. A strong cultural identity can contribute to people's overall wellbeing."[21]

Critics like Tully reject the grounding of indigenous claims on the liberal values of Western postcolonial states, arguing instead that indigenous communities are entitled to self-determination on the basis of their original self-government and independence prior to their forcible incorporation into new states through colonization.[22] The right to self-determination is central to a newly emerged global norm of indigeneity, reinforced by the UN Declaration on the Rights of Indigenous Peoples of 2007, endorsed in 2010 by New Zealand. Maori invoke the argument based on prior-existing sovereignty specifically in relation to the terms of the 1840 Treaty of Waitangi, over which there is some dispute: in the Maori-language version, the Maori retained sovereignty, but ceded to the Crown the right of governance. In the English-language version, the Maori ceded sovereignty. The current role of the Treaty, although it is not entrenched as a constitutional document, is so central in New Zealand that Maori claims in general are often referred to as Treaty claims. As Kymlicka notes, there are some disadvantages, however, to shaping the distinctive claims of indigenous peoples in terms of treaties, which tend neither to reflect current political realities, nor to address the current needs of indigenous peoples, inequalities, and issues in justice in contemporary terms.[23] As we shall see, the Treaty of Waitangi has been invoked to support both biculturalism and the distinct position of binationalism.

The prominence of the Treaty of Waitangi in Maori claims is recent; it was declared a nullity by the chief justice of the New Zealand Supreme Court in 1877, and subsequently a policy of Maori assimilation was accepted and pursued.[24] The Treaty was recovered, however, as a grounding for political claims during Maori political mobilization in the 1970s, and it has been incorporated into legislation since the mid-1980s. A key aspect of this historically has been the development of the policy of biculturalism. The Labour government elected in 1984 had committed itself before the election to reviving the Treaty, incorporating it into a bill of rights, and expanding the powers of the Waitangi Tribunal, established in 1975 with limited powers to consider claims based on breaches of the Treaty.[25] Once in government, Labour focused on the Tribunal and on incorporating the principles of the Treaty of Waitangi into legislation. In 1986, the *Puao-Te-Ata-Tu* report on a Maori perspective for the Department of Social Welfare recommended strategies to incorporate Maori cultural dimensions into the department's operations, and this became the model across state institutions.[26]

Also in 1986, the Royal Commission on the Electoral System "Towards a Better Democracy" heard submissions in Maori as well as English, and recognized the special status of the Maori as indigenous to New Zealand. In 1987, Te Reo Māori was accepted as an official language of New Zealand. These policies of cultural recognition and incorporation constitute the cultural redress dimension of Waitangi Tribunal recommendations, and form a key strand of what became the dominant policy of biculturalism. Biculturalism, the official recognition of both the dominant Pakeha and Maori cultures within public institutions purports to reform state institutions, policies, and regulations so that they include greater participation by Maori people, as well as Maori concerns, forms of expression and cultural practices.[27] This has meant a two-stranded strategy: the devolution of service provision to Maori organizations in partnership with the state, and the incorporation of Maori cultural practices into state institutions and processes—originally focused on those that deliver services to Maori, but now more widely adopted. Some of these cultural inclusion policies are more substantive, such as funding for Maori broadcasting and arts, and the inclusion of Maori history and culture in the school curriculum. The preschool curriculum is explicitly centered on Maori cultural values. Maori values are explicitly incorporated into the Resource Management Act, and into the activities of the Department of Conservation. In the social service provision ministries of Education, Social Development and Health, the use of Maori ceremonies, rituals, and language is more symbolic, although policies consistently emphasize the importance of establishing links to the extended family, or *whanau*, in Maori communities.[28]

Biculturalism was deemed by the 1986 report to be "the essential prerequisite to the development of a multi-cultural society."[29] The rhetoric of state institutions continues to emphasize the "unique place" of Maori culture, and the situating of polyethnic diversity within a bicultural context.[30] However, the relationship between the two founding cultures and subsequent cultural diversity was not spelled out, and the emphasis on cultural expression, recognition, and inclusion in multicultural terms has attracted some recent criticism on the part of Maori. Maori culture has become more visible in public life, but critics argue that rather than challenging Pakeha cultural and political hegemony in New Zealand, it reinforces it by positioning the Maori as a secondary, junior partner to the Crown.[31] Maori cultural identity is asserted in the context of Western political and bureaucratic institutions, rather than as a basis for self-determination through independent political structures. Critics argue that the changes introduced by biculturalism are merely window dressing, and that real power relations remain intact.[32] Cultural inclusion, or what Mason Durie calls "cultural capture" is in fact a strategy for managing and deflecting resistance.[33] Tom O'Reilly and David Wood claim that biculturalism's focus on cultural responsiveness is merely tokenism and point to the superficial use of cultural symbols and practices to satisfy Maori claims for recognition.[34] Nor is the problem simply the superficiality of cultural inclusion. Echoing a common critique of multiculturalism, Dominic O'Sullivan suggests that biculturalism assumes that Maori have developed into a single homogeneous identity and culture.[35] Cultural traditions are assumed to be homogeneous and frozen in time, rather than the products of continual negotiation within and between cultural communities. As a result, real struggles and conflicts within Maori communities over the changing meanings of cultural traditions are repressed. In response to these concerns, and to disputes over the role of Maori ceremonies in state institutions, the Maori Party has called for an investigation into the use of Maori customs, or *tikanga,* across the state sector. The party claimed that Maori customs are being used by the state to co-opt Maori into institutions that remain essentially hostile to them.[36]

The Treaty of Waitangi is interpreted by some Maori activists as authorizing claims not to the recognition and protection of culture, strategies which are seen as more suitable for polyethnic multiculturalism, but rather to self-determination and autonomy, based on retained sovereignty. This position sidesteps the question of diversity in non-Maori society: Maori are cast not as an ethnic group jockeying for recognition within an increasingly diverse society still dominated by Pakeha culture, but as an independent people negotiating with the Crown. These Maori claims are beyond the scope of this chapter, but I would note that they do not include secession, but focus rather on ownership of resources and the self-management of tracts of lands, resources, and social services. Nevertheless, they do incorporate real transfers of power, and the New Zealand state's reluctance to pursue self-determination (demonstrated by its refusal for three years to endorse the UN Declaration on the Rights of Indigenous Peoples) is not surprising.

Maori attitudes towards multiculturalism understood in terms of ethnic diversity and state recognition of minority cultures, are complex and evolving. There has been a long history since the nineteenth century of close relations between Maori and non-British immigrant groups, particularly the Chinese.[37] However in the 1990s, when the impact of liberalized immigration legislation was first becoming apparent, Maori concern about immigration emerged, on the grounds that a more diverse population would not necessarily support the fundamental status for Maori of the treaty relationship with the British Crown. Some Maori commentators, noting developments in Australia, where polyethnic multiculturalism long preceded recognition of indigenous rights, have fiercely opposed any characterization of New Zealand as multicultural. Ranginui Walker castigated the government in the late 1980s and 1990s for failing to consult with Maori over the extension of immigration policy to cover non-Europeans. Some of this reflected racist anti-Asian sentiments also expressed by Pakeha. Immigrants from Asia were, Walker claimed, driven by "egocentric" motives, rather than "a sense of altruism towards the host country."[38] They were insufficiently proficient in English, and their contribution to economic growth was low, since they "usually employ their own people."[39] In response, defenders of multiculturalism argued that non-European immigrants were being excluded from the debate on the New Zealand's identity and future. Drawing on the liberal philosophical arguments against recognition made by Chandran Kukathas, Ramesh Thakur argued that the state should give no preferential recognition to the language and culture of any ethnic group, including Maori, whom he characterized as immigrants.[40]

A succession of political groups, including the current Maori Party, have requested formal Maori input into immigration policy, and in 1991, a Waitangi Tribunal claim was launched in relation to the Immigration Act.[41] In 2015, a government report found that Maori (and Pacific) New Zealanders were less likely than other groups to hold positive views of migrants.[42] Maori concern about Asian immigrants and their commitment to the Treaty continued into the early twenty-first century.[43] In 2014, a survey found that Maori respondents disliked Asian immigrants more than any other demographic group.[44] Nevertheless, over the past decade, public Maori discourse has shifted and has become more explicitly anti-racist, perhaps in response to the expression of Pakeha racist sentiments against both immigrants and Maori. In 2007, the Maori Party co-leader Tariana Turia called for European migration to New Zealand to be reduced, claiming that the government was trying to stop the "browning of New Zealand" by stepping up immigration from Australia, Britain, and Canada.[45] In response to the 2010 Department of Labour report, prominent the Maori activist and academic Margaret Mutu advocated a cap on white immigrants to New Zealand, on the grounds that they brought with them "white supremacist attitudes." She added that Maori were "generally supportive" of immigration from Asian countries.[46] Then Maori Party co-leader Pita Sharples agreed that there was concern about "western" immigration to New Zealand, although the party was, he said, happy with Pasifika immigration, since it recognized commonalities of experience between Maori and Pasifika peoples.[47] Current Maori Party policy on immigration requires only that all new migrants complete a course on the history of the Treaty of Waitangi.[48]

The change in attitude among Maori leaders to multiculturalism, and especially the dropping of opposition to non-British migrants, undoubtedly reflects a shift in Maori political claims to binationalism and self-determination. While biculturalism seeks recognition for indigenous peoples on the grounds of cultural status, a strategy always open to extension to other cultural minorities, self-determination invokes a quite distinct set of political demands and justifications, and one that is not subject to competition from polyethnic groups.

THE LIMINAL STATUS OF PASIFIKA CULTURES

Pasifika peoples occupy a particular position in terms of cultural diversity: as immigrants they constitute a polyethnic community, but as Polynesians and the subjects of colonization elsewhere in the region, they are more closely linked to Maori than are other ethnic groups, and are key to the "branding" of New Zealand's identity as a Pacific nation. Moreover, they tend to be concentrated in low-skilled, low-wage employment, and are relatively disadvantaged in socioeconomic terms. This has meant that they are often grouped with Maori as the beneficiaries of affirmative action programs. The 1993 Human Rights Act prohibits discrimination on the grounds of race and ethnicity, among other categories, but specifically exempts provisions that are designed to ensure the equality of disadvantaged groups, such as training schemes and employment assistance measures. Several of these schemes, such as university entrance programs, have been set up to target Pasifika peoples as well as Maori. Pasifika peoples are also identified as the subjects of service provision: government departments such as Health, Social Development, and Education specifically target Pasifika as well as Maori New Zealanders, and there are special Pasifika courts for young offenders, similar to Maori courts.

These accommodations for Pasifika communities suggest that the immigrant/indigenous distinction is less important in shaping multiculturalist practices and policies than the ways in which national values and identity can be mobilized by the groups involved. As integrative multiculturalism has been justified in the past decade in terms of traditional New Zealand values of social justice and equality, provisions for immigrant groups that are systemically economically disadvantaged have been piggy-backed upon policies for Maori without objection. Potentially, this will benefit other disadvantaged polyethnic groups as well, such as refugees from Africa and the Middle East, but Pasifika peoples can also draw on discourse around national identity under globalization. Successive New Zealand governments have mobilized Maori, and increasingly, Pasifika culture, to promote the country as distinctive in the global trade and tourism market.

PUBLIC REACTIONS TO CULTURAL DIVERSITY

Maori concern about immigration must be interpreted in the broader context of anti-immigrant sentiment, particularly directed at Asians, in the wider community. As is not surprising in an overwhelmingly white and British postcolonial society positioned close to Asia and the Polynesian and Melanesian Pacific, New Zealand attitudes have historically reflected suspicion of and skepticism about nonwhite outsiders. The speed of policy changes in the 1980s and subsequent diverse immigration led to some strong social reactions around racial difference, sometimes expressed as moral panics. A notable example was the article "Asian Angst," by the conservative former politician Deborah Coddington, published in the mainstream magazine *North and South,* in which Coddington argued that Asian immigrants were involved in a "tide of crime." Coddington pointed to an increase in arrest figures for Asian New Zealanders over the prior decade—without mentioning, however, that the number of Asian New Zealanders had also increased in this period, and that the arrest rate of Asians as a proportion of the population had halved over the decade.[49] The article prompted much public debate, but it is worth noting that it attracted strong public opposition and was condemned by the Press Council. Anti-Asian sentiment has been boosted recently by the fast rise of house prices in New Zealand's major cities, which is commonly blamed on Chinese off-shore investors—a target often expanded by politicians and the popular media to include local New Zealander buyers of Asian ethnicity.[50]

The terrorist attacks of September 11, 2001, and in London and Bali in 2002 and 2005, and the Danish cartoon controversy the same year produced some anti-Muslim sentiment in public discourse in New Zealand. Opposition to multicul-turalism increasingly took the form of verbal attacks on the Muslim community for its alleged support—or at least failure to criticize strongly enough—extremist Muslim radicalism. This became a focus for criticism by the populist politician Winston Peters, who emphasized the theme in the lead-up to the 2005 election, linking increasing Muslim immigration into New Zealand with the threat of ter-rorism, suggesting that Muslim immigrants came from cultures with no respect for liberal values.[51]

Nevertheless, the government's 2015 *Community Perceptions of Migrants and Immigration* survey found that respondents were generally positive in their atti-tudes to migrants.[52] This suggests that there has been a recent decline in pub-lic anxieties about the cohesiveness of political community in New Zealand. Although these concerns focused on—or scapegoated—multiculturalism, they originated in broader social and economic changes. They arose in response to the neoliberal economic and administrative reforms imposed in the mid-1980s, which emphasized the country's need to compete in global markets, and reduced the state provision of social services and institutional support that had become accepted as part of the national identity in New Zealand. Community was rede-fined in terms of voluntary association, but was given no substantive content.[53] The cultural anxieties this produced were articulated, ironically, by neo-liberal advocate and then-leader of the conservative National Party Don Brash, in a well-publicized and controversial 2004 speech. In terms familiar from international critics of multiculturalism who argue that a common language and culture are essential to the shared practices that constitute the civic nation, Brash argued that state recognition and promotion of diversity detracts from a sense of common identity that holds the nation together.[54] Like other critics of multiculturalism from this perspective, Brash invoked liberal-democratic values as the content of that common identity, but implied in his argument that these are tied to a sub-stantive culture.

While Brash drew on a discourse of civic nationalism to reject biculturalism and express skepticism about state-sponsored multiculturalism, cultural diversity has also played positively in an emergent discourse about civic responsibility, citizenship, and movements for citizenship education in schools. These strands of civic nationalism emphasize intercultural dialogue, respect for difference, and democratic values over substantial cultural content.[55] In a 2002 statement of economic policy intent the Labour government under Helen Clark referred to New Zealand as "a land where diversity is valued and reflected in our national identity."[56] Moreover, while neoliberalism has seen a move away from state-sponsored discourse about egalitarianism and state support, these long-standing national values continue to have popular traction and are still invoked to justify social support and welfare policies addressing migrants and polyethnic communities, as well as the Maori.[57] In this way, discourses of distributive equality are not contrasted to recognition, as is frequently claimed by critics of multiculturalism,[58] but are mutually reinforcing.

MINORITY CULTURAL PRACTICES AND HUMAN RIGHTS

Critics of multiculturalism point to potential conflicts between the cultural practices of traditional society and prevailing Western norms of gender equality.[59] Controversies have arisen in New Zealand involving both Maori and polyethnic communities around particular cultural practices that have been interpreted as being contrary to central national values, entrenched in human rights law. In the case of Maori, this has occurred around the role of women in traditional Maori cultural practices. In 2005, a Pakeha female officer in the Department of Corrections protested publicly when she attended a farewell ceremony for male offenders organized by the Department. The ceremony, a *poroporoaki*, required women to sit behind men. Pakeha feminists spoke in support of her position; however, the overwhelming public response of Maori women was to reject their arguments, and to interpret the officer's actions as a refusal to accept the public expression of Maori culture.[60] This is despite the documented history of Maori women making feminist critiques of gendered roles in Maori ceremonies—and indicates that indigenous identification tends to trump gender in New Zealand.[61] In 2006, two conservative women members of Parliament refused to sit behind men at a Maori welcome ceremony, or *powhiri*, during a parliamentary visit to a Child Youth and Family Services event. New Zealand's Human Rights Act of 1993 prohibits discrimination on a number of grounds, including sex and culture, and these cases are usually interpreted to reveal an ongoing tension between biculturalism and Western human rights norms. But they also point to the difficulty of identifying fixed and stable interpretations of cultural meaning (another common critique of cultural recognition policies). As historians point out, the position of women in Maori culture shifted considerably after colonization.[62]

Similar conflicts have involved polyethnic cultural practices. In 2004, two women witnesses in an insurance fraud case in the Auckland District court requested permission to give evidence while wearing the burqa. Defense counsel objected, and the judge heard arguments about the issue outside the trial. Supporters of the women invoked the Human Rights Act of 1993 and the Bill of Rights Act of 1990, which prohibit religious discrimination. The judge decided that although wearing the burqa in court was a matter of right for the witnesses, this was outweighed by the impact it would have on the weight of evidence, since it prevented physical personal behavior and facial expression being assessed in cross-examination and was incompatible with the required public nature of the proceedings. In a compromise decision, the women were allowed to give evidence, without the burqa, behind screens, so that they were visible only to the judge, counsel, and female court staff.[63]

Cultural dress for women has in general attracted much less controversy in New Zealand than in Britain and Europe, and there is no movement to prohibit the head scarf, burqa, or other forms of concealing dress in public institutions. The Human Rights Commission advocates a "human rights framework" to balance and assess the conflicts caused by increasingly diverse ethnicity in New Zealand society, according to which rights to cultural expression are balanced against other individual human rights. (This framework has not, however, been explicitly invoked in response to disputes involving Maori.) State authorities in New Zealand have taken a generally pragmatic and conciliatory attitude to cultural dress requirements—women are allowed to wear the head scarf in passport photographs, for example, as long as the full face is shown, and female staff process the application if necessary.

CULTURE AND STATE LEGITIMACY

As we have seen, cultural diversity has played a complex role in conceptions of civic nationalism in New Zealand, deployed by both opponents and supporters of cultural recognition. As the nation moved in the 1990s to market its products in a global economy, a strong national identity was required to project New Zealand as a player on the international stage and distinguish it from competitors.[64] Particularly as New Zealand sought to enter Asian markets, cultural diversity has been emphasized as a key aspect of national identity, central to economic prosperity.[65] Polyethnic multiculturalism has been effectively marketed in Australia as a key aspect of modern national identity, as it has in Canada. In tourism and trade promotion, and in international trade shows, settler societies have emphasized their cultural diversity.[66] While polyethnic diversity is also promoted by New Zealand (notably in the area of selling education, at both school and university levels), particular emphasis has been given to Maori culture. To some extent this reflects long historical practice: since its colonial days, New Zealand has drawn on its Maori heritage to differentiate itself from Britain and other settler societies. As David Pearson points out, part of the process of emerging national independence in settler societies is the appropriation of indigenous culture. This allows these societies to distinguish themselves from the imperial center, on the basis of the particularities of insider/outsider relations between settlers and natives.[67] In the contemporary context, national identity is drawn upon in the global market as part of the "brand state"—the nation-state's image is a key aspect of its presentation to the world.[68] Jacqui True and Charlie Gao have shown that New Zealand has cultivated its image as "clean, green" and "100% Pure New Zealand," and aspects of Maori culture are also key to this distinctive brand.[69] The *haka* dance has been effectively deployed as a cultural symbol for New Zealand, as well as being marketed by Maori themselves. The ubiquity of this performance in international sporting events has been noted by critics, but generally, the marketing of national culture has mainly been criticized by Maori. Their concerns were recognized in the 2011 Waitangi Tribunal case Wai 262, which recommended, inter alia, that Maori be granted ownership over cultural practices and knowledge, which are to be treated as intellectual property, and protected from commercialization without the consent of their Maori owners.[70]

While niche national marketing accounts for New Zealand's promotion of Maori culture abroad, more complex reasons must be sought for the emphasis placed on biculturalism at home. As we have seen, biculturalism was developed as part of the response to Treaty of Waitangi claims, but its high level of support from both the state and Pakeha public suggest deeper social and ideological factors at work. Key here is the public concern noted above over the loss of traditional values of community and social support that has characterized political discourse in New Zealand since the neoliberal economic reforms of the mid-1980s.[71] Public attitudes to the role of the state and the value of community have not altered substantially to match the values inherent in neoliberalism. A study conducted by Louise Humpage suggests that despite the individualist and minimal state rhetoric of neoliberalism, support for the public provision of social services such health and education continued unchanged—66 percent of respondents favored free health care in 2005, despite over a decade of neoliberal "user pays" rhetoric. Similarly, support for increased government spending on education remained constant.[72]

These figures suggest that a majority of New Zealanders have continued to expect government to provide key social services notwithstanding the neoliberal rhetoric around personal responsibility and some popular enthusiasm for lower tax rates. Neoliberal rhetoric does not seem to have led New Zealanders to abandon their concern about the social impact of these reforms, especially upon families and children.[73] Moreover, support for the responsibility of the state to provide citizens with jobs remained fairly constant, despite the employment of "personal responsibility" rhetoric. Significant numbers saw the "laziness" of the unemployed as a factor in their circumstances, but Humpage's own qualitative survey in 2010 found that 82 percent of participants agreed with the statement "Government should take responsibility to ensure that everyone is provided for."[74] Humpage concludes from this that popular attitudes to social and economic policy do not shift neatly in line with changes in official discourse.[75]

In the context of this misalignment between the views of citizens and the state's own description of its role in maintaining and reinforcing social relations, Maori values of community, family, belonging, and tradition are drawn on by the state to supply a language that is missing in neoliberal rhetoric, but which continues to compel Pakeha New Zealanders.[76] The traditional cultural values supplied or quoted in Maori cultural practices adopted, promoted, and appropriated by the state are easily identified as those that neoliberalism had rejected: communal identification and responsibility, social hierarchies, reverence for history and tradition, spirituality, and an ontological connection to geographical place. Whereas liberal individualism is associated with rationality and communities of choice, Maori culture is presented as a positive alternative to this. As emotional, spiritual, given rather than chosen, and closely linked to the land, it "appreciates the mystical dimension and transcends reason."[77] As this suggests, cultural pluralism is useful to the state on several levels. By promoting polyethnic and Maori diversity abroad, New Zealand positions itself as a modern nation with a range of skills essential in the global market, but also with a distinctive attractive culture. Domestically, the promotion of Maori culture maintains legitimacy for the state by providing a discourse of belonging.

CONCLUSIONS

The absence of a comprehensive multiculturalism policy in New Zealand is best understood as resulting from the sensitive political relationship between long-standing indigenous claims and the newer demands of polyethnic diversity. As the latter have become more salient as an aspect of the social landscape, governments have responded by acknowledging multicultural realities, while maintaining the unique status of Maori under the Treaty of Waitangi. As the Ministry of Social Development's 2016 *Social Report* puts it: "They [the outcomes of social policy] recognise New Zealand is a multicultural society, while also acknowledging that Maori culture has a unique place. For example, under the Treaty of Waitangi, the Crown has an obligation to protect the Maori language."[78] The duties owed to other minority cultures are not spelled out. Current developments suggest that there is likely to be increasing public recognition of multiculturalism: the increasing shift in Maori political claims away from cultural inclusion and toward self-management and self-determination, evident in the Wai 262 recommendation and in accordance with international norms of indigeneity could potentially decrease tensions between the bicultural and multicultural aspects of New Zealand's identity. Moreover, the human rights framework advocated by the Human Rights Commission allows scope for greater formal minority cultural inclusion in public institutions.

As we have seen, the complex, mutually constituting relationship between cultural diversity policy on the one hand, and broader social values and governmental policies on the other, provide strong sources of impetus both for increased formal recognition of multiculturalism, and for a more systematic policy approach. Most importantly, New Zealand's need for growth will promote continued migration based on skills, which will, along with high birthrates in Maori and Pasifika communities, increase demographic diversity. The promotion and marketing of New Zealand in a competitive global market, as against other multicultural societies, will require it to emphasize its cultural and linguistic diversity, as shorthand for modernity, adaptability, and a skilled and flexible labor force. At the same time, the dislocations and upheavals of the global market under neoliberalism are likely to continue to reinforce the appeal of cultural values of community, belonging, and tradition. At the same time, the framing of cultural diversity as a contemporary grounding for national civic ideals of inclusiveness, social justice, and egalitarianism allows for pragmatic policies of cultural recognition in terms of service delivery to immigrants. This has already taken place with respect to Pasifika immigrants, and there is obvious scope to include polyethnic cultures and languages in, for example, schooling and social service delivery. Given current trends, it seems likely that multiculturalism as a discourse and policy program will become a stronger and more permanent aspect of the policy agenda in New Zealand, with a more sustainable future in a binational, rather than a bicultural, context.

NOTES

1. Maori are descended from Polynesian seafarers who arrived in New Zealand in the thirteenth century CE, and are occasionally and controversially described as the country's first immigrants.

2. Elizabeth Povinelli, *The Cunning of Recognition: Indigenous Alterities and the Making of Australian Multiculturalism* (Durham, NC: Duke University Press, 2002).

3. Mark Bevir, "Political Science after Foucault," *History of the Human Sciences* 24, no. 4 (2011): 81–96.

4. David Pearson, "Biculturalism and Multiculturalism in Comparative Perspective," in *Nga Take: Ethnic Relations and Racism in Aotearoa/New Zealand,* ed. Paul Spoonley, David Pearson, and Cluny MacPherson (Palmerston North, NZ: Dunmore Press, 1991), 207.

5. See Katherine Smits, "Multicultural Identity in a Bicultural Context," in *New Zealand Government and Politics* 4th ed., ed. Raymond Miller (Melbourne: Oxford University Press, 2006), 25–35.

6. See the essays in Michelle Harris, Martin Nakata, and Bronwyn Carlson, eds., *The Politics of Identity: Emerging Indigeneity* (Broadway, NSW, Australia: UTS ePress, 2013).

7. New Zealand, Labour and Immigration Research Centre, *Migration Trends 2015/2016* (Wellington: Ministry of Business, Innovation and Employment, 2016), 47.

8. Vince Marotta, "The Ambivalence of Borders: The Bicultural and the Multicultural," in *Race, Colour and Identity in Australia and New Zealand,* ed. John Docker and Gerhard Fischer (Sydney: University of New South Wales Press, 2000) 179–80.

9. For all statistical information, see Statistics New Zealand, http://www.stats.govt.nz.

10. "Projections Overview," ibid.

11. "Census Quickstats about Maori," ibid.

12. "Quick Stats about Culture and Identity," ibid.

13. Kerry Burke, "Review of Immigration Policy," *Appendices to the Journal of the House of Representatives G42* (Wellington: Government Printer, 1986).

14. Augie Fleras and Paul Spoonley, *Recalling Aotearoa: Indigenous Politics and Ethnic Relations in New Zealand* (Oxford: Oxford University Press, 1999).

15. New Zealand, Ministry of Social Development, *Connecting Diverse Communities,* www.msd.govt.nz/documents/about-msd-and-our-work/publications-resources/research/connecting-diverse-communities/cdc-public-engagement-2007.pdf.

16. Yasmin Alibhai-Brown, *After Multiculturalism* (London: Foreign Policy Centre, 2000,) 17.

17. New Zealand, Ministry of Social Development, *Connecting Diverse Communities.*

18. This culminated in speeches by David Cameron and Nicholas Sarkozy in February 2011 denouncing multiculturalism in Britain and France. See the discussion of Cameron's position in chapter 2 of this volume.

19. Will Kymlicka, *Multicultural Citizenship: A Liberal Theory of Minority Rights* (Oxford: Clarendon Press, 1995).

20. Charles Taylor, "The Politics of Recognition," in *Multiculturalism: Examining the Politics of Recognition,* ed. Amy Gutmann (Princeton, NJ: Princeton University Press, 1994).

21. New Zealand, Ministry of Social Development, *The Social Report 2016* (Wellington: Ministry of Social Development, 2016,) 175.

22. See James Tully, "The Struggles of Indigenous Peoples for and of Freedom," in *Political Theory and the Rights of Indigenous Peoples,* ed. Duncan Ivison, Paul Patton, and Will Sanders (Cambridge: Cambridge University Press, 2000).

23. Kymlicka, *Multicultural Citizenship.*

24. Four set-aside seats were granted to Maori in 1868 to reward loyal supporters of the Crown in the Land Wars. There are now seven set-aside seats, elected by voters who sign up to the Maori voting roll.

25. Jane Kelsey, *A Question of Honour: Labour and the Treaty, 1984–1989* (Wellington: Allen & Unwin, 1990) 46–47.

26. New Zealand, Ministerial Advisory Committee on a Maori Perspective and John Te Rangi-Aniwaniwa Rangihau, *Puao-te-ata-tu = Day Break: The Report of the Ministerial Advisory Committee on a Maori Perspective for the Department of Social Welfare* (Wellington: Department of Social Welfare, 1986).

27. Richard Mulgan, *Maori, Pakeha and Democracy* (Auckland: Oxford University Press, 1989), 10.

28. In 2011, the National Party government in partnership with the Maori Party introduced the Whanau Ora scheme, under which social services for Maori are coordinated and delivered to the *whanau,* rather than on an individual basis.

29. New Zealand, Ministerial Advisory Committee on a Maori Perspective and John Te Rangi-Aniwaniwa Rangihau, *Puao-te-ata-tu.*

30. New Zealand, Ministry of Social Development, *Social Report 2016,* 175.

31. Dominic O'Sullivan, *Beyond Biculturalism: The Politics of an Indigenous Minority* (Wellington: Huia, 2007), 3.

32. Augie Fleras and Jean Leonard Elliott, *The Nations Within: Aboriginal-State Relations in Canada, the United States and New Zealand* (Auckland: Oxford University Press, 1998).

33. Mason Durie, *Te Mana, Te Kawanatanga: The Politics of Maori Self-Determination* (Auckland: Oxford University Press, 1998).

34. Tom O'Reilly and David Wood, "Biculturalism and the Public Sector," in *Reshaping the State: New Zealand's Bureaucratic Revolution,* ed. Jonathan Boston, John Martin, June Pallot, and Pat Walsh (Auckland: Oxford University Press, 1991), 320–42.

35. O'Sullivan, *Beyond Biculturalism,* 21–22.

36. See Maori Party, "Call for Immediate Review on Govt Use of Tikanga," *Scoop Independent News,* November 1, 2005.

37. See Manying Ip, ed., *The Dragon and the Taniwha: Maori and Chinese in New Zealand* (Auckland: Auckland University Press, 2009).

38. Ranginui Walker, "Immigration Policy and the Political Economy of New Zealand," in *Immigration and National Identity in New Zealand: One People, Two Peoples, Many Peoples?* ed. Stuart Greif (Palmerston North, NZ: Dunmore Press, 1995), 293.

39. Ibid., 295.

40. Ramesh Thakur, "In Defence of Multiculturalism," in *Immigration and National Identity in New Zealand,* ed. Stuart Greif (Palmerston North, NZ: Dunmore Press, 1995), 271.

41. Waitangi Tribunal claim Wai 223. No report or recommendation was issued.

42. New Zealand, Ministry of Business, Immigration and Employment, *Community Perceptions of Migrants and Immigration: 2015 Community Survey* (Wellington: Ministry of Business, Immigration and Employment, 2015).

43. James Chang, "Maori Views on Immigration: Implications for Maori/Chinese Interactions," in *The Dragon and the Taniwha: Maori and Chinese in New Zealand,* ed. Manying Ip (Auckland: Auckland University Press, 2009).

44. Wepiha Te Kanawa, "Research Reveals Unstable Bond between Maori and Asian Immigrants," *Maori Television,* May 25, 2014.

45. See "Maori Party's Stance on Immigration Attacked," *New Zealand Herald,* February 27, 2013.

46. Marika Hill, "White Immigrants Row," *Sunday Star Times,* September 3, 2011.

47. Ally Mullord, "Pita Sharples on Maori and Immigration," TV 3 News, June 9, 2011.

48. See "Kawanatanga," *Maori Party,* http://www.maoriparty.org/kawanatanga.

49. Paula Oliver, "Press Council Condemns 'Asian Angst' Story," *New Zealand Herald,* June 11, 2007.

50. Aaron Lim, "Labour's Message to the Chinese Is Loud and Clear," *New Zealand Herald,* July 20, 2015.

51. Winston Peters, "The End of Tolerance" (speech, Far North Community Centre, Kaitaia, July 28, 2005), accessed November 19, 2018, www.scoop.co.nz/stories/PA0507/S00649.htm.

52. New Zealand, Ministry of Business, Immigration and Employment, *Community Perceptions of Migrants and Immigration.*

53. Patrick Fitzsimons, "Neoliberalism and 'Social Capital': Reinventing Community" (paper presented at the AREA Symposium "Neo-liberalism, Welfare and Education: The New Zealand Experiment," New Orleans, 2000).

54. See, e.g., Jean Elshtain, *Democracy on Trial* (New York: Basic Books, 1995), and Don Brash, "Nationhood" (speech, Orewa Rotary Club, January 27, 2004), accessed December 1, 2018, www.scoop.co.nz/stories/PA0401/S00220.htm.

55. See Katherine Smits, "Justifying Multiculturalism: Social Justice, Diversity and National Identity in Australia and New Zealand," *Australian Journal of Political Science* 46, no. 1 (2011): 87–103.

56. New Zealand, Office of the Prime Minister, *Growing an Innovative New Zealand,* (Wellington: Government Printer, 2002).

57. Louise Humpage, "Radical Change or More of the Same? Public Attitudes towards Social Citizenship in New Zealand since Neoliberal Reform," *Australian Journal of Social Issues* 43, no. 2 (2008): 215–30.

58. See, e.g., Brian Barry, *Culture and Equality* (Malden, MA: Polity Press, 2001).

59. There is a substantial literature; see esp. Susan Moller Okin, "Is Multiculturalism Bad for Women?" in *Is Multiculturalism Bad for Women?* ed. Joshua Cohen, Matthew Howard, and Martha C. Nussbaum (Princeton, NJ: Princeton University Press, 1994).

60. See Katherine Curchin, "Pakeha Women and Maori Protocol: The Politics of Criticising Other Cultures," *Australian Journal of Political Science* 46, no. 3 (2011): 375–88.

61. Ibid., 376.

62. Annie Mikaere, "Maori Women: Caught in the Contradictions of a Colonized Reality," *Waikato Law Review* 2 (1994): 125–50.

63. *Police v. Abdul Rohoor Azamjoo,* Auckland District Court (CRN 30044039397–8), January 17, 2005.

64. Peter Skilling, "National Identity in a Diverse Society," in *New Zealand Government and Politics,* ed. Raymond Miller (Melbourne: Oxford University Press, 2010), 60–61.

65. See, e.g., the promotion of New Zealand at the Shanghai World Expo in 2010.

66. Katherine Smits and Alix Jansen, "Staging the Nation at Expos and World's Fairs," *National Identities* 14, no. 2 (2012): 173–88.

67. David Pearson, "The Ties That Unwind: Civic and Ethnic Imaginings in New Zealand," *Nations and Nationalism* 6, no. 1 (2000), 94.

68. Colin Campbell-Hunt et al., *World Famous in New Zealand: How New Zealand's Leading Firms Became World-Class Competitors* (Auckland: Auckland University Press, 2001)

69. Jacqui True and Charlie Gao, "National Identity in a Global Political Economy," in *New Zealand Government and Politics* 5th ed., ed. Raymond Miller (Melbourne: Oxford University Press, 2010), 44.

70. The recommendation has not yet been enacted into law, and there is no sign that legislation is planned. For the report, see Waitangi Tribunal, *Ko Aotearoa Tenei: A Report into Claims Concerning New Zealand Law and Policy Affecting Māori Culture and Identity* (Wellington: Legislation Direct, 2011).

71. Katherine Smits, "The Neoliberal State and the Uses of Indigenous Culture," *Nationalism and Ethnic Politics* 20, no. 1 (2014): 43–62.

72. Humpage, "Radical Change or More of the Same?" 222.

73. Ibid., 225.

74. Louise Humpage, "What Do New Zealanders Think about Welfare?" *Policy Quarterly* 7, no. 2 (2011): 12.

75. Ibid., 12.

76. This argument is explored in more detail in Smits, "Neoliberal State."

77. Allan Hanson, "The Making of the Maori: Culture Invention and Its Logic," *American Anthropologist* 91, no. 4: (1989): 894.

78. New Zealand, Ministry of Social Development, *Social Report 2016,* 175.

Multiculturalism in the "New" Commonwealth

7

Multiculturalism in India

An Exception?

Rochana Bajpai, SOAS University of London

Theories of multiculturalism have been based substantially on the experience of Western democracies since the 1970s. However, several countries in the British Commonwealth have long-standing practices of ethno-religious pluralism that predate the establishment of liberal-democratic institutions. India is a key example. Its policies of group rights include legal pluralism in religious family law (Hindu, Muslim, Christian, Parsi), as well as affirmative action in the form of quotas in legislatures, government jobs, and educational institutions for caste and tribal minorities dating back to the nineteenth century. With territorial autonomy for several linguistic and tribal groups, India resembles a multinational federation in its institutional framework. India's Constitution of 1950 has been hailed as a prescient model of multicultural accommodation, ahead of its times in instituting the cultural rights of minorities and affirmative action for historically disadvantaged groups within a broadly liberal-democratic framework.[1] The subsequent development of a multinational federal framework from the 1950s is regarded as an exception to the unitary, centralized nation-state framework adopted by many postcolonial states.[2]

While concurring that India is a key case for evaluating multiculturalism, this chapter argues that claims of Indian exceptionalism need to be qualified. Focusing on the subset of group-differentiated rights, minority rights, and affirmative action, I elaborate three main claims. First, while accommodating some multicultural provisions, the Indian Constitution inaugurated a shift from consociationalism to affirmative action as the overarching framework of group-differentiated rights. Relative to the late colonial state, constitution-making marked a moment of containment in the long career of group rights in India. Second, the Indian

Constitution embodies two distinct approaches to the accommodation of group-differentiated rights, which might roughly be termed integrationist and restricted multicultural. The former underpinned provisions for quotas for ex-Untouchable and tribal groups; the latter is embodied in provisions of minority cultural protection and religious family laws. Third, the restricted multicultural approach has remained undersupported in India's constitutional vision. In particular, because of the confluence of liberal and nationalist concerns, there exists a normative deficit with regard to the protection of cultural *difference* and minority practices. Most acute in the case of religious minorities, this is the case to an extent for all minorities, whether defined by religion, language, caste, or tribe.

The normative deficit of multiculturalism at India's founding moment has persisted over time and has been politically influential. Since the promulgation of the Constitution in 1950, group-differentiated rights have been augmented, without, however, a concomitant elaboration of their rationale by policy-makers in terms of their society-wide benefits. This in turn has left minorities and disadvantaged groups more vulnerable to majoritarian resentment and backlash. Deficiencies in justifications of group-differentiated rights dating back to constitution-making have been a contributing factor in the ascendance of the Hindu Right.

Does the Indian example then suggest that liberal and nationalist frameworks inherently lack the normative-ideological resources for the accommodation of differential treatment, in particular, minority rights, as postcolonial theorists have suggested?[3] While Indian constitutional and parliamentary debates provide some support for this view, these also suggest that such claims are overstated. In Indian policy debates, considerations of secularism, religious freedom and social justice have been construed, often appropriately, as consistent with group-differentiated rights.[4] The main challenge for the accommodation of multicultural minority rights in India, as in many other countries, stems from policy-makers' overly narrow understandings of the requirements of national unity. The long shadow of the country's partition along religious lines in 1947 has limited political imagination in India regarding the accommodation of cultural difference. Furthermore, in India, as in many other countries in Asia and Africa, it is not so much liberal norms and institutions but their *weakness*—lack of support for rule of law, civil and political liberties for individuals in Indian liberal ideas—for instance, that renders minorities vulnerable to attack and discrimination.[5]

A note on terminology is in order at the outset. First, it might be asked whether the concept of multiculturalism is adequate for capturing the deep, multilevel diversity of the kind encountered in India and other countries of Asia and Africa. Multiculturalism can suggest a flattening of difference, a reduction of multiform diversity to a single level, more suited to the recent immigrant experience of North America and Europe, than to the long histories of pluralism in Asia, Africa, and the Middle East. It is also tilted toward *liberal* approaches to dealing with diversity, obscuring ways of dealing with difference in nonliberal traditions and societies

Terms such as "pluralism" might be preferred to denote the accommodation of difference in non-Western contexts. While these challenges have merit, multiculturalism remains a useful category for comparative analysis—for bringing non-Western experiences of group-differentiated rights into conversation with Western debates on multiculturalism—and is used as such here, with cognizance of its limits.

CHANGING FRAMES OF GROUP DIFFERENCE: FROM "MINORITY" TO "BACKWARD"

Two contrasting views of the Indian Constitution have been influential: that it represents a prescient model of multicultural accommodation within a liberal framework,[6] and that it marked a sacrifice of minority rights at the altar of the nation at independence.[7] Both views need to be nuanced. As I have detailed elsewhere, constitution-making (1946–49), which marked the formal institution of a liberal-democratic state, was also a moment of containment in the long career of group rights in India.[8] Nevertheless, unlike in many other postcolonial states, some minority rights were granted constitutional recognition, as were quotas for disadvantaged groups—the Indian Constitution was the earliest to institute affirmative action policies.

The Indian Constitution represented a cutback on minority representation provisions that had characterized both British policy and group demands in colonial India. Group-based representation in colonial legislatures dates back to the late nineteenth century, with Indians included in the representative institutions of the Raj as members of particular groups.[9] Special representation provisions (separate electorates, weightage, nomination) had expanded over the first half of the twentieth century to a range of groups, including most prominently Muslims and other religious minorities, as well as Untouchables (then called the Depressed Classes). During constitution-making, these came to be limited in several respects, as the paradigm for group-differentiated rights was comprehensively recast from consociationalism to affirmative action in the transition from colonial rule. The starkest case of retrenchment was to be found in mechanisms for guaranteed representation of religious minorities in legislatures and government employment, which came to be abolished. However, consociational type provisions were rejected in the case of Untouchables (Scheduled Castes or Dalits) as well.

To take some examples, initial constitutional proposals and the draft Constitution of 1948 included provisions for legislative quotas for religious minorities and Depressed classes under joint electorates (separate electorates were rejected) and recognized the "desirability of representation of minorities in the Cabinet."[10] By 1949, each of these provisions had come to be restricted mainly to the Scheduled Castes and Scheduled Tribes and some temporary provisions for Anglo Indians.[11] Cutback can also be observed, albeit to a much lesser extent, in the case of the "backward classes." Babasaheb Dr. Bhimrao Ambedkar's Depressed Class organizations' demand for separate electorates and guaranteed representation in the executive had been rejected in early deliberations, but the draft Constitution of 1948 included an Instrument of Instruction to the president and provincial governors regarding the desirability of representation of minorities in the Cabinet.[12] In the final stages of tidying up provisions in 1949, this provision was also deleted by the Constituent Assembly.[13]

The cutback in minority rights during Indian constitution-making was not limited to special representation provisions alone. Some have argued that the Indian Constitution marks not so much a containment of minority rights, as a shift from special representation provisions to cultural and educational rights of minorities.[14] It is true that the religious, cultural, and educational freedoms of minorities are protected in the text of the Indian Constitution as justiciable fundamental rights for individuals as well as groups (see Articles 25, 26, 29, and 30). My reading, however, suggests that minority cultural rights too came to be attenuated during constitution-making, albeit much less drastically than political representation provisions. The wording of cultural rights provisions was changed, diluting the focus on religious minorities; furthermore, the protection of minority languages and scripts would be a matter for individual and community initiative.[15] The constitution-makers declined to stipulate any obligation on the part of the state to preserve minority cultures, in contrast to the "backward classes," where the state's duties were written into the Constitution.[16] With regard to federal provisions, state rights also came to be limited after the partition of the country to create Pakistan in 1947. For instance, residuary powers earlier promised to the units, came to reside with the Central government.[17] State rights also came to be curtailed during constitution-making in several other areas, including the Emergency provisions allowing for the president to assume the functions of the state government in the event of constitutional breakdown.[18]

Does the Indian case represent a sacrifice of minority rights at the altar of the nation at independence, as in many other postcolonial contexts? Indian constitution-making offers a more complex story. Although Partition undeniably denuded religious minorities of constitutional protections,[19] the Constitution is not a majoritarian document. Against the demands of majoritarian nationalists, the religious, cultural, and educational rights of minorities were included in forms that were consonant with the concerns of minority representatives. For instance, a broad definition of the right to freedom of religion was adopted, including the right to "propagate" religion pressed for by several Christian representatives. Furthermore, in keeping with the wishes of several minority representatives, the state was not barred from aiding educational institutions that imparted religious instruction, despite objections by many staunch secularists. In the important area of religious family law, the demands of secularists and nationalists for a uniform civil code to supplant the different religious laws that governed family matters in colonial India were rejected.[20] In matters concerning marriage, divorce, inheritance, and adoption, Muslims, Christians, and Parsis were to be governed by their respective religious personal laws, which were constitutionally protected by rights to religious freedom.

A majoritarian reading of the Indian Constitution is also inaccurate when we turn to examine provisions for historically disadvantaged groups, the Untouchables and tribal populations. Here, the Indian Constitution recognized that the national community was not homogeneous, and that state action was required to tackle entrenched socioeconomic inequalities. From the early stages of constitutional deliberations, committee reports sought to emphasize the need for special treatment of the so-called backward groups.[21] The final constitutional draft included a range of affirmative action provisions, including mandatory legislative quotas, provisions enabling employment and educational quotas for the Scheduled Castes and Scheduled Tribes, as well as an undefined category of Other Backward Classes, expanding on colonial provision in some areas. In the case of Adivasis/Scheduled Tribes, there was some acknowledgement of cultural distinctiveness. Provisions included an element of self-government and sought to "balance improvement of their condition and a degree of assimilation with preservation of their distinctiveness and a measure of autonomy."[22] Overall, group-differentiated rights in the Indian Constitution are principally addressed to difference deriving from disadvantage. Differential treatment was envisaged for most part as a temporary measure for tackling socioeconomic disabilities and reducing intergroup difference over time, not as a permanent provision for the recognition of cultural difference.

The change in the regime of group rights during its passage from colonial to independent India was encapsulated in the declining fortunes of the term "minority" during constitution-making. At the start of the Constituent Assembly's deliberations in 1946, the representatives of most groups claiming special provisions emphasized that their group was a minority of some kind. This appears to have been a response to the colonial institutional framework where groups designated as minorities were the chief beneficiaries of special treatment. For instance, representatives of Untouchables called themselves "political minorities" on account of their historical exclusion from the governing structures of the country. In official categorization, however, Untouchables were removed from the purview of the term "minority." An amendment was adopted defining the term more narrowly so as to exclude the Scheduled Castes from its ambit, as well as deeming them part of the Hindu community.[23] This reflected nationalist dislike of the term "minority" and a desire to restrict its usage, as well as an anxiety about the separation of the Untouchables from the Hindu community that, it was feared, their categorization as minorities would encourage. Whether Untouchables ought to be distinguished from the Hindu community for purposes of representation had been a sensitive point for nationalists in the decades preceding independence, with Ambedkar and Gandhi emblematic of the adversarial positions in this debate. By the close of the Constituent Assembly debates in 1949, the term "backward" had become the favored designation to denote a group's entitlement to special treatment. Representatives favoring quotas for religious minorities now sought to establish that there were "backward" peoples among Muslims, Christians, and Sikhs.[24] The decline in the fortunes of the term "minority" during constitution-making, and corresponding popularity of the term "backward" classes, encapsulated the transformation that the regime of group-differentiated rights underwent during its passage from colonial to independent India.

APPROACHES TO GROUP-DIFFERENTIATED RIGHTS: INTEGRATIONIST AND LIMITED MULTICULTURAL

On closer examination, three broad positions on group rights in the Constituent Assembly debates emerge: opposition to all group-differentiated rights, which encompassed assimilationist and integrationist positions (these were distinct); support for maximal group rights, which can be termed multinational; and an intermediate, restricted multicultural position of support for some group rights. The classification is heuristic: individuals and parties moved from one position to another over time and across issue areas.[25] For instance, initially, minority parties such as the Muslim League, the Akalis, and the Scheduled Caste Federation, favored multinational policies; by the end, most had moved to restricted multicultural policies.

Constitutional outcomes varied across the different areas of group-differentiated rights. On quotas (termed "political safeguards" or "reservations") for religious minorities as well as ex-Untouchables and tribals (Scheduled Castes and Scheduled Tribes in official usage) in legislatures and government employment, the integrationist position won. On the cultural rights of religious minorities (including religious family laws), and territorial autonomy for linguistic minorities and tribal populations, a restricted multicultural position was embodied in the constitution. Both the integrationist and restricted multicultural positions represented a cutback on the multinational provisions that had characterized colonial constitutionalism and minority demands. However, both were *also* distinct from the assimilationist positions espoused by Hindu nationalists in the Constituent Assembly.

Indian nationalism comprised diverse ideological strands that were articulated in public arenas in their modern forms from the nineteenth century. Apart from the national movement led by the Congress party, several political movements based on caste, religion, class, and gender had contributed to the development of nationalist ideals. Two main conceptions of India's national identity are usually distinguished: secular and Hindu.[26] In secular nationalist conceptions, the nation was conceived in political terms, as a community united by its commitment to common political ideals, notably those of secularism, democracy and development: nationality was to consist in secular democratic citizenship. European models of nationalism based on language and descent were rejected; commonalities of language, religion, or any other cultural attribute were not to serve as the basis of India's national identity. In Hindu nationalist versions of India's national identity, articulated by a section of constitution-makers, Indian identity was defined in cultural terms, based typically on Hindi as the national language, descent from Indian religions particularly Hinduism, and other broadly Hindu themes. Minorities were assimilated in, or excluded from, the definition of the national identity.

In the Constituent Assembly debates, the normative-discursive repertoire of Indian nationalism comprised a constellation of inter-related concepts of secularism, equal citizenship rights, democracy, social justice, development and national unity. These were configured differently in the varied strands of nationalist opinion, generating multiple conceptions. For instance, national unity could denote political integrity, and/or social cohesion, and/or national identity. Secularism meant for some, equal citizenship for all individuals irrespective of religion, and for others, religious freedom for groups, distinct conceptions that supported policy implications that sometimes conflicted. Crucially, nationalists of different ideological hues, Hindu sympathizers on the right as much as staunch secularists on the left (these included minority representatives) *converged* on the view that quotas for religious minorities detracted from national unity and also from secularism, justice and democracy. By contrast, this convergence was less evident in the case of quotas for Scheduled Castes and Scheduled Tribes, as well as provisions for religious, linguistic and cultural autonomy, where secularists and Hindu sympathizers often spoke in different voices, and group rights were maintained in the Constitution.

Nationalist claims of our period that minority representation necessarily damaged national unity relied on a particular interpretation of the Indian past and of the history of minority safeguards under colonial rule. Against the colonial view that India was not a nation but a congeries of antagonistic nationalities, kept together by the exercise of imperial power, the nationalist account asserted that communal discord was the product of a deliberate colonial "divide and rule" strategy that set one community against another, to legitimize British presence as the guarantor of peace and of minority interests, and thereby prolong colonial rule in India. Special representation provisions for minorities, notably separate electorates, were the main instrument of the colonial divide and rule. These had bred community consciousness and rivalry, and once instituted, necessarily followed an escalating and separatist logic, leading to an ever-increasing number of groups demanding special measures, and ever-larger and more antagonistic claims, a process that culminated in the bloody partition of the country in 1947. In this narrative, the British as the architects of this policy were viewed as the chief culprits, the minorities, particularly Muslims, as pawns in the colonial game, culpable in allowing themselves to be misled, as blocking progress towards the national goal of liberation from British rule. The partition of the country on religious lines demonstrated, catastrophically, that nationalist fears about the dangers of minority safeguards were justified.[27]

Integrationist Approach: Legislative Quotas

The integrationist approach is most evident in the debates on reservations for religious minorities, ex-Untouchable and tribal groups. Reserved seats for religious minorities had been accepted in 1947 and were included the first draft of the Constitution of 1948. Nevertheless, nationalists sought to emphasize this was as "temporary" provisions and as measures of "compromise" or transition—in an ideal future, legislative quotas for religious minorities would no longer exist.[28] Legislative quotas for religious minorities were opposed as detracting from secularism, democracy, justice, development, and above all, national unity, a mutually reinforcing constellation of concepts that was invoked by an ideologically diverse cross-section of nationalists. Reservations for religious minorities required the recognition of a person's religion or caste in matters of public policy, and treated individuals differently depending on the community to which they belonged, which it was argued would undermine secularism. These were seen as detracting from democracy as these implied departures from the principle of the representation of individuals through territorial constituencies. But the overriding apprehension in this period was that the granting of special representation to religious minorities would undermine national unity. Several national-unity concerns coalesced here—the "mixing of religion and politics" in the case of separate electorates was thought to have hardened differences between Hindus and Muslims, and resulted in the bloody break-up of the country. National identity was another concern—quotas were instituted for groups defined in terms of the ascriptive criteria of religion, caste, and tribe, whereas the dominant conception of national identity in mid-20th century India, was civic rather than ethno-cultural, defined in terms of citizenship in a secular liberal-democratic state. And for some religion, caste, and other ethno-cultural affiliations were "backward," pre-modern relics, inconsistent with the task of building a modern nation-state.

The convergence of liberal and nationalist concerns meant that Hindu nationalists often used the language of secularism, equal rights, and democracy in the Constituent Assembly. It was perhaps their close links with national unity and shared hostility to group-differentiated policies that accounted for the widespread use of a liberal language in this period.[29] Secularist advocates of minority rights were also uncomfortable with mechanisms such as quotas that they saw as institutionalizing ethno-cultural groups. For instance, when legislative quotas for religious minorities were eventually withdrawn in 1949, Nehru commended their abolition as "a historic turn in our destiny," confessing that he had never been convinced about them, and that "doing away with this reservation business . . . shows that we are really sincere about this business of having a secular democracy."[30] At the same time, it is important not to overstate the overlap between nationalists on the left and the right. Convergence is not identity: secular and Hindu nationalists differed on several questions of minority rights in the Constituent Assembly.[31]

By contrast, reservations in the case of Untouchables and tribal groups were easier to accommodate within a liberal nationalist framework. It was argued that these would enable the economic and social advancement of these groups that was desirable from the standpoint of the goals of social justice, national unity and development. In the case of national unity, the assumption was that vertical levelling would produce horizontal integration: bringing Untouchable and tribal groups "up to the level of the rest" in economic terms would reduce the social gulf that separated them from the rest of the population. In the case of national development, "catching up" with the industrialized Western world was the desired goal; this in turn required quotas and other preferential provisions to boost the "backward" sections of the population in the short run; such measures would uplift sections that were dragging the nation down and inhibiting its progress.[32] The existence of "backward groups" was a symptom and a reminder of India's own "backwardness," the gulf that separated it from advanced Western countries, the club of powerful nations to which it wanted to belong. The register of such developmental arguments was one of paternalistic benevolence.[33] "Backward sections" were cast in dominant nationalist discourse as objects of compassionate and philanthropic action on their behalf, rather than as agents of their own improvement.[34]

While liberal nationalist and developmentalist ideals offered resources for the accommodation of special representation provisions for Scheduled Castes and Tribes, it is important to note that these supported quotas as temporary affirmative action provisions, and not as a multicultural right. In other words, nationalists rejected quotas as a means of recognizing social identity or protecting the distinct interests for *all groups:* special representation provisions were not intended as permanent instruments of self-government for any group. The case for special treatment of Untouchables and tribals was constantly distinguished from that of religious minorities through an emphasis on their poverty and "backwardness." Recast as a form of "'political' affirmative action,"[35] as short-term mechanisms[36] that would enable the realization of a future state of affairs in which special representation would no longer be necessary, legislative quotas for Dalits and Adivasis were not intended to serve as a form of *representation* as such.

In other words, as in the case of religious minorities, in the case of the Scheduled Castes and Tribes as well, nationalists rejected multicultural provisions as a means of recognizing the social identity or protecting the distinct interests of these groups.[37] There was, for instance, little recognition in nationalist opinion that on account of being historically marginalized, Untouchables and tribals had "a distinctive *perspective* on matters of public policy [emphasis in original],"[38] which merited representation, or that members of these groups were in a better position to understand and thereby represent these interests on account of their first-hand experience, better trust and communication with group members.[39] Nationalist and developmentalist concerns did not support quotas as a multicultural right, as a mechanism for minority representation as such.[40] And while some constitutional provisions in the case of the Scheduled Tribes did include an element of self-government, insofar as *legislative quotas* were concerned, these were advocated as an integrative mechanism. Acute as always about institutional effects, Dr. Ambedkar saw reserved seats for tribal groups as counterbalancing "the tendency towards segregation."[41]

Restricted Multicultural Approach: Religious Freedom, Family Law

A second approach to the accommodation of diversity in the Indian Constitution might be termed "restricted multicultural." This approach is discernable in the provisions for religious freedom and family laws, as well as the rights of linguistic and tribal groups; I focus here on the former.

Indian constitution-makers adopted a wide definition of religious freedom for individuals and groups. Unlike many other secular constitutions, the Indian Constitution allows associational and institutional autonomy, and includes specific provisions for the public profession of religious identity. Under religious freedom provisions in the Indian Constitution, all individuals have the freedom to "profess, practice and propagate" religion (Article 25) and every religious group or denomination has the right to "establish and maintain institutions for religious and charitable purposes," to "manage its own affairs in matters of religion," to own, acquire, and administer property "in accordance with law" (Articles 25 and 26 of the Indian Constitution). The wording of these rights in many cases assumed forms that were in keeping with the concerns of minority representatives. Thus, a broad definition of the right to freedom of religion was adopted after extensive debate, which included the right to practice religion in public spaces and, even more controversially in the face of vehement opposition of Hindu orthodox opinion, the right to "propagate" religion. The latter was in keeping with the demands of Christian representatives who argued that propagation was fundamental to the Christian faith. Religious denominations were permitted by right to hold property, and after extensive debate, the state was allowed to aid educational institutions that imparted religious instruction (including minority institutions), overriding the objections of those who sought to restrict the domain of religion.[42] Institutional pluralism is notably evident in the retention of separate religious family laws for Hindus, Muslims, Sikhs, and Parsis.[43] The demands of ardent secularists for a uniform civil code to supplant the different religious laws that had governed matters such as marriage and divorce in colonial India were rejected.

However, the approach remained limited multicultural overall. The right to freedom of religion is subject to other constitutional rights, including those of equality and nondiscrimination. State intervention is permitted, not just in the interests of public order, morality, and health, as common elsewhere, but also for purposes of social welfare and reform, departing from the colonial state's stance of nonintervention in the religious affairs of its subjects. Despite previous promises that religious family laws would be protected by specific constitutional provisions, no guarantees protecting religious laws from state intervention were included in the Constitution; explicit constitutional guarantees were rejected. The non-justiciable Directive Principles of State Policy include a provision for a uniform civil code, however, leaving open the door for legal unification in the future.

A restricted or weak multicultural approach has been defended by scholars as superior to strong or maximal multiculturalism in offering better protections for individuals and vulnerable groups within minorities, such as women.[44] In the case of the Indian Constitution, the problem was less with the approaches adopted for the accommodation of diversity than with the normative resources, which remained deficient for supporting restricted multiculturalism.

THE NORMATIVE DEFICIT OF LIMITED MULTICULTURALISM IN THE INDIAN CONSTITUTION

The repertoire of secular Indian nationalism did contain materials supporting limited multiculturalism. Thus, in a departure from the standard liberal position, groups as well as individuals were recognized as possessing rights and entitlements.[45] Speeches frequently emphasized, for instance, that individuals *and* groups should have the freedom to pursue their religions and develop their languages and cultures. Equality and justice were seen to require religious and cultural freedoms for all groups, including minorities; justice, it was said, demanded that no individual *or* group be subject to compulsion in matters of religion or language. Although secularism was construed as incompatible with legislative quotas for religious minorities, it was also seen to require religious and cultural freedom for all groups, including minorities. In most connotations of secularism in nationalist discourse,[46] the pursuit of religion and the preservation of language and culture on the part of citizens of all communities were held to be legitimate goals; their pursuit by citizens in both their individual and associational capacities was regarded as a corollary of the exclusion of religion from the political domain.

Nevertheless, for multiple reasons, justifications for multicultural provisions remained underdeveloped in nationalist opinion, unlike arguments for the integrationist type of group-differentiated provisions. Prominent among these in this period was the emphasis on individual over group rights.[47] Liberal individualist and developmentalist ideologies gained enormously from their convergence with nationalist concerns. The emphasis on the individual over the group, and on equal citizenship rights construed as the same rights for individuals from all groups provided a means for welding together a people divided by their group membership into a nation. It also provided the basis for a common national identity in a situation in which ethnic criteria were divisive. Given its links with national unity, it is unsurprising that a liberal language was espoused in the Constituent Assembly by a wide range of nationalists of diverse ideological moorings, Hindu nationalists as much as Westernized socialists.

The normative deficit of restricted multiculturalism derived also because special provisions for the protection of minority cultures remained undersupported in nationalist opinion. The move from *all* groups having rights to pursue their cultures to the *differential* rights of minorities remained unarticulated in nationalist opinion. In the case of "backwardness," the tensions between individual and group claims were confronted and arguments fashioned for special treatment of historically disadvantaged groups in terms of nationalist goals. By contrast, it is hard to find any elaboration in nationalist opinion on how the protection of minority cultures formed part of their vision of the common good. In particular, unlike in the case of the Scheduled Castes and Scheduled Tribes, there were no attempts to go beyond formal symmetrical notions of equality to substantive, contextual notions that could justify the differential treatment of cultures. There were, for instance, no arguments along the lines that minorities faced a greater threat to the integrity of their religion, language, or culture than the majority, whose practices are inevitably supported by society and the state.[48] Thus, in the context of the drafting of minority provisions Articles 29 and 30, the cultural rights of minorities were interpreted largely as negative liberties. The Constitution left open the possibility of state aid, but this was regarded as a concession rather than a duty of the state, whose responsibilities were limited to non-interference with the right of minorities to practice their cultures freely.[49]

The normative deficit in nationalist discourse with regard to the protection of cultural difference is also observable in the case of other minorities, notably tribal groups. There was some acknowledgement in nationalist opinion of a distinctive cultural identity,[50] but the need to protect tribal lands was qualified in important respects. Since a developmentalist perspective dominated discussions, progressive change in Adivasi cultures in the direction of greater integration with mainstream society was not ruled out, and protectionist provisions sought to give Adivasi communities greater control over the pace and nature of cultural change. Further, protectionist policies such as land rights and tribal councils were envisaged mainly for areas where tribals formed a local majority in a given territory. For areas in which tribals were a minority, or had successfully assimilated into the local population, cultural protection was rarely admitted as a goal.

So far I have suggested that in India's constitutional vision, there was a *normative deficit* with regard to the protection of cultural difference and minority practices, in large part on account of the limits of the liberal and developmentalist ideas of the time. Because of the recent partition of the country on religious lines, this was most acute in the case of religious minorities. It was also observable in the case of minorities defined by caste or tribe, and in relation to different types of group rights, such as legislative quotas, employment quotas, and rights to cultural autonomy. A normative deficit existed for group-differentiated rights in the case of legislative quotas for ex-Untouchables and tribals as well, but this was easier to overcome within a liberal nationalist framework. In other words, the accommodation of special representation provisions for caste and tribal minorities was based on *reframing* these as temporary affirmative action provisions, rather than as permanent instruments of self-government for culturally distinct groups.[51] As such, the Indian Constitution did not mark as radical a departure "from accepted liberal practices of the time" as scholars have suggested.[52]

Against my argument so far, however, it might be contended that India's linguistic federalism is a form of multicultural accommodation. In Will Kymlicka's influential schema, based largely on Canadian experience, subnational autonomy is the paradigm form of multiculturalism. The relationship of multiculturalism to territorial self-government policies therefore needs greater examination.

FEDERALISM AND MULTICULTURALISM IN INDIA

Indian experience suggests that the relationship of territorial self-government policies to multiculturalism is complex. Self-government rights can of course help protect group cultures, insofar as *all* relevant groups have such rights, but these are not necessarily instances of group-differentiated rights. During Indian constitution-making, federal provisions were not seen as an instance of a group-differentiated right. All units were granted the same rights, and a single citizenship was instituted.[53] Kashmir's special status (Article 370) was not based on recognition of its ethnic or religious distinctiveness.[54] Even in the case of princely states, technically sovereign once British rule ceased, proposals for separate constitutions and different relations with the federation were rejected.[55]

It might be argued, however, that policies of self-government based on language seek to compensate for disadvantages faced by their speakers in relation to the dominant majority language that forms the basis of nation-building. In other words, as with affirmative action programs, self-government rights can be said to "asymmetrically distribute rights or opportunities on the basis of group membership."[56] Such an interpretation of self-government rights assumes, however, nation-building centered on a single national language, whereas Indian nationalism emerged in the second half of the nineteenth century as a coalition of regional nationalisms and was envisaged as multilingual.[57] A "sense of region and nation emerged together, through parallel self-definitions," and so being Bengali-, Marathi-, or Tamil-speaking was regarded as congruent with, and reinforcing, a common Indian identity.[58] The Congress Party recognized language-based units in its internal organization from the early twentieth century onwards (and particularly after 1920), advocating linguistic states as a more rational basis of provincial organization than the British administrative boundaries.[59] Thus, although during constitution-making there were pressures for the adoption of Hindi as a national language from Hindu nationalists and others, these were opposed from within the dominant Congress party by non-Hindi speakers.

Ultimately a compromise formula was adopted. Hindi in the Devanagari script was designated as an official language, to be used for "inter-provincial communication."[60] English would also continue as an official link language, initially for fifteen years, extended since. Fourteen regional languages (now twenty-two) were also listed in the Constitution as national languages entitled to state support, and to be used in public service examinations. Furthermore, while adopting a federal framework, constitution-makers declined, despite pressures from linguistic nationalists to do so, to specify the basis for defining subnational units, i.e. whether this would be on linguistic lines. Although the many proponents of linguistic provinces in the Constituent Assembly pressed their case, they "did not consider themselves separatists,"[61] in contrast to the level of conflict between centralizers / federalists and provincialists / states' rights advocates in Canada and the United States.[62] The delineation of subnational units in India from the 1950s occurred as a result of a political process involving contentious mobilization, and was a "symmetrical reform, recognizing minority languages, but [only] on a symmetrical basis."[63]

Finally, as self-government rights facilitate nation-building at sub-state levels, in India, as in the United States and other countries, they have in practice conflicted with the rights of minorities of religion, caste, tribe, or language. During constitution-making, the protection of minorities was often cited against the rights of states, and in favor of strengthening the central government.[64] This concern has been borne out subsequently in the many instances of collusion by state government and the police agencies they control in violence against religious minorities.[65] Most Indian state governments have passed laws against beef-eating and religious conversion that discriminate against religious minorities.

Indian experience thus suggests that while territorial self-government policies are instances of group rights, these do not necessarily constitute group-differentiated rights, as all groups may have the same rights. Nor are they strictly speaking minority rights, since the relevant territorial units are often dominated by religious, caste and language groups that form majorities.

NEW CONJUNCTURES, OLD CONSTRAINTS

Since the promulgation of the Indian Constitution in 1950, group-differentiated rights have expanded in several areas. Employment and education quotas have expanded since the 1990s to include large new groups of mainly intermediate lower castes (the so-called Other Backward Classes, or OBCs). Stronger multicultural policies were instituted for Muslims in 1986, when the Indian Parliament passed a law that exempted the Muslim community from provisions of a common criminal code in the area of family law. On the other hand, the rise of Hindu nationalism since the 1990s has been accompanied by growing discrimination and violence against minorities, particularly Muslims, which has intensified since the election of a Hindu Right government in 2014.[66] Many factors have contributed to the complementary expansion of group-differentiated rights and of Hindu nationalism since the 1980s. In India, as elsewhere, majoritarian nationalism appears to be a reaction to multicultural and affirmative action policies, and a popular revolt against a liberalism seen as elitist.[67]

The paradigm shift in constitution-making from consociationalism to affirmative action remains influential. Its long term, systemic effects can be observed in the fact that all substantial extensions of quotas have been to groups designated as "backward," and in the shape of group rights claims, where "backward" has become the inclusive term to denote a group's eligibility for special treatment, just as "minority" was in the late colonial period. Based on findings of Muslim socio-economic deprivation, the 2004–14 Indian government sought to extend affirmative action to Muslims in a limited form.[68] Muslim parties and leaders have pressed for the inclusion of Muslims in the list of Scheduled Castes (currently Muslims are included in state lists of OBCs and STs, but not SCs),[69] on grounds of economic and educational "backwardness," invoking constitutional values of nondiscrimination and religion-neutrality of state policy.

The normative deficit of group-differentiated rights has remained and has been accentuated in some respects. In the case of cultural protection, for instance, although communitarian conceptions of secularism were advanced during the Shah Bano debate regarding the independence of Muslim personal law, policy-makers failed to justify special treatment in terms of nondomination or group oppression.[70] Why Muslims ought to have greater freedom from state intervention than the Hindu majority, whose religious laws were subjected to state reform in the 1950s, remained unarticulated. During the expansion of educational and employment quotas to include intermediate castes since the 1990s, policy-makers neither elaborated justifications for these in terms of the common good, nor imposed institutional limits that would render them consistent with nondiscrimination and equality of opportunity. How benefits for lower castes would enable a more equal or just society for all, for instance, was not elaborated. As such, the expansion of quotas underpinned by the new discourse of social justice has remained vulnerable to criticisms that these are sectional benefits to court electorally powerful constituencies at the expense of the national good. The attempts by the Congress-led United Progressive Alliance government (2004–14) to include religious minorities within the ambit of affirmative action have been executive-led and ad hoc. These attempts have been unaccompanied by actions that could build a broader consensus, or the elaboration of reasons for affirmative action for religious minorities in terms of the common good.

As scholars have argued, differential treatment of minority personal law in India can be justified on several different grounds: on the basis of equal respect for all individuals, as minority religions are disadvantaged in relation to the majority religion; on the basis that imposition of reforms on subordinated groups compounds injustices; and because minorities are under-represented in state institutions, and so disadvantaged with respect to collective self-determination in religious matters, unlike Hindus. Similarly, quotas for disadvantaged caste or religious minorities in education and employment can be justified as a universal benefit from the standpoint of democratic citizenship, since they offer individuals from different social backgrounds the opportunity to interact in ways that makes them better citizens,[73] or better equipped to live together on terms of equality.[74]

There have, however, been few attempts by policy-makers to construct a robust, normative ideological basis for such policies in terms of the common good, as universal benefits that serve the national interest. The dominant narratives of national unity and national identity in India continue in a sense to be imprisoned in the Partition era, with successful examples of the recognition of group rights since then (e.g., the decline in demands to secede after the accommodation of linguistic claims through subnational territorial autonomy) having little impact on official discourse and popular understandings. Policy evolution and political change in India continues to be shaped by the resolutions arrived at, and those left unfinished, at its founding moment. In terms of policy, religious freedoms of minorities have been truncated by the enactment of laws against cow slaughter and conversions in most states. In politics, the continuing normative deficit of group-differentiated rights has meant that state assistance for particular groups is perceived as an illegitimate concession detracting from the national good and motivated solely by electoral considerations, rather than a matter of justice. Unsurprisingly, the Hindu Right, with its rhetoric of putting the national interest first, and criticism of minority appeasement—that special provisions for minorities are a form of group partiality, unjust favoritism with little principled basis—has benefitted.

Hindu nationalism in India, like majoritarian nationalisms elsewhere, reflects a "minority complex,"[75] a sense that the majority religion is not getting its due share of recognition and resources from the state. Following V. D. Savarkar's influential *Hindutva* (1923), Hindu nationalists locate Indian identity in Hindu civilization (*sanskriti*), defining a Hindu as a person who regards India as their father-land as well as holy-land. This definition includes members of Indic religions—Buddhists, Jains, Sikhs—but excludes Muslims and Christians. The duty of Hindu nationalists is to restore the lost "grandeur of Hindu culture and their supremacy over a land that had been invaded by foreigners" (Muslim and Christian invaders) through fashioning a more muscular, disciplined, and masculine Hindu identity.[76] During the movement for Indian independence and constitution-making, Hindu nationalism was overtaken and, to an extent, subsumed within the Congress-led secular nationalism, held in check by leaders such as Gandhi and Nehru.[77] However, Hindu nationalism has remained a powerful undertow throughout India's political history, with the educational and social work at the grassroots level carried out by the RSS and its affiliates. It achieved its electoral breakthrough on the national stage in the 1990s, with the decline of the Congress Party creating the space for the rise of the Bharatiya Janata Party. The BJP has consistently opposed multicultural policies such as religious family laws and special status for Kashmir, and in support of normative Hindu food habits and attitudes to religion, has enacted or strengthened laws against cow slaughter and conversions. The BJP's rise and periods in power have been accompanied by an increase in incidents of violence, intimidation, harassment, and hate speech against religious minorities, notably Muslims, as well as political dissidents. Since the election of a BJP majority government in 2014, instances of violence and lynching of Muslims by Hindu mobs have increased.

The BJP government since 2014 has resisted calls for strong condemnation of anti-Muslim violence, retained and elevated ministers who have made hate speeches against Muslims, and appeared to support the cultural domination of minorities, demoting public holidays associated with minorities such as Christmas and Easter and official Eid celebrations. In the routine violations of the basic human rights of religious minorities and dissidents, and growing authoritarianism, India looks less like a democratic exception, and more like its neighbors Pakistan, Sri Lanka, Myanmar, and many other countries in Asia and Africa.

CONCLUSIONS

In the emerging literature on comparative multiculturalism, India is often regarded as an exceptional case.[78] The Indian Constitution of 1950 recognizes the rights of religious and linguistic minorities, and indigenous groups and castes. Predating policies of multiculturalism in Western democracies by several decades, the constitutional entrenchment of group rights in India derived from colonial and nationalist legacies, both informed by longer historical, political and social practices of dealing with difference.[79]

Multicultural provisions in India encounter similar challenges to those that have hindered their adoption in other Asian states.[80] At independence, in India, as in other countries of the British Commonwealth, minorities were seen as "illegitimately privileged" by the colonial state, and there was a desire "to roll back the privileges accorded to minorities under colonialism."[81] Relative to the late colonial state, the Indian Constitution marked a cutback in multicultural provisions. Historical association with Western imperialism continues to pose a challenge to defenders of minority rights in India and other postcolonial countries. Moreover, the influence at constitution-making of a mid-twentieth-century developmentalist ideology meant that in India, as elsewhere,[82] the nationalist hope was that religious, caste, linguistic, and other ethnic conflicts would fade away once modernization, arrested under colonial rule, got underway. From a nationalist developmentalist standpoint, exemplified by Nehru, ethnic claims were regarded as reminders of India's "backwardness," out of step with the times, and distractions from the real problems, which were economic.[83]

Although liberal ideas in the Indian Constituent Assembly were more accommodating of group-differentiated rights than their Western counterparts,[84] a normative deficit remained with regards to minority rights.[85] Group-differentiated rights were accommodated predominantly as temporary affirmative action provisions for the uplift of "backward" sections, a means toward the ideal of ethnicity-blind citizenship.[86] In India, as elsewhere, liberal opposition to differentiated citizenship was conjoined with nationalist concerns about the divisiveness of special treatment in ways that constrained the normative-ideational space for group-differentiated rights. An "acceptance of the existing cultural plurality" was not accompanied by "a positive evaluation of diversity that provided the rationale for the multicultural framework."[87]

As in other countries of Asia and Africa,[88] in India, too, group rights predate the institution of a liberal-democratic framework of equal individual rights Although liberal ideas have been more prevalent and influential in India than is commonly believed,[89] their proponents there have rarely expanded on the need for constraints on state power for the sake of personal freedoms. The enforcement of rule of law and protections for individual freedoms remains weak, whereas communitarian ways of thinking have been more powerful. In India, as in other states of Asia and Africa affected by geopolitical insecurity, minorities have been seen as a threat to the security of the state, "a potential 'fifth-column', prone to collaboration with a neighbouring enemy."[90] Since the partition of India to create Pakistan, Muslims in particular have been accused of divided loyalties, exacerbated by continuing India-Pakistan tensions and the conflict over Kashmir. With the growing violence, hate-speech, and discrimination against Muslims that has accompanied the ascendancy of Hindu nationalism, India is similar to other countries in Asia and Africa where ethnic majoritarianism prevails, unconstrained by rule of law.

Even though the Indian experience has many features in common with those of other states in Asia and Africa, it remains conceptually significant, bringing to the fore important features of multiculturalism often neglected in Western debates. For example, Indian Constituent Assembly debates highlight a close affinity—often overlooked in the West—between liberal concerns of equal citizenship and nationalist concerns of political unity and social cohesion. Liberal opposition to group-differentiated rights has been underpinned by nationalist considerations to a much greater extent than contemporary defenders of liberalism acknowledge.[91] This is not, however, to suggest that liberal values are inextricably embedded within a unitary homogenizing nation-state, and so necessarily opposed to group-differentiated rights, as postcolonial theorists have tended to suggest.[92] In Indian policy debates, considerations of secularism, equal citizenship, and equality of opportunity have been construed, often appropriately, as consistent with group-based rights, as I have detailed elsewhere.[93] It is, however, to suggest that owing to overly narrow understandings of the requirements of national unity, the resources that liberal-democratic principles offer for the justification of group rights remains to be elaborated by policy makers in India and elsewhere.

The Indian case also highlights the need to make a distinction between multicultural rights in general, and minority rights, between *group* rights, on the one hand, and *group-differentiated* rights, on the other. Multicultural policies enhance the autonomy of majority as well as minority groups; minority rights or policies for the protection of cultural difference are a subset of multicultural rights. This distinction remains underdeveloped in contemporary theories of multiculturalism. In Kymlicka's framework, for instance, the paradigmatic form of multicultural right is territorial self-government for national minorities. Subnational autonomy, however, can apply to majority groups (e.g., the English in the United Kingdom), as well as minorities (e.g., the Scottish and Welsh in the UK). India's multinational federalism that recognizes the claims of self-government of several linguistic and tribal groups is an example of a multicultural policy that is not a group-differentiated right, and has weakened protections for religious, caste, and linguistic minorities. This could be a sequencing issue;[94] scholars have suggested that basic individual rights need to be entrenched before group rights are recognized. However, majoritarian multiculturalism in India and elsewhere also suggests that arguments for cultural protection need to be supplemented with those for the protection of cultural *difference* and minority practices.

Lastly, Indian debates highlight a complex fact: liberal frames are insufficient, but also remain *necessary* for the elaboration and evaluation of multiculturalism. On the one hand, a framework for multiculturalism in Asia and Africa needs to recover resources from a range of traditions—socialist, radical democratic, republican, and religious—for the justification of group rights. For example, Indian arguments for group rights have invoked considerations of national unity and development, communitarian conceptions of secularism, democratic values of equality and of status and dignity for the disadvantaged. On the other hand, for group rights to be more multicultural in terms of recognizing minority rights, these need to be more liberal in terms of respecting individual freedoms. In India, as elsewhere, most minority demands pertain to the lack of enforcement in the case of minorities of universal protections offered by liberal states to all citizens—physical security and freedom from arbitrary arrest and detention, freedom of religion, nondiscrimination and equal opportunity in employment. Indian experience reminds us that standard liberal freedoms remain important and unrealized for religious, political, and sexual minorities.

NOTES

1. See, e.g., Gurpreet Mahajan, *Identities and Rights: Aspects of Liberal Democracy in India* (Delhi: Oxford University Press, 1998), and Rajeev Bhargava, "Democratic Vision of a New Republic: India,

1950," in *Transforming India: Social and Political Dynamics of Democracy*, ed. Francine Frankel, 26–59 (Delhi: Oxford University Press, 2000).

2. See, e.g., Will Kymlicka, *Multicultural Citizenship: A Liberal Theory of Minority Rights* (Oxford: Clarendon Press, 1995). Following common practice, the term "multiculturalism" is used in a broad sense, to denote "group rights," "minority rights," "preferential treatment," and "special treatment" in a relatively loose and inclusive fashion (Will Kymlicka and Wayne Norman, eds., *Citizenship in Diverse Societies* [Oxford: Oxford University Press, 2000], 2). Such policies are distinguished by the fact that these go beyond common rights for all citizens. Debates on policies for minorities and lower castes have distinct historical trajectories in India—see Rochana Bajpai, *Debating Difference: Group Rights and Liberal Democracy in India* (Delhi: Oxford University Press, 2011).

3. E.g., Partha Chatterjee, "Secularism and Tolerance," in *Secularism and Its Critics*, ed. R. Bhargava, 345–79 (Delhi: Oxford University Press, 1998).

4. For details, see Rochana Bajpai, "The Conceptual Vocabularies of Secularism and Minority Rights in India," *Journal of Political Ideologies* 7, no. 2 (2002): 179–97, and Bajpai "Secularism and Multiculturalism in India: Some Reflections," in *The Problem of Religious Diversity: European Challenges, Asian Approaches*, ed. Anna Triandafyllidou and Tariq Modood, 204–27 (Edinburgh: Edinburgh University Press, 2017).

5. Rochana Bajpai, "Beyond Identity? UPA Rhetoric on Social Justice and Affirmative Action," in *New Dimensions of Politics in India: The United Progressive Alliance in Power*, ed. Lawrence Saez and Gurharpal Singh (London: Routledge, 2012).

6. E.g., Gurpreet Mahajan, "Indian Exceptionalism or Indian Model: Negotiating Cultural Diversity and Minority Rights in a Democratic Nation-State," in *Multiculturalism in Asia*, ed. Will Kymlicka and Baogang He (Oxford: Oxford University Press, 2005), 288–313; Mahajan, *Identities and Rights*; and Bhargava, "Democratic Vision."

7. E.g., Iqbal Ansari, "Minorities and the Politics of Constitution Making in India," in *Minority Identities and the Nation State*, ed. D. L. Sheth and G. Mahajan, 113–37 (Delhi: Oxford University Press, 1999).

8. Rochana Bajpai, "Constituent Assembly Debates and Minority Rights," *Economic and Political Weekly* 35, no. 21–2 (2000): 1837–45, and Bajpai, *Debating Difference*.

9. Groups defined in terms of social and economic criteria (landholders, universities, and trade associations) were also represented in legislative bodies. See Judith Brown, *Modern India: The Origins of an Asian Democracy* (Oxford: Oxford University Press, 1990), 142; and Sunil Khilnani, *The Idea of India* (London: Hamish Hamilton, 1997).

10. India, *Constituent Assembly Debates: Official Report* (New Delhi: Lok Sabha Secretariat, 1946–50), 5: 246, 249; and Ralph Retzlaff, "The Problem of Communal Minorities in the Drafting of the Indian Constitution," in *Constitutionalism in Asia*, ed. R. N. Spann (Bombay: Asia Publishing House, 1963), 72.

11. See B. Shiva Rao, *The Framing of India's Constitution: Select Documents* (Delhi: Indian Institute of Public Administration, 1967), 770–80, and Bajpai, *Debating Difference*.

12. Retzlaff, "Problem of Communal Minorities," 72

13. For details, see Bajpai, *Debating Difference*.

14. Mahajan, *Identities and Rights*.

15. Z. H. Lari in India, *Constituent Assembly Debates*, 7: 900–903.

16. For details, see Bajpai, *Debating Difference*.

17. Granville Austin, *The Indian Constitution: Cornerstone of a Nation* (1966), 1st Indian ed. with new preface (Bombay: Oxford University Press, 1972), 197.

18. For details, see ibid., esp. chaps. 8, 10, and 11.

19. Ansari, "Minorities and the Politics of Constitution Making," 134.

20. From the late eighteenth century on, parts of religious law pertaining to family law, caste, and religious endowments were exempted from the purview of state regulatory action. See J. Duncan M.

Derrett, *Introduction to Modern Hindu Law* (Oxford University Press [Indian Branch], 1963), and Archana Parasher, *Women and Family Law Reform in India* (New Delhi: Sage, 1992).

21. See, e.g., Rao, *Framing of India's Constitution,* 2: 416, on the first minority rights report of 1947.

22. Marc Galanter, *Competing Equalities, Law and the Backward Classes in India* (Delhi: Oxford University Press, 1984), 153.

23. K. M. Munshi in *Constituent Assembly Debates,* 5: 227.

24. See, e.g., Mohamed Ismail Sahib and Sardar Hukam Singh, cited in Bajpai, *Debating Difference.*

25. Some of the most vocal supporters of the integrationist position were from minority backgrounds. Most women representatives in the Constituent Assembly espoused an integrationist position.

26. Ashutosh Varshney, "Contested Meanings: India's National Identity, Hindu Nationalism, and the Politics of Anxiety," *Dædalus* 122, no. 3, *Reconstructing Nations and States* (Summer 1993): 227–61.

27. Although the Congress party had endorsed separate electorates up until the 1930s, by the time of the Constituent Assembly debates, it was an article of nationalist faith that "history" had shown that separate representation destroyed national unity.

28. E.g., S Radhakrishnan in *Constituent Assembly Debates,* 5: 283–84.

29. See, e.g., Mahavir Tyagi in *Constituent Assembly Debates,* 5: 219.

30. *Constituent Assembly Debates,* 8: 329, 332.

31. For details, see Bajpai, *Debating Difference.*

32. See, e.g., K. T. Shah in *Constituent Assembly Debates,* 7: 655.

33. Niraja Gopal Jayal, *Democracy and the State, Welfare, Secularism, and Development in India* (Delhi: Oxford University Press, 1999).

34. In its role as the director of the project of development, the postcolonial state assumed a stance that was very similar to its colonial predecessor, that of guardian and protector of "weaker groups" (Chatterjee 1995, 218), which served to legitimize the nationalist elite as the leaders of society, rescuing the "masses" from backwardness.

35. Kymlicka, *Multicultural Citizenship,* 141.

36. Galanter, *Competing Equalities,* and Mahajan, *Identities and Rights.*

37. See, e.g., Vallabhbhai Patel in *Constituent Assembly Debates,* 5: 272.

38. Melissa Williams, *Voice, Trust, and Memory: Marginalized Groups and the Failings of Liberal Representation* (Princeton, NJ: Princeton University Press, 1998), 6.

39. Kymlicka, *Multicultural Citizenship,* and Jane Mansbridge, "What Does a Representative Do? Descriptive Representation in Communicative Settings of Distrust, Uncrystallized Interests, and Historically Denigrated Status," in *Citizenship in Diverse Societies,* ed. Kymlicka and Norman, 99–123.

40. As Kymlicka notes of special representation provisions as a form of affirmative action, "it is unclear in what sense this is a form of *representation,* for there are no mechanisms in this model for establishing what each group wants, or for ensuring that the 'representatives' of the group act on the basis of what the group wants" (Kymlicka, *Multicultural Citizenship,* 148).

41. Rao, *Framing of India's Constitution,* 587.

42. Ibid., vol. 2.

43. All Indian citizens are governed by a common criminal law, but in matters of family law pertaining to marriage, divorce, succession, adoption, guardianship, and maintenance, members of four major religious communities—Hindu, Muslim, Christian, and Parsi—are governed by their respective religious laws. The post-independence Indian state has undertaken reforms in Hindu law, but like some other states (e.g., Israel), it has largely adopted a stance of nonintervention vis-à-vis the personal laws of minority communities.

44. Kymlicka, *Multicultural Citizenship,* and Ayelete Shachar, "Group Identity and Women's Rights in Family Law: The Perils of Multicultural Accommodation," *Journal of Political Philosophy* 6, no. 3 (1998): 285–305.

45. See also Mahajan, *Identities and Rights,* and Bhargava, "Democratic Vision."

46. On different meanings, see Bajpai, "Conceptual Vocabularies."

47. See, e.g., G. B. Pant in *Constituent Assembly Debates,* 2: 332.

48. See, e.g., Kymlicka, *Multicultural Citizenship.*

49. On the general point, see, e.g., Henry Shue, *Basic Rights: Subsistence, Affluence, and U.S. Foreign Policy.* (Princeton, NJ: Princeton University Press, 1980).

50. Galanter, *Competing Equalities,* and Mahajan, *Identities and Rights.*

51. On the distinction, see, e.g., Kymlicka, *Multicultural Citizenship,* 33.

52. Mahajan, *Identities and Rights;* Mahajan, "Indian Exceptionalism or Indian Model"; and Bhargava, "Democratic Vision."

53. See Austin, *Indian Constitution* (1972), 189.

54. Louise Tillin, "United in Diversity? Asymmetry in Indian Federalism," *Publius: The Journal of Federalism* 37, no. 1 (2007): 56–57, notes that the Indian Constitution's asymmetrical arrangements in the case of tribal areas in northeast India (Sixth Schedule) are "peripheral" units distinct from the rest of India and do not represent "an official commitment to constitutional asymmetry" in general.

55. Austin, *Indian Constitution* (1972), 252–53. The retreat from constituent powers for state legislatures was explained thus: "the idea of separate constitutions being framed for the different . . . units of the Indian Union was a legacy of the Rulers' polity and that in a people's polity there was no scope for variegated constitutional patterns" (Vallabhbhai Patel, *Constituent Assembly Debates,* 10: 162–63, cited in Austin, *Indian Constitution* (1972), 252.

56. Kymlicka, *Multicultural Citizenship,* 222n8.

57. Jyotirindra Dasgupta, "India's Federal Design and Multicultural National Construction," in *The Success of India's Democracy,* ed. Atul Kohli (Cambridge: Cambridge University Press, 2001).

58. Khilnani, *Idea of India,* 153.

59. Neera Chandhoke, "Negotiating Linguistic Diversity: A Comparative Study of India and the United States," in *Democracy and Diversity: India and the American Experience,* ed. K. Shankar Bajpai (New Delhi: Oxford University Press, 2007), 120.

60. Granville Austin, *The Indian Constitution: Cornerstone of a Nation,* 1st ed. (Oxford: Clarendon Press, 1966), 266.

61. Austin, *Indian Constitution* (1972), 239.

62. Austin, *Indian Constitution* (1966), 186.

63. Tillin, "United in Diversity?" 48. Subsequently, states with substantial tribal groups have also been carved out of linguistic states—e.g., Chattisgarh and Jharkhand in 2000.

64. Austin, *Indian Constitution* (1966), 238.

65. Notably in Gujarat in 2002 and in Assam in 2012.

66. For an account, see Amrita Basu, "More Than Meets the Eye: Sub Rosa Violence in Hindu Nationalist India," Institute for Religion, Culture and Public Life (IRCPL) Conference on Democracy and Religious Pluralism, Columbia University, New York, February 12–13, 2016.

67. On Hindu nationalism as a form of "elite revolt" by upper castes against the growing political power of lower castes, see Stuart Corbridge and John Harriss, *Reinventing India: Liberalization, Hindu Nationalism and Popular Democracy* (Malden, MA: Polity Press, 2000).

68. For details, see Bajpai, "Beyond Identity?" Reports commissioned by the government on the status of minorities, notably the Sachar Commission in 2006 and the Ranganath Misra Committee in 2007, have provided evidence of substantial social discrimination and economic exploitation among Muslims in particular.

69. As per the Constitution (Scheduled Caste) Order of 1950, only Hindu and Sikh dalits were eligible for SC benefits. In 1990, this was extended to Buddhists (following Dr. Ambedkar, a substantial portion of Dalits had converted to Buddhism). Dalit Christians and Dalit Muslim communities are included in lists of Backward Classes in several states, but are not yet eligible for Scheduled Caste status, which brings a higher level of benefits. The Scheduled Tribes category, in contrast, does include Christian and Muslim groups.

70. For details, see Bajpai, *Debating Difference.*

71. Jeff Spinner-Halev, "Feminism, Multicultural Oppression, and the State," *Ethics* 112, no. 1 (2001): 84–113.

72. Uday Mehta, "Gujarat—Hindu Rashtra Laboratory," in *Religion, Power and Violence: Expression of Politics in Contemporary Times,* ed. Ram Puniyani (Thousand Oaks, CA: Sage, 2005). See also Pratap Bhanu Mehta, "Reason, Tradition and Authority: Religion and the Indian State," in *Toleration on Trial,* ed. Ingrid Creppell, Russell Hardin, and Stephen Macedo, 193–214 (Lanham, MD: Lexington Books, 2008).

73. Martha Nussbaum, "Affirmative Action and the Goals of Higher Education" (paper presented at Conference on Affirmative Action in Higher Education in India, the United States and South Africa, New Delhi, March 19–21), 2008.

74. Elizabeth Anderson, "Integration, Affirmative Action and Strict Scrutiny," *New York University Law Review* 77 (2002): 1195–1271.

75. Stanley J.Tambaiah, *Sri Lanka: Ethnic Fratricide and the Dismantling of Democracy* (London: I. B. Tauris, 1986).

76. Christophe Jaffrelot, "The Hindu Nationalists and Power," in *The Oxford Companion to Politics in India,* ed. Niraja Gopal Jayal and Pratap Bhanu Mehta (Delhi: Oxford University Press, 2011), 206.

77. The Constitution contains some Hindu nationalist elements, including the desirability of prohibiting cow slaughter and the subsumption of Sikhs, Buddhists, and Jains within the category Hindu in matters of religious personal law. For more details, see Pritam Singh, "Hindu Bias in India's 'Secular' Constitution: Probing Flaws in the Instruments of Governance," *Third World Quarterly* 26, no. 6 (2006): 909–26.

78. See, e.g., Kymlicka and He, eds., *Multiculturalism in Asia.*

79. For details, see Bajpai, *Debating Difference.*

80. Kymlicka and He, eds., *Multiculturalism in Asia.*

81. Ibid., 7.

82. Ibid., 12.

83. See Partha Chatterjee, *Nationalist Thought and the Colonial World: A Derivative Discourse?* (London: Zed Books, 1986), 140–41.

84. Mahajan, *Identities and Rights,* and Bhargava, "Democratic Vision."

85. Liberalism in India remains understudied and usually assimilated into nationalism, but represented a distinct strand of ideas, as I have argued elsewhere. See Rochana Bajpai, "Liberalisms in India: A Sketch". In: *Liberalism as Ideology: Essays in Honour of Michael Freeden.* ed. Ben Jackson, and Marc Stears 53–76 (Oxford: Oxford University Press, 2012).

86. Constitution-makers saw this category as including Untouchable and tribal groups, but not religious minorities. For a leading example of how affirmative action provisions are less problematic for liberals than multicultural provisions, see, e.g., Brian Barry, *Culture and Equality: An Egalitarian Critique of Multiculturalism* (Malden, MA: Polity Press, 2001), 114.

87. Mahajan, "Indian Exceptionalism or Indian Model," 291–92.

88. Kymlicka and He, eds., *Multiculturalism in Asia.*

89. Bajpai, "Liberalisms in India".

90. Kylicka and He, eds., *Multiculturalism in Asia,* 9.

91. As Kymlicka notes, historically, liberals have objected to minority rights on grounds of "stability, not freedom or justice" (Kymlicka, *Multicultural Citizenship,* 68–69).

92. E.g., Partha Chatterjee, "Secularism and Tolerance."

93. Bajpai, *Debating Difference.*

94. Kymlicka and He, eds., *Multiculturalism in Asia.*

8

Secularism in India

A "Gandhian" Approach

Farah Godrej, University of California, Riverside

M. K. Gandhi is sometimes thought of as the "spiritual father" of Indian secularism, despite the fact that he is clearly not a secularist in the common Western sense of the term.[1] This contradiction arises from what appears to be ambivalence in Gandhi's thought toward the notion of secularism. On the one hand, he insists that politics must be infused with religion or spirituality (terms he uses interchangeably). At other times, he expresses a strong sentiment that religion and the state should remain separate, and that the state should never interfere with matters of religion. How might this apparent contradiction be explained? I argue that this requires distinguishing between the different senses in which Gandhi used the term "religion." Gandhi uses the term idiosyncratically: religion understood in one particular way is to be brought to bear on politics, while understood in another way, religion is a pernicious force in political life. His multifaceted understanding of religion challenges the conceptual distinction between "public" and "private" as understood within Western discourses on secularism. In so doing, he both offered an idiosyncratic understanding of religious "freedom," and challenged traditional Western secularist understandings of the relationship between individuals and communities.

This chapter also traces the dynamic and contested trajectory of "secularism" in post-Independence India, demonstrating that while many contemporary Indian thinkers have attempted to engage Gandhian understandings of secularism, few have recognized precisely how prophetic his opposition was to Westcentric secularism. I identify a continuum along which thinkers are more or less inclined to see Western liberal secularism as appropriate for the Indian context, with those most critical of secularism's applicability in India closest to Gandhi. Although these

150

critics do not always explicitly offer a distinctly Gandhian approach to Indian secularism, reading their critiques in conjunction with my interpretation of Gandhi explains some contradictions of contemporary Indian secularism in ways that also illuminate Gandhi's own concerns.

THE CHALLENGE: AN APORETIC GANDHI

"For me," Gandhi observes, "every . . . activity is governed by what I consider my religion."[2] "I cannot conceive of politics as divorced from religion," he says. "[R]eligion should pervade every one of our actions."[3] Gandhi made no distinction between the spiritual and the moral,[4] and considered each of these realms as synonymous with truth-seeking. Thus, when he claims that "politics are not divorced from morality, from spirituality, from religion,"[5] he means simply that politics is to be guided by the quest for truth, which to him is synonymous with *dharma* (duty or moral order) or spirituality.[6] For those who understand secularism as strict separation of religion from politics, Gandhi's views thus seem anti-secular.

Yet at other times Gandhi expresses a deep, abiding commitment to what he calls secularism. "If I were a dictator, religion and state would be separate," he asserts. "I swear by my religion, I will die for it. But it is my personal affair. The state has nothing to do with it. The state would look after your secular welfare . . . but not your or my religion. That is everybody's personal concern!"[7] Elsewhere he claims that the state "should undoubtedly be secular. Everyone in it should be entitled to profess his religion without . . . hindrance."[8] In what sense, then, can we speak of Gandhian "secularism" or "religious freedom," given his apparent desire for politics and religion to be complementary, rather than separate? Of course, one possible explanation is that Gandhi conceived of politics quite apart from the state, as occurring in the realm of daily personal interaction, not simply in the impersonal and bureaucratic sphere of statecraft. But I suggest that there is more to the story. A deeper exploration of Gandhi's idiosyncratic usage of the term "religion" will reveal a foresighted critique of modern liberal notions of secularism, one which coincides remarkably with contemporary critiques of secularism in India.

In what follows, I offer a reading of Gandhi's position on religion, religious freedom and secularism that is syncretic, rather than strictly exegetical. That is, it deliberately constructs an interpretive view through reliance on a combination of textual material and interpretations by other scholars. Gandhi's writings are deeply aporetic: he rarely offers analytically unambiguous conclusions following from clearly stated assumptions. His political thinking is often scattered across treatises, pamphlets, newspaper articles, editorials, letters, and speeches, and characterized by ambiguity and nuance. The interpretive challenge this presents is compounded by the fact that many of his works were written in English, while many others (such as the seminal *Hind Swaraj*) were written in Gujarati, and subsequently translated either by himself or by close associates. Linguistic nuances have often intervened to introduce interpretive plurality into the meaning of a concept or category, and even his own retranslation of his work multiplies rather than limits the possible meanings of his statements.

Gandhi's writings have long been the subject of multiple, conflicting interpretations, and extrapolating his views requires engaging creatively with this polyvocality.[9] Arriving at a single, ostensibly "accurate" or "authentic" interpretation of Gandhi belies this understanding of the interpretive process as necessarily polyvocal, and so is deeply problematic. Nevertheless, polyvocality should not lead to impressionistic or relativistic interpretations that float free of a rigorous connection to the texts, ideas, or life-worlds they are intended to illuminate. All interpretations are appropriations of a sort; yet we can distinguish between those that are respectful, careful, and credible, and those that are disrespectful, ungenerous, or epistemically violent.[10] My reading here seeks to reconstruct a Gandhian understanding of religious freedom and secularism, excavating his understanding of the relationship between the state and religious groups (commonly called "church-state relations" in the West), and among various religious groups, in a multireligious polity.

RELIGION 1: "PRIVATE" TRUTH-SEEKING

Religion 1 (hereafter R1) is my term for Gandhi's conception of religion as a "private" activity of truth-seeking. When he calls religion one's "private" or "personal" affair, he has a very specific meaning of "private" in mind. Understanding this requires a brief detour through Gandhi's metaphysical views, including the crucial distinction between Absolute and relative truth that is foundational to the entirety of his political thinking. Having been deeply influenced in his early life by the Jain tradition in his home state of Gujarat, Gandhi always acknowledged the debt of his metaphysical position to the Jain doctrine of *anekantavāda*, or "many-sidedness."[11] Like some of the Vedic texts from which it stems (but from which it ultimately departs), Jain doctrine holds that reality manifests itself within a plurality of material forms and phenomena, many of which may conflict with one another. Truth and reality are perceived differently from diverse points of view, and no single point of view is the complete truth.[12] Human beings are only capable of partial knowledge; consequently, no single, specific, human view can claim to represent absolute truth. Apparent contradictions in the earthly world of human ideas are thus an indication of the flexibility, fluidity, and plurality of ultimate reality.[13] On this view, to hold any particular viewpoint as final is to hold a limited picture of reality. Rather than relying on establishing the validity of any given proposition, solutions to moral problems become concerned with investigating the multiplicity of truths and working through them in a nondichotomous fashion.

This way of inquiring into problems defies the absolutist logic employed by many normative frameworks in Western political thought. Gandhi repeatedly emphasized that his own understanding of various truths, even as he held steadfastly to them, was always provisional and contingent, until further examined and tested through the nonviolent encounter. He distinguished between "Absolute" and "relative" truths. Absolute Truth was "the Eternal Principle, that is God," while relative truths are our own individual perceptions of the many-sided and pluralistic Absolute Truth.[14] Absolute Truth is so pluralistic, many-sided, and fluid, that no single human mind can capture it entirely. Human life is most often a struggle to approximate a series of "relative" truths. Because human knowledge of this Absolute Truth is fallible, human beings are destined to see Truth only through the fragmented prism of their relative, everyday perceptions.[15] This leads to an epistemic fallibility, a sense of contingency about one's conclusions, and an ability to keep them open to correction at all times.[16]

It is important to emphasize that Gandhi privileges the *activity* or *process* of truth-*seeking* over *definitive knowledge* of truth. That is, he is mainly interested in arriving at less ambitious and provisional truths about the right action to be taken in a specific situation for a specific reason.[17] While the goal of attaining Absolute Truth is always present, Gandhi reminds us of the danger of resting with the belief that we have in fact attained it, because it takes us away from the continued *activity* of seeking. Gandhi scholars have reminded us that there is a privileging in Gandhi of truth as experiential rather than cognitive.[18] Truth is instantiated through everyday practices of truth-seeking, rather than in any formal, doctrinal, or final manner. It is not to be understood as an abstraction, but rather as something experienced through the everydayness of practice.[19]

To connect this back to R1: when Gandhi claims that religion should be a "private matter," he is using religion to mean the *dharma* (duty) of truth-seeking as a private process, activity, or practice, rather than a steady state. Gandhi's R1 conception of religion is private in a very particular way. The individual conscience is central for Gandhi in every endeavor of truth-seeking. The conscience, for Gandhi, is "the voice of God . . . of Truth."[20] The "call of the individual conscience" is the main vehicle for accessing truth, and the practices of truth-seeking are to constitute a kind of systematic training of the individual will.[21] Thus, when Gandhi calls religion a "private" and "personal affair," he means this in an existential sense: it is between you and your God.[22] R1 is a deeply experiential and interactive relationship with the deepest part of the self, the part which Gandhi believes has a special connection to the Truth that is God.[23]

But crucially, this does not mean that those private practices of truth-seeking driven by the conscience cannot be brought to bear on collective, public life. In fact, the opposite is the case: Gandhi was particularly adept at taking "private" practices of truth-seeking—such fasting or celibacy—and bringing them to bear on public matters.[24] In so doing, he would exemplify his experience of a relative truth-claim rather than engage in dogmatic declarations of truth as principled commitment. When Gandhi says there can be no politics without religion, he is referring to R1, characterized by private activities and experiences of truth-seeking.

Of course, there is also a communitarian sense in which Gandhi uses the term "religion," as something shaped by the power of tradition and community. Yet, as many scholars have demonstrated, Gandhi was hardly univocal on the question of deference to traditional community guidance: time and time again, he ran afoul of Hindu religious authorities in reinterpreting traditional religious guidance in ways that were reformist, claiming to do so on the basis of individual epistemic authority legitimated by the call of conscience.[25] Religious communities for him function as a support or supplement to the truth-seeking of the conscience, "ancestral practices" that serve as "*action heuristics,* instructing the individual on how to become a better human being."[26] Such supporting or supplementary guidance comes precisely in the form of everyday practice, rather than through the belief in Absolute Truth.[27] These guiding practices derive their truth from the fact that they have been handed down from generation to generation. Practice and experience continue to take precedence over doctrinal belief.[28]

We are now in a position to understand why Gandhi may be thought of as an anti-secularist. He is keen that practices and experiences of truth-seeking be brought to bear on actions in the political realm, leading to a marriage between political life and truth-seeking.[29] Certainly, one's relationship to Truth, God, the Inner Voice, is deeply private in the sense that it is subject to one's own inner experience. At the same time, Gandhi would want R1 and private truth-seeking to serve as the "repository or expression of moral values," available for checking corruption, violence, and other ills of public life.[30] Moreover, when this form of private faith is brought to bear on public political matters, Gandhi insists that it be done in an experiential, exemplary, and action-oriented manner: that is, not through declaring principled commitment to doctrinal truths, but through practices that demonstrate through exemplary engagement the activity of truth-seeking. We can now make sense of Gandhi's claim that politics cannot be divorced from spirituality or religion, when religion is understood in a very particular way as R1.

RELIGION 1 VERSUS RELIGION 2: PRIVATE TRUTH-
SEEKING VERSUS DOCTRINAL TRUTH

Gandhi's R1 can now be explored through a contrast with what I call Religion 2 (hereafter R2). In contrast to R1 understood as private practices of truth-seeking, R2 may be understood as principled commitment to absolute or doctrinal truth. I argue that Gandhi is deeply troubled by and suspicious of R2. He is referring to this conception of religion when he says the state should be "secular," or remain apart from religion. In describing R2 as doctrinal truth or principled commitment, I rely on analyses by scholars who have described the Semitic or Abrahamic concept of religious truth, in which religions are seen as a matter of mutually exclusive truth or falsity of doctrines, propositions, and beliefs.[31] Each of these religions claims to be a unique revelation to humanity, and that its own doctrines are therefore the true self-disclosure of the divine.[32] Other traditions are seen as false doctrines or rival claims to truth. This leads in turn to the obligation to proselytize, for if one believes in a universally valid truth, all others are necessarily false, and one is obliged to combat false doctrines. In contrast, the overall ethos of *anekantavāda* permeates most non-Abrahamic faiths of the subcontinent, even as its conceptual roots can be traced specifically to Jain theology and metaphysics. Hindu, Jain, Buddhist, and Sikh traditions do not ascribe "exclusive" truth predicates to their doctrines or beliefs.[33] As we have seen, other traditions are viewed not as competing doctrines, but rather as the transmitted "ancestral practices" of communities.[34]

Why might Gandhi be troubled by the intervention of this R2 conception of religion into political life? Gandhi repeatedly claims that "all faiths are true and divinely inspired, and all have suffered through the necessarily imperfect handling of men."[35] There is, he states, "no such thing as one true religion, every other being false."[36] Elsewhere he claims that "my Hindu instinct tells me that all religions are more or less true."[37] Or: "Religions are different roads converging to the same point. What does it matter that we take different roads so long as we reach the same goal?"[38] Such statements are consistent with his understanding of *anekantavāda:* ultimate Truth cannot be completely grasped by finite human perception, and religious doctrine is a result of such finite perception. In such a world, all religious traditions are seen as parts in an ongoing human search for ultimate truth, containing portions of some truth and some error. Gandhi suggests therefore that it is best to follow one's own, but hold others as dear and close.[39]

In addition, let us recall that Gandhi's commitment to *anekantavāda* involves an "epistemic humility" that leaves him skittish about claiming to have reached the Absolute Truth.[40] It is not simply that it is difficult to know the truth; one must come to know it through a lifetime of practice rather than belief. Thus, the notion that one "has reached" the truth leads to an emphasis on belief and doctrine over practice and experience. It takes us away from constant seeking, allowing us to rest in the certainty that we "have" the truth. Gandhi believes this R2 conception of religion as inflexible or principled commitment to be a destructive force in politics. He repeatedly warns us that the claim to infallibility, in having reached Absolute Truth, "would be a most dangerous claim to make."[41] Karuna Mantena has reminded us that Gandhi is sensitive to the danger that idealism and attachment to principle can facilitate ideological entrenchment in politics. "The worry is that when political disagreements are framed as arguments over fundamental principles, the potential for political progress may dissipate in an atmosphere of increasing hostility and polarization."[42]

There is yet another sense in which Gandhi fears the preponderance of R2 over R1. When Gandhi says religion is a "personal" or "private" affair, I read him as being deeply concerned that this private conception of religion (R1) should not be subject to the doctrinal authority of institutionalized faiths (R2) attempting to control the conscience.[43] If an R2 conception of religion gains predominance over R1, then the individualized, everyday, action-based understanding of religion as conscientious truth-seeking could be displaced by a doctrinal and absolutist one, privileging "truth professed" over "truth lived." One way we can see this is by following the debates around Gandhi's aversion to proselytizing, to which he was staunchly opposed. In his often tense communications with Christian missionaries, Gandhi insists that Christianity is simply one among many true religions (each of which also contain some measure of error). He repeatedly questions the missionary goal of obtaining the confession of cognitive belief in Christian principles, instead of simply practicing truth through exemplary action and encouraging others toward such action.[44]

For Gandhi, when religions function as rival movements entitled to gather as many adherents as they can, this encourages the view of religion as "private" in the wrong sense. It turns the realm of belief into an ideological battlefield where doctrinal belief systems square off against each other by attempting to win the allegiance of individual consciences. The conscience, that delicate instrument of R1, comes under pressure to pledge allegiance to doctrinal principles, rather than engaging in *practices* of truth-seeking. This conception of the "private" sphere is exactly the wrong one, if it means that the privacy of the individual's struggle with her own conscience (R1) becomes the object of appropriation by doctrinal religions attempting to win validity for their truth claims (R2). This model of religious competition in the so-called "private" sphere is focused on pursuing commitments to abstract ideals more than on providing guidance regarding exemplary practices for living well. When the notion of "freedom of conscience" is reduced to competition among doctrinal truth systems, religion is no longer "private" in the sense that truly matters for Gandhi. Instead, the tendency is to reify doctrine, belief, and principle over practice and exemplary lived experience.

We are now in a position to understand how Gandhi envisioned the appropriate relationship between individuals and religions in a multireligious polity. When he claims that everyone should be allowed to profess their religion without hindrance, he means that each person should be left alone on their own private path to truth-seeking. Here, I do not use the phrase "left alone" in a literal sense: Gandhi clearly sees a role for traditional ancestral guidance. Rather, I use "left alone" in an existential sense, as individuals struggle to find truth for themselves through repeated practice and struggle. Gandhi envisions a truly individual, conscience-driven search for truth, instantiated through practice, with the occasional guidance of a community, to be accepted or rejected as conscience sees fit. When this traditional guidance in the *practice* of truth-seeking gets transformed into a competition among the inflexible doctrinal truth *claims* of various religions, the relationship between individuals and religious communities starts to go awry. Individual consciences can come under pressure and be led away from the private activity of truth-seeking, rightly understood, as communities focus on ideological entrenchment grounded in the certainty of one's own truth and the falsity of others'. In contrast, Gandhi suggests that the individual activity of truth-seeking (R1) should not be subject to appropriation by the forces of religious doctrine (R2). Instead, individual truth-seeking must not only focus on habituation and practice, it must be brought to bear on public matters through exemplary actions, rather than through doctrinal belief. It is in this sense that Gandhi claims that there should be no separation between religion and politics. Let us now see what role the state might play in all of this.

SECULARISM IN POST-INDEPENDENCE INDIA

For most Western theorists, secularism means the strict disestablishment of religion from state, or the strict exclusion of religion from all state affairs for the sake of promoting the religious liberty and equal citizenship of all individuals.[45] Rather than conforming strictly to the Westcentric model of church-state separation, secularism has been defined in India, not as neutrality toward all religions, but as "equal respect" for all religions (*sarva dharma sambhava*). The precise meaning of this is rarely clear, but it has often manifested itself as equal tolerance toward, intervention in, and sometimes embrace of, myriad public and private expressions of faith. Meanwhile, the state's intervention in the majority religion (Hinduism) through the legal abolition of untouchability coexists uneasily with its reluctance to intervene in the gender-biased legal practices of Islam, a minority religion in India. Rather than requiring a strict distance and equal neutrality from all religions, the Indian state reserves the right to selectively intervene in and engage with religions and religious practices. The Indian Constitution, even as it implies the strict separation of state and religion, recognizes the rights of religious minorities, commits the state to give aid to educational institutions established and administered by religious communities, and permits religious education in institutions partially funded by the state.

Contemporary theorizing about secularism in India has long been divided around the question of whether the liberal-democratic institutions adopted in post-independence India were Western theoretical impositions alien to indigenous ideas and practices. This issue has become particularly salient since the emergence of a religious and caste-based politics of identity in India. The rise of an assertive political Hinduism has been accompanied by: instances of mass religious violence; the reemergence of a sociopolitical hegemony privileging the Hindu majority; a desire to reassert the rights of upper-caste Hindus; and subsequently, rising anxiety about the rights of minorities such as Muslims, Christians, and lower-caste

Hindus.[46] By the turn of the millennium, both the conceptual apparatus and practice of secularism in India were said to be in crisis.[47] Such anxiety has been heightened by the election as prime minister of Narendra Modi, a right-wing politician who is widely known to have incited religious riots involving the massacre of Muslims by Hindus.

One can identify several discernible strands along a continuum of contemporary Indian political thinking about the purpose and place of secularism in Indian political life.[48] On one end we have Nehruvians or liberal democrats committed to the secularist project in the accepted Western sense. Nehru's concept of secularism was recognizably modern, rationalist, and rooted in European Enlightenment ideals.[49] It is well known that Gandhi's religiousness was both puzzling and mildly annoying to Nehru, an agnostic who wished the state to observe neutrality with regard to all religions, considering most Indian forms of religious belief backward, superstitious, and antithetical to modernity. Nehruvian secularists insist that it is precisely because of India's religious diversity that it requires something like the Western model of secularism, understood in terms of the religious neutrality of the liberal state. Moreover, "to people like Nehru, to conceive of the high ideals of rationality, secularism, or even socialism as 'European' was a mistake. These were intrinsically universalist ideals that were generated by early modern European debates."[50] For proponents of this position, secularism represents progress, liberty, and the "operation of scientific temper and rationality."[51] The persistence of communalism represented the failure of Indians to modernize adequately and of religion to take its proper place in the private sphere.

In the middle of the spectrum, there are discourses that argue that some modification of the Westcentric secularist conception is required in order to apply it to the distinctiveness of the Indian situation, a "deliberate crafting of different rules to respond to a historically distinct situation."[52] Rajeev Bhargava argues, for instance, that Indian secularism can be redefined as "principled" distance, a doctrine through which the state can reserve the right to intervene in and engage with religions and religious practices for the purpose of promoting certain values constitutive of secularism (however these are defined).[53] Meanwhile, Partha Chatterjee proposes a criterion by which the long history of intricate involvement of the Indian state in the affairs of religious institutions can be justified as legitimate and fair. Nonintervention in the affairs of a religious community should be predicated on internal representativeness and democratic structures: those members of minority religious groups who demand noninterference from the state should also demand that their group publicly obtain from its members consent for those practices that have regulatory power over the lives of members.[54] Other thinkers in this range of the spectrum argue that secularism is in fact "an empty category devoid of any stable meaning," which has meant different things in different circumstances of its contestation.[55] In her excellent history of Indian secularism, Shabnum Tejani lists a variety of Indian thinkers who have addressed the profound ambivalence at the heart of the secularist project, arguing that secularism in India can only be understood when situated in the particularities of its historical context.[56]

Finally, at the other end of the continuum, we have discourses that question the very viability of secularism within India, arguing that secularism is a Western transplant with almost no intelligibility in the Indian context. It is this set of discourses that allows us to best understand the relevance of Gandhi's thinking to contemporary debates about secularism. One of the earliest proponents of this position, T. N. Madan, called secularism "an alien cultural ideology, which lacks the strong support of the state [and] has failed to make the desired headway in India."[57] Madan claims that the creation of the secular state relies on the intellectual history of Christianity, and on a peculiarly Christian culture.[58] "The transferability of the idea of secularism to the countries of South Asia . . . should not be taken for granted," he writes.[59] "Neither India's indigenous religious traditions nor Islam recognize the sacred-secular dichotomy . . . therefore, the modern processes of secularization . . . proceed in India without the support of an ideology that people . . . may warm up to."[60]

Other scholars say that secularism is a Western transplant that migrated to India without its larger world view and conditions of intelligibility. It therefore has little meaning in the Indian context, partly because there is no equivalent understanding of the separation between religious and secular, or even an equivalent understanding of what religion is. In such a situation, using the language of secularism only exacerbates rather than ameliorates conflicts among religious groups.[61] Ashis Nandy, a prominent neo-Gandhian, alleges that the statist model of secularism in India is itself responsible for much interreligious strife, because of its attempt to exorcise religion from public life.[62] Secularism is linked to an unnecessary emphasis on modernization and rationality, understood as a loss of meaning, a desacralization and erasure of religion from public life, a neglect of religious community and sensibility, and a misplaced valorizing of statist intervention. If a religious way of life "cannot find normal play in public life, it finds distorted expression in fundamentalism, revivalism and xenophobia."[63] As Madan argues, "it is not religious zealots alone who contribute to fundamentalism . . . but also the secularists who deny the very legitimacy of religion in human life and . . . provoke a reaction."[64]

Thinkers in this last group of discourses are also concerned with the question of the relationship *between* the state and various specific religions, and *among* the adherents of these different religions. S. N. Balagangadhara and Jakob de Roover argue convincingly that the problem of religious conflict in post-independence India has been exacerbated rather than ameliorated by the so-called neutrality of the state.[65] The position of liberal neutrality, according to which the state is to remain strictly neutral with respect to all religions in a multireligious state, has been considered the benchmark for a secular state. The framers of the Indian Constitution tried to transplant the theory of the Western liberal state into Indian soil. Its cognitive framework construed non-Semitic traditions like Hinduism as the structural equivalents of Christianity, viewing them as embodiments of doctrinal truth claims. This continued the colonial mechanism that had compelled Indian religious traditions to refashion themselves according to the Semitic model of religion, gradually pushing what were once fluid and open-ended religious communities to transform into rigid bodies that required specific religious texts and doctrines as canonical for each community. Non-Semitic religious traditions like Hinduism were forced to "semiticize" by aggressively defending their own practices and demonstrating their foundations in terms of "religious doctrines" and "sacred texts."[66] When the post-independence Indian state adopted this Semitic model of religions by allowing proselytization, it implicitly privileged the notion that religion was a matter of doctrinal truth and falsity.[67] This further transformed the relationship between its religious communities from one in which all religions were seen as equally legitimate paths to truth into a zero-sum conflict of competing doctrines, in which communities now saw other religions as rivals to truth claims.

Religious conflict was exacerbated as each tradition's orthodox factions entrenched their attempts to establish their "doctrines" as the superior form of religion in Indian society. Balagangadhara and de Roover cite this as the most compelling explanation for the rise of Hindu fundamentalism and the consequent breakdown of cultural pluralism and interreligious harmony in contemporary India. Ashis Nandy claims that distorted or perverted versions of religion circulating in modern or semi-modern India owe their origins to the perception of the triumph of secularism.[68] Religious zealots looked longingly at more "monotheized" Western faiths and attempted to replicate their doctrinal power and authority.[69] As Ajay Skaria notes, religion for Gandhi only became undemocratic and intolerant when identified with the modern Western conception of it.[70]

How might we connect all of this back to Gandhi's seemingly idiosyncratic and contradictory understanding of "secularism"? The cited criticisms of secularism's "transplanted" nature would seem to explain the contradictions of secularism in India in ways that converge most closely with Gandhi. His thought can be interpreted as a warning to Indians about the dangers of the modern secular state adopting the R2 conception of religious truth, moving us away from a conception of religion as activity and practice (R1), and toward religion as a set of doctrinal truth-claims (R2). These warnings are visible in contemporary critiques of secularism in which Gandhi's R1 and R2 conceptions, and the primacy of *anekantavāda*, are reflected. These critiques point to the problems of ideological entrenchment stemming from a conception of religion as reified doctrinal truth rather than as exemplary individual practice based on truth-seeking by the conscience.

The Western secular liberal state is able to sustain its claim to neutrality with respect to the truth-value of religious claims—while extending the freedom of proselytization to all religions—*only* because it shares with Semitic religions their beliefs about what constitutes religion.[71] In so doing, it has privileged a certain conception of religious truth. When the postcolonial Indian state adopted this model of liberal secular neutrality after independence, making proselytization legally permissible as a condition of "religious freedom," it implicitly took a position on the nature of religion, and adopted a Semitic theology that was hardly neutral, especially in comparison to *anekantavāda.* The ostensibly neutral, secular state has seemed all the more intrusive and violent in a society constituted mainly of non-Semitic faith traditions. The state's commitment to a specific understanding of religious truth—and thus to a *non-neutral* metaphysical claim—is at odds with the non-Semitic one that has historically been predominant among its citizens.[72] The Indian state encourages an understanding of religion as closer to R2 in Gandhi's sense, and further away from R1 and *anekantavāda,* exerting a cultural, interpretive power over social understandings of religion.[73]

Thus, Gandhi's contention that proselytization should be impermissible is more than a seemingly odd and oppressive stance toward what is construed as religious "freedom" in the West. Instead, it can be understood as a decoding of, and a resistance to, the underlying Semitic metaphysical commitments of the liberal secular state. It can also be seen as a reenvisioning of the meaning of religious freedom as R1 rather than R2, a call to remain free from the imposition of an R2 conception. The fact that the modern secular state wishes to extrapolate politics away from truth-seeking is only one reason—albeit perhaps the most commonly cited one[74]—that Gandhi finds such a state to be flawed. But on the reading I have offered, the modern state is intrusive and coercive for Gandhi because it has implicitly privileged an R2 (or Semitic) view of the relationship between religions. In turn, this leaves non-Semitic faiths at a disadvantage, subject to proselytizing by Semitic faiths, while their own notions of religion are ignored and pressured to change in favor of a Semitic one.

CONCLUSIONS

My reading of Gandhi's approach to secularism and religious freedom is not taken from a literal or strict exegetical approach to his textual *corpus.* Gandhi himself did not use the terms R1, R2, Semitic or non-Semitic religions, liberal neutrality, and so forth. Rather, I suggest he was responding to the categories that were invading India through the colonial process, providing a reception to epistemically loaded terms from Abrahamic traditions. Whether or not he directly engaged the framework from which these terms arose, he was able to anticipate the dangers with which their reception in India was fraught. It is this responsive reception that I have attempted to excavate here. Gandhi's suspicion of an R2 conception of religion over an R1 one had to do with precisely the sorts of critiques that contemporary critics of Indian secularism raise: an emphasis on doctrinal truth claims over practice and action, and a lack of epistemic humility stemming from the inflexible or doctrinal commitments of religion understood as R2. I have also argued that Gandhi was concerned about the atmosphere of hostility and polarization that results when religions are seen as competitors attempting to win validity for truth claims. Indeed, this appears to be precisely the scenario that contemporary India finds itself in, since the language of modern secularism has forced communities to conform to an alien understanding of religious truth, while introducing a steady stream of distortion into their self-understandings. Meanwhile, it destroys a historically stable, age-old model of interfaith harmony, in which adherents of various religions saw their respective practices as complementary, nonexclusive paths to truth, often involving fluid processes of intercultural borrowing and assimilation. The secular Indian state presents itself as a "neutral" power standing above competing claims to religious truth, while all along privileging the Semitic conception of religious truth.

What has resulted is exactly what Gandhi appeared to have feared: a competition among the inflexible, principled doctrinal truth *claims* of various religions (R2). Meanwhile, the individual conscience, rather than engaging in the activity of truth-seeking understood as "private" in Gandhi's sense (R1), becomes engaged in the work of ideological entrenchment grounded in the certainty of knowledge about doctrinal truth, and the concomitant falsity of "other" truths (R2).

To say that Gandhi was resistant to the modern liberal language of secularism, and found it to be a "parochialism claiming universal provenance,"[75] is not news to us. But he prophetically reminds us that the language and operation of the liberal secular state violate the assumption of *anekantavāda* according to which all religions are equally "true" paths. When the state takes a position on what religion is, this leads to a competition among abstract doctrinal truth claims, while getting in the way of the truly private practice of religion in Gandhi's sense. This allows us to understand Gandhi's apparently contradictory claims—that "the state should undoubtedly be secular" and that he "cannot conceive of politics as divorced from religion"—in a way that relies on more than simply the semantic distinction between "the state" and "politics." Gandhi's understanding of secularism may be read as a warning about the violence inflicted by the secular state when culturally-specific notions of "religion" and "neutrality" are transplanted into non-Semitic contexts. While Gandhi's usage of terms such as "religion," "secularism," "private," and "public" was admittedly aporetic and idiosyncratic, I have offered here a knitting-together of meaning, suggesting that he refigures the private/public distinction in Westcentric discourse, and gives the "private" practice of religion a whole new meaning. He also offers an understanding of religious "freedom" predicated on an understanding of the relationship *between* individuals and communities, as well as *among* different religious communities. Above all, I have attempted to show that his fears about the encroachment of Westcentric conceptions of religion in the non-Western context were not entirely unfounded. Rather, they coincide with contemporary discourses about the distortions wrought by postcolonial secularism in India, resulting from the transplanting of secularism from the Abrahamic to the Indian cultural context.

NOTES

1. T. N. Madan, *Modern Myths, Locked Minds: Secularism and Fundamentalism in India* (Delhi: Oxford University Press, 1997), 235.

2. Mohandas K. Gandhi, *The Collected Works of Mahatma Gandhi* (Delhi: Government of India, Ministry of Information and Broadcasting, Publication Division, 1958–94), 55: 443.

3. Ibid., 77: 292.

4. Ibid., 81: 424.

5. Ibid., 53: 396.

6. See ibid., 96: 74: "Is not politics too a part of *dharma!*" See also ibid., 18: 255: "I take part in politics because I feel that there is no department of life which can be divorced from religion." For a fuller account of the relationship between spirituality and politics in Gandhi's thought, see Raghavan Iyer, *The Moral and Political Thought of Mahatma Gandhi* (Santa Barbara, CA: Concord Grove Press, 1983), chap. 3; Bhikhu Parekh, *Gandhi's Political Philosophy: A Critical Examination* (Notre Dame, IN: University of Notre Dame Press, 1989), chap. 4; and Anthony Parel, "Introduction," in *Gandhi, Freedom, and Self-Rule*, ed. Anthony J. Parel (Lanham, MD: Lexington Books, 2000).

7. Gandhi, *Collected Works*, 92: 190.

8. Ibid., 96: 238.

9. Ashis Nandy, one of India's preeminent scholars and interpreters of Gandhi, writes of the "distinct Gandhis" who have survived, asserting bluntly that the interpretive task is not motivated by "car[ing] who the real Gandhi was or is." See Nandy, "Gandhi after Gandhi: The Fate of Dissent in Our Times," *Little Magazine* 1, no. 1 (May 2000). Vinay Lal also points out that there is "no singular Gandhi," and that many have "authored their own Gandhi." See Lal, "The Gandhi Everyone Loves to Hate," *Economic and Political Weekly*, October 4, 2008.

10. Farah Godrej, *Cosmopolitan Political Thought: Method, Practice, Discipline* (Oxford: Oxford University Press, 2011), 94–97.

11. Gandhi, *Collected Works*, 33: 410; 59: 496

12. See Tara Sethia, ed., *Ahimsa, Anekanta and Jainism* (Delhi: Motilal Banarsidass, 2004); Acharya Mahaprajna, *The Quest for Truth in the Context of Anekanta* (Ladnun, India: Jain Vishva Bharati Institute, 2003); Y. J. Padmarajiah, *A Comparative Study of the Jaina Theories of Reality and Knowledge* (Delhi: Motilal Banarsidass, 1963); Umrao Singh Bist, *Jaina Theories of Reality and Knowledge* (Delhi: Eastern Book Linkers, 1984); Satkari Mookerjee, *The Jaina Philosophy of Non-Absolutism: A Critical Study of Anekantavada* (Delhi: Motilal Banarsidass, 1978); Bimal Krishna Matilal, *The Central Philosophy of Jainism (Anekanta-vada)* (Ahmedabad: L. D. Institute of Indology, 1981); and Nathmal Tatia, *Studies in Jaina Philosophy* (Banaras: Jain Cultural Research Society, 1951).

13. John M. Koller, "Why Is Anekantavada Important?" in "*Syadvada* as the Epistemological Key to the Jaina Middle Way Metaphysics of Anekantavada," ed. Tara Sethia, *Philosophy East and West* 50, no. 3 (2000).

14. Mohandas K. Gandhi, *An Autobiography: The Story of My Experiments with Truth* (Boston: Beacon Press, 1993), xxvii. See also Farah Godrej, "Nonviolence and Gandhi's Truth: A Method for Moral and Political Arbitration," *Review of Politics* 68, no. 2 (2006); *The Moral and Political Writings of Mahatma Gandhi*, ed. Raghavan N. Iyer (Oxford: Clarendon Press, 1986), 2, chap. 5: 1–15, 160–77, 188–90, 205, 539, 564–69.

15. Godrej, "Nonviolence and Gandhi's Truth," and Gandhi, *Moral and Political Writings*, ed. Iyer, 2: 160. See also Margaret Chatterjee, *Gandhi's Religious Thought* (Notre Dame: University of Notre Dame Press, 1983), 67.

16. "I am far from claiming any finality or infallibility about my conclusions," Gandhi states in his autobiography. "For me they appear to be absolutely correct, and seem for the time being to be final. . . . but at every step I have carried out the process of acceptance or rejection and acted accordingly" (Gandhi, *Autobiography*, xxvii). "I claim . . . nothing more than does a scientist who, though he conducts

his experiments with the utmost accuracy, forethought and minuteness, never claims any finality about his conclusions, but keeps an open mind regarding them" (ibid.). A seeker after truth, Gandhi claims, "must always hold himself open to correction, and whenever he discovers himself to be wrong he must confess it at all costs" (ibid., 350). See also Gandhi, *Moral and Political Writings,* ed. Iyer, 2: 167, 188–89.

17. See Godrej, "Nonviolence and Gandhi's Truth."

18. Ajay Skaria, "Gandhi's Politics: Liberalism and the Question of the Ashram," *South Atlantic Quarterly* 101, no. 4 (2002); Akeel Bilgrami, "Gandhi the Philosopher," *Economic and Political Weekly* 38, no. 9 (2003); and Uday S. Mehta, "Gandhi on Democracy, Politics and the Ethics of Everyday Life," *Modern Intellectual History* 7, no. 2 (2010).

19. As Bilgrami puts it, "it is only our moral experience which is capable of being true" (Bilgrami, "Gandhi the Philosopher," 4164).

20. Gandhi, *Collected Works,* 61: 219–20. The volume of references to conscience or "inner voice" in Gandhi's corpus—e.g., ibid., 15: 273; 21: 112–13; 26: 260; 51: 308—is difficult to enumerate.

21. For the primacy of the individual conscience in truth-seeking, see both Godrej, "Nonviolence and Gandhi's Truth," and Gandhi, *Moral and Political Writings,* ed. Iyer.

22. In other words, Gandhi "wished to be alone with himself and his God." See Sudhir Chandra, *Continuing Dilemmas: Understanding Social Consciousness* (New Delhi: Tulika Books, 2002), 282.

23. For a compelling account supporting this view of Gandhi's "private," experiential and existential understanding of truth-seeking, see "An Unresolved Dilemma: Gandhi on Religious Conversion," in Chandra, *Continuing Dilemmas,* 271–306.

24. For a fuller account of this, see Farah Godrej, "Ascetics, Warriors and a Gandhian Ecological Citizenship" *Political Theory* 40, no. 4 (2012): 437–65.

25. See Bhikhu Parekh, *Colonialism, Tradition and Reform: An Analysis of Gandhi's Political Discourse* (Thousand Oaks, CA: Sage Publications, 2003), and Parekh, *Gandhi's Political Philosophy.* See also Farah Godrej, "Towards a Cosmopolitan Political Thought: The Hermeneutics of Interpreting the Other," *Polity* 41, no. 2 (2009): 135–65.

26. Sarah Claerhout characterizes Gandhi's understanding of religion and religious belief as defined by ancestral practice, rather than by propositions about truth or falsity. "When Gandhi discusses [religious] 'beliefs,' he does not refer to propositions about the world that are either true or false, but rather intends to refer to the transmitted action heuristics or practical instructions handed down by a community." See Sarah Claerhout, "Gandhi, Conversion, and the Equality of Religions: More Experiments with Truth," *Numen—International Review for the History of Religions* 61, no. 1 (2014): 70–71.

27. "The role of such heuristics is to generate certain kinds of action . . . the best way to express such instructions for action is by *embodying* the kind of actions and attitudes they generate. The best way to learn such heuristics is not through verbal expression and reproduction but through mimesis of actions and attitudes" (ibid., 6).

28. This illustrates Akeel Bilgrami's claim that truth for Gandhi is experiential rather than cognitive: "It is not propositions purporting to describe the world of which truth is predicated, it is only our own moral experience which is capable of being true." See Bilgrami, "Gandhi the Philosopher," 4164.

29. Ashis Nandy is certainly right to claim that if secularism means the evacuation of all religion understood as truth-seeking from politics, this is definitely not Gandhi's conception of secularism. See Ashis Nandy, "An Anti-Secularist Manifesto," *Seminar* 314 (1985), and Nandy, "The Politics of Secularism and the Recovery of Religious Tolerance," *Alternatives: Global, Local, Political* 13, no. 2 (1988): 177–94.

30. Nandy, "Anti-Secularist Manifesto," 17.

31. S. N. Balagangadhara and Jakob de Roover, "The Secular State and Religious Conflict: Liberal Neutrality and the Indian Case of Pluralism," *Journal of Political Philosophy* 15, no. 1 (2007): 73–74. See also de Roover and Balagangadhara, "The Dark Hour of Secularism: Hindu Fundamentalism and Colonial Liberalism in India," in *Making Sense of the Secular: Critical Perspectives from Europe to Asia,* ed. Ranjan Ghosh (New York: Routledge, 2013), 111–30.

32. Balagangadhara and de Roover, "Secular State and Religious Conflict," 73. See also de Roover and Balagangadhara, "Dark Hour of Secularism."

33. Balagangadhara and De Roover, "Secular State and Religious Conflict," 74–76. This is, of course, a large claim, and I do not intend to dismiss the complexity that lies at the heart of characterizing an entire group of religions in this fashion. This is not to argue that the question of religious "truth" does not occur in these religions, or that Hindus, Buddhists, or Sikhs do not speak in terms of "religion" and "truth." This complexity notwithstanding, however, it is not too contentious to argue that the discussion of truth in Indian languages and religious texts appears to be of a completely different kind from the doctrinal truth claimed by Semitic religions.

34. Ibid., 76. While it is true that Islam, the largest minority religion in India, is in principle an Abrahamic faith, the practice of Indian Islam, through centuries of proximity to and fusion with its Indian non-Abrahamic counterparts, has tended to be far more fluid, flexible, open-ended, and syncretic. For more on Islam's syncretic nature in India, see J. J. Roy Burman, "Hindu-Muslim Syncretism in India," *Economic and Political Weekly* 31, no. 20 (1996): 1211–15.

35. Gandhi, *Collected Works,* 48: 334.

36. Ibid., 71: 1.

37. Ibid., 25: 56.

38. Ibid., 10: 271.

39. "I came to the conclusion long ago . . . that all religions were true and also that all had some error in them, and that whilst I hold by my own, I should [hold] others as dear as Hinduism, from which it logically follows that we should hold all as dear as our nearest kith and kin and that we should make no distinction between them" (ibid., 41: 112).

40. Godrej, "Nonviolence and Gandhi's Truth."

41. Gandhi, *Collected Works,* 38: 296.

42. Karuna Mantena, "Another Realism: The Politics of Gandhian Nonviolence," *American Political Science Review* 106, no. 2 (2012): 458.

43. Chandra, "Unresolved Dilemma," 282.

44. The depth of Gandhi's discomfort with proselytizing—and particularly its insistence on solidification of doctrinal commitment—is explored at length in Robert Ellsberg, ed., *Gandhi on Christianity* (Maryknoll, NY: Orbis Books, 1991), and Chandra, "Unresolved Dilemma."

45. This is hardly to suggest that the concept of secularism admits of no multiplicity or variation even in the West; on this point, see Madan, *Modern Myths, Locked Minds,* chap. 1; Rajeev Bhargava, "Indian Secularism: An Alternative, Trans-cultural Ideal," in *Political Ideas in Modern India: Thematic Explorations,* ed. V. R. Mehta and Thomas Pantham (New Delhi: Sage Publications, 2006); and Andrew Davison, *Secularism and Revivalism in Turkey: A Hermeneutic Reconsideration* (New Haven, CT: Yale University Press, 1998).

46. Sudipta Kaviraj, "Languages of Secularity," *Economic and Political Weekly,* December 14, 2013.

47. See Rajeev Bhargava, *The Promise of India's Secular Democracy* (New Delhi: Oxford University Press, 2010); Anuradha Dingwaney Needham and Rajeswari Sunder Rajan, eds., *The Crisis of Secularism in India* (Durham, NC: Duke University Press, 2007); Madan, *Modern Myths, Locked Minds;* and T. N. Srinivasan, ed., *The Future of Secularism* (New Delhi: Oxford University Press, 2007).

48. In her excellent summary of secularism in India, Shabnum Tejani identified four positions on secularism in contemporary Indian debates. See Shabnum Tejani, *Indian Secularism: A Social and Intellectual History, 1890–1950* (Bloomington: Indiana University Press, 2008). While I am in broad agreement with her, I do differ slightly from her in how I understand the spectrum of positions, and how I categorize thinkers along such a spectrum. This characterization is in no way intended to diminish the richness, plurality, and complexity of Indian thinking about secularism, but rather to identify and group several kinds of discourses together.

49. See Madan, *Modern Myths, Locked Minds,* 238–48; de Roover and Balagangadhara, "Dark Hour of Secularism," 20.

50. Kaviraj, "Languages of Secularity."

51. H.S. Verma, "Secularism: Reflections on Meaning, Substance and Contemporary Practice," in *Secularism and Indian Polity,* ed. Bidyut Chakrabarty (New Delhi: Segment Books, 1990), cited in Tejani, *Indian Secularism,* 8. See also P.C. Chatterji, *Secular Values for Secular India* (Delhi: South Asia Books, 1984); Asghar Ali Engineer, *Communal Challenge and Secular Response* (Delhi: Shipra Publications, 2003); Amartya Sen, "Secularism and Its Discontents," in *Unravelling the Nation: Sectarian Conflict in India,* ed. Kaushik Basu and Sanjay Subrahmanyam (Delhi: Penguin, 1996); Meera Nanda, *Prophets Facing Backward: Postmodern Critiques of Science and Hindu Nationalism in India* (New Brunswick, NJ: Rutgers University Press, 2003); and Meera Nanda, *Breaking the Spell of Dharma and Other Essays* (New Delhi: Manohar Publishers, 2003).

52. Kaviraj, "Languages of Secularity."

53. See Bhargava, *Promise of India's Secular Democracy;* Bhargava, "Indian Secularism."

54. Partha Chatterjee, "Secularism and Tolerance," *Economic and Political Weekly* 9 (July 1994); Chatterjee, "Religious Minorities and the Secular State: Reflections on an Indian Impasse" *Public Culture* 8 (1995).

55. Tejani, *Indian Secularism,* 11.

56. Neera Chandhoke, *Beyond Secularism: The Rights of Religious Minorities* (New Delhi: Oxford, 1999), and Aditya Nigam, *The Insurrection of Little Selves: The Crisis of Secular-Nationalism in India* (New Delhi: Oxford University Press, 2006).

57. T.N. Madan, "Secularism in Its Place," *Journal of Asian Studies* 46, no. 4 (1987): 757.

58. Kaviraj, "Languages of Secularity."

59. Madan, "Secularism in Its Place," 754

60. Madan, *Modern Myths,* 261.

61. See Jakob De Roover, Sarah Claerhout, and S.N. Balagangadhara, "Liberal Political Theory and the Cultural Migration of Ideas: The Case of Secularism in India," *Political Theory* 39, no. 5 (2011): 571–99; see also Jakob de Roover, "The Vacuity of Secularism: On the Indian Debate and Its Western Origins," *Economic and Political Weekly,* September 28, 2002.

62. Ashis Nandy, "The Twilight of Certitude: Secularism, Hindu Nationalism, and Other Masks of Deculturation," *Alternatives: Global, Local, Political* 22 no. 2 (1997): 157–76; Nandy, "Politics of Secularism"; and Nandy, "Anti-Secularist Manifesto."

63. Nandy, "Twilight of Certitude," 167.

64. Madan, "Secularism in its Place," 757

65. Balagangadhara and de Roover, "Secular State and Religious Conflict."

66. Ibid., 86; Nandy, "Politics of Secularism," 187; and Nandy, "Twilight of Certitude," 171.

67. Balagangadhara and de Roover, "Secular State and Religious Conflict."

68. Nandy, "Twilight of Certitude," 158.

69. Nandy, "Anti-Secularist Manifesto," 22–23.

70. Skaria, "Gandhi's Politics," 959.

71. Balagangadhara and de Roover, "Secular State and Religious Conflict," 82.

72. Jakob de Roover, "Is Secularism the Solution to Communal Conflict in India?" http://indianrealist.wordpress.com/2010/05/16/is-secularism-the-solution-to-communal-conflict-in-india; page no longer available. But see Claerhout, "Gandhi, Conversion and the Equality of Religions," 75.

73. Relatedly, although slightly differently, Nandy argues that secularism depends on coercive power of state. See Nandy, "Twilight of Certitude," 164, 169.

74. Parekh, *Gandhi's Political Philosophy,* and Thomas Pantham, "Thinking with Mahatma Gandhi: Beyond Liberal Democracy," *Political Theory* 11, no. 2 (1983).

75. Skaria, "Gandhi's Politics," 960.

9

Contesting Multiculturalism

Federalism and Unitarism in Late Colonial Nigeria

Wale Adebanwi, University of Oxford

This chapter examines the different approaches to multiculturalism among Nigeria's three core and competing regions in the period of decolonization.[1] The key questions that are confronted here in focusing on the contention over the nature and dynamics of multiculturalism in this era are these: Is multiculturalism the best way to deal with diversity in an emerging but divided (African) nation-state? Is multiculturalism antithetical to nation-building and mutual recognition of equal value among different ethnic-nationalities within African polities? What happens when multiculturalism simultaneously constitutes the basis of political architecture as well as the fundamental problem of political organization in a multi-ethnic state?

I suggest that engaging with these questions can be helpful in understanding the unending political instability in contemporary African states caused largely by the unremitting antagonism between the constituent groups. The chapter explains the historical sociology of the politics of ethno-cultural diversity in Nigeria in relation to the struggle to construct a suitable political architecture for the governing of a vast country, an architecture that was strong enough to respond to as well as manage Nigerian's diversity while ensuring unity. Generally, I suggest that contemporary problems in multi-ethnic postcolonial African states concerning the best approaches to national unity, diversity, party politics, power sharing, and so on, are rooted in different visions of multiculturalism, as exemplified in the Nigerian case.

Will Kymlicka recently argued that "ideas about the legal and political accommodation of ethnic diversity have been in a state of flux around the world for the past 40 years."[2] However, Kymlicka reflects a dominant trend in the literature in the West,[3] in which contemporary multiculturalism is assumed to be largely a Western experience or problem.[4] Even while admitting that multiculturalism is a phenomenon that has been around for many centuries and that even in the contemporary era, "in very few countries can the citizens be said to share the same language, or belong to the same ethnonational group,"[5] thus making multiculturalism "a normative response to that fact,"[6] yet the focus and examples drawn by many scholars from, or based in, the West are almost always from Euro-American contexts (extending sometimes to Australia). In this context, multiculturalism, for the most part, is captured either as a phenomenon defined by the social, economic, political, and policy responses to increased immigration from the developing world to the West,[7] or as represented in the challenges faced by minorities (racial, ethnic, religious, or gender) in contemporary Western societies[8]—or both. Perhaps because of its peculiar experience of state racism that survived up the last decade of the twentieth century, South Africa is the only country in Africa that has attracted sufficient attention in the literature on multiculturalism.[9]

Kymlicka, among others, also dates the "struggle for multiculturalism and minority rights" as having emerged "in the late 1960s," as one of the three "waves" of movements that arose against the backdrop of "this new assumption of human equality [which] generated a series of political movements designed to contest the *lingering presence or enduring effects of older hierarchies* [emphasis added]."[10] Contrary to this position, the Nigerian case—as evident in several other African countries, including Kenya, (South) Sudan, South Africa, Cameroon, Uganda, the Democratic Republic of the Congo, Mauritania, and the Central African Republic—shows that the struggle for multicultural diversity in Africa preceded this period, even if the specific language of "multiculturalism" was not used at this point. Also, many cases in Africa point to the fact that the struggle for multiculturalism regarding "the lingering presence or enduring effects of older hierarchies" is not only one in which minority groups are pitched against dominant majority groups. In some cases, such struggles set dominant or marginal majority groups against one another or even marginal majority groups against dominant minority groups.

Against this backdrop, Amy Gutmann's definition of multiculturalism as "the state of a society or the world containing many cultures that interact in some *significant way* with each other [emphasis added],"[11] is one of the most useful ways of approaching this phenomenon. However, as the African experience has shown, although multiculturalism is potentially a positive principle in multi-ethnic societies and states, its practices may not necessarily produce beneficial consequences. The uses to which dominant groups, systems, or parties put multiculturalism may in fact portend danger for the democratic principles inherent in the idea. As Asef Bayat has argued, although multiculturalism "calls for equal coexistence of different cultures within a national society," its politics is paradoxically also steeped in "the language of separation and antagonism [as well as] cultural superiority and ethnocentrism."[12]

To account for this, it is important to pay attention to the historical context of multiculturalism in understanding its contemporary successes or failures in actually existing societies. Examining particular contexts of multiculturalism also helps to explain what it means in different societies and at different points. Here, I examine the debate between those who have imagined multiculturalism as (semi-)separatism—called by all sorts of names, including "Pakistanisation" and "tribalism"—and those who have approached multiculturalism as a critical basis for the survival of a deeply divided and plural society, such as Nigeria. I want to use the "solutions" provided in the Nigerian experience to reflect on the questions I pose above by reflecting on British colonial legacy in Nigeria, the decolonization-era debates on the best political architecture for a multi-ethnic state, the principles that inform the positions taken, the responses that these positions generated, and how the Nigerian experience speaks to the phenomenon of multiculturalism in general.

THE (POST)COLONY AND THE CHALLENGE
OF MULTICULTURALISM

Since 1914, the British Government has been trying to make Nigeria into one country. But the people are different in every way, including religion, custom, language and aspirations. . . . We in the North take it that Nigeria's unity is only a British intention for the country they created . . .

—ALHAJI SIR ABUBAKAR TAFAWA BALEWA, NIGERIA'S FIRST PRIME MINISTER

In August 2014, over five hundred delegates, representing different groups, particularly ethno-regional groups, concluded five months of contentious deliberations on the existing divisive political structure and the future of Nigeria. The fundamental crisis of nation-building that provoked the convocation of the National Conference, the fourth of its kind in post-independence Nigeria, as the BBC reported, "has seen bitter conflicts between [Nigeria's] numerous ethnic, religious and linguistic groups."[13] At the end of the conference, over six hundred resolutions were passed. Based on these resolutions, a 335-page report was produced and submitted to President Goodluck Jonathan. The chairman of the National Conference Committee, former Chief Justice Idris Kutigi, reportedly stated that fears expressed in some parts of the country that the conference would lead to the disintegration of the country had been dispelled.[14]

However, the fact that questions are still being raised about basic issues of national unity fifty-four years after independence and six decades after the key structural issues regarding unity were assumed to have been resolved at the pre-independence constitutional conferences points to the lingering problems regarding the multicultural nature of Nigeria. Mohammed Haruna, a leading journalist and one of the most vociferous defenders of northern interests and Islam in Nigeria and an antagonist of the idea of a national conference in Nigeria, told the BBC that "virtually every [post-independence] constitutional conference in this country has come with a *hidden agenda* by its convener and virtually all of them have come to grief [emphasis added]."[15] What Haruna calls a "hidden agenda" is the suspicion among the political elite of the core northern region that post-independence national conferences in Nigeria promoted by the southern political elite were designed to limit the influence of the north in the country. Therefore, the region has always been opposed to all post–civil war national conferences and the struggle for "political restructuring" of the federation, championed mainly by southerners. Indeed, it is significant that all the successful (national) constitutional conferences were the ones held in the late colonial period. These conferences determined the fundamental structures of the Nigerian federation. Every other major successful instance of tinkering with the structure of the federation since independence was by the military, mostly led by northern soldiers. The only major change under a non-northern military ruler, General Aguiyi Ironsi, an Igbo (southern) military ruler, was one of the factors that provoked a countercoup (in July 1966), which ultimately led to civil war (1967–70). The Ironsi regime had abolished the federal system and replaced it with the unitary system (of provinces). This was reversed after Ironsi's assassination in July 1966.

In the light of the fact that all attempts to fundamentally reshape the Nigerian federation through democratic processes has failed, it is important to reexamine the original positions and debates among the country's three regions and their leaders, which continue largely to determine the current attitudes toward multiculturalism in Nigeria.

Diversity or plurality is one of the most important issues constantly raised in, and about, Nigeria. The recognition of the multicultural nature of the country evident in the old national anthem,[16] and the national "aspirations" encoded in it, could as well have served as a reflection of the controversies and contestations over Nigeria's unity and nationalism in the two decades preceding Nigeria's independence. This was especially true as the leaders of the different ethno-regional formations fought hard to ensure the recognition of their different political and cultural identities. The Nigerian experience is no surprise, though, given that, as David Theo Goldberg argues, "multiculturalism and commitments to diversity emerged out of [the] conflictual history of resistance, accommodation, integration, and transformation."[17] Against this backdrop, a central question that arose in late colonial Nigeria, as reflected in the struggles between those who wanted independent Nigeria to be a federal state and those who favored a unitary state, was this: Is multiculturalism a menace?[18]

Indeed, before the British amalgamated the northern and southern protectorates in 1914 to form Nigeria as a single colony, and even more so since, difference and multiculturalism *were* largely constructed by important sections of the national political elite—including even those who affirmed their own identities—as a menace. The British colonialists themselves also believed and exhibited this, even while insisting that the fate and fortunes of the different ethnic, cultural, and religious groups in Nigeria were tied together. As Sir Abubakar Tafawa Balewa, one of the leaders of the Northern People's Congress (NPC)—who later became Nigeria's first and only prime minister—put it, since the amalgamation "the British Government has been trying to make Nigeria into one country." Balewa saw this as a futile effort, because he considered the people who made up the country as "different in every way, including religion, custom, language and aspirations." He concluded that "Nigeria's unity is only a British intention for the country they created." The differences among the components parts of Nigeria, Balewa submitted, were too deep to make unity possible.

John N. Paden, biographer of Sir Ahmadu Bello, the late first premier of the Northern Region of Nigeria, recalls an encounter in the mid-1960s between two of the three Nigerian leaders whose attitude to multiculturalism helped to shape Nigeria's future—against the backdrop of the powerful effects of the colonial architecture. Bello and Dr. Nnamdi Azikiwe, the first premier of the Eastern Region of Nigeria and, later, the country's first ceremonial president, are said to have had a meeting in which the latter demanded of Bello, "Let us *forget* our differences . . . " to which Bello responded, "No, let us *understand* our differences. I am a Muslim and northerner. You are a Christian and easterner. *By understanding our differences, we can build unity in our country* [emphasis added]."[19]

Even though Bello and Azikiwe did not specifically use the language of multiculturalism in this encounter, their preceding and succeeding statements and actions constitute further evidence of their different and differing attitudes to cultural diversity among Nigeria's many ethnicities and faiths. If multiculturalism is, at the core, "a principle [that indicates] respect for the pluralism of cultures,"[20] then *forgetting* differences might connote disregarding the pluralism of cultures, while *understanding* difference might mean accepting the reality of such plurality, just as Bello insisted. He and his party, the Northern Peoples' Congress (NPC), strongly challenged the assimilationist policy championed by Azikiwe and his party, the National Council of Nigerian Citizens (NCNC), even though Bello envisaged multiculturalism in restrictive terms, as applying only along ethno-regional and religious lines.[21]

Before Bello and Azikiwe had this encounter, Chief Obafemi Awolowo, the third of the triumvirate Nigerian nationalist leaders and first premier of the Western Region, had led a contentious debate between his political party, the Action Group, and Azikiwe's NCNC about the best structural political and constitutional arrangement to guarantee Nigeria's multicultural realities. This debate revolved around whether federalism or unitarism would be the best political system for a multi-ethnic state such as Nigeria after independence from Britain. Incidentally, the two sides agreed that the question of Nigeria's multi-ethnic and multi-religious nature was a critical one that ought to be confronted through the political arrangement that would succeed British colonial rule. Azikiwe and the NCNC, for the most part, identified the multicultural nature of Nigeria as a *menace* or a *problem* that ought to be transcended, if not *solved*, through assimilationist or (politically) *centralizing* policies, starting with a unitary system of government. In this model, a central government would be supreme, and all subnational units would exist by the authority of the central government. On the contrary, Awolowo, and later Bello—both with different inflections—argued that Nigeria's multiculturalism should be approached as a *strength* that ought to be recognized and honored, through *decentralizing* policies, which would constitute essential building blocks in the struggle for national unity and development.

This debate was not limited to Nigeria; in much of Africa during the late colonial and early independence era multiculturalism was regarded as a "menace." Colonialism created most modern African states, with the possible exception of Somalia, as multi-ethnic entities, but federalism was viewed in most parts of the continent as disuniting, separatist, or secessionist.[22] In many instances, federal systems collapsed, among them the federation of Rhodesia and Nyasaland (1953–63), where Nyasaland became Malawi and Northern Rhodesia became Zambia at independence in 1964; Cameroon (which switched to a unitary system in 1972); Kenya (where the Majimbo ("regions") constitution with federal features was changed to a unitary system under Kenyatta); and Uganda (where President Milton Obote dropped the asymmetrical relations between the center and the provinces in 1955).[23] The dominant attitude in African states to federalism has produced different consequences, including authoritarian rule, the silencing of ethnic, religious, and cultural minorities, the imposition of unitarist forms of government, and one-party (or one-dominant-party) states. At independence and for much of the first two decades thereafter, most African states attempted officially to *forget* their inherent multiculturalism rather than *recognize* it. In the few cases where multiculturalism was accommodated to some extent, extreme centrifugal forces eventually encouraged the victory of centripetal forces. In the late colonial and early independence eras in Africa, multiculturalism was thus regarded as a threat to nation-building, "national unity," "peace," "progress" and economic, political and social "development."[24] Despite this, however, no African country could avoid the challenges of multiculturalism. Each country faced these in different forms and responded in different ways, depending on their historical circumstances.[25]

MULTICULTURALISM, BRITISH COLONIALISM, AND INDIRECT RULE

No robust analysis of multiculturalism in Africa can proceed without understanding the historical context. In the case of Nigeria, in particular, the structuring—as well as epochal—powers of the indirect rule system introduced by the British colonial administration and its consequences in determining the nature of the multiethnic state are critical. The "principle of ruling through the native chiefs" imposed on Nigeria, as its chief architect, Frederick Lugard,[26] the first British governor-general of amalgamated Nigeria, described the indirect rule system (or Native Authority System), was one in which "racial dualism" was "anchored in a politically enforced ethnic pluralism," as the Ugandan academic Mahmood Mamdani puts it.[27] And because this "ethnic pluralism" was underlined by "the contradictory character of ethnicity,"[28] when the bifurcated states created by colonialism were deracialized in much of Africa, they were not democratized.[29] Hence, though inherently a democratic phenomenon, process, and policy, multiculturalism has remained more of a (democratic) potential than reality in much of Africa. In most of the countries, struggles to achieve democratic multiculturalism—whether violent or nonviolent—have been the rule rather than the exception.

Given that the indirect rule system was a form of "decentralized despotism,"[30] multiculturalism was *produced* and *entrenched* as a technology of rule rather than as a democratic tool for recognizing difference and diversity. The multi-ethnic African postcolonial states that succeeded the colonial states therefore reproduced forms of multiculturalism that were a dimension of power as well as a form of resistance, part of the problem as well as part of the solution.[31]

From 1900 to 1906, Lugard was the high commissioner of the British Protectorate of Northern Nigeria where he established the practice of administering the colony through emirs and local chiefs.[32] In 1914, he was appointed as the governor-general of the amalgamated territories (of the Northern and Southern Protectorates) called the Colony and Protectorate of Nigeria. Although the indirect rule system was most suitable for the Northern Protectorate (largely dominated by the Fulani emirs), less so for the western part of the Southern Protectorate (with its monarchical system), and most unsuitable for the acephalous societies of the Igbo areas of the eastern part of the Southern Protectorate, it was nonetheless extended over the whole of colonial Nigeria, thus producing specific forms of struggles for multiculturalism that Nigeria still contends with today.

In the early years of the twentieth century, the British approached multiculturalism in contradistinction to unity. Lugard's successor, Sir Hugh Clifford, found the idea of a "Nigerian" *nation* "dangerous" and encouraged multiculturalism as a means to "divide and rule." He observed:

> Assuming . . . that the impossible were feasible—that this collection of self-contained and mutually independent Native States, separated from one another, as many of them are, by great distances, by differences of history and traditions, and by ethnological, racial, tribal, political, social and religious barriers, were indeed capable of being welded into a single homogeneous nation—a deadly blow would thereby be struck at the very root of national self-government in Nigeria, which secures to each separate people the right to maintain its identity, its individuality and its nationality, its chosen form of government; and the peculiar political and social institutions

which have been evolved for it by wisdom and by the accumulated experience of generations of its forebears.[33]

Evidently, Clifford did not accept the "premise of multiculturalism as a principle [of] respect for the pluralism of cultures."[34] What he articulated was fear of such pluralism as the basis for constructing mutual peace, justice, and equity among cultures. In his *Background to Nigerian Nationalism,* James Coleman captures this attitude, which didn't change significantly as Nigeria approached independence: "The artificiality of Nigeria's boundaries and the sharp cultural differences among its peoples point to the fact that Nigeria is a British creation and the concept of a Nigerian nation is the result of the British presence. . . . The present unity of Nigeria, as well as its disunity, is in part a reflection of the form and character of the common government—the British superstructure—and the changes it has undergone since 1900."[35]

Such was the depth of the differences between the administration of the two hitherto separate northern and southern protectorates that "the different policies and conceptions of colonial administration which evolved in each of the two protectorates during the fourteen years of their separate existence continued to dominate official thought and action."[36] The bureaucracies in the two areas operated separately, and the colonial officials in the two protectorates also represented the two areas as if they were representatives of two different countries.

However, the process that led to the bifurcation of the north and the south and the further bifurcation of the south into western and eastern regions, for the most part, glossed over the several minority groups in these three regions, thus imposing the three largest majority groups, Hausa-Fulani (north), Igbo (east), and Yoruba (west) over more than three hundred minority groups. By the late 1940s and 1950s, it became apparent that "ethnicity, and the need to accommodate disparate ethnic nations within the proposed Nigerian independent territory, would pose a sizeable challenge. . . . [Because the] ethnic minorities were not to be pacified by the usual rhetoric and promises."[37] Given the agitations of the minority groups as Nigeria approached independence—as evident in the 1957 Conference on Nigeria's (Independence) Constitution at Lancaster House in London—a Minorities Commission was set up by the British government. Despite this, before, and even a few years after the creation, in 1963, of the first minority region in Nigeria (the Mid-West Region), the struggle for multiculturalism in Nigeria was largely defined by the tripartite arrangement involving the original three regions, that is, the Northern Protectorate and the western (including the Lagos colony) and eastern sections of the Southern Protectorate. This rendered "cultural minorities vulnerable to significant injustice at the hands of the majority, while exacerbating ethnocultural conflict."[38] The hierarchical subdivision of the country during colonial rule into provinces, and districts or divisions, which were supposedly based on "territorial boundaries of indigenous political units,"[39] encouraged these provinces and districts—in which the minority groups were the majority—to "become the focus of a new loyalty and thus . . . [progress] from the status of an artificial administrative unit to that of a political unit possessed of its own individuality."[40]

These two factors—indirect rule and hierarchical subdivision of the country during colonial rule—as Nigeria moved toward independence particularly in the 1950s, when different regions of the country fought for and gained a measure of autonomy, ensured that, to use Mamdani's words, "participatory forms ("empowerment") that stress[ed] the autonomy of a bounded group—only to undermine any possibility of an alliance-building majority-based representation" eventually justified and strengthened "the most undemocratic forms of central power."[41] In the context of the British government's attempt to develop Nigeria into a unitary state, which Awolowo dismissed as "patently impossible,"[42] multiculturalism thus became a big challenge for the emergent country.

"Nigeria is not a nation [but] a mere geographical expression," Awolowo had contended in his *Path to Nigerian Freedom* (1947).[43] The Oxford historian of the British empire Margery Perham shared that view, observing in her foreword to Awolowo's book: "There is at present . . . no Nigeria but the one traced on the map by Britain and held together in a state-system maintained by this country [Britain]."[44] She added: "If Mr. Awolowo is right, as I believe he is, that in face of the deep divisions of race, culture and religion in Nigeria, political advance through natural groups and regions is the only way to a wider unity, then Britain may for long be required to provide the framework which holds three groups together until they are able to fuse into unity or federation."[45] One of the most salient controversies in this era, therefore, was whether the best system by which "the main groups [could] come together at the centre to pool and share their traditions and resources" was a federal or a unitary system.[46] Thus, in the decolonization period, the colonial government and the representatives of the Nigerian groups confronted the question of how to protect and preserve multiculturalism within the independent nation-state.

Multiculturalism can be understood in the Nigerian context as a strategy for the political management or protection of the country's multi-ethnic reality (including the imbrication of this with religious differences, especially along ethnoregional lines. It also connotes, as evident in many parts of Africa, what Tariq Modood calls "political accommodation of minorities."[47] However, the politics of *minoritization* in Nigeria is politically salient and thus more regularly expressed in the language of *marginalization.* Thus, minoritization or marginalization is not limited to ethno-linguistic groups that are politically categorized as minorities; it also involves majority groups that at one point or the other have imagined themselves to have been, or likely to be, marginalized by other groups. Furthermore, in Nigeria, multiculturalism is not only a response to the politics of identity; it is also critical for the politics of resource distribution and access to political power.

Additionally, it can be argued that, in the decolonization and immediate post-independence eras, multiculturalism in principle constituted a rhetoric for preventing the breaking up of the country in the light of the threats or attempts by the three regions of the country to secede at different points.

"WHEN WAYS OF LIFE COLLIDE"

Nigeria is one of the stark examples of "what actually happens when issues of group identity are made the focal point of public attention and political argument in the inevitably rough and ready tumble of real politics [in Africa]."[48] The leaders of both the Northern Region and the Southern Region approached the question of when Nigeria would achieve self-government as one that reflected the "essential" difference between the two hitherto separate territories. In one strand of what I describe as the *cultural discourse of duality*—which in colonial Nigeria constituted the backdrop to this difference—northerners, generally, were constructed by their leaders and the British colonial officers as "restrained," "dignified," "cultured," "respectable," and "respectful" of their British overlords; southerners were constructed by the same people (northern leaders and the British) as "rash," or "impatient," "aggressive," "disdainful of the 'backward' north," "eager to dominate the north," and "disrespectful" of their British overlords. In the alternative strand of the cultural discourse of duality, southerners, generally, were constructed by their own leaders as "progressive," or "radical," "freedom loving," "forward-looking," "modernity-embracing," "enlightened," "developed" (comparatively) and opposed to perpetual foreign domination; northerners were constructed by the southerners as "backward," "conservative," "feudal," "unenlightened stooges of imperialists," and opposed to the unity and independence of Nigeria.[49]

No doubt the reality was far more complex than the simplistic attitudes and discourses alternatively deployed by these leaders, their supporters, the press, and British colonial officers; but this cultural discourse of duality was at the center of the question of multiculturalism in colonial Nigeria, reflecting both the dimensions and the limitations of multiculturalism in the late colonial era. As the pressure for self-government became more intense after the end of World War II, with the British Empire expressing willingness to bring its former colonial possessions into the British Commonwealth, the challenge of managing multiple identities in these colonial possessions moving toward independence became a central concern. However, managing the multiple identities could not be done in a vacuum, and the pressure for self-rule also quickened the pace of constitutional advance,[50] given that the constitutional or legal process was the best guarantor of the right to difference. The pace of constitutional development in the colonies, in turn, stimulated the development of political parties,[51] given that the power to protect difference and identities during that period could not also be acquired in a vacuum—particularly, where cultural, ethnic, communal, and other identity groups were insufficiently powerful to dictate the sharing of political power.

In the case of Nigeria, the indirect rule system, which promoted decentralization, left a contradictory political legacy in relation to the emergent need for centralized parliamentary democracy. Although British imperial interests and conservative chiefs and traditionalists favored the continued development of the native authority system, most Nigerian nationalists favored a move toward parliamentary institutions.[52] However, even among those who favored the latter, there were deep disagreements regarding the details and the pace.

Given the existing unitary structure imposed by the British, the first constitutional attempt at federalism in Nigeria was the constitution promulgated in 1945 under Governor Sir Arthur Richards.[53]. The concept of regionalism was the most important and acceptable feature of this constitution.[54] This was a compromise between regional separatists, who wanted three separate states, and the strong federalists, who wanted a central parliament. For Richards, the "embryonic, quasi-federal structure" created by the 1945 constitution was a "practical means" of ensuring two major objectives. It had the potential both to promote national unity in Nigeria, and to accommodate diversity within that unity.[55] Responding to those who argued that regionalism would promote separatism, Sir Bernard Bourdillon, one of Richards's predecessors, stated that "in fact, this measure represents not the division of one unit into three, but the beginning of the fusion of innumerable small units into three and from these three into one."[56] Despite the objections of the three regions to some parts of this constitution, all the major parties and the leaders of the three regions, particularly the Northern Region, applauded the regional arrangement.

Why did all the regional leaders at this point embrace regionalism in the context of multiculturalism? What constituted the historical circumstances that dictated this position in each case, and what were the responses? What were the differences in their approaches to regionalism in relation to multiculturalism and nationalism? I will attempt to answer these questions in the following sections.

MULTICULTURALISM: BETWEEN BURKEAN AND JACOBIN NATIONALISM

As I suggested earlier, the constitutive challenge of multiculturalism in Nigeria should be understood and analyzed mainly against the backdrop of the legacy of colonialism, particularly late colonialism—a period during which "prevailing communal forces reinforced regional networks of power and patronage that dominated political behavior."[57] By bringing together two separate territories and governing these for a few decades as two or three separate territories with two or three "distinct" *cultures,* the British, with the ironic collaboration of the leaders of the ethno-regional political parties in the colonial era, created a politics in which multiculturalism became a *crisis* or a problem to be confronted and transcended, rather than an asset to be embraced and managed. In Nigeria ethnic and ethno-regional self-consciousness thus produced a situation in which "relationship among groups was one of ethnic stratification…rather than ethnic coexistence."[58] This problem was exacerbated, as Coleman correctly noted, by the uneasy balance between the main three groups, which left them "as in all situations of bi- or tripolarity, vulnerable to the delicate balance of their ethnic duality or plurality suddenly giving way to a polarization into total ethnic bloc opposition or rivalry."[59]

Since no territorial or political unity had existed before, no real unity was achieved, despite the fact that most of the nationalists paid lip service to, or indeed desired, national "unity-in-diversity." As Rupert Emerson observed: "Where there is original unity, nationalism serves further to unite; where there is a felt ethnic diversity, nationalism is no cure."[60] It is important, therefore, to understand the different approaches of the major pre- and immediate post-independence ethnoregional blocs, political parties, and regional leaders to multiculturalism through the lens of the traditions of Jacobin and Burkean forms of nationalism.

Jacobin Nationalism: Azikiwe, the NCNC, and the Eastern Region

The National Council of Nigerian Citizens, under the leadership of the Nigerian nationalist, journalist, and anti-colonial agitator par excellence, Dr. Nnamdi Azikiwe—an Igbo from eastern Nigeria—was Nigeria's earliest example of a political party driven by a Jacobin approach to multiculturalism. Although the NCNC was later identified with the Igbo-dominated eastern region of Nigeria, it was founded, Azikiwe stated, "in order to unify the various elements of our communities … and to emancipate our *nation* from the manacles of political bondage [emphasis added]."[61]

The mantra of the Jacobin form of nationalism, emerging from the French experience, is *la nation une et indivisible* (the nation, one and indivisible). Its goal was to combine "the heritage of the different regions . . . in one national heritage; producing a republican monocultural universalism from disparity."[62] As Tom Furniss would have described it, the NCNC's form of nationalism was a "modernizing nationalism that sought to replace local identities and differences with a homogenized national politics and culture."[63]

Among the nationalist leaders, Azikiwe, using the NCNC and his chain of newspapers, particularly the *West African Pilot*, was the most vociferous about creating a nation that sidestepped or transcended the existing "tribal" (ethnic) groups and emergent ethno-regional arrangements. Despite Azikiwe's rather ironic position as the president of the Ibo State Union, and his statement at the 1949 conference of the union that "it would appear that the God of Africa has specially created the Ibo [Igbo] nation to lead the children of Africa from the bondage of the ages,"[64] he and his chain newspapers were opposed to the building of what the *Pilot* called "ethnic shrines." Azikiwe, the NCNC, and the *Pilot* insisted that they were championing an "integral nationalism" and offered themselves "as the protector of morally superior national values and interests," to use André van de Putte's words.[65] Azikiwe argued that the recognition and validation of ethnic particularities were antithetical to the emergence of a strong and united Nigeria. Despite its multicultural heritage, Nigeria ought to become a melting pot rather than a potpourri, he argued. This position was adopted by many Igbo leaders and intellectuals in late colonial Nigeria and thus became not only the NCNC's position, but also the "Igbo position," given the preponderance of Igbo support for the party and its leader. The *Pilot* dismissed any contrary position as "pakistanization," a metaphor for the feared balkanization of Nigeria (along Indian/Pakistani lines) by those championing federalism.

Azikiwe at some points supported the adoption of a federal system for Nigeria, even though federalism involves a fundamental recognition of difference and diversity, allowing complex societies to manage their common affairs at a central level while also guaranteeing the independence of constituent units in the management of their local affairs.[66] Between 1943 and 1948, he advocated that Nigeria be divided into eight protectorates, some of which roughly coincided with ethnic boundaries, in a federal colony. In 1948, in its Freedom Charter, the NCNC also advocated a federal system based strictly on ethnic units.[67] This was a clear acknowledgement of the country's multiculturalism.

However, in 1951, Azikiwe and the NCNC leaders suddenly changed their minds. The party stated that "in view of recent *divisionist tendencies* in the country and to accelerate the attainment of our goal for a united Nigeria, a unitary form of government with the acceptance of the principle of constituencies will be better for Nigeria [emphasis added]."[68] The excuse for the new position was that the colonial government "and anti-NCNC Nigerians were using *federalism as a cloak for dismembering Nigeria* [emphasis added]."[69] As Coleman correctly notes, other, perhaps more critical, reasons for the change were the emergence of a strong and well-organized political party in the Western Region, the Action Group (AG), and the structure and organization of the 1951 Macpherson Constitution—which succeeded the Richards Constitution. Based on a more democratic process than was followed in the adoption of the Richards Constitution, the Legislative Council in Lagos appointed a select committee to consider the question of the status of the national capital, Lagos. As a member of the committee (representing the NCNC), Azikiwe wrote a minority report in which he objected to the tripartite division of the country into regions, or what he called a "tri-sected Pakistanized country."[70] He argued for "the division of the country along the main [ten] ethnic and/or linguistic groups in order to enable each group to exercise local and cultural autonomy."[71] The position of Azikiwe and the NCNC might seem inconsistent, but the emergence of the Yoruba-dominated AG in the Western Region (which at some point included Lagos), where the NCNC had held sway, meant that the party faced the possibility of defeat in the Regional House of Assembly under a federal system, as indeed happened later in the 1951 elections.[72]

Azikiwe and NCNC members insisted that their party—unlike the others, particularly the AG, and later the Northern People's Congress (NPC)—was championing the building of a "homogeneous" nation. It was not until 1954 that Azikiwe and the NCNC again accepted the federal system in the march toward Nigeria's independence. However, it was obvious to the other parties and regions of Nigeria, that this was a grudging acceptance of the reality, resulting from the rigidity of the stances of the Action Group/Western Region and the NPC/Northern Region. Indeed, Azikiwe and the NCNC never abandoned their position that regionalism and ethno-regional parties were manifestations of "division" rather than diversity. In the rhetoric and writings of Azikiwe and the spokesman of the NCNC, multiculturalism was portrayed as a problem for any emerging African nation-state. What the others saw as the refusal of Azikiwe and the NCNC/Eastern Region to accept the reality of Nigeria's multicultural composition by canvassing for a unitary system was linked to fears of what the other two major ethno-regional groups described as an attempt at "Ibo [Igbo] domination" of Nigeria. This continued to hover above ethno-political relations, thus defining the relationship among the three major groups. It also partly provoked the countercoup led by northern soldiers against the Igbo-led military regime in July 1966 and, eventually, the Nigerian Civil War (1967–70).

Burkean Nationalism: Awolowo, the AG, and the Western Region

In contrast to the Jacobin form of nationalism championed by Azikiwe and the NCNC, Chief Obafemi Awolowo and the Action Group articulated a Burkean notion of nationalism, which fitted Nigeria's multicultural nature, even though it had the potential to acerbate ethnic tension and deepen existing conflicts, particularly between the two major southern ethnic groups, the Igbo and the Yoruba.

In arguing against French "revolutionary nationalism . . . whose centrist and potentially totalitarian tendencies he represents as destructive of the sense of nation,"[73] Edmund Burke supported "such divisions of our country as have been formed by habit, and not by a sudden jerk of authority," adding that "the love to the whole is not extinguished by this subordinate partiality."[74] For Burke, local attachments, identifications, and loyalties were not barriers to national ones, but only prepared the mind for larger loyalty. In advocating for a hierarchy of loyalties, "each supreme in its own sphere,"[75] Burke pointed to the form of multicultural nationalism that Awolowo and AG advocated for Nigeria.

Unlike the NCNC members and its leader, who emphasized their pan-Nigerian identity, Coleman argues that, "more in the tradition of Burke, Awolowo had always been a Yoruba nationalist first and a pan-Nigerian nationalist second."[76] Therefore, from "the beginning . . . there was a fundamental difference in attitude regarding the ends toward which the nationalist movement should be directed."[77] When the Egbe Omo Oduduwa (Society of the Descendants of Oduduwa) was formed as a cultural organization for the Yoruba, first in London in 1945 and later in Nigeria in 1948, the group advertised two of its objectives to include the acceleration of "the emergence of a virile modernized and efficient Yoruba state with its own individuality within the Federal State of Nigeria," while striving "earnestly to cooperate with existing ethnic and regional associations and such as may exist thereafter, in matters of common interest to all Nigerians, so as to thereby attain to unity in federation."[78]

The Egbe later became the basis of the creation of a political party, the Action Group, devoted to capturing power in the Western Region in the decolonization period. The party, led by Awolowo, resolved that "under the circumstances then prevailing in [late colonial] Nigeria the only certain avenue to power was a regional political party."[79] Thus, one of its most important campaign strategies for mobilizing support in the region was opposition to Azikiwe, the NCNC, and the threat of "Igbo domination" under the unitary system.

In his autobiography, Awolowo states that he wanted to rebuild Yorubaland to ensure that every cultural group would have its rightful place in a multicultural Nigeria. This attitude and the activities geared toward validating it were dismissed by the NCNC and Azikiwe's *Pilot* as a process of the "pakistanization" of Nigeria. The *Pilot* regarded AG's version of multiculturalism as a "determination to remain difficult to Nigerian unity" through the imposition of "the evils of regionalization."[80] The AG was described as a "parochial party," pursuing "parochial nationalism" and engaging in "tribalistic demarcation of the country,"[81] as opposed to the NCNC, which had a "national policy."[82]

In *Path to Nigerian Freedom*, Awolowo emphatically rejected the unitary system, arguing that "since the amalgamation, all the efforts of the British Government have been devoted to developing the country into a unitary state. . . . This is patently impossible." He added that although the existing three regions were "designed for administrative convenience, a truly federal system would require boundary readjustments to ensure that each group, however small, is entitled to the same treatment as any other group, however large. . . . Opportunity must be afforded to each to evolve its own peculiar political institution."[83]

In the end, by leveraging Yoruba cultural nationalism, Awolowo and the Action Group not only contested the Jacobin "revolutionary nationalism" preached by Azikiwe and the NCNC but successfully promoted a Burkean recognition of a hierarchy of loyalties in a multicultural federal state in which each component part of the federation, at least notionally, was supreme in its own sphere. However, Awolowo and the AG did not succeed in making ethno-linguistic units the component parts of a multicultural Nigerian state. The units remained three (later four) multi-ethnic regions until 1967, when they became states.

Neo-Burkean Nationalism: Bello, the NPC, and the Northern Region

Given its delayed and reluctant encounter with European modernity, the Northern Protectorate, the huge, conservative laager constructed around the Fulani-led caliphate that emerged from the 1804 jihad, had an understandably different attitude to the struggle for national unity as Nigeria moved toward independence. Apart from the factors already mentioned above, several other factors also provided the context for the specific approach that the Northern Region, its dominant party, the Northern People's Congress (NPC), and its preeminent leader, Sir Ahmadu Bello, adopted in responding to the challenges of national unity after the two protectorates were amalgamated to form a single British colony.[84]

These included the insulation of the Northern Protectorate from Christian missionary conversion and the enlightenment campaign—including expansion of opportunities for Western education—which strengthened existing differences and ratified it strongly along ethno-regional lines; a shift in the production of cash crops for export;[85] and the expansion and consolidation of Islamic influence and dominance based on the numerical strength of the combined ethnicities of the Hausa and the Fulani (Hausa-Fulani) in much of the Northern Region. The British colonial officers in the Northern Protectorate too were instrumental in this process. Such was their commitment to making the north distinct from the south, despite the amalgamation, that between 1923 and 1947, the northern leaders were not represented in the central Nigerian Legislative Council in Lagos, the capital of colonial Nigeria. Therefore, the north lagged behind the south in engaging with modern democratic institutions and practices. These led to fears of southern domination, the policy of "northernization" in the late colonial and early postcolonial eras, the north's initial opposition to Nigeria's independence in the mid-1950s and a unique outlook on multiculturalism that admitted of a different standpoint for the multicultural region from the one adopted for the whole of Nigeria. Thus, while northern leaders, led by Ahmadu Bello, were eager to unify the Northern Region and transcend cultural, ethnic, and religious differences within the region, particularly among the region's many minority groups,[86] they insisted that Nigeria was a multicultural polity, in which the Northern Region must be recognized as a single cultural whole as well as a united political community. This was despite the fact that "the Northern Region is not a cultural or a historical unit."[87] Indeed, "from a tribal standpoint," Coleman observed, "the north is far more heterogeneous than the south," notwithstanding that the "integrative bonds of Islam and the Fulani Empire, however, [gave] a large part of the north a certain feeling of identity."[88] This background is important, because the reality in the north, or the way in which that reality was understood by the leaders of the NPC in relation to the rest of Nigeria, dictated their approach to multiculturalism, particularly in response to the most suitable political system for Nigeria as the country approached independence in the late 1940s and the 1950s.

Even though both Bello and Awolowo preached Burkean nationalism, the Bello NPC's articulation of why and how federalism was the most suitable political system for "understanding" and protecting differences was qualitatively different from the Awolowo AG's. It emerged from a different reading of history and comparative experience. The AG-Awolowo position emerged from a deliberate, elaborate analysis of both local and global experiences of multiculturalism and was influenced by desire for power in the emerging political configuration, whereas the Bello-NPC position was influenced largely both by fears of southern domination in a unitary system and the associated disagreement with the southern leaders over a proposal, favored by the AG and NCNC, that Nigeria be granted independence in 1956. The leaders of the Northern Region felt that the region was not ready and thus risked the substitution of internal (Southern Nigerian) "colonialism" for the British variety. The northern leaders' position followed a pattern adopted by groups that felt disadvantaged by the move toward independence and thus attempted "to slow down the march to independence or to gain special concessions," as famously noted by Donald Horowitz.[89]

While Bello and NPC focused on and campaigned for *regional multiculturalism,* that is, the recognition of each region as a cultural unit within the federation of Nigeria, and the primary form of affiliation/nationalism, Awolowo and the AG favored *ethno-linguistic multiculturalism,*[90] that is, a federation of nationalities, with ethnic nationality as the primary form of affiliation/nationalism. Awolowo emphasized the country's multiculturalism, noting that groups called "tribes" were actually "nations," and cited ten such groups recorded during the 1931 census, the Hausa, Ibo (Igbo), Yoruba, Fulani, Kanuri, Ibiobio, Munshi or Tiv, Edo, Nupe, and Ijaw.[91] There was "as much difference between them as there is between Germans, English, Russians, and Turks," he observed, and the fact that they had "a common overlord [the British] does not destroy this fundamental difference." The languages of these groups "differ. . . . Their cultural backgrounds and social outlooks differ widely; and their indigenous political institutions have little in common. Their present stages of development vary. . . . It is evident from the experiences of other nations that incompatibilities such as we have enumerated are barriers which cannot be overcome by glossing over them. They are *real,* not imaginary, obstacles."[92] Bello shared this position only to the extent that the differences were limited to external regional differences, not differences internal to the region, particularly his own Northern Region. Thus, for Bello, the Northern Region was a cultural unit, while for Awolowo, the ethno-linguistic group ought to be the cultural unit. Therefore, for Awolowo, the Hausa-Fulani (ethno-cultural group) would be a federating unit rather than the north (region), as favored by Bello.

After the crisis over the date of independence, as Bello notes in his autobiography, the Northern Region decided to "take a modified line."[93] He elaborated on this by stating that the Northern Region "must aim at a looser structure for Nigeria while preserving its general pattern—a structure which would give the regions the greatest possible freedom of movement and action; a structure which would reduce the powers of the Centre to the absolute minimum and yet retain sufficient national unity for practical and international purposes."[94] He advocated for a "federal principle" in which "what happened in Lagos [the federal capital, would not be] of great consequences . . . in the north."[95]

Eventually, the federal system adopted by Nigeria at independence was largely a compromise between the Bello-NPC-Northern Region and Awolowo-AG-Western Region positions. As one of the earliest scholars of Nigerian federalism notes, these two were the most vociferous in "repeating that they would not be dominated by other areas of tribal groups."[96] However, even while notionally encouraging multiculturalism, structurally, the federal system adopted in Nigeria before independence leveraged multiculturalism while limiting it largely to ethnoregional differences. This became a problem in the post-independence era, since minority groups in the three regions demanded greater recognition of their differences from the three big ethnic groups.[97]

THE LIMITS OF REGIONALIST FEDERALISM

Some scholars have argued that one of the primary steps that must be taken to achieve a "fuller conception of multiculturalism" in the quest to "deal with diversity" is to break down "the false opposition between unity and difference, between solidarity and diversity, or . . . between universalism and particularism."[98] Against this backdrop, they propose that multiculturalism should be approached in multiple ways as (i) "a critical-theoretical project," (ii) "an exercise in cultivating new conceptions of solidarity in the context of dealing with the realities of pervasive and increasing diversity," (iii) "a response—or a set of responses—to diversity that seeks to articulate the social conditions under which difference can be incorporated . . . and order achieved from diversity."[99] Hartmann and Gerteis argue for bringing these different approaches into a "productive tension with each other" in order to reconcile different "visions of difference."

The Nigerian case examined here illustrates the fundamental challenges faced in the attempt to reconcile "visions of [multicultural] difference," as well as the problem of constructing a workable political system to accommodate and address the difference. Even though the federalists won the debate in the late colonial era, with Nigeria becoming a federation at independence, it was specifically the *regionalist version* of multiculturalism that triumphed, insofar as the struggles by minority groups for recognition beyond tokenism were largely ignored in the tripartite arrangement—a Hausa-Fulani-dominated Northern Region, an Igbo-dominated Eastern Region, and a Yoruba-dominated Western Region—that was established. However, the attempt to return the country to a unitary system after the January 1966 coup had disastrous consequences including the civil war, in which more than a million people died. Multiculturalism is not antithetical in principle to nationbuilding, but it has served contradictory purposes in the Nigerian federation. Though the multicultural nature of the country is not always respected and honored, recognition of the multicultural nature of the federation and the limitations and responsibilities this imposes on political leaders have, on the one hand, prevented Nigeria from fully achieving its potential as a rich, powerful nation in the developing world, and, on the other hand, averted the total disintegration of the country. Also, although there is a popular view in Nigeria that the recognition of the country's multiculturalism has thwarted national integration, there is also a conflicting popular recognition of the fact that even the existing instrumental recognition of multiculturalism helps in the unending struggle to ensure that all the major cultures are given a measure of, if not equal, space and value.

Shortly before the civil war, the political elite seemed to have reached a consensus regarding the wisdom of some of the country's leaders who had earlier advocated multiple territorial division of the country beyond the three regions (later four in 1963) inherited from colonial rule. Even though the twelve states that emerged from the four regions before the outbreak of civil war did not exactly match the ethno-linguistic divisions proposed in the 1940s and 1950s—apart from the fact that this was specifically geared toward discouraging the minorities in the old Eastern Region from supporting the Igbo-led attempted secession—the creation of more states pointed to greater recognition of the multicultural reality of the Nigerian federation. It was evident, as James Coleman had predicted in his 1958 book *Nigeria: Background to Nationalism*, that the country could not survive on the basis of exclusive regional multiculturalism with the (structural) region-based federalism that was adopted at independence.

The end of the civil war (1967–70) witnessed greater recognition and accommodation, even if not totally satisfactory, of minority interests, and a greater embrace of Nigeria's multicultural realities. Structural unitarism was adopted by a succession of the misnamed federal military governments (1966–79; 1983–99) in the guise of federalism, but in spite of the structural unitary system, the division of the country into more and more states (three regions, four regions, twelve states, nineteen states, twenty-one states, thirty states, and now thirty-six states) has to some extent decreased tension over the nonrecognition of difference. Nonetheless, this solution constitutes what Eghosa Osaghae calls a "broad catch-all" policy.[100] Still, the fundamental questions regarding the terms of national relations remain critical and in "productive tension," in Nigeria,[101] particularly because bi- or tri-polarity still largely determines the nature of power sharing at the highest level of national relations. This has since been further divided administratively into six zones: north-west, north-east, north-central, south-east, south-west, and south-south.

CONCLUSIONS

The Nigerian experience, as reflected in the debates on the best political system in the late colonial era, points to the failure of assimilationism in multi-ethnic polities in Africa. The attempt to deny the mediating role of ethnic and cultural groups and "deal with difference by removing it,"[102] championed by the Azikiwe NCNC, did not succeed. What triumphed in the late colonial era was what Hartman and Gerteis have described as "fragmented pluralism," based on "strong preexisting group boundaries," with a strong emphasis on the maintenance of "distinctive group cultures."[103] This is the opposite of assimilationism, of course, and it was what the Bello NPC and the Awolowo AG supported and practiced. The orientation to diversity in this model is "closest to the standard definition of multiculturalism." In late colonial Nigeria, the ethno-regional group was regarded as the *valid* group. In this sense, because the three (later four) regions and even the ethnic groups subsumed under them were also based on what Durkheim described as "mechanical solidarity," "group boundaries [were] policed in the way that social boundaries [would have been] in assimilationism."[104]

Yet, although fragmented pluralism was triumphant in the pre- and immediate post-independence period, what the pluralists actually *preached* in the emphasis on "understanding difference," as Bello articulated it, was a "better" form of pluralism, that is, "interactive pluralism." I suggest that this is what the Burkean notion of nationalism actually aims for. It is what Nigeria's postcolonial leaders, despite their actions, have also publicly valorized. As explained by Hartman and Gerteis, interactive pluralism emphasizes "mutual recognition and respect of difference," even while insisting on "the importance of the [ethno-regional] groups as primary basis for association in society."[105] However, because the "groups in interaction" were based on mutual fears and negative evaluations of the other groups' assumed intention, Nigerian multiculturalism in the late colonial and early postcolonial era was fragmented rather than interactive. Though much hope was expressed for an emergent unity in the future that would honor and respect multiculturalism, token efforts were undertaken in terms of "substantive commitments" to produce sustainable democratic federalism. However, despite the fact that federalism has survived without being entrenched in post-independence Nigeria,[106] the survival has been sufficient in keeping the multicultural state together, even if the nature and ideal of multiculturalism continue to be contested.

NOTES

1. A version of this chapter was published in *Commonwealth and Comparative Studies* (2017). The author thanks the publishers of the journal, Taylor & Francis, for permission to republish it.

2. Will Kymlicka, *Multiculturalism: Success, Failure, and the Future* (Washington, DC: Migration Policy Institute, 2012), 1.

3. See also Bhikhu Parekh, *Rethinking Multiculturalism: Cultural Diversity and Political Theory* (Cambridge, MA: Harvard University Press, 2002); Anne Phillips, *Multiculturalism without Culture* (Princeton, NJ: Princeton University Press, 2007); Tariq Modood, *Multiculturalism* (Malden, MA: Polity Press, 2007); Paul Sniderman and Louk Hagendoorn, *When Ways of Life Collide: Multiculturalism and Its Discontents in the Netherlands* (Princeton, NJ: Princeton University Press, 2007); and George Crowder, *Theories of Multiculturalism: An Introduction* (Malden, MA: Polity Press, 2013).

4. For a few exceptions, see Charles R. Hale, "Does Multiculturalism Menace? Governance, Cultural Rights and the Politics of Identity in Guatemala," *Journal of Latin American Studies* 34 (2002): 485–524.

5. Will Kymlicka, *Multicultural Citizenship: A Liberal Theory of Minority Rights* (Oxford: Clarendon Press, 1995), 1, and Crowder, *Theories of Multiculturalism*, 2.

6. Parekh, *Rethinking Multiculturalism*, 6.

7. See Will Kymlicka, *Finding Our Way: Rethinking Ethnocultural Relations in Canada* (Oxford: Oxford University Press, 1998); Kymlicka, *Politics in the Vernacular: Nationalism, Multiculturalism, and Citizenship* (Oxford: Oxford University Press, 2001); Kymlicka, *Multicultural Odysseys: Navigating the New International Politics of Diversity* (Oxford: Oxford University Press, 2007); Kymlicka, *Multiculturalism*; Kymlicka, *Multicultural Citizenship*; Charles Taylor, "The Politics of Recognition," in *Multiculturalism: Examining the Politics of Recognition*, ed. Amy Gutmann (Princeton, NJ: Princeton University Press, 1994); Crowder, *Theories of Multiculturalism*; Modood, *Multiculturalism*; and Parekh, *Rethinking Multiculturalism*.

8. See, among others, Phillips, *Multiculturalism without Culture*.

9. See Donald L. Horowitz, *A Democratic South Africa? Constitutional Engineering in a Divided Society* (Berkeley: University of California Press, 1991); Crain Soudien, "Dealing with Race: Laying Down Patterns for Multiculturalism in South Africa," *Interchange* 25, no. 3 (1994): 281–94; and Simon Bekker and Anne Leidé, "Is Multiculturalism a Workable Policy in South Africa?" *International Journal on Multicultural Societies* 5, no. 2 (2003): 121–36.

10. Kymlicka, *Multiculturalism*, 6.

11. Amy Gutmann, "The Challenge of Multiculturalism in Political Ethics," *Philosophy & Public Affairs* 22, no. 3 (1993): 171.

12. Asef Bayat, *Life as Politics* (Stanford, CA: Stanford University Press, 2009), 186.

13. Abdullahi Tasiu Abubakar, "Analysis: What Did Nigeria's National Conference Achieve?" BBC, August 24, 2014.

14. Ibid.

15. Ibid.

16. "Though tribe and tongue may differ / In brotherhood *[sic]* we stand," the anthem proclaims.

17. David Theo Goldberg, "Introduction," in *Multiculturalism: A Critical Reader*, ed. David Theo Goldberg (Malden, MA: Blackwell, 1994), 7.

18. Hale, "Does Multiculturalism Menace?" contends that even if multiculturalism is not inherently a menace, it nevertheless has the potential *to menace*.

19. John N. Paden, *Ahmadu Bello, Sardauna of Sokoto: Values and Leadership in Nigeria* (London: Hodder & Stoughton, 1986), 3.

20. Sniderman and Hagendoorn, *When Ways of Life Collide*, xi.

21. Bello viewed the northern regional community "as a 'trans-ethnic' community, or a federation within a federation," Paden argues (*Ahmadu Bello*, 314), but in fact, he approached multiculturalism primarily in terms of the differences between the northern region (with majority Muslim population) and the southern region (with majority Christian population).

22. Nigeria and Ethiopia (since 1995) are the two fully federal systems in Africa. A few other nations have quasi-federal systems or systems with federal features.

23. See Isawa Elaigwu, "Federal Systems Not New to Africa," *Federations*, December 2010–January 2011.

24. One of the most important factors that also informed this attitude was authoritarian rule prevalent in independent African nations.

25. See Bekker and Leidé, "Is Multiculturalism a Workable Policy in South Africa?" and Soudien, "Dealing with Race."

26. Frederick Lugard, *Dual Mandate in British Tropical Africa* (Edinburgh: William Blackwood & Sons, 1922), 199. See also Anthony Hamilton Millard Kirk-Greene, *Lugard and the Amalgamation of Nigeria: A Documentary Record* (London: Frank Cass, 1969), 70.

27. Mahmood Mamdani, *Citizen and Subject: Contemporary Africa and the Legacy of Late Colonialism* (Princeton, NJ: Princeton University Press, 1996), 7.

28. Ibid., 8.

29. Ibid.

30. Ibid., 52.

31. See, e.g., ibid., 8; and Olufemi Vaughan, "Ethno-Regionalism and the Origins of Federalism in Nigeria," in *Democracy and Prebendalism in Nigeria: Critical Interpretations,* ed. Wale Adebanwi and Ebenezer Obadare (New York: Palgrave Macmillan, 2013), 230.

32. Richard L. Sklar, *Nigerian Political Parties: Power in an Emergent African Nation* (Princeton, NJ: Princeton University Press, 1963), 18

33. James S. Coleman, *Nigeria: Background to Nationalism* (Berkeley: University of California Press, 1958), 194.

34. Sniderman and Hagendoorn, *When Ways of Life Collide,* xi.

35. Coleman, *Nigeria,* 45–46.

36. Ibid., 48.

37. Michael Vickers, *A Nation Betrayed: Nigeria and the Minorities Commission of 1957* (Trenton: Africa World Press, 2010), 3.

38. Kymlikca, *Multicultural Citizenship,* 5.

39. Coleman, *Nigeria,* 48.

40. Kymlicka, *Multicultural Citizenship,* 5.

41. Mamdani, *Citizen and Subject,* 298–99.

42. Obafemi Awolowo, *Path to Nigerian Freedom* (London: Faber & Faber, 1947), 47.

43. Ibid.

44. Margery Perham, "Foreword," in Obafemi Awolowo, *Path to Nigerian Freedom* (London: Faber & Faber, 1947), 14.

45. Ibid.

46. Ibid.

47. Modood, *Multiculturalism,* 5.

48. Sniderman and Hagendoorn, *When Ways of Life Collide,* xi.

49. Strands of these discourses are gleaned from the major accounts by the leaders, their biographers, the classic texts on Nigerian politics, and Nigerian newspapers in the 1940s and 1950s. See also Wale Adebanwi, *Nation as Grand Narrative: The Nigerian Press and the Politics of Meaning* (Rochester, NY: University of Rochester Press, 2016).

50. Sklar, *Nigerian Political Parties,* 87.

51. Ibid., 87.

52. Coleman, *Nigeria,* 273.

53. British colonial officials who supported the northern region were also fearful of a unitary system in Nigeria because the "educated elements in coastal towns [meaning Lagos and other parts of the south] would become predominant." See Coleman, *Nigeria,* 275.

54. Ibid., 276.

55. Ibid.

56. Ibid., 276–77.

57. Vaughan, "Ethno-Regionalism," in *Democracy and Prebendalism in Nigeria,* ed. Adebanwi and Obadare, 231.

58. Coleman, *Nigeria,* 129.

59. Ibid., 129.

60. Cited in ibid., 130.

61. Nnamdi Azikiwe, *Zik: A Selection from the Speeches of Nnamdi Azikiwe* (Cambridge: Cambridge University Press, 1961), 163.

62. André van de Putte, "Nationalism and Nation," *Ethical Perspectives* 1 (1994): 114.

63. Tom Furniss, "Cementing the Nation: Burke's *Reflections* on Nationalism and National Identity," in *Edmund Burke's Reflections on the Revolution in France: New Interdisciplinary Essays,* ed. John Whale (Manchester: Manchester University Press, 2000), 138.

64. Coleman, *Nigeria*, 347.

65. Van de Putte, "Nationalism and Nation," 14.

66. K. C. Wheare, *Federal Government* (Oxford: Oxford University Press, 1963), 19.

67. Coleman, *Nigeria*, 347.

68. Ibid., 324.

69. Ibid., 348.

70. Azikiwe, *Zik*, 173

71. Quoted in Coleman, *Nigeria*, 348.

72. The late Nigerian political scientist Billy Dudley pointed out, however, that the Western and Northern regions, which benefitted most from rising commodity prices in the 1950s, were the strongest advocates of federalism, and that Nigeria's political leaders were "positively attracted" by the Australian academic Sir Kenneth Clinton Wheare's collegial model of federalism as a "method of dividing powers so that the general and regional governments are each within a sphere co-ordinate and independent" (K. C. Wheare, *Federal Government*, 4th ed. (London: Oxford University Press, 1963), 11). These may have been supporting factors, but I think that the leaders' articulation of their reasons, as examined here, do not support Dudley's conclusion. See B. J. Dudley, "Federalism and the Balance of Political Power in Nigeria," *Journal of Commonwealth Political Studies* 4, no. 1 (1966): 16–29.

73. Furniss, "Cementing the Nation," 136.

74. Quoted in ibid., 138.

75. Carlton Hayes, *The Historical Evolution of Modern Nationalism* (New York: Macmillan, 1931), 93.

76. Coleman, *Nigeria*, 351.

77. Ibid., 351.

78. S. O. Arifalo, *The Egbe Omo Oduduwa: A Study in Ethnic and Cultural Nationalism, 1945–1965* (Akure, Nigeria: Stebak Books, 2001), 107–8, and Wale Adebanwi, *Yoruba Elites and Ethnic Politics in Nigeria: Obafemi Awolowo and Corporate Agency* (New York: Cambridge University Press, 2014), 53.

79. Coleman, *Nigeria*, 350.

80. *Pilot*, July 19, 1952, 2.

81. *Pilot*, October 1, 1952, 2.

82. *Pilot*, July 19, 1952, 2.

83. Coleman, *Nigeria*, 324.

84. See ibid.; C. S. Whitaker Jr., *The Politics of Tradition: Continuity and Change in Northern Nigeria, 1946–1966* (Princeton, NJ: Princeton University Press, 1970); and Vaughan, "Ethno-Regionalism," in *Democracy and Prebendalism in Nigeria*, ed. Adebanwi and Obadare.

85. Coleman, *Nigeria*, 353.

86. "Our aim," Bello said in an address to the people of the northern region, "is to unify the North and make all tribes living in the Region feel that they are one and the same people. The people of the North are in fact already one" (Paden, *Ahmadu Bello*, 151n32).

87. Coleman, *Nigeria*, 354.

88. Ibid.

89. Donald Horowitz, *Ethnic Groups in Conflict* (Berkeley: University of California Press, 1985), 4.

90. In his *Political Blueprint of Nigeria* (1943), Azikiwe, too, "envisaged a federal commonwealth of Nigeria made up of eight "protectorates," whose boundaries roughly followed ethnic lines" (Coleman, *Nigeria*, 324). He later changed his mind.

91. Awolowo, *Path to Nigerian Freedom*, 48.

92. Ibid., 48–49.

93. Ahmadu Bello, *My Life* (Cambridge: Cambridge University Press, 1962), 136.

94. Ibid.

95. Ibid., 227.

96. John P. Mackintosh, "Federalism in Nigeria," *Political Studies* 10, no. 3 (1962): 223.

97. See Eghosa E. Osaghae, "Federalism, Local Politics and Ethnicity in Nigeria: Do Ethnic Minorities Still Exist in Nigeria?" *Journal of Commonwealth & Comparative Politics* 24, no. 2 (1986): 151–68; Osaghae, "Ethnic Minorities and Federalism in Nigeria," *African Affairs* 90, no. 359 (1991): 237–58; Osaghae, "Managing Multiple Minority Problems in a Divided Society: The Nigerian Experience," *Journal of Modern African Studies* 36, no. 1 (1998): 1–24; Rotimi Suberu, *Federalism and Ethnic Conflict in Nigeria* (Washington, DC: United States Institute of Peace Press, 2001); and Suberu, "Federalism in Africa: The Nigerian Experience in Comparative Perspective," *Ethnopolitics* 8, no. 1 (2009): 67–86. For the background to this, see Vickers, *Nation Betrayed*.

98. Douglas Hartmann and Joseph Gerteis, "Dealing with Diversity: Mapping Multiculturalism in Sociological Terms," *Sociological Theory* 23, no. 2 (2005): 221.

99. Ibid., 222.

100. "By taking states rather than ethnic groups as the units to be represented and balanced, the federal character principle favored majorities and powerful minorities, as opposed to the ordinary (or 'residual') minorities which were dominated in the states" (Osaghae, "Managing Multiple Minority Problems," 19).

101. Such "productive tension" is partly responsible for the rise of fundamentalist religious groups such as Boko Haram that seek to obliterate Nigeria's multicultural society and establish an Islamic state.

102. Hartman and Gerteis, "Dealing with Diversity," 226.

103. Ibid., 230.

104. Ibid.

105. Ibid.

106. See, e.g., Suberu, "Federalism in Africa," 67.

10

Arrested Multiculturalisms

Race, Capitalism, and State Formation in Malaysia and Singapore

Daniel P. S. Goh, National University of Singapore

Malaysia and Singapore are often hailed as pluralistic postcolonial countries that have succeeded in institutionalizing peaceful and stable ethnic relations. Malaysia is a federal constitutional monarchy spread over nearly 330,000 square kilometers and divided into Peninsular Malaysia and East Malaysia on the island of Borneo. Of the country's over twenty-nine million people, around half consider themselves Malays, and another one-tenth are indigenous peoples, both making up the important political category of *bumiputera* (literally, "son of the soil" in the Malay language) peoples. The two largest minority groups are the Chinese and the Indians, mostly second- and third-generation descendants of migrants, comprising a quarter and one-fourteenth of the population respectively. Non-naturalized new migrants make up a tenth of the population. Singapore is a republic and island city-state of only over 710 square kilometers sitting at the tip of the Malay Peninsula. Over a third of its 5.3 million population are non-citizens. Among the citizens, almost three-quarters are Chinese, 13 percent are Malays, and 9 percent are Indians.

The achievement of peaceful ethnic relations is remarkable, given that the tumultuous post–World War II decades witnessed the alignment of class struggles and ethnic conflicts. Both countries are successor states to the swath of colonial territory that was known as British Malaya and British Borneo. After the war, the British prepared for decolonization and promoted multiracial citizenship to integrate the disparate ethnic groups making up the local population. The next two decades saw policy reversals and nationalist machinations, guerrilla insurgency and civil strife, and the merger of Malaya, British Borneo, and Singapore into

Malaysia, culminating in the fatal Chinese-Malay racial riots in Singapore in 1964, which led to the separation of Singapore from Malaysia, and in Malaysia in 1969.

These traumatic events pushed forward divergent economic development programs aimed at resolving the political conflict, and institutional arrangements that utilized different forms of multiracialism as the foundation for nation-building. Patronage multiracialism was institutionalized in Malaysia, and corporatist multiracialism in Singapore, aligned with economic policy to promote *bumiputera* and statist capital accumulation respectively. Now, after decades of political stability and economic growth, the old multiracialism is fraying due to economic crises, and the new multiculturalisms envisioned in the 1990s in the midst of reforms in response to globalization have failed to take off.

In this chapter, I discuss the divergence of multiracialism and the arrested development of multiculturalism in Malaysia and Singapore. Against conventional explanations privileging nationalism as the main theoretical register, I argue that both the divergence and arrested development were primarily influenced by state formation in relation to capitalist development. In turn, the trajectories of capitalist development and state formation were heavily shaped by the contradictions of colonial racial formation and the political responses to these contradictions by both colonial and postcolonial actors. In other words, I argue that the divergent multiracialisms and the arrested multiculturalisms in contemporary Malaysia and Singapore have deep origins in the intertwining of race and economic development in colonial Malaya, particularly in the provision of migrant labor for the important tin-mining and rubber plantation export sectors.

Economic histories of Malaya tended to be written in the vein of J. S. Furnivall's theory of the plural society, which postulates the making of a medley of racial groups who interact in the marketplace but do not cohere as a nation.[1] The question has been framed as whether the plural society of disparate Chinese, Indian, and Malay groups was "the outcome of conscious government policies ascribing roles and capitalising on ethnic separation to make overall control easier and to promote British economic interests."[2] For the most part, scholars have interpreted the evidence to answer in the affirmative, that the colonial government promoted "deliberate segregation of labour along racial lines,"[3] or encouraged "a racialized division of labour."[4] For Charles Hirschman, the colonial political economy underpinned the racial ideology that saw each race as biologically programmed to fulfill specific economic functions, and this ideology in turn was used for the colonial census that informed economic and social developmental policy.[5]

While the theory of colonial pluralism could be fruitfully used as an analytical frame to understand the making of multiracialism in Malaysia and Singapore, historical narratives employing the frame tend to revert to a functionalist view of the relationship between state, economy and society.[6] These narratives treat racial ideology as functional in the production and maintenance of political control and economic exploitation, as though state actors had the clarity of mind and the institutional capacity to engineer political economies with mere racial ideas. This neglects the disruptive influence of events on historical processes that produce the possibility and probability of the events occurring in the first place. It also ignores the autonomy of racial discourses and their lineage in scholarly histories and colonial archives, and the political contestations between myriad groups of state and nonstate actors seeking to appropriate and subvert the discourses.

The approach I adopt here follows Michael Omi and Howard Winant's racial formation perspective, which takes race as a concept signifying social conflicts by indexing phenotypical features of the human body. Racial formation refers to the process of "historically situated projects" of interpreting and representing human bodies and society in order to organize and distribute resources along racial lines.[7] Colonial racial formation in Malaya refers to the process of ethnographic projects representing native bodies and colonial society in order to organize and distribute land and labor along racial lines in order to develop and maintain the colonial state. This privileges a focus on state actors but is justified because the colonial state, through gradual centralization and expansion over the decades from the 1870s to 1930s, was the single most powerful transformative agent in the colony. However, the racial formation perspective requires that my analysis also account for historical contingencies, including the discursive contestation, politics, and unintended consequences that flow from the underlying contradictions of colonial racial formation.

THE CONTRADICTIONS OF COLONIAL
RACIAL FORMATION

Nineteenth-century British interests in Southeast Asia led to the establishment of the Straits Settlements of Penang, Singapore, and Malacca as free ports, to which laissez-faire colonialism attracted Chinese merchants. Chinese mining and trade interests penetrated the neighboring Malay states on the peninsula using the Straits Settlements as their base. This exacerbated succession crises in the sultanates and fostered widespread political instability in the Straits region. Throughout the 1870s, local governors intervened in the Malay states of Perak and Selangor of their own accord, but London forced the governors to implement Resident rule by advice rather than direct rule. To pay for the start-up costs of government, the British supported development of Chinese tin mining, controlled by triad secret societies. Up till the turn of the century, Perak and Selangor state revenues depended heavily on a duty on tin, mining land rents, and taxing Chinese labor consumer goods such as opium. However, the colonial government did not see dependence on Chinese mining as tenable in the long run and encouraged European planting to supplant Chinese mining.

Shortage of labor hindered the development of the European estates. Some officials wanted to protect the customary authority of the Malay rajas, which entailed keeping the Malay peasantry in their kin-ordered villages. In any case, most offi-cials thought that their bountiful environment had made the Malay peasants too lazy and self-indulgent to supply useful labor to the European plantations. Chinese workers were favored for their industry, but they were "inclined to be disorderly, cost more in police and supervision, and give more trouble," the British surmised from frequent riots among the Chinese in the Straits Settlements. Tamil workers, however, were seen as "well-behaved and docile" and "accustomed to British rule."[8] Moreover, since southern India was under direct British rule, the supply of labor from there was better assured. The British therefore preferred Tamils. To keep up with the rubber boom in the 1900s, the government promoted free-wage labor by assisting in the recruitment and shipment of Tamil workers.

The state apparatus was greatly expanded and centralized in this period to deal with the exigencies of the boom. The Federal Council was established as a legisla-tive body structured along the lines of the Straits Legislative Council to better represent the interests of the increasing number of European planters and busi-nessmen resident in the Federated Malay States. An elite colonial civil service aided by a subordinate native service staffed mostly by Malays was expanded to oversee the rapid economic development. The Malay elites were no longer seen as a martial group to be salvaged by careful diplomacy. They were now racial resources valued for their local knowledge and to be deployed in the subordinate bureaucracy as assistants to British officers in rural districts.

Chinese labor, previously left alone, came under increasing governmental regu-lation in efforts to aid the previously neglected European tin-mining sector, which depended on heavy capital investment in machines, as opposed to labor-intensive Chinese mining. Malay farmers, who quickly caught onto the rubber boom and switched to rubber trees, also came under increasing regulation. Concerned about potential Chinese usurpation of Malay smallholdings, the colonial government enacted the Malay Reservations Act in 1913 "to provide protection for the Malays against themselves" by limiting land transactions in reservations to Malays.[9] To resolve food shortages during World War I, the colonial government also enforced rice cultivation on lands alienated to Malay farmers.

By the time the war ended, the key features of colonial racial formation in Malaya had become discernable. The state held a monopoly on the land in the name of the Malays, recruiting Malay elites to manage it. Malay peasants, meanwhile, were tied to the land and segregated from both market forces and the Chinese through the promotion of customary rice production. The distrusted Chinese were increasingly displaced from tin mining, obstructed in agricultural settlement, and left to fend for themselves in urban areas. Tamils, apparently obedient and docile, were imported to work the plantations. European capital dominated the tin and rubber sectors, and Chinese capital, pushed or locked out of these, remained largely mercantile.

This colonial racial formation deepened in the interwar years, and its contradic-tions began to show. Rubber production restrictions during the postwar commod-ity slump and the Great Depression saw Malay smallholders further segregated from the market economy and pushed toward customary rice cultivation. Malay reservations were expanded to curb Chinese agrarian development and lock in Malay rice planting, which deepened Malay underdevelopment.

Policy toward the Chinese crept toward exclusion. In response to political demands from local-born Chinese elites who actively supported the empire during the war, native representation was expanded in the Straits Settlements Legislative Council from one to seven unofficial members in 1923 to reflect the multiracial character of the colony. But this concession was counteracted by the increasing use of Malay indigeneity to keep the Chinese at bay throughout Malaya. When the unofficial members in the newly expanded council called for the civil service to be opened to non-Malays, the government replied that the British were trustees of the Malays, "the owners of the soil," who possessed "special rights in this matter more than any others."[10] Placed on the defensive, conservative local-born Chinese turned to a Chinese racialism that repudiated their centuries-long Malay acculturation. The Malacca-based unofficial council member Tan Cheng Lock opposed the compulsory learning of the Malay language, claiming that Peranakans (Straits-born Chinese) "with a strong Malay admixture revealed . . . dire physical and moral depravity," and that it was the "continual infiltration of pure Chinese blood" through immigration that saved the Straits Chinese. and allowed them to prosper."[11]

Labor unrest in the late 1930s caught the colonial government by surprise. In 1937, despite labor segregation, Chinese and Indian workers in urban sectors and rural estates and mines struck. The involvement of the latter was a revelation, because the Indians were supposed to be docile and well taken care of, and officials had fondly portrayed the Tamil as a simple, childlike figure. The Labour Department had taken special care to prevent them from being politicized, turning the barracks of Tamil laborers into family housing, promoting gardening, and improving vernacular education. After the strikes, the colonial government did an about-face and established state-supported labor unions and industrial courts. These modern institutions of labor representation had important postcolonial consequences, forming the grounds of struggle between centrist and radical-leftist nationalists after World War II, but the government did not have time to develop the unions before war broke out. The unions were unable to challenge the leftists, who had developed strong support on the ground during the decades-long political vacuum caused by British neglect of Chinese workers. Even patronage ties to the estate Indians were not as strong as they seemed, British officials being too blinded by the ethnographic caricature of Tamil docility to see that the Tamils also harbored nationalist sentiments.

DECOLONIZATION AND THE POLITICAL ECONOMY OF RACIAL CONFLICT

After World War II, the contradictions of colonial racial formation intensified. The Chinese-dominated, communist-led leftists who had formed the local resistance to Japanese occupation now controlled the countryside, ready to stage revolution if their demands for equal political representation of the non-Malay masses were not met. Many Indians had joined the Indian National Army and fought alongside the Japanese to win Indian independence, and widespread public support for the INA during the Red Fort trials of its captured officers for treason meant that the British could no longer ignore Indian nationalism in Malaya. Many of the Malay elites collaborated with the Japanese, but the British could not replace them easily with functionaries who were equally loyal and able to command authority over the Malay masses.[12]

Political calculations led to the Malayan Union in 1946, which federated the Malay states and the Straits Settlements states of Penang and Malacca under a single government, with the Malay rulers surrendering their sovereign powers to the British Crown and granting equal rights to most non-Malays domiciled in Malaya. But this led the Malay elites to unite under the United Malays National Organization (UMNO), staging civil disobedience campaigns and withdrawing from participation in the government bureaucracy. The government machinery ground to a halt, and the Union collapsed in 1948. The Federation of Malaya was established, restoring the sovereignty of the Malay rulers and the special rights and position of the Malay people, while tightening citizenship requirements for the non-Malays. The communists revolted and fought the British in a long insurgency.

The British proceeded to establish interethnic bargaining. The Communities Liaison Committee, comprised of six Malays, six Chinese, and one representative apiece of the Indian, Ceylonese, Eurasian, and European communities, was set up in 1949. It was tasked with discussing and make recommendations on the Chinese aiding the economic position of the Malays, political relations between Malays and non-Malays, and the Malayanization of education.[13] The Committee served not only as the platform for interethnic bargaining but to institutionalize the dominant model of multiracial political rule. Conservative noncommunist Chinese and Indian leaders formed the Malayan Chinese Association (MCA), led by Tan Cheng Lock, and the Malayan Indian Congress (MIC), and joined UMNO to form the coalition Alliance Party, which won elections in 1955, 1959, 1964, and 1969 and governed throughout the period. The "consociational democracy" stabilized ethnic relations through quid pro quo bargaining between communal leaders, supported by the communities, mobilized in discrete racial silos.[14] Through the coalition, the non-Malay minorities recognized the special position of the Malays in exchange for equal citizenship rights, while the coalition provided a platform for the negotiation of material concerns specific to each group. As T. N. Harper succinctly summarizes it, the Chinese were concerned with "land rights, and an openness to new leadership which could guarantee a minimum of interference in their economic and cultural affairs," the Indians with "unionism and movements of social reform," and the Malays with "the root cause of Malay poverty, through self-help and political mobilisation."[15] The communist insurgency was defeated and, with ethnic relations stabilized in the consociational compact, Malaya became independent in 1957.

The Singapore Question

The one thing that was the constant throughout the whole period was the exclusion of Singapore from the politics of decolonization, from both the Malayan Union and the Federation of Malaya. The British kept Singapore out of the Union so as to keep the demographic balance between Malays and non-Malays, numbering almost 2.5 million people in each category. Postwar Singapore had a population of almost a million, one-fifth that of Malaya, with the Chinese making up around three-quarters of it. The democratization of the colonial racial formation as nationhood approached meant such calculations were necessary to maintain British influence after decolonization. After all, British capital was still heavily invested in the mining and plantation sectors, and rubber and tin remained important strategic resources, especially when the Allies got sucked into the Korean and Vietnam Wars. Singapore mattered directly in this regard because it was the trade and services hub for capital and export of the commodities. By keeping Singapore out of the Union and Federation, the British retained economic control.

Still, it was an anomaly that had to be addressed once Malaya became independent. Singapore clearly could not be kept as a colony indefinitely, while the rest of Southeast Asia achieved independence. Through the 1950s, leftist nationalist influence made its presence felt in Singapore. The Singapore question became acute when it became clear that the sinophone leftists dominated the political scene and the conservative anglophone Straits Chinese leaders supported by the British had no clout after the advent of mass politics. If the British continued to dither on granting Singapore independence, then either the city would eventually be lost to a mass uprising or the Malayan economy would collapse due to political instability caused by the use of force to maintain control. But if the British were to grant Singapore independence quickly, then the city would be handed to the leftists through legitimate elections. The option to integrate Singapore into Malaya, belatedly, was unacceptable to the UMNO leaders, since it would upset the racial balance, inject even greater Chinese power into the economy, and introduce a large group of highly educated non-Malays into the civil service.

Fortuitously for the British, the issue was resolved by a group of anglophone Fabianists, led by a young lawyer, Lee Kuan Yew, who formed the multiracial People's Action Party (PAP) in alliance with sinophone leftists, providing English-educated respectability to the latter. When the PAP pressed for early elections, knowing that it would easily win, the British took a chance and supported Lee's faction so as to outmaneuver the sinophone leftists, whom they suspected of being communist sympathizers. In May 1959, with expanded suffrage, the PAP won the first general election in Singapore under the new Constitution, which allowed for self-governance. UMNO won three of the eight seats it contested, signifying the strong presence of Malay nationalists in the city-state.

The split between the two camps came when Lee's group started preparing with the British and UMNO to unite Singapore with Malaya, whose prime minister, Tunku Abdul Rahman, viewed merger as more acceptable than having sinophone leftists control Singapore, and hence Malaya's economy. The merged state would also include the two territories of British North Borneo, Sabah and Sarawak, thus maintaining the demographic balance between Malays and non-Malays. Opposed to merger, because they saw it as hampering their goals of quickly establishing an independent socialist state, the sinophone leftists left the PAP to form the Barisan Socialis (Socialist Front). But months before the merger referendum and general election proceeding the referendum, this new party was crippled by crackdowns and administrative detentions of its leaders and unionists on grounds of communist subversion.

In September 1963, the Singapore electorate voted for merger, and five days later, the PAP was returned to government of what was now an autonomous state in the Federation of Malaysia, with less than half the popular vote and a reduced parliamentary majority. Crucially, UMNO broke an agreement with the PAP not to campaign on each other's turf, and supported the Singapore Alliance Party, a multiracial coalition of communally organized parties mimicking the Alliance Party across the causeway, which came third in the popular vote. Despite the vote in favor of a merger, within two years, Malaysia and Singapore would go their separate ways. The reasons for this split relate directly to their divergent political economies, which were both rooted in colonial racial formation.

The Political Economy of Racial Conflict

As much as the economies of the two previously separate political entities of Malaya and Singapore were interlinked and interdependent, the differences were stark and significant. The postwar economic growth of Malaya was still driven by primary commodity exports, with the steady rise in world prices for tin and rubber from 1947 to 1960 fueling the growth of the public sector.[16] Agriculture was still the primary economic sector in Malaya, accounting for nearly 62 percent of workers in 1957, but there was a shift in the distribution of labor from agriculture to the secondary industries of manufacturing and construction, and to the tertiary sectors of commerce and services. In Singapore in 1957, secondary industries accounted for 21 percent and tertiary for 72 percent of the workforce, compared to 10 and 28 percent respectively in Malaya. Much of the increased labor engagement in secondary industries in Malaya was in construction, whereas in Singapore, it was in manufacturing.[17] Thus, Singapore was industrializing while retaining its trading and export hub functions for Malaya, and Malaya was deepening its agrarian economy in the midst of urbanization and the growth of commercial activities among the Chinese.

From the perspective of the PAP leaders in Singapore, the way forward for the economy was to push for industrialization led by the Chinese, who dominated the secondary and tertiary sectors and held the stock of local capital. Goh Keng Swee, the minister of finance, wrote in 1965 that the strategy was to mobilize domestic savings by relying on profit-oriented business enterprises rather than on a rentier class, and to pursue import substitution in the context of the commodity export economy, since imports accounted for more than a third of the gross national product of Malayam.[18] A few years before merger, in order to attract foreign multinational corporations to drive industrialization, rather than rely on local Chinese capital, Goh created the Economic Development Board and began development of the Jurong industrial estate. Goh believed that the Chinese would be the modernizers of the postcolonial state because they were uprooted migrants shorn of traditionalist institutions, while the Malays remained steeped in the ethos of an agrarian society.[19] He was skeptical, however, of the ability of traditional capital to turn away from the primary commodity sectors.,[20] and so saw his task as recruiting (with the help of foreign manufacturing capital) a new class of industrial labor from the Chinese population.

In contrast to Singapore, economic growth in Malaya was still very much grounded in the agrarian export sector, buoyed by a commodities boom in the world market. However, the situation was getting dire, and the sustainability of growth was threatened by the lack of new planting and replanting, especially for Malay smallholdings. Progress was made belatedly in the late 1950s with committed planting schemes, but a lack of administrative expertise caused attempts to kick-start rural development oto falter.[21] In addition, problems of capital and experience meant that enterprise in Malaya could not progress beyond cottage industries and contract work. As a result, from 1957 to 1970 the average monthly income in Malaya climbed by 23 percent, to U.S.$172, for ethnic Malays, and by 26 percent, to U.S.$381, for the Chinese.[22] The postcolonial state tried to tackle the inequality by preferring Malays in government work and specific economic sectors, while leaving the urban sector, rural plantations, and mines dominated by the Chinese and Western corporations alone. Progress was slow, and it did not help that the Chinese opposed the learning of Malay as the national language and medium of instruction and the integration of Chinese and Tamil vernacular schools into the state system.

These economic and political issues led to the deterioration of cooperative consociationalism and threatened the prospect of democracy without consensus. Just as this was occurring, the PAP encouraged an alternative vision.[23] The PAP accused the Alliance Party of fostering "Malay Malaysia" racialism, and in contrast called for a multiracial "Malaysian Malaysia" with equal rights for all. Singapore's minister of culture, S. Rajaratnam, described this vision as one of gradual and equal acculturation toward a Malayan culture by enlarging the overlapping areas of cultural beliefs and practices shared by the Malay, Chinese, and Indian cultures.[24] Arguably, however, the PAP's vision was not free of racialism, as it both tapped into the widespread fear of assimilation into Malay culture among Malaysian

Chinese, and presumed that the Chinese and Indians would have to modernize the nation because the Malays lacked the capacity to do so.

Following the 1963 Singaporean elections, relations between UMNO and the PAP, with their competing multiracial visions quickly soured. Kuala Lumpur dragged its feet in establishing a common market, which would have benefited Singapore's industrialization and led to further entrenchment of non-Malay economic power. These tensions began to be reflected in strained Malay-Chinese relations in Singapore, which were exarcebated when the Singapore-based PAP won a seat in the suburbs of the federal capital, Kuala Lumpur, in the general election in peninsular Malaysia in April 1964 by campaigning on the slogan of a "Malaysian Malaysia." In this toxic political climate, the usually peaceful Malay procession to celebrate the Prophet Muhammad's Birthday in Singapore quickly deteriorated in July 1964 into riots between Chinese secret society and Malay ultranationalist gangs. Curfews were imposed for almost two weeks, but less than two months later, riots broke out again. Thirty-six people died, over five hundred were injured, and over three thousand were arrested, in the worst violence yet seen in postwar Singapore. Chinese-Malay tensions continued to brew, and in an attempt to defuse them, Tunku Abdul Rahman thus decided to expel Singapore from the Malaysian Federation, making Singapore an independent country on August 9, 1965.

However, Chinese-Malay tensions continued to brew in West Malaysia, particularly in the context of widening wealth and income inequality between Chinese and Malays. Things came to a head at the 1969 general election. Having had a glimpse of the PAP's "Malaysian Malaysia" vision, the Chinese swung their support from the Malayan Chinese Association (MCA) to two new left-wing Chinese-dominated parties, the Parti Gerakan Rakyat Malaysia (Malaysian People's Movement Party) and the successor to the PAP, the Democratic Action Party (DAP). Many Malays also swung from UMNO to the Pan-Islamic Party (PAS), indicating unhappiness with the widening racial-class inequality and lack of governmental intervention in the economy.[25] The Alliance Party suffered its worst result, barely getting the majority of the popular vote and a slim four-seat buffer for its parliamentary majority. An opposition victory parade in Kuala Lumpur and a UMNO countermarch led to riots, on May 13, 1969, that spread across much of the city and neighboring areas in Selangor. The rest of the country remained relatively calm, but hundreds, mostly Chinese, died in the violence, the causes of which remain controversial and disputed to this day.

CAPITALIST DEVELOPMENT AND DIVERGENT POSTCOLONIAL MULTIRACIALISMS

The 1964 and 1969 race riots disrupted the existing organization and distribution of land and labor along racial lines in Malaysia and Singapore. As we saw earlier, these configurations were crucial to the development and maintenance of the colonial state, yet they contained contradictions which ultimately altered the postcolonial trajectories of both countries. These contradictions were expressed in both the disjuncture of "Chinese" capital, "Malay" land and "Indian" labor, and the recurring claims by left-wing movements to represent "Chinese" labor. Yet racial formation is not simply a matter of economic or political arrangements; it also requires ethnographic projects that represent the bodies of workers—and society itself—in ways that support the arrangement of labor and land. It is therefore significant that the underlying contradictions of colonial *political economy* exploded in racial violence by way of the *cultural* practices of processions and parades. These processions required interactions between individual bodies, and were a popular expression of communal life in the colonies. As cultural practices they therefore embodied and represented various individuals and communities in different ways. Yet the racial violence of the 1960s left these dual bodies indelibly marked as racial bodies, as "Chinese" and "Malay".

In the aftermath of the 1964 and 1969 riots, the already divergent multiracialisms in Singapore and Malaysia, the former favoring equal citizenship rights and the latter involving the recognition of the special Malay position in exchange for citizenship rights, developed in very different directions. Given the existing political economy, both, however, favored capital. In Malaysia, the Malay special position became the basis for rapid capital accumulation using the UMNO-captured state to build up a Malay capitalist class on par with the non-Malays. In Singapore, the PAP entrenched formal equality as the basis for extensive autocratic interventions in society, brushing aside the old bourgeoisie to build a state-based capitalism in alliance with multinational capital. *Post*colonial racial formation in both Malaysia and Singapore therefore refers to the process of *political* projects representing Chinese and Malay bodies and society in order to accumulate *capital* along racial lines to develop and maintain the new nation-state.

Malaysia: Malay Capital Accumulation and Patronage Multiracialism

After the 1969 riots, the National Operations Council was established and ruled by decree in a state of emergency in Malaysia. Deputy Prime Minister Tun Abdul Razak became director of the Council and the de facto head of government. Tunku Abdul Rahman was subsequently forced to resign in Tun Abdul Razak's favor in September 1970, and then as UMNO president in June 1971, a few months after parliamentary rule was reestablished. During the period of Council rule, a debate ensued between mainstream economists in the government and a group of political economists associated with the Department of National Unity. The former group involved many highly educated non-Malay elites and "liberal" Malays led by the minister of finance, who was the MCA representative. Two of the National Unity political economists, the Norwegian Just Faaland and the Malaysian Rais Saniman, went on to document the work that led to the adoption of the New Economic Policy in 1971 in a book published in 1990, *Growth and Ethnic Inequality*.

For Faaland and Saniman, the problem was Malaysia's dual economy, in which a wealthy modern sector existed "side by side with mass rural poverty and underemployment in the traditional sector." Malays were overwhelmingly concentrated in the latter.[26] Mainstream economists saw the problem as Malays not being responsive to capitalism and not working as hard as the Chinese and Indians.[27] Assistance for the poor would help uplift the Malays, and the trickle-down effect of growth would do the rest. Malays were trapped in structural imbalances in income, employment, and ownership of capital.[28] The New Economic Policy aimed, first and foremost, to improve the income balance for Malays, and then secondarily, to maximize employment creation for all races through promotion of labor-intensive production and export-led industrialization.[29] This was to be achieved by tearing down the "system of 'apartheid' constructed against the Malays, openly or indirectly, by the colonial masers," promoting "active participation and equal partnership rather than of disruptive distribution and hand-outs to the Malays," and developing Malay capability for active and equal participation through education and training.[30]

Faaland and Saniman's approach recognized the political and sociological factors in colonial racial formation, but the treatment of the problems remained racial. One of their key recommendations was to design programs that would increase Malay rural income and employment, while stemming Malay migration to the cities and slowing Chinese and Indian migration to Malay-dominated states with principally rural economies. The intention was not to permanently segregate the races, but to foster political stability through integration of races as economic peers.[31] Nevertheless, the progressive project involved the marking and separation of racial bodies.

Furthermore, like mainstream economists, Faaland and Saniman believed that "disunity among the Malays is a historical 'adat' [custom] . . . born out of their instinct, [and] perfected by. . . practice."[32] The New Economic Policy aimed to unite the Malays, but an additional challenge was to construct "a new alliance of moderate elements (Malay, Chinese, and Indian) within the nation."[33] In 1973, to support the New Economic Policy, a new alliance, the Barisan Nasional (National Front), was formed by the component parties of the Alliance—UMNO, the MCA, and the MIC—and a slew of other political parties, including the Parti Gerakan. Barisan went on to win the next four general elections handsomely. In this period, 1974 to 1990, the New Economic Policy formed the bedrock of Malaysian state formation and the political bargaining between the parties representing various racial constituencies.

Faaland and Saniman criticized the five-year plans after 1975 for deviating from the New Economic Policy by focusing on growth rather than racial income equity.[34] They pointed out that Malays accounted for only 13.6 percent of corporate ownership at par value in 1990, up from 3.6 percent in 1975, whereas non-Malays accounted for 56.7 percent, up from 37.5 percent; the greatest loss was to foreign ownership, which dropped from 53.3 percent to 23.7 percent.[35] The ratio of non-Malay to Malay income fell from 1.71 in 1967 to 1.40 in 1985, but Faaland and Saniman appear to lament that this improvement had come at a cost to racial economic equality in terms of capital ownership.[36] The New Economic Policy aimed for a 30 percent Malay share of corporate ownership by 1990, but together with the trust agencies for Malay interests, only 20 percent was achieved.[37]

The implementation and outcome of the New Economic Policy have been well analyzed; scholars note the strengthening of the state's hand in the economy, particularly in relation to the ownership and management of corporate assets. Beginning with the replacement of the MCA's leader as finance minister by Prime Minister Tun Abdul Razak himself, UMNO elites took control of the administrative-legal levers of the state to make deals on their own behalf with local Chinese and foreign capitaliststs.[38] Consociational bargaining between peer parties in a coalitional political framework gave way to communal trading of patronage political capital and access to economic privileges dispensed through the UMNO-dominated state.[39]

For UMNO, especially after Mahathir bin Mohamad became prime minister in 1981, political control of both the new Malay and old non-Malay economic elites became the chief objective in the pursuit of national unity. A new Malay capitalist class and middling business class rose up through state patronage within UMNO. Non-Malay capitalists shared in the spoils of nationalizing foreign corporate property and privatizing state assets through the other Barisan Nasional parties, and so were also tied to the political fortunes of UMNO.[40] Export-led growth in commodities, especially in the oil and gas sector, became the focus of the "state-capitalist network."[41]

Singapore: State-Led Industrialization and Corporatist Multiracialism

In the 1970s and 1980s, Singapore's trajectory was similar to Malaysia's in its underlying thrust: the deepening of state intervention in plural society to maintain political stability and drive economic development, which were seen as mutually reinforcing and necessary condition for each other. The difference was that whereas Malaysia started from the premise of the special position of the Malays as first among equals, Singapore began from a foundation of formal multiracial equality. The New Economic Policy reoriented Malaysia's economic development toward the modernization of the rural sector and the nationalization of the commodity sector to boost Malay income and capital accumulation. After the separation from Malaysia and the loss of the hinterland, there was very little room for Singapore to move as a mercantile city-state. Singapore moved in exactly the opposite direction to Malaysia by seeking to urbanize the island completely for industrialization and proletarianization. Without a large domestic market, import-substitution industrialization was no longer viable, and export-oriented industrialization, following in the footsteps of Japan, South Korea, Taiwan, and Hong Kong was the way forward. Local capital was too deeply involved in production and trade in the Malayan commodity sector, so the state moved to participate directly in development.

Goh Keng Swee's nascent industrialization program introduced in the early 1960s proved to be a prescient hedge. The newly minted Jurong industrial estate was expanded for export production in the context of heightened regional demand fueled by U.S. intervention in Vietnam. The Economic Development Board took the lead in attracting multinational corporations to invest in the country. A new ideology of survival as a small city-state surrounded by potentially hostile neighbors was formulated, which emphasized a disciplined social organization and competitive labor costs as necessary conditions and therefore implied, politically, the corporatist cooptation of unions and other social groups.[42]

Coupled with forced resettlement of villagers, farmers, and shop house residents into public housing flats, which eventually came to house over 80 percent of the population, the corporatist cooptation of unions and suppression of dissent represented nothing less than a brutal social and cultural revolution that transformed Singapore society into an urban proletarian society dependent on state provision of welfare. For Goh, this was inevitable. Speaking to Australian radio in 1967, Goh cited Max Weber's Protestant Ethic and spelled out the need for an "integrated, comprehensive, all-embracing approach" to modernization. Unapologetically, mentioning the examples of Victorian England and Stalinist Russia, Goh stated that there was "no easy way to grind out of the mass of poor people the economic surplus or savings needed to finance capital accumulation."[43]

The multiracialism that was forged turned out to be corporatist too, with institutions formed to represent racial and religious groups within the ambit of the state, while community grassroots organizations were formed and placed under the direction of the state's People's Association. Mobilized as a cultural resource to cultivate Singapore's social ethic, ethnicity was, however, neutralized as a discursive and electoral resource for oppositional parties and other groups. Speaking at the University of Singapore in 1972, Goh refuted the notion that the government should set norms of good behavior and motivation for individuals to adjust to modernization, citing the difficulty of legislating such matters, and of communicating these needs. "In a multiracial community, there are different criteria by which good conduct is assessed.," he said.[44]

This was disingenuous, since modernization by way of public housing and myriad social engineering campaigns that followed resettlement was already shaping the Singaporean worker, whose work ethic was expected to mimic that of the Chinese. The multiracialism of equal differences represented by the linking of Chinese, Malays, Indians, and Eurasians arms was used to convey the message that the Singaporean social ethic was to be one of disciplined national unity, with the government acting as a neutral arbiter for the universal good of society regardless of race. But the equivalent relativity of differences was also used to cut off political organizations from speaking up for any particular group by claiming that it would open the arena to completing cultural claims that could not be reconciled. The auto-cratic government tagged dissidents as racial, ethno-linguistic, or religious chauvin-ists who threatened communal strife, or as agents of neocolonialism or communism.

In a belated move to recognize the persistent socioeconomic marginality of the Malays for historical and structural reasons (and worsened by economic develop-ment relying on the proletarian work ethic of the Chinese), the state set up the Council for the Education of Muslim Children in 1982 to fund additional educa-tional programs to help the Malays. By that time, the education system, reformed by Goh to emphasize race-blind academic streaming for the general population, but special education catering to the Chinese elites, had already entrenched the centrality of economic capital and cultural capital for educational outcomes.[45] Thus, the socioeconomic marginality of the Malays was dealt with in a differenti-ated corporatist manner, in which the Malays were given state funding to help themselves achieve better social mobility through education, because racial self-help was ostensibly the best method to do so given the relativity of racial differ-ences. A decade later, reflecting the state's corporatist multiracialism, equivalent Chinese, Indian, and Eurasian self-help groups were formed to target uplifting of low-income workers—the reproduction of labor through education and the reskilling of labor through training—in racial terms.

GLOBALIZING CAPITAL AND ARRESTED MULTICULTURALISMS

By the 1980s, the contradictions of postcolonial racial formation were surfacing in both countries. In Malaysia, the focus on Malay capital accumulation moved the society toward racial equality in terms of class structure and inequality. UMNO came to be dominated by Malay businessmen and grew detached from both grassroots labor and the growing Malay urban middle classes. Nationalization of foreign corporate holdings was hitting the limits, thus reducing the scope of patronage dispensation to the non-Malay capitalists and the ability of the state to keep the multiracial alliance tight.

In Singapore, resettlement of the population was completed, thus ending the supply of new workers and eroding the labor cost competitiveness that multina-tional corporations were sensitive to. Growing Malay marginality, with politically destabilizing consequences, was only starting to be addressed in a long-term man-ner through the education of children of low-income families. A policy of foreign immigration distinguishing between low-skilled transient workers and skilled long-term residents, was accelerated to keep labor costs low, but came with an increasing price for corporatist multiracialism, since the migrants could not be integrated into the existing institutions tailored for control of the working-class citizenry.

The contradictions were expressed politically as democratizing pressures. In 1987 and 1988, the Singapore government used the colonial-era Internal Security

Act to arrest over a score of Catholic Church social workers, civil society activists, and opposition party members. Accused of engaging in a "Marxist conspiracy" to overthrow the state, they were kept under indefinite extrajudicial detention. In Malaysia, the government launched copycat crackdowns on civil society and the opposition. In both crackdowns, the need to keep the multiracial peace was used to justify the actions, though it was clear to international human rights organizations and the local middle classes that the governments were trying to stem the tide of democratization hitting East Asia.

The two ruling parties saw large swings against them. Barisan saw its vote share drop from over 60 percent in 1982 to 53 percent in 1990, with the opposition just short of capturing one-third of the parliamentary seats to block constitutional changes. The PAP's vote share dropped from nearly 78 percent in 1980 to 65 percent in 1984, and, during the crackdowns, to 63 percent in 1988 and 61 percent in 1991, with the disorganized opposition prying open four parliamentary seats in that election. The PAP did better than Barisan did in Malaysia because it established a couple of new multiracial institutions in the late 1980s that hampered the opposition parties: group representation constituencies for the election of a slate of candidates that had to include a candidate of a specified minority race; and the ethnic integration policy to prevent minority ethnic enclaves from forming voting blocs in public housing estates.

Malaysian Prime Minister Mahathir's response to the political swing was belated but far more liberal and progressive, at least rhetorically, than that of the PAP. In 1991, in line with a new national development policy to promote manufacturing and accelerate Malay capital accumulation, Mahathir announced a grand Vision 2020 program to mold a single "ethnically integrated" nationality, the "Bangsa Malaysia" (Malaysian Race), which would underpin an advanced industrialized economy, mature democratic polity, and tolerant multicultural society.[46] In Singapore, the new prime minister Goh Chok Tong promised liberalization and to build a kinder and gentler Singapore, as opposed to the brutally disciplined decades of industrialization and proletarianization. Economic reforms to move the economy up the value chain to advanced manufacturing and research-based industries emphasized middle-class formation. Singapore began to see the influx of skilled migrants, and in the early 2000s the government announced that it aimed to foster a new cosmopolitan multiculturalism.

The new multicultural visions resonated with the sustained economic development. The collapse of the Soviet Union and the opening up of Communist China through to the 1990s accelerated global capital flows and kept growth rates high in industrializing Malaysia and reindustrializing Singapore. Singapore's GDP growth averaged 9.0 percent in the decade prior to the Asian Financial Crisis, from 1988 to 1997, compared to the 8.9 percent in the previous two decades marked by primary industrialization.[7] Malaysia's growth rate was more impressive, with corresponding figures of 9.3 percent from 1988 to 1997 compared to 6.5 percent from

1968 to 1987.[48] Helped by a disorganized political opposition starved of discursive resources to challenge its ideological hegemony and unable to present a multicultural alternative, the PAP regained its peak of electoral support with 75 percent of the votes in the 2001 general election. Barisan garnered 65 percent in the 1995 general election.

However, the contradictions of patronage and corporatist multiracialisms soon redoubled in the era of financial crises. The old postcolonial multiracialisms were still institutionally dominant, and the new multiculturalisms remained largely visionary and saw only minor translations into policy. In Malaysia, the 1997 financial crisis brought about a grave challenge from the progressive wing of UMNO led by Deputy Prime Minister Anwar Ibrahim, which was purged and suppressed by draconian crackdowns. Drastic capital and currency controls stabilized the economy and maintained a slower but sustainable pace of growth, thus largely shielding the economy from the further vagaries of global capital in the 2000s.[49] The rural plantation and commodity sectors were protected, and the industrializing and financial sectors were the most affected. The government extended its share of the economy, bailing out and absorbing Malay-owned companies and Chinese banks, while failing to promote local small and medium-sized enterprises (many of which were either non-Malay or interethnic partnerships) because of its focus on Malay capital accumulation.[50]

The main opposition parties, Anwar Ibrahim's Parti Keadilan Rakyat (People's Justice Party), the PAS, and the DAP—respectively representing the urban Malays, rural Malays, and non-Malays—formed a loose multiracial coalition, Pakatan Rakyat (People's Alliance), in 2004 to challenge the Barisan Nasional. In the 2008, in the continued low-growth situation, Barisan saw its electoral support dip to 50 percent, and Pakatan broke Barisan's two-third parliamentary majority and formed the state governments of industrialized Penang and Selangor and rural Kedah and Kelantan. In response, the new prime minister, Najib Razak, launched a "One Malaysia" campaign to promote national unity and expounded a New Economic Model to attract foreign investments to sustain growth. Communal patronage trading and political support from the non-Malays collapsed, as Chinese ownership of the economy plunged, while Malay capital accumulation stalled.[51] The more liberal aspects of Najib's model, such as the move away from Malay capital accumulation and affirmative action, were dropped after the reactionary factions of UMNO revolted. In the 2013 general election, Barisan's electoral support slipped to a record low of 47 percent, its parliamentary majority kept intact by political support from resource-rich Sarawak and Sabah.

In Singapore, the 1997 crisis hastened economic restructuring, and the economy began to shift from a manufacturing to a service base. Foreign immigration accelerated, with the percentage of citizens in the population dropping from 86 percent in 1990 to 74 percent in 2000 and 64 percent in 2010. At the same time, wage growth lagged behind cost-of-living inflation. The socioeconomic marginality of the Malays persisted, corporatist multiracialism faltered, and younger generations ceased to participate in the grassroots activities organized by the People's Associations. Anti-foreigner sentiment spread in this period, as socioeconomic inequality widened between the top 20 percent income bracket of elite managers and professionals who moved in the same social circles as the foreign expatriates and the rest of the population living in the public housing heartlands. In the 2006 general election, electoral support for the PAP swung downward by almost 9 percent, and in 2011, it fell to a record low of 60 percent. Losing a group representation constituency for the first time, it also lost a key cabinet minister.

Even before the new multiculturalisms could be translated into institutions to secure political stability for development in the context of globalizing capital, the old postcolonial multiracialisms were therefore, eroded by the political-economic contradictions it engendered. Though Malaysia and Singapore went their separate ways and developed their political institutions and economies on different multiracial premises, they ironically came to share the same characteristics of arrested development. Direct involvement of the state in the economy resulted in the underdevelopment of local enterprises and dependence on foreign multinationals. Overlapping racial and class inequalities persist in a slow-growth environment.

CONCLUSIONS

Malaysia and Singapore represent a paradox in the making of postcolonial multiculturalism, where peaceful ethnic relations that have been achieved by the building of strong states depend on the enduring context of racial conflict. This chronic racial conflict has deep roots in the contradictions of colonial racial formation, manifested economically in the racial division of labor, and politically in the divergent native policies of the Federated Malay States and the Straits Settlements, and then the successor postcolonial states of Malaya and Singapore. While attempts were made by postcolonial state builders to meet each other halfway in the merged state of Malaysia, the state builders eventually fell out, because Singapore looked toward transforming its mercantile economy into an industrial hub, while Kuala Lumpur privileged agrarian and natural resource capitalist development. Due to the racialized character of the economic division of labor, each side pushed for a political multiracialism that suited its economic approach.

After their 1965 separation, the multiracialisms of Malaya and Singapore diverged, based on the differing political-economic logic of capital accumulation and state formation in the two polities. By the 1990s, state formation matured, and their multiracialism became inadequate for a new era of globalization. From the 1990s on, with each deepening capitalist crisis, the contradictions of the old multiracialism and the new economy have shown up in deepening social conflicts, thus arresting the development of more liberal multiculturalisms to match the political economy of globalization. At the time of writing, both countries stand at a cross-roads. Their state-led multiculturalisms have been arrested, and their economic engines are spluttering. The Chinese-Malay conflict, formed by colonial conceit and hardened during decolonization, remains as real as ever. Both countries are thus marked by peaceful ethnic relations that co-exist with enduring racial conflict, a paradox which has historically been mitigated by strong state-building. Yet attempts to resolve the contradictions of the colonial political economy and then economic globalization have deepened the paradox. The postcolonial states must continue to maintain the precarious balance between peace and conflict if they are to endure. Fifty years after the race riots of the 1960s, racial conflict in Malaysia and Singapore has once again become a frightening prospect.

NOTES

1. J. S. Furnivall, *Colonial Policy and Practice: A Comparative Study of Burma and Netherlands India* (Cambridge: Cambridge University Press, 1948).

2. John H. Drabble, *An Economic History of Malaysia, c. 1800–1990: The Transition to Modern Economic Growth* (New York: St. Martin's Press, 2000), 102.

3. G. Missen, "Wage Labour and the Political Economy in West Malaysia," in *Industrialisation and Labour Force Processes: A Case Study of Peninsular Malaysia,* ed. T. G. McGee et al. (Canberra: Australian National University, 1986), 74.

4. Azlan Tajuddin, *Malaysia in the World Economy (1824–2011): Capitalism, Ethnic Divisions, and "Managed" Democracy* (Lanham, MD: Lexington Books, 2012), 56.

5. Charles Hirschman, "The Making of Race in Colonial Malaya: Political Economy and Racial Ideology," *Sociological Forum* 1, no. 2 (1986): 330–61; and Charles Hirschman, "The Meaning and Measurement of Ethnicity in Malaysia: An Analysis of Census Classifications," *Journal of Asian Studies* 46, no. 3 (1987): 555–82.

6. Daniel P. S. Goh, "The Plural Society and Multiculturalism in Malaysia and Singapore," in *Multicultural Challenges and Redefining Identity in East Asia,* ed. Nam-Kook Kim, 211–32 (Farnham, Surrey, England: Ashgate, 2014).

7. Michael Omi and Howard Winant, *Racial Formation in the United States: From the 1960s to the 1990s,* 2nd ed. (New York: Routledge, 1994), 56.

8. United Kingdom, Colonial Office, Federated Malay States Sessional Papers, Legislative Council Proceedings and Papers, Labour Commission, 1891, CO275/44, 66, Public Records Office, National Archives, Kew, London.

9. Ibid., Federated Malay States Sessional Papers, Federal Council Proceedings and Papers, July 9, 1913, CO576/8, B23.

10. Ibid., Federated Malay States Sessional Papers, Legislative Council Proceedings and Papers, April 14, 1924, CO 275/111, 35.

11. Ibid., February 12, 1934, CO273/135, 18.

12. Keat Gin Ooi, "The Japanese Occupation and the Peoples of Sarawak," in *Southeast Asian Minorities in the Wartime Japanese Empire,* ed. Paul H. Kratoska, 133–52 (London: RoutledgeCurzon, 2002) 143.

13. Wan Asna Wan Mohd Nor, "Political and Economic Accommodation in Peninsular Malaysia," in *Political Economy of Development in Malaysia,* ed. B. N. Ghosh and Muhammad Syukri Salleh, 21–44 (Kuala Lumpur: Utusan Publications, 1999), 25.

14. Arend Lijphart, *Democracy in Plural Societies: A Comparative Exploration* (New Haven, CT: Yale University Press, 1977), 150.

15. T. N. Harper, *The End of Empire and the Making of Malaya* (Cambridge: Cambridge University Press, 1999), 9.

16. Chong-Yah Lim, *Economic Development of Modern Malaya* (Kuala Lumpur: Oxford University Press, 1967), 23–24.

17. Soo Ann Lee, *Economic Growth and the Public Sector in Malaya and Singapore 1948–1960* (Singapore: Oxford University Press, 1974), 24.

18. Keng Swee Goh, *The Economics of Modernization* (1972; Singapore: Federal Publications, 1995), 55, 67–68.

19. Ibid., 38.

20. Ibid., 56.

21. Lee, *Economic Growth and the Public Sector,* 143.

22. Tajuddin, *Malaysia in the World Economy,* 147.

23. Karl von Vorys, *Democracy without Consensus: Communalism and Political Stability in Malaysia* (Princeton, NJ: Princeton University Press, 1975).

24. S. Rajaratnam, "Our Cultural Heritage," in *S. Rajaratnam on Singapore: From Ideas to Reality,* ed. Kwa Chong Guan (1960; Singapore: World Scientific Publishing, 2006).

25. Edmund Terence Gomez and K. S. Jomo, *Malaysia's Political Economy: Politics, Patronage and Profits* (Cambridge: Cambridge University Press, 1999), 21.

26. Just Faaland, J. R. Parkinson, and Rais Saniman, *Growth and Ethnic Inequality: Malaysia's New Economic Policy* (London: Hurst, 1990), 37.

27. Ibid., 30.

28. Ibid., 32.

29. Ibid.

30. Ibid., 70.

31. Ibid., 250.

32. Ibid., 202.

33. Ibid., 247.

34. Ibid., 97.

35. Ibid., 142.

36. Ibid., 62.

37. Ibid., 142.

38. James V. Jesudason, *Ethnicity and the Economy: The State, Chinese Business, and Multinationals in Malaysia* (Singapore: Oxford University Press, 1989), 78, 84.

39. K. S. Jomo, *Growth and Structural Change in the Malaysian Economy* (London: Macmillan, 1990), 230–32.

40. Gomez and Jomo, *Malaysia's Political Economy,* 117–65.

41. Tajuddin, *Malaysia in the World Economy,* 159.

42. Garry Rodan, *The Political Economy of Singapore's Industrialization: National State and International Capital* (London: Macmillan, 1989), 88–93.

43. Keng Swee Goh, *The Practice of Economic Growth* (1977; Singapore: Federal Publications, 1995), 39.

44. Ibid., 192.

45. Lily Zubaidah Rahim, *The Singapore Dilemma: The Political and Educational Marginality of the Malay Community* (Singapore: Oxford University Press, 1999).

46. Noor, "Political and Economic Accommodation," 37.

47. At 2010 market prices, Department of Statistics, Singapore.

48. At 2005 market prices in U.S. dollars, World Bank.

49. Sook Ching Wong, K. S. Jomo and Kok Fay Chin. *Malaysian "Bail Outs"? Capital Controls, Restructuring and Recovery* (Singapore: Singapore University Press Press, 2005).

50. Edmund Terence Gomez, "The Politics and Policies of Corporate Development: Race, Rents and Redistribution in Malaysia," in *Malaysia's Development Challenges: Graduating from the Middle,* ed. Hal Hill, Tham Siew Yean, and Ragayah Haji Mat Zin, 63–82 (London: Routledge, 2012).

51. Ibid., 65.

11

The Cunning of Multiculturalism

A Perspective from the Caribbean

Viranjini Munasinghe, Cornell University

CARIBBEAN MULTICULTURALISM AS EXCEPTION

When Prime Minister Kamla Persad-Bissessar, a Trinidadian of Indian descent, announced in her Indian Arrival Day speech in 2010 that the Republic of Trinidad and Tobago's Ministry of Arts and Culture was being renamed the Ministry of Arts and *Multiculturalism,* she triggered a heated public debate about the formal adoption of multiculturalism as policy. This was, in many ways, a predictable response for Trinidadians, who are acutely aware of the mutual entanglement between politics and culture and ever vigilant of instances of it.[1] The Indo-Trinidadian[2] journalist Kris Rampersad, chair of UNESCO's T&T National Commission, had this to say:

> While we reel at the emphatic denouncement of multiculturalism [by leaders in Germany and the U.K] in Germany . . . , the local Ministry of Multiculturalism hosted a conference "Towards a Multiculturalism Policy for Trinidad and Tobago." Its keynote . . . speakers were foreign academics and technocrats from . . . Canada and the United Kingdom, who admitted that they had no answers for us on our efforts. . . .
>
> Apart from the few . . . voices . . . from the Caribbean . . . trying to represent what this region can bring to the debate [on multiculturalism and cultural policy] . . . Caribbean Governments and States have been largely inaudible, invisible and relatively inactive in the international discussion.
>
> Compared to our societies, which are already multicultural, the multicultural conversation in the international arena . . . has largely been a reaction to "globalisation" and directed at immigrants, who are seen to be potentially disruptive of the "mainstream." . . .
>
> . . . We have largely evolved a unique brand of multiculturalism from many migration streams.[3]

Despite both the critical interventions of postcolonial theory and empirical evidence to the contrary, identification of the North Atlantic as the originary site of events and ideas of global (universal) significance—industrialization, modernity, human freedom, liberal democracy, and the nation, to name a few—remains widely accepted.[4] Rampersad's remarks reference this temporality, which distinguishes between those who set the pace and those fated to follow, and highlight the paradox contained in this distinction for Caribbean countries like Trinidad, which have long been presumed to be multicultural. Rampersad captures, in measured language, an array of concerns expressed by Afro- and Indo-Trinidadian scholars, public intellectuals, politicians, and concerned citizens in their critical assessment of formalizing multiculturalism as policy.[5] The rallying concern driving Trinidadian protests was alarm at introducing a policy that leaders of the developed world, where it was first implemented, were already declaring a failure and a threat to national integration.[6] The general anxiety haunting the debate over multicultural policy was the possibility that state intervention directed at fostering diversity would compromise the hard-won common ground, or national cohesion, that had organically developed in Trinidad in spite of its legacy of colonial racialization.

The varied claims and positions informing the debate on multiculturalism may seem at odds with normative understandings of diversity (heterogeneity; impurity) and unity (homogeneity; purity) conditioned as they are by nation-building trajectories of former metropolitan and settler societies where the initial goal of homogeneity through assimilation was later, in the face of radical alterity, redirected to managing diversity through multiculturalism (non-Anglo/Euro immigrants). I flatten the experiences of former metropolitan and settler societies, not because I think the differences between them are insignificant, but because these nation-builders had access to a viable, if tenuous, native subject who could signify the cultural core of their respective nations.[7] When multiculturalism came to these societies, the dominant race and class, through nation-building projects of homogenization, had already fixed the cultural coordinates of civil society as the symbolic core of the nation.[8] Given the early decimation of Native American populations first by Spanish and later by English colonizers, no such option was available to Caribbean nation-builders, who faced the formidable task of making Old World ancestries native to the New World. This "symbolic lack" is fundamental to understanding how nation-building in Trinidad simultaneously incorporated both heterogeneous and homogeneous principles.

The temporal sequence of homogeneity giving way to heterogeneity is undone by Trinidadians' simultaneous claim to an a priori multiculturalism ("natural multiculturalism") and common ground for Trinidad. Furthermore, given that the two are asserted to coexist, fears that formal adoption of multiculturalism might fragment this common ground are puzzling. This chapter analyzes these seeming contradictions by attending to the empirical particulars directing Trinidad's passage from extractive colony to "a United Nations in miniature," a postcolonial nation reputed for its cosmopolitan excess even by Caribbean standards.[9] In so doing it adds another layer of complexity to the tenuous claim of multicultural inclusion from the vantage point of Caribbean exceptionalism.

Given the trend toward multiculturalism based on liberal aspirations to inclusiveness, nations are now expected simultaneously to straddle unity and diversity, and the demand that they do so is commonplace. Yet despite multicultural "inclusion," specific ancestral groups continue to argue that they suffer symbolic marginalization, and this chapter addresses how such exclusion operates in the postcolonial context of Trinidad despite—or through formal—inclusion. The Trinidadian example suggests that classical nationalism—which is to say, the impulse to homogenize and to create "purity" out of "impurity"—has hardly been crushed by multiculturalism. Although the putatively hybrid and cosmopolitan subjectivities of this age of late capitalism are widely celebrated, Trinidad shows that even multicultural nations constituted on the basis of cultural/racial difference may mask the homogenizing narratives of nationhood often relegated to the safety of eighteenth- and nineteenth-century models of nationhood.

REVISITING CARIBBEAN MULTICULTURALISM

The formal emergence of multiculturalism, understood as a strategy for ensuring national cohesion by incorporating minority and immigrant groups as full participating members of society, without their losing their cultural distinctiveness, is seen as having occurred first in Canada in 1971, followed by Australia in 1973.[10] As the term "multiculturalism" spread to metropolitan centers and postcolonial nations the meanings invested in it varied.[11] Despite critical assessments of multiculturalism informed by postcolonial theory and ethnic and cultural studies, liberal theorizations of multiculturalism remain for the most part in thrall of its association with non-Anglo/European minorities and immigrants, beginning in the 1970s, as a term to describe, analyze, and manage what might be called "new" diversity, the Third Worlding of the First World.[12] The dominant theorizations of cultural difference thus remain confined to the register of cultural Other without referencing the mutual entanglements that make all identities, dominant and subordinate, open and vulnerable to one another.[13] As a consequence, theorizations of multiculturalism that preserve the symbolic core of the nation reproduce the fiction of equivalence of the different cultural units implied by the term itself. The multicultural discourse in Trinidad provides an intriguing contrast to such familiar multicultural formulations because the issue of which ethnic group can more legitimately represent the nation remains unsettled. Indeed, in the case of Trinidad, it is precisely the lack of a legitimate culture-history referent for the nation, or an undisputed symbolic core to it, that drives the multicultural struggle between different ethnic groups over, and on behalf of, that nation.

Nation-builders and scholars with liberal leanings debate whether liberal democracies should recognize cultural groups in politics, and if so, how best to do this without compromising fundamental liberal values. Meanwhile, critical analyses of the politics of recognition foreground the moral and cultural constitution of liberalism's subject, the "abstract universal citizen," against which the particularity of other citizens is measured and evaluated.[14] The disclosure of particularity does not necessarily undermine liberal claims to the universal provided the cultural and moral foundations of liberalism are still assumed to possess a singular capacity to generate that universal. This allows for a conceptualization that locates the very generative conditions of the demand for recognition in the contradictory workings of late modern democracy, and, more specifically, in the compromise between two cherished liberal principles, individual freedom and social equality.[15] This is a significant analytical departure from prevailing liberal formulations of the politics of recognition that view the politics of difference as an external and potential obstacle to liberal values underpinning democratic nation-states. Contrary to the anxieties expressed by defenders of the liberal order, subjects' demands for recognition of their difference based on memories of historical injury tend to reinscribe—rather than threaten—liberal values and institutions, in part because the injured seek recompense that aligns their identification with liberal bureaucratic desires.[16]

Liberalism's subject, the "abstract universal citizen," leaves open the possibility of including previously excluded groups, yet the privileges of "equal citizenship" have been found to be highly unequal.[17] "For racialized subjects [in the United States] the fiction of 'equal citizenship' can mean denying the continuing effects of racial exclusion through the government's failure to protect civil, political and social rights of people of color," according to Leti Volpp.[18] Parsing four registers of citizenship—as status, rights, politics, and identity—Volpp argues that for Asian Americans in the United States, citizenship as identity is not derived from political and legal rights, and that their cultural identity can hinder their access to these rights. Writing of "the general failure to identify Asian Americans as constituting American national identity," Volpp claimed in 2001 that "to be Asian American suggests in the American imagination the idea that one acts according to cultural dictates somehow fundamentally different from those known in the United States. One's Asianness seems to be the difference one must suppress in order to be a full citizen."[19]

By foregrounding the relation between culture and citizenship (citizenship as identity), Volpp draws attention to the moral and cultural limits of multicultural inclusion through political and legal rights.[20] The privileges and costs attached to cultural citizenship are in turn determined by the extent of overlap or dissonance between a particular culture indexing diversity and the culture-history referent for the nation. The power to fix the cultural coordinates of civil society, which set the terms for incorporating diverse Others, is thus highly privileged, and not always transparent and open to contestation, as with the multicultural discourse in Europe and Anglo/European settler colonies. But, in the New World context of Trinidad the debate over multicultural policy addresses precisely this struggle over the symbolic definition of the nation.

Trinidadian Multiculturalism

Multiculturalism as official policy, with its liberal promise of realizing equality through recognition of cultural difference, came to Trinidad relatively late (in May 2010) compared to Canada and Australia, which are credited with implementing it in the early 1970s. The hesitance of earlier Trinidadian political leaders to adopt it is puzzling, because in this region of the oldest colonies of the West the imprint of racialization is pervasive, from Trinidad's celebrated cosmopolitanism to Trinidadians' reputation for "racial voting." From the period leading up to and since independence in 1962, the pivotal challenge for nation-builders has been to define *the* common ground (distinct from liberal common good) of the nation (a culture-history referent) in relation to the ancestral groups comprising Trinidad. At a formal level, the challenge of nation-building in Trinidad—forging the relation between the particular (different ancestral groups) and the universal (common ground)—is similar to the challenge of recognizing multicultural distinctions (particular) in relation to the foundational principles of a liberal-democratic nation (universal). The critical question for the latter is how to incorporate diverse individuals or groups so as to enable their full participation in the nation without loss of their cultural distinctiveness or threat to fundamental liberal values of the nation embodied by the universal rights-bearing citizen.[21] Substantively, however, there are fundamental differences between how "multiculturalism" operates in Trinidad's national project, which is democratic and liberal in spirit, and the normative script for multiculturalism in liberal-democratic nations. Trinidadian specificity can be understood only through a reading of its colonial history, founded on operations of racialization peculiar to extractive colonies in the New World.

Contrary to received wisdom that relegates the problem of heterogeneity to new states, Robert Young and Wolfram Schmidgen among others have questioned the cultural homogeneity attributed to the old states of Europe.[22] Academic disclosures of "impurities" aside, the fact remains that "historic" nations are deemed such precisely because they have been, for the most part, successful in their claim to homogeneity. The New World context of the Caribbean, however, resists the sentiment of a single kind of belonging, because as descendants of immigrants, slaves, and bonded labor, nation-builders of these societies have no option but to acknowledge the diversity of their Old World ancestors in staking a claim in the New World. Historical memory of Old World origins runs counter to claims of autochthony, a pivotal moral criterion for establishing belonging to the nation.

The challenge for nation-builders in the Caribbean was to transform Old World distinctions into New World purities.

First ruled by Spain (beginning in 1498), then Britain (from 1796 until independence in 1962), Trinidad's population also has a significant French component—a result of an agreement between Spain and France in 1783—"the Cedula [schedule] of population"—that saw the influx of a number of French Catholics and their African slaves into the island.[23] Between 1845 and 1917, almost 143,000 indentured laborers from India also came to Trinidad to work in the sugar plantations to replace the labor of African slaves after emancipation in 1834. In addition, some Trinidadians also trace their ancestry to China, Madeira, Syria, Lebanon, Venezuela, and the smaller Caribbean islands. Shaped by a historical legacy of plantation slavery and its attendant racial hierarchy, the significance of ancestral diversity was amplified by the rigid correspondence between occupation and ancestral origin—Europeans as masters, Africans as slaves, and East Indians as indentured laborers.[24] This history of voluntary and forced immigration from diverse areas of the Old World, and the life experiences imposed by the hierarchical relations structuring the plantation-slavery complex, significantly inform Trinidadians' understanding of their society as composed of people with diverse ancestries.[25]

This colonial history posed specific challenges for nation-building in Trinidad. Unlike in settler societies where Anglo/European immigrants were able to transform Old World ancestral diversities into New World purities, in Caribbean extractive colonies independence called for the transfer of state power from European colonizers to formerly subordinate groups.[26] And, unlike in Asia and Africa, where nation-builders could fashion indigenous native subjects to justify nationhood, the contenders for inheriting the state in Caribbean societies could not claim ancestral cultures that were either indigenous or had the capacity to transcend their particularisms, imprisoned as they were by a heritage of colonial racialization. The problem of reconciling the sociological fact of difference with the national imperative of unity—a general Caribbean predicament—was heightened in Trinidad, because the racial hierarchy encompassing the European and African mix typifying Caribbean societies was complicated by the significant presence of East Indians. As such, Trinidad could not even count on the tenuous unity based on a shared African ancestry claimed by other anglophone Caribbean societies. Much has changed since independence, but the current debate over formal multiculturalism and the anxiety that it will erode the existing common ground, reinscribes a tension fundamental to Trinidad, which has historically resisted attempts to resolve heterogeneity (multiculturalism) and homogeneity (national unity; common ground).

This tension is powerfully illustrated by the tendency of Trinidadians to use either "callaloo" (a stew made with the leaves of the dasheen bush, and flavored with okra and coconut milk) or "tossed salad" as metaphors for the nation. Trinidadians, mostly of African descent, see callaloo as a fitting metaphor, because this stew made of local ingredients conveys both native origins (in the New World) and the containment of *diverse* elements within a *single* unit. In the "callaloo" metaphor homogeneity trumps heterogeneity and thereby attests to a common ground legitimizing the nation, thereby creating a single New World purity through a homogenizing narrative. Alongside callaloo, however, is the metaphor of "tossed salad," which is not as ubiquitous as callaloo, but references an equally significant different model for Trinidadian society. This metaphor is primarily used by Trinidadians of Indian ancestry, who take exception to the callaloo metaphor, because the diverse ingredients in a callaloo are boiled down to an indistinguishable "mush," which erases the specific (taste) identities of the original ingredients, flattening them all into a homogeneous taste. Many Indo-Trinidadians thus find this metaphor inappropriate. Instead, they opt for the metaphor of "tossed salad," which also permits the containment of diversity within a single unit, but here, unlike in the callaloo, each diverse ingredient maintains its original unique identity. This subtle but significant distinction attests to a complex dialectical relationship informing Trinidadian national narratives, which were founded on colonial racializations that presented African and Indian as radically different, leaving the privilege of representing the nation open to contestation.

The "projected" incapacity of African and Indian cultures to transcend their particularities (and effectively symbolize the nation) can only be understood in relation to Anglo/Euro cultural claims to a monopoly of universals, which may be academically challenged, but remain formidable in setting the political and cultural agenda for "the rest." In Trinidad, the question of which group's culture is suitably equipped to represent the nation remains open, thereby rendering visible the cultural claims backing power that have been neutralized in more normative contexts of multiculturalism, such as in former Anglo/European settler colonies and metropoles. In short, the multicultural debate in Trinidad unsettles the claims of North Atlantic liberal multiculturalism to monopolize universals, and foregrounds the issue of culture in politics.

Examining a variety of texts that depict a positive vision of the Trinidadian nation for the benefit of tourists, foreign investors, and foreign scholars, Daniel Segal has argued that the projected "cosmopolitanism" of Trinidadian society—the image of a "United Nations in miniature"—suggests a nationalist narrative that emphasizes the continuity of ancestral diversities into the present.[27] The plurality or heterogeneity embodied by the various immigrant groups on their arrival in Trinidad is said to continue into the present. According to Segal, the Trinidadian nationalist narrative celebrates "not the creation of unity from heterogeneity—not the capacity to invent a new identity out of many old identities—but the coexistence of diverse ancestral kinds in 'harmony.'"[28] The original ancestral types reproduce themselves as discrete elements, preserving purity at the level of each and every group. This *cosmopolitan* narrative of Trinidad, which emphasizes the continuity of original ancestral types, resembles a *multiculturalist* narrative that corresponds to the metaphor of "tossed salad." Mixture here is nominal, a mere juxtaposition of different types (or purities).

The Trinidadian nationalist narrative of the continuity of pure ancestral types, however, exists in dialectical tension with another, equally visible Trinidadian (or anglophone Caribbean) nationalist narrative that pivots around the notion of mixture as symbolized by local understandings of their identities and societies as creole. A conception of Trinidadian national identity as oscillating between the polarities of mixture and purity is necessary for understanding how certain groups deemed pure (like East Indians) are symbolically positioned outside an imagined national community that ironically purports to celebrate precisely such ancestral purities. Such a dialectical reading complicates the very notion of purity, forcing one to recognize that not all purities represented in the cosmopolitan narrative of Trinidad are accorded the symbolic privilege of nativeness.

Creole understood as signifying the synthesis of new cultural and racial identities indigenous to the New World, provided a powerful counternarrative to the depiction of Caribbean societies as "a patchwork of not-yet-sewn together fragments."[29] This latter view was epitomized by M. G. Smith's "plural society" model, which posited the absence of a consensus of cultural values between Europeans and Africans in the anglophone Caribbean.[30] Smith argued that West Indian (or anglophone Caribbean) societies consisted of culturally distinct social segments—"Whites," "Coloreds," and "Blacks"—who practiced different forms of the same institution, and that these societies were held together by the political power exercised by a dominant demographic minority. "The connection between culture and nationalism was highly problematic in the West Indies," Smith asserted. "The common culture, without which West Indian nationalism cannot develop the dynamic to create a West Indian nation, may by its very nature and composition preclude the nationalism that invokes it. This is merely another way of saying that the Creole culture which West Indians share is the basis of their division."[31]

This projected lack of a common, unifying culture dovetailed with the widely held image of Caribbean societies as excessively dependent on the metropole—hence, V. S. Naipaul's caricature of Caribbean peoples as "mimic men."[32] To counter the idea that cultural identity was somehow problematic for West Indian peoples, West Indian scholars advanced the "creole society thesis," which emphasized the role of a distinctive common culture as a basis for national unity. Although the "creole thesis" was, in fact, the ideology of a middle-class intelligentsia seeking a leading role in an integrated, newly independent society, it nevertheless enhanced the emerging Caribbean nationalism of the third quarter of the twentieth century, forming a significant element in the Caribbean decolonization process.[33]

The term "creole" refers in common Caribbean usage to "a local product which is the result of a mixture or blending of various ingredients that originated in the Old World, suggesting an appropriate site of unity. Nationalists and local and foreign scholars alike saw creolization as a process of cultural interaction, synthesis, and change, whereby diverse Old World forms combined to create novel forms indigenous to the New World. This not only supplied the basis of common cultural identity for Caribbean people, it was also a narrative of indigenization. Anything and anybody native to the New World as a consequence of mixing was "creole." In Bolland's words "'Creole' refers to people who are *culturally distinct* from the Old World populations of their origin [emphasis in original]."[34] The principle of the creole narrative is in tension with the Trinidadian cosmopolitan narrative—creole signifying *distinctions* from Old World origins and the cosmopolitan narrative signifying *continuity* of Old World ancestries. In contrast to the cosmopolitan narrative, creolization was all about the creation of new (World) identities out of the many old (World) identities. In Trinidad, the colored and black middle-class intelligentsia's efforts to elevate calypso, steelband, and carnival (formerly the culture of the urban black lower-classes, whom the local elites despised) as *the* national symbols of the nation during the period leading up to independence rested on the premise that such cultural forms, while influenced by Old World strains, *originated* in the New World.[35] In this sense, one could argue that all things Creole—people, cultural forms, and languages—constitute core symbols of nativeness or indigeneity in Trinidad.

Trinidad's popular national narrative of cosmopolitanism, in which pure ancestral identities continue to the present, echoes M. G. Smith's analytical model of pluralism. The nationalist narrative of mixture (or creolization), on the other hand, as embodied in the term "creole," corresponds to the creole society thesis. These correspondences are somewhat jarring in that they juxtapose lay and analytic models, which seem in principle to be at odds. On the one hand, the analytic model of pluralism, which characterized these societies as deeply divisive and held together only by the power wielded by the white minority, is positioned in a paradigmatic relation to the lay model of the cosmopolitan, multicultural society with its promise of inclusion to all citizens. On the other hand, the creole society model, which emerged as an anti-imperialist discourse that emphasized the creative capacity of Caribbean peoples, is annexed to lay understandings of Creole, which excludes some Trinidadians from native status.[36] In order to understand how the various pure ancestral types represented in the cosmopolitan/multicultural narrative are differentially privileged in their claims to native status, the second narrative of mixture must be considered.

The ideology of mixing, variously conceived, was integral to defining native status in the Americas. But not all ancestries were privileged with the capacity to mix. In his analysis of Trinidad's colonial racial order, Segal illustrates how East Indians were excluded from the mixed category.[37] Trinidad's colonial racial order was built on the premise that pure races (representing different parts of the Old World) came to Trinidad, and subsequent mixing of these pure races was a feature peculiar to Trinidad and the Caribbean in general. This colonial rule of racialization located pure races outside of Trinidad, and those that embodied race mixture as indigenous to Trinidad. This legacy of racialization constituted a major ideological axiom through which East Indians later came to be defined outside the nation of Trinidad.

The idea that East Indians were "unmixables" was premised on Orientalist caricatures of Indians as persons saturated with an ancient (albeit inferior) culture that militated against mixing: as such, Indians remained of the "East" regardless of their ties to Trinidad.[38] Africans, in contrast, were seen as lacking an ancestral civilization, and their imputed status of "cultural nakedness" permitted the African, through mixing, to incorporate new elements and thereby become West Indian, or native.[39]

Mixing, which defined nativeness, was represented in the color spectrum defined by the end point values of black and white. All persons with some European and African ancestry were considered colored, and in this way both a pragmatic and ideological connection was established between the two groups: a connection thought to be particular to Trinidad yet reminiscent of the entire Caribbean. Even though blackness was devalued, the fact that the category black constituted a crucial axis in this pervasive system of social classification indicated recognition of the black or colored person's place in Trinidad. In contrast, East Indians were excluded from accountability within this system or any other that would have represented their ties to other groups and by extension to Trinidad. As such, there is a conspicuous lexical absence for East Indian mixing, an absence all the more telling when contrasted to the plethora of terms—both pseudo-scientific historical terms such as mulatto, quadroon, octoroon, and others and more popular contemporary terms such as black, black black, red, light black, brown, colored, French Creole, white, so-called white, and Trini white, among others—to account for different proportions of black and white mixing. Despite the ample empirical evidence that pointed to East Indians mixing with other groups, what is significant to my argument is the absence of *social* recognition of such mixing.

East Indians were also excluded from the term Creole, which applied to all persons of white and black extraction (those represented in the color spectrum). Excluded from accountability within the color spectrum, East Indians were not considered an ingredient in this resulting mixture. If mixing was the principle through which nativeness was defined, then to be native or local was also to be Creole. Denied the capacity to mix and denied social recognition of their local connections to other ancestral groups, East Indians never became Creoles. Accordingly, even today East Indians are not designated by the term Creole. The exclusion of East Indians from Creole status had significant implications for this group's positioning vis-à-vis the incipient nation of Trinidad during the decolonization period when Creole came to metonymize Trinidadian national identity.[40]

The narrative that to be Trinidadian is somehow also to be racially mixed is as prevalent as the narrative of the continuity of ancestral purities. Paradoxical as it may seem, these two nationalist narratives—emphasizing purity and impurity—are not mutually exclusive. Many Trinidadians "know of six or more racial . . . strains in their ancestry," Daniel Crowley observed. "Such people are proud of their mixed origins, and boast that they are 'a real mix-up,' or 'a West Indian callallu.'"[41] Even whites, whom one might assume to have a vested interest in claims to purity, readily acknowledge the illicit mixings in their genealogies. A member of a respectable upper-class French Creole family in his early fifties recounted his Portuguese, English, Scottish, and East Indian ancestry to me with amusement, adding that the term "French Creole" designates "so-called whites"—"so-called" because in fact they are all mixed. "Perhaps the epitome of a Trinidadian is the child . . . with a dark skin and crinkly plaits who looks at you out of decidedly Chinese eyes and announces herself as Jacqueline Maharaj," the Trinidadian novelist Merle Hodge observed.[42] On the other hand, Trinidadians continuously dissect or calibrate different proportions of mixture by resorting to the original ancestral categories, thereby insisting on defining persons or behavior on the basis of pure types—hence, even in Crowley's example, people display their mixedness by breaking it up into its constituent pure parts. Similarly, each feature of Hodge's Trinidadian child is isolated and attached to different ancestral types. Even in this instance when East Indian elements are recognized in the mix, the name "Maharaj," as an isolated trait, denotes culture not phenotype.[43] In a speech at a forum on the subject "What Is the Culture of Trinidad and Tobago?" the renowned carnival bandleader and designer Peter Minshall eloquently summed up Trinidadians' penchant for specifying the diverse purities that make up their native selves:

> I created several years ago a character called Callaloo. He was in everyman, with particular reference to these islands, in that who ever you were if you look at him it was your own self you would see. If you were black and you looked at he it was your own black self you going to see. White, brown or anything . . . it was your self you going to see in. *He was all of us in one.* Callaloo had a speech and in the course of the speech he said to de people and dem, "de differences is here to delight not divide and destroy."[44]

Insistence on racial accounting on the basis of pure ancestral types subverts the coherence and integrity of narratives of homogenization. That is, when a Trinidadian accounts for a person's racial makeup by saying "he half white and half black," mixture is acknowledged, but the insistence on accounting on the basis of pure types subverts complete flattening of heterogeneity to homogeneity. This narrative of mixture, which insists on racial calibration posits two stages. The first signifies the mixing of the originally pure types—Africans, various European groups, Chinese, and Amerindians—and the second signifies the calibration of the resulting mixtures on the basis of the pure types. In this national representation, East Indians who circumvented the cauldron of mixture (and hence the first stage)—at least in terms of social recognition of their mixture—enter into the second unamalgamated stage as yet another pure type like all other pure groups representing cosmopolitan Trinidad. The implication is that East Indians can be considered just as Trinidadian as those groups represented in the color spectrum that were subject to miscegenation. But such a reading is misleading, eclipsing more subtle principles of exclusion. Given that mixture embodied in the term Creole remains a defining principle for nativeness in Trinidad, pure ancestral types represented in the cosmopolitan or multicultural narrative of the nation are not symbolically equivalent. Trinidadian nationalist narratives distinguish between two types of purity that are differentially positioned in relation to national identity—*the purity of ancestral types that never passed through the cauldron of mixture and the purities that constitute parts of a mixture.* The latter type of purity never represents a whole in and of itself; it is the purity that is created through the calibration of mixed instances. In contrast, the purity supposedly embodied by ethnic groups who never mixed, like the East Indians, does constitute wholes, and as such they were placed at a considerable ideological disadvantage with respect to claiming native status in the New World.

The Trinidadian example complicates cosmopolitan or multicultural narratives that posit equivalence between racially subordinate groups. Colonial racialization combined with national imperatives to indigenize and mediate diversity through mixing, so as to fix African ancestry as the nation's ideological culture-history referent, making Afro-Creoles the legitimate inheritors of the state and the nation. Afro-Trinidadian claims on the postcolonial state were legitimized by the narrative of creolization for almost three decades. Creolization, however, was a narrative of homogenization that also allowed for the recognition of ancestral diversity, or heterogeneity. Claiming both indigeneity and ancestral diversity, Afro-Creoles were able to harness this tension better than any other group. Ironically, however, their political and cultural hegemony was buttressed by the representation of cosmopolitan/multicultural difference—which is to say, all ancestral differences in Trinidad— as fundamental to Trinidadian nativeness. Yet, as I have illustrated, creole difference and cosmopolitan difference are not equals in relation to native privilege. Such multicultural inclusion is nominal when they draw sustenance from homogenizing national narratives that invest only some groups in the multicultural nation with native privilege.

Elsewhere I have analyzed how, from a position of considerable disadvantage, Indo-Trinidadians gradually secured economic and political power.[45] Beginning in the 1980s, Indo-Trinidadians challenged Creole definitions of the nation and battled for national inclusion on the basis of their Indian ancestry. Indo-Trinidadians sought to displace the privileged creole narrative of mixture by redefining the nation's culture-history referent to include "purities" that were not mixed. It was this struggle around the symbolic definition of the nation that polarized the national narratives invoking callaloo and tossed salad. Indo-Trinidadians, intent on preserving their projected ancestral purity as Indians and also asserting their claims as authentic Trinidadians, sought to displace the callaloo/creole narrative (which they perceived to be an ideology of homogenization and assimilation) with that of tossed salad.

The political landscape has transformed dramatically since the struggles in the 1980s and 1990s over the symbolic definition of the nation. Since independence, political parties have largely relied on ethnic constituencies, with Afro-Trinidadians dominating politics and Indo-Trinidadians in opposition. Indo-Trinidadians were never seen as legitimate contenders for the postcolonial state because of the cultural particularities defining them and their "sectional" interests. Even in the early 1990s, the sentiment that an Indo-Trinidadian could not legitimately be prime minister prevailed. The elections of 1995 changed the political trajectory of the country, however, when an Indo-Trinidadian party and its leader, Basdeo Panday, came to power.

The political landscape has been significantly transformed, so that the state is no longer the preserve of Afro-Trinidadians, and Indo-Trinidadians are no longer perennial outsiders. Nevertheless, in negotiating the balance between common ground and cultural diversity, the former is aligned with Afro-Trinidadian and the latter with Indo-Trinidadian interests. The debate around multiculturalism thus remains animated by differing narratives of ancestral purity that contrast those who are mixed (calibrated purities), with those who never mixed (whole purities). Indeed, the official rationale for the adoption of multiculturalism as policy addresses Indo-Trinidadian pleas for such a policy. In 2011, the renamed Ministry of the Arts and Multiculturalism noted:

> Local Calls for a platform for Multiculturalism have traditionally revolved around perceived inequity in distribution of state resources amongst disparate ethnic groups in Trinidad and Tobago. This call has been most popular amongst the Hindu artistic and cultural fraternity as evidenced by the [Hindu charitable organization] Maha Sabha's request that the Ministry of Culture be labelled the Ministry of Multiculturalism. . . . The Honourable Prime Minister has clearly demarcated the focus of Multiculturalism on greater equity in the distribution of state resources in the Cultural Sector.[46]

The justification for multiculturalism in Trinidad as a corrective for previous state bias that cultivated Afro-Creole forms foregrounds the particularity attributed to those of both African and Indian ancestries. While Afro-Creole culture symbolized the Trinidadian nation until as recently as the 1980s, it was nevertheless always open to contestation. The elevation of Afro-Creole culture to national culture did not render invisible its particularities. Ironically, it was the particularity assigned to Indo-Trinidadians, even though subordinate, which continually interrupted narratives of homogenization that would exhaust the symbolic space of the nation. Even when East Indians were situated as outsiders, Afro-Trinidadian nation-builders were compelled to acknowledge East Indian difference and thereby admit to their own difference—if only to qualify their culture and history as the most suited referent for the nation. The retrospective Indo-Trinidadian charge of state bias in sponsorship of Afro-Trinidadian culture is possible because homogenizing national narratives of creolization did not or could not establish an uncontestable new purity. The significance of this Caribbean exception is borne out if we reflect on the absurdity of directing the same accusation at Anglo/Euro purities defining English, American, Canadian, or Australian native subjects. The doxa of these purities making up the symbolic core of each nation may be tweaked to accommodate multicultural difference, but this difference always remains the difference of the Other, rarely challenging Anglo/European symbolic ownership of the nation. In Trinidad, the dialectical play between homogenizing and cosmopolitan narratives, founded on colonial race hierarchies, continues to resist consolidation of either African or Indian ancestry as the nation's symbolic core. And the relentless proclivity of Trinidadians to read Indian or Creole interests into any instance that mixes culture and politics reveals the stakes tied to cultural citizenship, which transcend the Caribbean exception. The Trinidadian case, where the work of culture in politics is for the most part transparent and legible, provides a unique angle from which to critically engage privileges of liberal citizenship attached to other, more familiar formulations of liberal multiculturalism.

NOTES

1. The ethnic composition of the two islands comprising the nation-state of Trinidad and Tobago is significantly different. People claiming African descent largely populate Tobago. Since this paper is on the dynamics between Afro- and Indo-Trinidadians, I focus on Trinidad. Between 1834 and 1917, 426,623 indentured laborers were brought from India to labor in the sugar plantations of the Caribbean (see Walton Look Lai, *Indentured Labor, Caribbean Sugar: Chinese and Indian Migrants to the British West Indies, 1838–1918* [Baltimore: Johns Hopkins University Press, 1993], 19). They were essentially brought to compete with the labor of the newly freed former slave population—this is especially true of colonies such as Trinidad and Guyana. Many of the indentures did not return, as was the initial plan, and in some countries today, like Trinidad, Guyana, and Surinam, their descendants constitute a substantial part of the population. The ethnic breakdown of Trinidad and Tobago's population of 1.3 million according to the 2011 census was East Indian 35.43 percent, African 34.22 percent, mixed 22.8 percent (of which 7.7 percent are "Douglas" of African and East Indian mix, and 15.16 percent classified as "mixed other"), other ethnic group 1.4 percent, and not stated 6.2 percent. Trinidad and Tobago, Ministry of Planning, *Housing and Population Census Demographic Report* (Port of Spain: Central Statistical Office, 2011).

2. Ethnic terminologies are complex, and an array of terms specific to each ethnic group are often used interchangeably by Trinidadians. The choice of terminology, rarely consciously articulated, signify nuanced understandings of each group's capacity to embody the nation. For example, the terms "Indian," "Indo-Caribbean," "East Indian," and "Indo-Trinidadian" all refer to those claiming Indian ancestry in the New World and in particular Trinidad. The term "East Indian," the historically familiar referent for those of Indian ancestry, now competes with terminologies considered more progressive, like "Indo-Trinidadian," because of the symbolic exclusions invested in the "East Indian." Similarly, of the range of terms signifying those of African ancestry, "African," "negro," "black," "Creole" (as a noun), and "Afro-Trinidadian," pejorative racializations such as "negro," while fairly common in lay discourse, are consciously avoided in local academic and political discourse. I opt for "Indo-Trinidadian" and

"Afro-Trinidadian," which are not popular terms but those considered most politically correct. My use of terminologies differs from that of most Trinidadians because I wish to emphasize *projected* differences as opposed to claimed *natural* ones. I use "Indo-Trinidadian" and "Afro-Trinidadian" as analytical terms to refer to the projected dichotomy between Trinidadians claiming Indian and African descent except in contexts where the issue is the symbolic status attributed to Indo-Trinidadians. There, I opt to use "East Indian" for reasons of local historical and contextual consistency and also to connote a degree of marginality not conveyed by "Indo-Trinidadian."

3. Kris Rampersad, "Multikulti Is Dead! Long Live Multiculturalism!" October 18, 2010, accessed December 4, 2018, http://kris-rampersad.blogspot.com/2010/10/multikulti-is-dead-long-live.html.

4. I use "North Atlantic" here as a generic (as opposed to a geographic) term to encompass areas and societies variously identified as "Western," "Northern" "Global North" "First World," and "developed," which include metropolitan centers (UK, France, Germany) and former settler colonies (the United States, Canada, Australia), and in particular those nations that have implemented some form of multicultural policy.

5. Rampersad's critique contrasts markedly with those that polarize the debate by identifying multiculturalism as a strategy to consolidate Indo-Trinidadian and, more pointedly, Hindu interests. See, e.g., Selwyn Cudjoe, "Multiculturalism and Its Challenges in Trinidad and Tobago," *Global Society* 48 (2011): 330–41. Given the proclivity of people in creole societies to "operate with understandings and expectations concerning fundamental *differences* that set apart persons in their society" (Lee Drummond, "The Cultural Continuum: A Theory of Intersystems," *Man* 15 [1980]: 353), the default even when indexing intercultural situations is difference, which carries the potential for polarization.

6. Germany's Merkel and England's Cameron are the figures most often cited. See Richard Ashcroft and Mark Bevir's chapter 2 in this volume, "British Multiculturalism after Empire: Immigration, Nationality, and Citizenship," which addresses the retreat from multiculturalism in the United Kingdom.

7. For a lucid discussion of these differences, see Sneja Gunew, *Haunted Nations: The Colonial Dimensions of Multiculturalism* (London: Routledge, 2004).

8. As Michel-Rolph Trouillot remarks, "the nation is the culture and history of a class-divided civil society, as they relate to issues of state power. It is that part of the historically derived cultural repertoire that is translated in political terms." Trouillot, *Haiti: State against Nation: The Origins and Legacy of Duvalierism* (New York: Monthly Review Press, 1990), 25.

9. Caribbean colonies are called "extractive" because, unlike settler colonies in America and Australasia and colonies in Asia and Africa, they were established solely for the benefit of the metropole.

10. Christine Inglis, *Multiculturalism: New Policy Responses to Diversity* (Paris: UNESCO, 1996), cited in Kenwyn Taylor, "Multiculturalism and the Political Process in Trinidad: A Case Study," *Journal of the Department of Behavioural Sciences* [University of the West Indies, St Augustine Campus, Trinidad and Tobago] 1, no. 1 (2012): 100.

11. Gunew, *Haunted Nations.*

12. Ibid.; Elizabeth Povinelli, *The Cunning of Recognition: Indigenous Alterities and the Making of Australian Multiculturalism* (Durham, NC: Duke University Press, 2002); Leti Volpp, "'Obnoxious to Their Very Nature': Asian Americans and Constitutional Citizenship," *Citizenship Studies* 5, no. 1 (2001): 57–71; and Daniel Goh, "From Colonial Pluralism to Postcolonial Multiculturalism: Race, State Formation and the Question of Cultural Diversity in Malaysia and Singapore," *Sociology Compass* 2, no. 1 (2008): 232–52.

13. See, e.g., Charles Taylor, "The Politics of Recognition" in *Multiculturalism: Examining the Politics of Recognition,* ed. Amy Gutmann (Princeton, NJ: Princeton University Press, 1994). Even in those moments when Taylor concedes that human identities are dialogically constituted, as in his use of Gadamer's "fusion of horizons," the comparative engagement with "our" background of evaluation with those of formerly unfamiliar cultures, the onus lies on the latter to prove compatibility with "our" liberal values. "The 'fusion of horizons' operates through our developing new vocabularies of comparison,

by means of which we can articulate these contrasts. *So that if and when we ultimately find substantive support for our initial presumption* [emphasis added], it is on the basis of an understanding of what constitutes worth that we couldn't possibly have had at the beginning. We have reached the judgment partly through transforming our standards" (ibid., 67).

14. Amy Gutman, "Introduction," in *Multiculturalism: Examining the Politics of Recognition,* ed. Amy Gutman (Princeton, NJ: Princeton University Press, 1994), and Taylor, "Politics of Recognition.".

15. Wendy Brown, *States of Injury: Power and Freedom in Late Modernity* (Princeton, NJ: Princeton University Press, 1995).

16. Ibid.

17. A feature amply documented and analyzed in the voluminous literature on indigenous, minority, and ethnic groups in all parts of the world.

18. Volpp, "Obnoxious to Their Very Nature," 61.

19. Ibid., 67.

20. The title of Volpp's essay, "'Obnoxious to Their Very Nature': Asian Americans and Constitutional Citizenship," is indeed revealing.

21. See Kenwyn Taylor, "Multiculturalism and the Political Process in Trinidad," 100. I am not concerned here with critiquing the liberal distinction between private and public or the idea that public institutions should not be influenced by particulars of identity to ensure they remain neutral. However, it is worth noting that, from this perspective, it is the private/public distinction that allows for the neutrality of the public sphere, which protects citizens' freedoms and equality. Those characteristics common to all "our universal needs, regardless of our particular cultural identities, for 'primary goods' such as income, health care, education, religious freedom, freedom of conscience, speech, press . . . the right to vote, and the right to hold office" (Gutmann, "Introduction," in *Multiculturalism,* ed. id., 4).

22. Robert Young, *Colonial Desire: Hybridity in Theory, Culture, and Race* (London: Routledge, 1995), and Wolfram Schmidgen, *Exquisite Mixture: The Virtues of Impurity in Early Modern England* (Philadelphia: University of Pennsylvania Press, 2012).

23. James Millette, *Society and Politics in Colonial Trinidad* (Trinidad: Zed Books, 1985).

24. Daniel Segal, "Living Ancestors: Nationalism and the Past in Postcolonial Trinidad and Tobago," in *Trinidad Ethnicity* ed. Kevin Yelvington, 221–39 (Knoxville: University of Tennessee Press, 1994).

25. See Drummond, "Cultural Continuum, 353. The ethos captured by Drummond for Guyana prevails also in Trinidad: "Members of a creole society . . . operate with understandings and expectations concerning fundamental *differences* [emphasis in original] that set apart persons in their society. . . . Diversity and divisiveness are fundamental to the system. Differences can operate as representations because they take their significance from a pool of shared myth and experience."

26. Munasinghe "Narrating a Nation through Mixed Bloods," Social Analysis: The International Journal of Social and Cultural Practice 49, no. 2 (2005): 155–63.

27. Segal, "Living Ancestors."

28. Ibid., 226.

29. Helen Safa, "Popular Culture, National Identity, and Race in the Caribbean," *New West Indian Guide* 61, nos. 3–4 (1987): 115–26.

30. Smith's "plural society" model was borrowed from John Furnivall, who used the term to describe colonial societies in British Burma and the Dutch East Indies, where diverse groups existing side by side without mixing were held together by the power of the colonizer. See Furnivall, *Colonial Policy and Practice: A Comparative Study of Burma and Netherlands India* (Cambridge: Cambridge University Press, 1948).

31. See M. G. Smith (1965) quoted in Nigel Bolland, "Creolization and Creole Societies: A Cultural Nationalist View of Caribbean Social History," in *Intellectuals in the Twentieth- Century Caribbean,* vol. 1: *Spectre of the New Class: The Commonwealth Caribbean,* ed. Alistair Hennessy (London: Macmillan, 1992), 51.

32. V. S. Naipaul, *The Mimic Men: A Novel* (London: André Deutsch, 1967).

33. Bolland, *Creolization and Creole Societies,* 53.

34. Ibid., 50. Given the diverse meanings conveyed by the terms "creole" and its derivatives in various parts of the Americas, the discussion here is limited to the anglophone Caribbean. "Creole" operates in various registers: as theory; as dynamic process of cultural creation (creolization), and as a noun signifying persons of mixed African and European ancestry. "Creole" is capitalized when used as a noun to signify a person, or adjectivally in the terms "French Creole" and "Afro-Creole"; other adjectival uses are lowercased (e.g., "creole culture"), as are abstract nouns derived from "creole" (e.g.,"creolization").

35. See Lloyd Braithwaite, "The Problem of Cultural Integration in Trinidad," *Social and Economic Studies* 3, no. 1 (1954): 82–96; Stephen Stuempfle, *The Steelband Movement: The Forging of National Art in Trinidad and Tobago* (Philadelphia: University of Pennsylvania Press, 1996), and Peter van Koningsbruggen, *Trinidad Carnival: A Quest for National Identity* (London: Macmillan Education, 1997).

36. Viranjini Munasinghe, "Creating Impurity Out of Purity: Nationalism in Hybrid Spaces," *American Ethnologist* 29, no. 3 (2002): 663–92.

37. Segal, "Living Ancestors."

38. See ibid; and Viranjini Munasinghe, "Culture Creators and Culture Bearers: The Interface between Race and Ethnicity in Trinidad," *Transforming Anthropology* 6 no. 1–2 (1997): 72–86.

39. Segal, "Living Ancestors."

40. See Viranjini Munasinghe, *Callaloo or Tossed Salad? East Indians and the Cultural Politics of Identity in Trinidad* (Ithaca, NY: Cornell University Press, 2001), and Munasinghe, "Creating Impurity Out of Purity."

41. Daniel Crowley, "Plural and Differential Acculturation in Trinidad," *American Anthropologist* 59, no. 5 (1957): 819–20.

42. Merle Hodge, "The Peoples of Trinidad and Tobago," in *David Frost Introduces Trinidad and Tobago,* ed. Michael Anthony and Andrew Carr (London: André Deutsch, 1975), 1.

43. The author thanks Richard Ashcroft for this acute observation.

44. Recorded by the author, City Hall, Port of Spain, Trinidad, May 3, 1990.

45. Munasinghe, *Callaloo or Tossed Salad?*

46. Trinidad and Tobago, Ministry of the Arts and Multiculturalism, "Rationale for Policy Framework for Multiculturalism" (2011), accessed November 28, 2018, www.culture.gov.tt/wp-content/uploads/2015/07/2012-02-National-Multiculturalism-Policy-Framework-Rationale.pdf.

12

Comparative Perspectives on the Theory and Practice of Multiculturalism

Lessons from the Commonwealth

Richard T. Ashcroft, University of California at Berkeley
Mark Bevir, University of California at Berkeley

In this concluding chapter we explore the implications of this volume for the theory and practice of multiculturalism. We provide clear answers to the central questions raised at the outset: What is "multiculturalism," and how did it come about? What dilemmas has it posed for liberal-democratic governance? How have these been responded to in theory and practice, and are the different responses adequate? Are there alternative approaches to cultural diversity that have been overlooked? The chapters in this volume demonstrate that multiculturalism has implications that stretch beyond its current formulations in both public and academic discourse, casting doubt on basic assumptions of modern liberal democracy, and even on the viability of the nation-state in its present form.

Decolonization caused a significant increase in internal cultural diversity in many liberal democracies, which gave rise to multiculturalism as a social fact, related set of policy challenges, and normative debates. Yet the legacies of the British Empire also conditioned the various responses to cultural diversity, thereby helping to construct different forms of "multiculturalism." The dominant understanding of multiculturalism in political practice is in terms of the accommodation and integration of minority immigrants. The political theory of multiculturalism is broader in scope, including national minorities and indigenous peoples as well as immigrants, but nevertheless generally only ascribes self-government rights to the former two, and then only in certain circumstances. Conceptualizations of multiculturalism in current theory and practice have been conditioned by decolonization, which affected countries differently depending on both their domestic history and their position within the Empire. Comparing forms of multiculturalism across the British Commonwealth demonstrates that "multiculturalism" properly understood has profound ramifications for modern societies. The putative "siloing" of multiculturalism in theory and practice is problematic, and the holistic account of multiculturalism provided by this book points toward a radical approach to cultural diversity, which is to reform governance to make it much more polycentric, i.e. operating through an overlapping set of formal and informal institutions, no single one of which is empowered to trump all the others. Polycentric institutions, and an emphasis on pluralism within them, would better be able to accommodate the fluid, interrelated, and mutually constructing nature of the relevant issues and groups. In so doing, we might unwind unhelpful forms of social construction that occurred during imperialism, decolonization, and the creation of "multiculturalism" itself.

MULTICULTURALISM IN POLITICAL PRACTICE: IMMIGRATION AND INTEGRATION

The dominant political and public understanding of multiculturalism is in terms of postwar immigration and the dilemmas this has posed for traditional forms of liberal-democratic governance. In response to these challenges, many states have granted cultural minorities exemptions from putatively neutral and difference-blind laws, complemented by more positive assistance, such as language rights, education reforms, and funding for minority cultural activities. The explicit or implicit aim of these multicultural "regimes" is to help immigrants integrate into a polity understood as having a dominant cultural majority. These policies and laws are therefore aimed primarily at immigrant groups, rather than national minorities or indigenous peoples, who are usually seen as falling outside of the ambit of debates about "multiculturalism." Comparison of different countries across the Commonwealth undermines this narrative, however, in several key ways.

For example, the different issues raised by cultural diversity are not cleanly separable from each other, suggesting that neither are the different "types" of multiculturalism. In both Singapore and Malaysia, the forms of multiracial consociationalism adopted around independence have political, economic, and cultural aspects that affect each other, and thereby "multiculturalism," in various ways. Political tensions followed the ascription of individual citizenship rights within the context of an overarching group politics. In turn, this political competition is itself entangled with cultural practices, as seen in the community processions and parades that helped trigger the Malaysia/Singapore split. Yet economics has demarcated these different ethno-cultural groups even further by way of programs of development seen as necessary for political stability and cultural harmony. The entanglement of politics, economics, and culture can likewise be seen in India, where the adoption of Western liberal secularism has exacerbated political conflict between religious groups. The constitution adopted at independence also recast issues that are ostensibly religious or cultural—such as discrimination against the

Scheduled Castes—in socioeconomic terms, embroiling multiculturalism even further in interest group politics. These cases show that multiculturalism raises cross-cutting issues that affect the way groups relate to each other and to the state. In turn, this suggests that "integration" is not a unitary process, but takes place across a number of different "spheres," including the political and economic, and through processes that span public and private, individual and group. We therefore should not automatically prioritize *cultural* integration above all other forms, or assume it can/should take place in splendid isolation. Nor can we simply assume that integration in one sphere inevitably aids integration in another, or even that this would be desirable.

Although the cases cited above are from the "New" Commonwealth, the underlying point has traction elsewhere.[1] For example, recent public discourse in the United Kingdom has been dominated by calls for immigrants to integrate into British culture more completely.[2] Yet this ignores both the historical specificity of articulations of the cultural nation and the long-term degradation of the welfare state that aids integration. The pluralistic nature of integration thus suggests that even in cases such as the British one, which seem to fit the paradigmatic model of immigrant multiculturalism, we need to be aware of the historical nuances of particular "regimes" of integration, and the ways in which modern debates may gloss over underlying factors that are not overtly cultural. In turn, this reinforces the need to ensure that multicultural policy frameworks and the accompanying public rhetoric are open and holistic, rather than rigid and totalizing, in their approach to integration.

The interrelated nature of politics, economics and culture not only affects the way we should approach the integration of immigrants, however. It also embroils multiculturalism in debates over the treatment of national minorities and indigenous peoples, even if this is not always clearly understood in public discourse. For example, one reason behind the Brexit vote was the widespread perception that the welfare state—and the postwar British national identity of which it is a part—is being threatened by immigrant multiculturalism. Yet immigration and "Britishness" are understood and valued differently in different parts of the United Kingdom, which each have their own underlying national identity.[3] The dominant public understanding of British multiculturalism in terms of immigration and race therefore masks direct political connections to issues involving national minorities, in particular Brexit and renewed pressure for Scottish independence. In New Zealand "multiculturalism" is also understood primarily in terms of immigrant integration, yet again it is entangled at a deeper level with issues relating to national minorities/indigenous peoples. Its multiculturalism is shaped by debates over civic values and national identity, which take place against the background of official biculturalism. The neoliberal reforms that created immigrant multiculturalism threatened key aspects of New Zealand's national identity rooted in social justice, provoking a public backlash. Related government attempts to co-opt communal values based in indigenous culture were resisted by the Maori, who distinguished themselves from immigrant groups by articulating their claims in terms of bina-tionalism. Yet in recent years the Maori have softened their stance on immigration, seeing immigrant groups as potential allies in their struggle to resist racism and maintain a robust biculturalism. Both the British and New Zealand cases therefore illustrate the inevitable entanglement of multiculturalism in contests over national identity, which means immigrant multiculturalism cannot be neatly separated from issues relating to national minorities and indigenous peoples.

It is therefore unsurprising that government attempts to treat immigrants, national minorities and indigenous peoples separately can be ineffective, with the different groups influencing each other even as they try to distinguish their claims. This process occurs in both Britain and New Zealand, but is perhaps clear-est in Canada. Canada's reputation as a world leader in multiculturalism is in part built on features of its legal system that have helped to accommodate a variety of groups and claims. Ironically, however, this has had negative consequences. A crucial effect has been the siloing of discourses surrounding Quebec, indigenous peoples, and the integration of nonwhite immigrants, with "multiculturalism" in public discourse construed predominantly in terms of the latter. Not only does this gloss over connections prominent in the philosophical literature, it has also resulted in unhelpful politicization of debates. Multiculturalism is presented as a mechanism by which Anglophone Canada can intrude in Quebec's political and cultural autonomy, and as potentially undercutting the distinctive claims of indige-nous peoples. These difficulties are exacerbated by the legal doctrine of "reasonable accommodation," which facilitates opportunistic resistance to liberal egalitarian norms by local majorities, and by the potentially essentializing treatment of indig-enous cultures by the courts. Variegated legal arrangements and constitutional protections therefore interact with interest-group politics in Canada, meaning that even as the different groups and issues are perceived as separate in law and policy, they interact at a deeper level.

Attempts to treat immigrant groups, national minorities, and indigenous peo-ples separately are also ineffective in the New Commonwealth. We have already seen that in Malaysia, Singapore, and India, multiculturalism raises political, eco-nomic, and cultural issues that cut across each other, and that this has contributed to its politicization. A similar process can be seen in in Trinidad and Tobago, where the recent adoption of "official" multiculturalism draws on policy discourses that construe it primarily in terms of integration. Yet this multiculturalism has dis-turbed the precarious balance between the organically developed commonality aligned with Afro-Trinidadian interests and the self-conscious cultural diversity favored by Indo-Trinidadians.[4] Overall, therefore, the cases show that even nar-row conceptualizations of multiculturalism are implicated in contests over state resources, national identity, and cultural recognition. "Multiculturalism" thereby helps to construct competing groups as social entities through policy, law, and public discourse, even as they try to keep themselves separate.

Lastly, cases in the New Commonwealth highlight that the association of integration with immigration is contingent. Malaysia, Singapore, India, and Trinidad and Tobago have all struggled to blend different cultural groups together, yet of these states only Malaysia and Singapore have received significant numbers of postwar immigrants, many of whom are treated like guest workers who do not require permanent integration. The Nigerian case provides the clearest illustration, however, that framing multiculturalism in terms of immigrant integration may be unhelpful. Nigerian independence was shaped by political competition between three main groups, none of which formed an overall majority, with no clear way of integrating the groups into a single cohesive polity. The cases thus highlight that integration is a key issue even in the absence of mass immigration or a dominant majority.[5]

Casting multiculturalism in public discourse in terms of immigrant integration appears to be conditioned by historical experiences in Britain and the "Old" Commonwealth. Even in those countries, attempts to separate immigrant multiculturalism cleanly from other groups and issues—in particular those relating to indigenous peoples and other national minorities—are often ineffective, and perhaps counterproductive. Just as multicultural "issues" cut across politics, economics, and culture, the different groups—immigrants, national minorities, indigenous peoples, and other "cultural" groups—mutually construct each other, even in the absence of a dominant cultural majority. Confining "multiculturalism" to policy approaches aimed at immigrant integration is therefore historically conditioned, theoretically unconvincing, and practically impossible.

MULTICULTURALISM IN POLITICAL THEORY: CULTURE, IDENTITY, AND GOVERNANCE

The dominant understanding of multiculturalism in political theory draws on the typology of groups and rights conditioned by historical experiences in the Old Commonwealth and made famous by the Canadian philosopher Will Kymlicka. In political theory "multiculturalism" thus encompasses national minorities and indigenous peoples as well as immigrant groups, and potentially supports rights to special political representation, self-government, and historical reparations. Prominent claims made in support of these multicultural rights are that culture facilitates individual autonomous choice, supports self-respect, and grounds shared identities vital for democratic governance.[6] Unlike policy discourses, however, political theorists do not simply assume that the polity contains a cultural majority into which minorities must integrate. Rather, prominent advocates—and sometimes even critics—of multicultural rights support altering political structures in order to track the boundaries of individual cultural groups, in particular national minorities or indigenous peoples.[7] These structural changes are often supplemented with "polyethnic" multicultural rights aimed at integrating—but not assimilating—immigrant groups into the dominant (usually national) culture. On the face of it, therefore, this means that multicultural political theory supports our claim that casting multiculturalism purely in terms of immigrant integration is unhelpful. Yet even this more expansive understanding of multiculturalism in political theory is too rigid to accommodate the complexity of postwar multiculturalism.

A comparison of different countries across the Commonwealth casts doubt on the central claims in multicultural political theory in ways that build on the critiques from the previous section. Postcolonial polities are often defined by cultural hybridity or pluralism rather than homogeneity or unity, and therefore may lack fixed identities either at the state, substate, or even individual level. For example, while Afro-Creoles have historically dominated postcolonial Trinidadian politics, the hybridity that is definitional of creole culture destabilizes even this identity, preventing consolidation of either African or Indian ancestry as the nation's symbolic center. In India and Nigeria, the sheer scale of diversity within the state has arguably militated against the construction of a clear, stable shared identity, and even in the much smaller Britain there is pluralism at the heart of the cultural nation. Decolonization and multiculturalism have fundamentally—and perhaps irrevocably—destabilized British national identity, and postwar articulations of an inclusive Britishness continue to be pressured by resistance to immigration, economic globalization, and a suspicion of Islamic groups. This instability has been exacerbated by differences between England, Scotland, Wales, and Northern Ireland. Even these underlying nationalisms are too fluid to secure productive shared identities in the way many multicultural theorists presume.[8] National and cultural identities are dynamic and variegated, which indicates that their hybridity must be taken into consideration by both the theory and practice of multiculturalism, undercutting simple accounts of their role in governance that are common in the literature.[9]

Even where there are relatively clear forms of group identity, the nature of the relevant "culture" or "nation" can change in ways that undercut common assumptions regarding their effects and the neat separation of groups/rights. For example, in resisting the shift to neoliberalism, Pakeha (white/European-descended) and Maori New Zealanders drew on *shared* values that were grounded in *divergent* forms of national identity. Yet even these dual forms of identity are dynamic, with the Maori simultaneously defending domestic binationalism and rejecting the homogenized version of their culture co-opted by the state to "brand" New Zealand internationally. In addition, the elision of state services for the Maori and Pasifika immigrants means that the latter sometimes occupy a liminal status between the two dominant "nations." Similar issues occur in Canada, where Anglophone citizens form a clear cultural majority, albeit one that must co-exist with Francophone Canada and the First Nations. Yet variations between Quebec's "interculturalism," Federal "multiculturalism," and the legal treatment of indigenous cultural rights, demonstrates that the multiple cultural nations and groups in Canada are not immutable, but are expressed differently depending on context and fora, as is their response to cultural difference. Even in Australia the Anglophone "core" of the nation is not static. An early exclusionary ethno-nationalism was replaced by an assimilative cultural nationalism, which in turn has been tempered by a liberal nationalism that stresses integration. Australian multiculturalism is in part a pragmatic compromise between competing aspects of national identity, predicated on the ever-changing nature of the nation in response to cultural diversity. Comparison of cases across the Commonwealth therefore indicates that multicultural theorists can neither simply assume that "shared" values or identities rooted in culture or nation are identical at a deeper level nor that they will remain constant across time and domestic context. The relevant groups are not fixed and stable entities that play a predictable role in liberal democracy, but rather are dynamic, fluid, and contested.

Even a "political" nation that could potentially bridge underlying diversity may become entangled with thicker cultural nationalisms, as can be seen in India's post-independence nation-building. India has a distinctive approach to cultural diversity, rejecting overt group consociationalism in favor of more individualized forms of liberal governance, which are then supplemented by a "limited" multicultural regime of group-differentiated rights. Yet this approach came about largely because constitution-making at independence led to a compromise between different forms of liberalism and nationalism. Liberals and secular nationalists valorized difference-blind individual citizenship and a political conception of the nation, whereas conservative nationalists sought greater social unity through a cultural understanding of the polis. The growing power of Hindu nationalism suggests, however, that this convergence of interests was temporary and therefore unstable. Parallel difficulties can be seen in Britain, where public figures frequently suggest that a British national identity construed primarily in terms of shared values and institutions can unite different groups. Yet the "rebalancing" of British multiculturalism by forms of liberal nationalism potentially excludes more conservative cultural minorities, and Brexit has been accompanied by a resurgence in ethno-nationalism. The tendency of British debates over national identity to draw (often reflexively) on thicker aspects of British history and culture suggests that attempts to use a thin version of "Britishness" to unify the polity are misplaced.

Our comparative study of multiculturalism thus indicates that any given "culture" or "nation" is complex, dynamic, and alters across different contexts. The cases also suggest that the "political" nation is not robust enough to resist thicker forms of cultural and even ethno-religious nationalism. Yet the claims of multicultural theorists typically revolve around the function of culture in supporting autonomous choice, self-respect, and useful shared identities. This volume thus supports prominent "cosmopolitan" critiques of liberal multicultural theory alleging that it—and thereby the literature more broadly—implicitly relies on a simplistic account of culture.[10] The crux of this critique is that individuals simultaneously participate in multiple and overlapping forms of culture and identity. If true, this means that assigning rights to particular cultures on the basis that they play a necessary role in individual or group life is both unwarranted and potentially counterproductive.[11]

Cultures are socially constructed in two key senses that make rigid and monolithic accounts of it unsustainable. Firstly, since cultural meanings are necessarily abstract generalizations of concrete individual meanings, they are subject to human agency, as demonstrated by cultural change.[12] Secondly, any attempt to identify a culture is itself a form of social construction, and therefore placing an individual in one clearly identifiable culture with a precise boundary would require reducing it to a stipulative list of features. It is therefore unpersuasive to claim that an individual is necessarily located in a single culture that functions as an exclusive context for choice or identity. Since cultures are socially constructed, we have reason to suppose that individuals are located in multiple cultures and have several cultural identities, and therefore that whatever role "culture" plays will vary with how we define it. There may be different levels of overlapping understandings and identities that have important social effects, but there are many different levels of abstraction from individuals, of which any particular culture is only one.

Overall, therefore, the cases discussed in the preceding chapters support the contention that tracking the boundaries of specific cultural groups is empirically and philosophically problematic, undermining attempts to separate groups typologically and ascribe them different rights on this basis. This volume therefore casts doubt on the main reasons given in multicultural theory for wanting to prioritize particular cultures, and on the ability to do so in practice.[13]

MULTICULTURALISM, LIBERALISM, AND EMPIRE

Dominant accounts in philosophy and politics are thus fundamentally flawed in their conceptualization of multiculturalism. Since various "multicultural" issues and groups are interrelated and mutually constructing in *both* theory and practice, attempting to separate them cleanly is bound to fail. Our analysis of multiculturalism only shows us, however, that our response to cultural diversity must be holistic. It does not offer us positive guidance as to what type of rights, for which sort of groups, are justified. Should we treat all minority groups like immigrants or as equivalent to national minorities? Is the correct response to cultural diversity centralization and integration, devolution and local political autonomy, or something else entirely? Is it possible to have an integrated response to multiculturalism that productively spans both theory and practice?

In order to find a way out of this impasse, we must move up a level of analysis and examine multiculturalism in greater historical depth, and in its international as well as domestic contexts. The interaction of liberal and colonial forms of governance has conditioned the forms taken in each by multiculturalism, which not only challenges liberal-democratic norms and conceptions of the nation, but has remade states at a fundamental level. Modern multiculturalism is itself part of the process of decolonization, which continues to affect relationships both within and between the Commonwealth states. Tracing the roots of current philosophical and political debates foregrounds the depth of the dilemmas it poses to traditional liberal democracy, starting to bring into focus the issues that a fruitful form of multiculturalism must address.

The clearest examples of the entanglement of liberalism, colonialism, and multiculturalism are in the New Commonwealth. In what are now Malaysia and Singapore, the colonial state maintained itself by limiting ethnic groups to different economic roles: "Chinese" capital, "Malay" land, and "Indian" labor. This crude division showed strains under the Empire, and at decolonization the British advocated blending the diverse populations into unified polities through equal citizenship rights. A purely individualized approach was rejected by local elites, however, in favor of multiracial consociationalism that drew on the categories of colonial political economy. The state's capacity to balance the different groups has depended on economic growth, and so fluctuating fortunes have amplified calls for democratization and newer forms of multiculturalism. These efforts at reform have been undercut, however, by highly mobile labor and capital, and by recent financial crises. Nation- and state-building in both countries is thus still conditioned by the consociationalism drawn from racialized colonial governance, and its interactions with globalized liberal economics. Similar factors in Trinidad and Tobago have affected the development of nation and state, and thereby the way cultural diversity has been managed. Plantation slavery resulted in a rigid racial hierarchy, with Europeans as masters, Africans as slaves, and East Indians as indentured laborers. The annihilation of indigenous peoples led to recasting the descendants of enslaved Africans as "native," however, and so as the legitimate inheritors of the postcolonial nation and state. Afro-Creoles have therefore dominated domestic post-independence politics, but recently this has been challenged by Indo-Trinidadians, in part through an official multiculturalism that draws on policy discourses from Europe and the Old Commonwealth. The intertwined effects of colonial and liberal governance therefore contribute directly to the hybridity at the heart of the nation and colors political competition between subnational groups.

Colonialism also caused some polities to reject aspects of liberal governance, or to adopt aspects of it unsuited to local contexts. For example, the form of federalism adopted at Nigerian independence was the result of British influence, yet this tripartite division was inherently unstable, and cut across important religious and linguistic differences. In addition, the way the three main groups understood one another politically and culturally was conditioned by strategies employed by the British, as can be seen in their leaders' private statements and rhetoric in their party-controlled newspapers. British colonial governance therefore contributed to the distrust between the Igbo, Yoruba, and Hausa-Fulani, who favored different balances of federalism and nationalism. The entanglement of liberalism with colonialism in Nigeria helped to cast both cultural diversity and decentralization as threats, delaying the institution of a more radical federalism suited to Nigeria's deeper underlying cultural diversity.

Indian elites were also suspicious of British divide-and-rule strategies, and some had a strong commitment to universalist forms of liberal governance, including secularism. A pragmatic compromise between liberals and nationalists at independence reinforced resistance to colonial-era decentralization and group-rights, resulting in a rejection of consociationalism in favor of a "limited" multicultural framework. Subsequent expansion of multicultural policies and rights in India has thus occurred through ad hoc concessions to lobbying rather than the consistent application of political principle. This "normative deficit" plays into the rhetorical strategies of the Hindu Right, which also portrays multiculturalism as a threat to the nation. The interaction of liberalism, colonialism, nationalism, and religion is therefore vital for understanding multiculturalism in India. Although the early liberal state was defined by its relegation of religion to the private sphere, European colonialism was often justified by attempts to spread the Christian religion around the globe, and this dual inheritance altered the trajectory of both religion and politics in India. The Abrahamic faiths understand religion in terms of absolute doctrinal truth, and thereby prioritize the conversion of individuals through missionary work. Yet the religious traditions native to India do not share these commitments, but rather see truth as partial, perspectival and subject to open-ended pursuit from within one's own community. The imposition of Western secularism therefore incentivized the reconstruction of Indian religious traditions and communities in competitive "Semitic" terms, feeding ethno-religious conflict. Cases in the New Commonwealth therefore illustrate the deep historical connection between liberalism and colonialism, which has conditioned not just multiculturalism, but the structure, nature, and development of the postcolonial nation, state, and even religious groups.

The entwined legacies of liberalism and colonialism are also at work in the Old Commonwealth. In New Zealand, the Maori resisted the commodification of their culture for purposes of both domestic politics and international trade, and in so doing asserted their status as a distinct and equal founding group. Yet in responding to the neoliberalism that sought to open New Zealand more widely to global economic forces, they articulated their claims to internal political autonomy through emerging norms relating to indigenous peoples, which in turn drew on the international human rights law created by the postwar crisis in liberal governance. The influence of these international discourses led to significant domestic legal changes, such as the renewal of treaty claims and human rights legislation, which in turn have interacted with debates over immigrant multiculturalism and national identity. A parallel process has occurred in Australia, where multiculturalism—although it ostensibly also applies to indigenous peoples—is understood primarily in terms of nondiscrimination and equality of opportunity. These universalist liberal principles, and the political institutions and forms of citizenship through which they are expressed, are a key part of the British legacy in Australia. Unlike in Nigeria and India, however, where the experiences under colonial governance tainted liberal principles and practices, these aspects of the imperial inheritance have been readily accepted as central parts of Australian national identity and state governance. Australian multiculturalism also draws on inter- and transnational discourses, however, including a mix of norms and practices from other Commonwealth countries.[14] Yet Australia is unique in the way it has blended these international and domestic elements, maintaining a balance between cultural nationalism, liberal democratic principle, and the forces of globalization released by decolonization. In the Old Commonwealth, liberalism and colonialism have thus conditioned multiculturalism in both its domestic and international aspects—which are themselves not cleanly separable—and thereby altered the basic structure of both state and nation.

The United Kingdom lacks a written constitution or formal federalism, and so has addressed cultural diversity through policy and legislation rather than an overt restructuring of the state. Nevertheless, multiculturalism has reconstituted Britain at a fundamental level, and there has been a failure fully to acknowledge the deep connection to empire. Colonization provided a common project for the different nations of the United Kingdom, helping to form both the modern British state and a new "national" identity. The end of empire therefore not only challenged Britain's status as a world power but destabilized "Britishness" itself. The overall result was a postwar transformation of UK nationality, citizenship, and immigration law, which in turn has meant that multiculturalism focuses on integrating immigrants into the British nation. Yet there is no consensus regarding what that nation is, or should be. Thinner political identities compete with thicker forms of "muscular liberalism" and cultural nationalism, which in turn often slide into ethnocentrism. These different forms of British national identity cut across underlying nationalisms, which have different relationships with multiculturalism, immigration, and a welfare state under pressure from domestic neoliberalism and economic globalization. These cleavages and their historical roots are rarely foregrounded in debates over British multiculturalism. The resulting public discourse therefore also suffers from a "normative deficit," which stems from a failure to address directly the ways in which liberalism and colonialism have conditioned Britain's self-understanding. British national identity continues to be expressed through a Whiggish exceptionalism that alternates between sanitizing and celebrating British imperial history, ignoring the effects of the end of empire on the plural identities it held together. The refusal to face the intertwined nature of Britain's colonial past and multicultural present thus masks the depth of the challenge cultural diversity poses to the British nation and state, suggesting that efforts to limit its scope to immigrant integration will be counterproductive.

Domestic cultural diversity thus cannot be understood without reference to international discourses, and forms of modern multiculturalism are conditioned by the historical legacy of liberalism and colonialism. Postwar multiculturalism challenges traditional liberal-democratic norms and practices that are themselves entangled with the history of colonial governance. Multiculturalism, and the decolonization of which it is a part, have also altered the basic form of the nation and structure of the state, albeit that these processes have varied in their mechanisms, effects, and how they are understood. Comparison of different cases across the Commonwealth indicates that a productive response to postwar cultural diversity must address its multiple contexts, but still acknowledge the depth of its challenges to nation and state. In particular, any fruitful form of multiculturalism must remain cognizant of the ongoing effects of colonialism on its own theory and practice, and on liberal-democratic governance more broadly.

MULTICULTURALISM IN THE BRITISH COMMONWEALTH: NEW, OLD, AND ORIGINARY

The dilemmas posed by the end of Empire looked very different from the center than at its periphery, and therefore the categories of colonizer, settler-colony and colonized which structure this volume help to explain important features of the different cases. For example, polities in the New Commonwealth, which had to balance multiple competing groups after decolonization, all encompass a degree of cultural diversity that cannot readily be encapsulated by the Westernized conceptualizations of multiculturalism that arose in the 1970s.[15] Racialized colonial governance has conditioned Trinidadian national identity, fixing Afro-Creole, East Indian and White Settlers as the organizing groups, even as these categories are constantly pressured by hybridity within and across the correlated identities. Multiculturalism in Malaysia and Singapore has been determined by economic development rather than political institutions, but both of these are beholden to racialized categories inscribed by the British. And in India, the legacy of colonial missionary work and Western liberalism has masked the underlying normative or cultural issues and exacerbated ethno-religious conflict.[16] Meanwhile, in Nigeria, resistance to decentralization in reaction to the colonial divide-and-rule strategy had disastrous consequences. Multiculturalism in the contemporary New Commonwealth therefore cannot be understood without reference to the ongoing effects of governance rooted in the intersection of liberalism and colonialism.

The legacy of colonial governance is significantly different in the nations of the Old Commonwealth. As "Greater Britain" these colonies all had longer experiences of self-rule, preferential treatment by the United Kingdom, greater initial homogeneity, and more controlled transitions to independence. The privileged status of these countries bolstered the stability of their political institutions and economic development, which aided the creation of a robust welfare state. These political, economic, and cultural factors supported the integration of new arrivals following immigration reforms, which in turn drew out policies that self-consciously addressed cultural diversity. The unique position of the Old Commonwealth within the Empire thus facilitated the development of forms of official bi- and multiculturalism that were able to blend traditional liberalism, domestic reformulations of it, and newer international discourses. The nature of the nation in the Old Commonwealth, and its relation to Britishness, is also very different. Stuart Ward has demonstrated that the collapse of the imagined community of "Greater Britain" after World War II forced the countries of the Old Commonwealth to develop forms of nationalism to fill the void.[17] Even as these settler-colonies shifted away from the imperial metropole, however, the articulation of their "new nationalisms" drew on aspects of their British inheritance. The dominant *cultural* nation was still presumed to be anglophone, albeit that it was self-consciously reconstructed in relation to national minorities, indigenous peoples, and immigrant groups.[18] In addition, the "Anglo-Saxon" cultural inheritance could be construed in broadly homogenous terms, without looking through the anglophone "core" to potential tensions within it among the English, Scots, Welsh, and Irish elements.[19] This stable cultural core has helped the Old Commonwealth countries evolve gradually in the face of cultural diversity, facilitating the adoption of "multiculturalism" as part of their national identity. All of the above factors are plausibly the result of their position within the Empire, and seem to have helped these states tailor their responses to local conditions, aiding their ability to meet the challenges of postwar cultural diversity.

Such opacity has not been a long-term option within the United Kingdom itself, however. Before World War II, Britain had never existed without empire, and the attempt to manage post-imperial foreign relations—including issues related to race—via nationality reforms caused mass nonwhite immigration. Britain developed a bifurcated form of multiculturalism in response, which conditioned the public understanding of it in terms of immigrant integration. Modern British multiculturalism is therefore also a direct legacy of colonial governance and the way it interacted with liberal norms (such as anti-racism) both domestically and internationally. Ironically, however, this hides its connection to basic issues regarding the nation and state. "Britishness" is a distinctive identity, but is constructed out of underlying nations that have all reacted differently to multiculturalism, as Brexit and renewed calls for Scottish independence have shown. The British nation is inherently unstable in a postcolonial setting, which casts doubt on the postwar attempt to integrate migrants into a single national identity. It may well be, therefore, that Britain requires more a fundamental and deliberate legal restructuring in response to multiculturalism than the nations and states in the Old and New Commonwealth, who have addressed its challenges more self-consciously and more systematically.

Exploring the ways in which experiences of multiculturalism have been conditioned by both local factors and countries' positions within the Empire therefore reinforces and deepens our analysis. The different conceptualizations of multiculturalism are functions not just of geography and history but also of different forms of power, and of how these were instantiated both during and after empire. Colonial governance at least partly constructed the issues and groups in each locale, and its legacy affected attitudes to, and interpretations of, liberal democracy. In turn, this altered the trajectory of nation- and state-building in each case, and conditioned understandings of multiculturalism in theory and practice. Our narrative demonstrates that not only does "multiculturalism" cut across the borders of policy and theory, it also straddles the boundaries of nations and states, and undercuts traditional accounts of their origin. Prominent narratives in the social sciences, humanities, and law see the formation of modern nations, states, and liberal democracy as taking place within Europe, and only then exported to other parts of the world. Yet this volume strengthens claims that this story is a myth, and an unhelpful one at that.[20] The countries of the British Commonwealth have never existed in complete independence from one another, and the legacy of the Empire continues to affect their development. The multiple layers of identity and governance engaged by multiculturalism stretch across individual countries, none of which exist in splendid isolation from each other. Modern polities are not closed political, economic, or even moral communities, but rather are related parts of an interdependent global system. It is not just the different "multicultural" groups and issues that are interrelated and mutually constructing, but the Commonwealth nations and states themselves.

This volume therefore leads us back to venerable struggles over the proper nature and scope of liberal democracy, helping to clarify what form our response to multiculturalism should take, and at what level it should be applied. Multiculturalism must be understood holistically, as a process by which different groups—including nations and states—construct each other, and "multiculturalism" itself, through a series of overlapping debates regarding politics, economics, and culture. Our responses must be similarly flexible, yet nevertheless engage the deep-rooted issues of identity and governance raised by cultural diversity and the end of imperialism. Our form of multiculturalism must therefore be wide-ranging, traversing politics, economics, and culture, and all manner of different groups and rights. It must be radical in its scope, questioning long-standing presumptions regarding the history, nature, and function of both nation and state. And it must address the depth of the challenge posed by multiculturalism to traditional liberal-democratic governance, suggesting that we must reform not just principles and practices, but also the basic structure of the polity.

MULTICULTURALISM AS THEORY AND PRACTICE: POLYCENTRIC AND PLURAL GOVERNANCE

In this final section, we bring together the different strands of our analysis, and this volume more broadly, sketching the central lessons of our comparative study for the theory and practice of multiculturalism.[21] We have seen that across the postwar Commonwealth cultural diversity has called into question not just whether the nation-state in fact facilitates liberal democracy, but whether it is even viable in its traditional form. Multiculturalism presses directly on potential cleavages in the modern world, revealing the contingency of cherished national narratives and fundamental forms of governance, and engaging identities grounded in the former as well as norms relating to the latter. The interrelationships between culture, meaning, and identity, and their normative ramifications for governance, are crucial issues for any form of multiculturalism. Yet current understandings of multiculturalism in theory and practice are unhelpful in the way they generally attempt to separate out different "multicultural" groups, rights, and issues. Instead, we need to reconstitute our basic forms of our governance to be radically polycentric and pluralist.[22]

The dominant understanding of multiculturalism in contemporary politics is in terms of immigration, but this is unduly narrow. It underplays historical interactions between different groups and the way these have influenced the policy and legal frameworks applying to each. The politicization of public discourse surrounding multiculturalism and national identity also discourages some groups from framing their claims in multicultural terms, glossing over important philosophical problems and deeper connections between different issues. In public debates over national identity, the overarching goal is to articulate an inclusive form of it that can integrate a multicultural citizenry. Yet current popular discourse fails to address the pressing question as to whether nonexclusionary forms of identity can have the desired effects, not just on immigrants but on the wider populace. Integration is not a unitary process but rather takes place in different ways, across many locales, and into multiple groups. This suggests we should not focus on the participation of immigrants in specific spheres of public life, such as the majority culture or national identity, or through narrow mechanisms such as policy and law. Cultural meanings and identities are fluid, dynamic, and overlapping, which means that generalized calls for "integration," "assimilation," or even "cohesion" may be misplaced.

Current practices of multiculturalism may therefore have something to learn from the philosophical issues addressed in multicultural political theory, and its wider scope. It is clear that multiculturalism stretches far beyond the challenges posed by postwar immigrant integration, potentially justifying a radical remaking of the state, including grants of political autonomy to national minorities. Yet political theory may also have something to learn from our historical study of multiculturalism. For example, many postwar immigrants to the United Kingdom already possessed the equivalent citizenship status to natural-born British citizens by the time they arrived, and so do not fit the standard typology in multicultural political theory. Nor do the many of the various substate groups reconstructed by colonial and liberal governance in the New Commonwealth, many of which straddle the boundaries between politics/economics/culture, nation/national minority, and even indigenous/alien.[23] This volume therefore suggests that claims to self-government on the basis of culture are not necessarily limited to peoples subject to colonization, or to minority national groups such the Québécois who were co-colonizers. Rather, immigrants from former colonies, and a wide variety of autochthonous groups within them, may have a plausible claim to more substantive rights, including political autonomy.[24] A blanket asymmetry of rights is therefore unpersuasive.

The division between groups and rights employed at the level of theory thus potentially ignores important aspects of history. The standard typology is also philosophically unconvincing, arbitrarily valorizing the role and nature of culture in some groups at the expense of others. What sort of rights can be justified on the basis of cultural difference has been a recurring issue in the philosophical literature, as have connected concerns about the reification and essentialization of cultures.[25] We have suggested above that liberal multiculturalists—and perhaps some of their critics—are committed to the claim that particular cultures play a necessary role in individual choice, ground self-respect, and facilitate useful shared meanings and identities. Yet philosophical holism rules out a rigid view of culture, indicating instead that it is plural, fluid, overlapping, and contested.[26] Our historical study of the Commonwealth supports these philosophical claims, demonstrating that multiculturalism straddles multiple and interconnected historical, geographical, temporal, and discursive contexts. The intersection of multiculturalism and liberal democracy, and—through imperialism—the intertwining of the nations and states of the postwar Commonwealth themselves, means that any attempt to separate groups and issues in policy and theoretical discourse is unconvincing. It is therefore presumptively problematic to assign rights on the basis of culture to particular groups of individuals but not to others. Identification of individuals as members a group to which we might ascribe multicultural rights—such as a culture, national group, or perhaps even a state—is itself an act of social construction, which means that the difference between those inside and those outside the group may be unclear and contested. In fact, an anti-essentialist account of culture seems to rule out any fixed cultural identities, and thereby undercut claims for their protection based directly in culture itself.

The issues multiculturalism raises cannot simply be ignored or dismissed, however. The forms of identity and governance that multiculturalism challenges are deep-rooted, and our case studies also show that sensitivity to local history and conditions is important. Superficially similar groups may therefore have distinctive claims in different contexts, and require tailored forms of "multiculturalism."[27] This means we should be suspicious of one-size-fits-all and one-time-only solutions, whether it be in terms of moral values, political practice or the composition of the polity itself. Yet, although we have good reason to believe that cultural identities and groups are fluid, some people will believe—and act as if—they are not. Any "multicultural" regime must therefore be flexible enough to account for those that experience culture as singular and natural and those that see it as plural and constructed. Our holistic understanding of multiculturalism thus points toward the value of radically restructuring polities to be more polycentric, and thereby better suited to the plural patterns that constitute our social world. In order to move beyond the impasse between current forms of multicultural theory and practice, therefore, we should treat all "cultural" groups akin to national minorities or indigenous peoples rather than immigrants. Such reforms would address the fundamental issues raised by multiculturalism, be sensitive to historical context, but also philosophically and normatively robust. All of the chapters in this volume speak to this claim, although not all of our authors would necessarily make it as forcefully as the editors, or even at all.

More open-ended forms of social organization would better reflect the fluid and interrelated nature of the various issues and identities that multiculturalism engages, allowing different groups to determine their boundaries, practices, and norms for themselves. It would enable individuals to express different aspects of their identity according to their own priorities, and thereby accommodate those who wish to embrace cosmopolitan forms of identity, yet would also open spaces for others to focus on more traditional practices. Multiple and overlapping forms of governance may also help to foster partial—and context-sensitive—forms of integration that serve purposes of justice or social cohesion.[28] Polycentric institutions would thus accommodate deep diversity and help to secure social stability. Yet they would also facilitate social change. Since our theories and practices are mutually constructing, our reasoning is best instantiated in lived practices, which will inevitably take many experimental forms whereby our plural forms of life are constantly remade in different ways. Allowing genuine self-governance for those who reject dominant norms could productively utilize the different ways in which the understandings and identities of individuals overlap and interact. We hope greater polycentricity and pluralism in governance would encourage political experimentation, economic innovation, and cultural renewal.[29]

Yet any systematic response to deep diversity, whether by direct state action or otherwise, risks constructing groups in precisely the way that philosophical critiques of multiculturalism allege.[30] We suggest that reorganizing our institutions to be more polycentric minimizes these risks, however, even if it cannot eliminate them entirely. Structural changes will inevitably have effects on groups—in the main by increasing exit and thus experimentation—but these more flexible forms of self-governance will allow the evolution of a group in any direction, including multiple variations of it. Such effects are materially different from the state imposing fixed rights from outside the group, which necessarily affect the rate of change (or condition its form) by privileging some interpretations of the group over others.[31] We do not claim that structural reforms and pluralist public discourse will automatically produce beneficial practices, rather that it is plausible that they will. Harmful forms of social construction are inevitable, but the sheer complexity of identities and issues at play suggests that they cannot be prevented by top-down control. Rather, they must be reformed through countervailing practices led from below, which will be facilitated by polycentric institutions and pluralistic practices. Nor do we suggest that it is impossible or unjustified to draw boundaries between different groups in order to ascribe rights. Legal rights are an important tool for correcting historical injustices against a particular group, and the bounds of the group and scope of the right can be identified by tracing the negative effects of previous practices of social construction on its members. For example, race is a social construction, but one that has clearly benefited those identified as "white" rather than those who are not, and rights for the latter may therefore be justified as a corrective. Yet the nature of the difficulty addressed implies that these rights should be temporary rather than permanent, more akin to affirmative action than constitutional principle.

We also suggest that structural changes, if instituted correctly, will encourage pluralist discourses, which can make our inevitable practices of social construction more transparent, and thereby potentially more productive. Political practice and theory evolve in tandem, but this is often through messy historical processes that obfuscate the empirical effects and normative issues, as this volume demonstrates. Part of the process of instituting polycentric reforms could be public discussion of why and how they address multiculturalism as we have conceptualized it here. Emphasizing in public discourse and education the history behind our current cultural pluralism would help to foreground the realities of empire and its afterlife, in particular those that relate to race and national identity. Polycentric structures, and an emphasis on pluralism within them, may thereby make us more self-conscious of previous instances of social construction and assist attempts to unwind them. We must also be cognizant of the new social realities we create, some of which may even flow from attempts to deconstruct older ones. For example, valorizing *any* identity, even a cosmopolitan one, will exclude those who do not meet its criteria, and thus is potentially divisive. And while listening to the voices of people who have traditionally been silenced is a vital part of overcoming injustice and exclusion, we must be cautious in our embrace of those who claim to speak with authority for fellow members of marginalized groups, lest we turn the historical experiences of some into reified identities that silence others.

Holism means that individual judgments and identities are always provisional, and must be understood as such. As societies we therefore should not attempt to instantiate ahistorical principles, protect fixed identities, or track "objective" boundaries between groups. No matter how important we feel any of these to be, they cannot form completely fixed, foundational points in social life. In turn, this suggests that we should not attempt to impose specific values—including the robust forms of autonomy or equality that inform many theoretical accounts of liberalism and cosmopolitanism—but rather focus on persuasion. We therefore sympathize with accounts of multiculturalism such as those offered by Seyla

Benhabib and Sarah Song, who both emphasize the socially constructed nature of cultures and foreground the importance of deliberation in negotiating changes within and across them.[32] Nevertheless, we must guard against focusing too narrowly on disputed liberal values or formal democratic processes, which we have seen are often historically implicated in the forms of social construction we are trying to address.[33] Rather than valorizing moral rules or particular political procedures, it may be more productive to cultivate a pluralist ethic of openness to difference, and to encourage free exchanges between and within groups. In any event, uncertainty as to the relative importance in their members' lives of the multiple groups/identities present indicates that the precise structures of governance adopted cannot be fixed in advance. Reforms must be tailored to local conditions, subject to negotiation and deliberation, and take diverse forms. We should therefore be wary of theoretical arguments that prioritize governance at one level over another, whether it be the claims of postnationalist cosmopolitans such as Arash Abizadeh regarding the global demos, liberals such as David Miller regarding the nation, or the communitarians and civic republicans who gravitate toward smaller-scale communities.[34]

The challenges presented by multiculturalism, and our advocacy of polycentric institutions in response, connects current debates to long-standing tensions between the central and local. The juxtaposition of centralization and localism occurs in all contexts, either directly in debates over liberal-democratic governance, or indirectly through contests over national identity. Our preference— particularly within Britain, the case the we know best—is for radical devolution to a wide range of groups and associations. In part, this is because we would like to re-empower the local, which we feel has been systematically devalued, even as we continue to look upward towards international organizations. The pull toward the local is itself contingent, however, and is not tied to a particular physical space. Rather polycentric governance may furnish a variety of overlapping 'local' contexts, between which individuals could move both literally and figuratively. Radical polycentricity maximizes the ability of individuals to self-sort into the associations that are the most beneficial to them, and to learn from forms of life that are not. We therefore suggest that the state must facilitate the movement of people through guaranteeing both a potent form of the right of exit, and substantive freedom of information within and across the different levels of organization.

Drawing on postanalytic philosophy, and nonstatist aspects of the socialist tradition such as the guild socialism of G. D. H. Cole, Ashcroft will argue elsewhere that as well as guaranteeing the right of exit, the polycentric multicultural state must provide the economic and cultural capital to utilize it, including shelter, sustenance, and education. The state must provide a physical and social space for those moving around within it to exit into, where they may engage in reflection, enquiry, and reassociation. Perhaps this version of the "welfare" state would function more like Michael Walzer's "hotel" than a permanent home, but would be more than this, containing information about other associations and ways of life.[35] The state would thus also be a library, a rail network, and a marketplace of ideas. We are therefore committed to a much more robust state than other theorists who advocate polycentricity, such as Chandran Kukathas, in part because we offer a thicker (albeit nonessentialist) account of cultural identity and meaning, and in part because of our own political and philosophical commitments.[36]

Our overall position therefore bears a passing resemblance to John Stuart Mill's "experiments in living." Yet our postfoundationalism severs our account from the individualism, romanticized cultural essentialism, and substantive autonomy central to Mill, but which also can be seen in much contemporary liberal, multicultural, and cosmopolitan theorizing. Our form of pluralism is thus distinctive, drawing on a variety of intellectual traditions, yet is still multicultural in a meaningful sense. And our polycentricity forms a generally applicable—but not homogenizing—approach to cultural difference that is normatively justifiable, yet still allows for a degree of historical nuance. By providing a holistic response to multiculturalism that bridges both theory and practice, polycentric and pluralist governance may therefore help to mitigate the tension between historical specificity and normative principle that is particularly acute within multiculturalism, and which runs throughout post-Enlightenment philosophy and politics.

Ultimately, however, the way forward lies not in following the plaintive cries of political theorists, but rather in harnessing the extraordinary variety that originates in everyday lives. By opening ourselves to the radical diversity of human beliefs and practices through which individuals and communities remake themselves, we can move forward without becoming disconnected from the past, and look to the global without abandoning the local. If we do, we may start to address the underlying tensions in our thought and practice that are both old and new, and central to the many worlds we share.

NOTES

1. We use "Old" and "New" Commonwealth to distinguish Canada, Australia, and New Zealand from other colonies in the Empire, which were never intended to be permanently settled by the British, and whose relationship to Great Britain was marked by more nakedly extractive practices. We do not include South Africa and Zimbabwe within the former, for reasons we discuss in the introductory chapter, as part of a detailed discussion of these terms and our other vocabulary choices.

2. We use the terms "United Kingdom" and "Britain" interchangeably, i.e., including Northern Ireland in both.

3. Richard Ashcroft and Mark Bevir, "Pluralism, National Identity and Citizenship: Britain after Brexit," *Political Quarterly* 87 (2016): 355–59.

4. The island of Tobago is much less ethnically diverse than Trinidad, since it is almost entirely populated by people of African descent. Its population is around 60,000, compared with 1.3 million in Trinidad. The overwhelming weight of political and economic power therefore resides in Trinidad, as do the dominant narratives of nationhood. We therefore follow Viranjini Munasinghe in frequently using "Trinidad," "Indo-Trinidadian," and "Afro-Trinidadian" as shorthand.

5. We argue elsewhere that Kymlicka's theory of multiculturalism is part of a broader family of liberal positions—along with, e.g., David Miller's *On Nationality* (Oxford: Oxford University Press, 1995)—that see the cultural nation as vital for the functioning of modern democracy (Richard T. Ashcroft and Mark Bevir, "Liberal Democracy, Nationalism and Culture: Multiculturalism and Scottish Independence," *Critical Review of International Social and Political Philosophy* 21, no. 1 [2018]: 65–86). The influence of Kymlicka's early work means these presumptions have shaped much of the political theory literature, particularly work by liberal supporters of multiculturalism. Even those theorists who do not fall squarely within that camp came to share key assumptions regarding culture and governance. For example, the "politics of recognition" made famous by Charles Taylor overlaps with liberal multiculturalism as it relates to identity and self-respect, and shares a similar commitment to the cultural group as the primary locus of governance, especially when it coincides with the nation. See *Report of the Commission on Accommodation Practices Related to Cultural Difference* (Quebec: Government of Quebec, 2008), which Taylor co-authored with Gérard Bouchard; Charles Taylor, "The Politics of Recognition," in Amy Gutmann, ed., *Multiculturalism: Examining the Politics of Recognition* (Princeton, NJ: Princeton University Press, 1994); and for an excellent discussion of the "Herderian" aspects of Kymlicka's argument that push him closer to Taylor, see Helder de Schutter, "The Liberal Linguistic Turn: Kymlicka's Freedom Account Revisited," *Dve domovini//Two Homelands*, no. 44 (2016): 51–65. For an overview of "cultural nationalism" broadly compatible with ours, see Arash Abizadeh, "Does Liberal Democracy Presuppose a Cultural Nation? Four Arguments," *American Political Science Review* 96, no. 3 (2002): 495–509.

6. This is clearly true of Kymlicka and Taylor and thus forms the dominant view in the theoretical literature, albeit subject to caveats and critiques. Multicultural political theory therefore tends to emphasize the relationship between culture and governance, but unlike some liberal nationalists, such as David Miller, both Kymlicka and Taylor disconnect the "cultural" nation or group from the state. Postcolonial theorists tend to share the presumption that some minority cultural groups, particularly indigenous peoples, should be self-governing: see James Tully, *Strange Multiplicity: Constitutionalism in the Age of Diversity* (Cambridge: Cambridge University Press, 1995), and Glen Sean Coulthard, *Red Skin, White Masks: Rejecting the Colonial Politics of Recognition* (Minneapolis: University of Minnesota Press, 2014). Likewise, Iris Marion Young endorses claims to self-government by indigenous peoples, albeit "more as a means to the achievement of structural equality . . . than an end in itself" (Young, "Structural Injustice and the Politics of Difference," in Anthony Simon Laden and David Owen, eds., *Multiculturalism and Political Theory* [Cambridge: Cambridge University Press, 2007], 60–88, at 61). Even Chandran Kukathas, who does not think culture grounds specific rights, grants self-rule to any group or association that desires it, and thus allows for the possibility of self-governing cultures (Kukathas, *The Liberal Archipelago: A Theory of Diversity and Freedom* [Oxford: Oxford University Press, 2003]). We therefore think it is uncontroversial to state that the norm in theoretical accounts of multiculturalism is to focus on immigrants, national minorities, and indigenous peoples as separate groups, and only seriously to contemplate substantive self-rule for the latter two. Our critique will proceed on that basis, although we must admit it has greater traction on Kymlicka and Taylor than some other political theorists in this area.

7. Ashcroft and Bevir, "Pluralism, National Identity and Citizenship," and "Liberal Democracy, Nationalism and Culture."

8. Ashcroft and Bevir "Liberal Democracy, Nationalism and Culture," and Abizadeh "Does Liberal Democracy Presuppose a Cultural Nation?"

9. Ashcroft and Bevir, "Pluralism, National Identity and Citizenship" and "Liberal Democracy, Nationalism and Culture."

10. This accusation is most often leveled at Kymlicka's theory and liberal variants thereof, but also has traction on Taylor and possibly also theories that foreground indigenous claims. Kymlicka's central claim is that that culture forms the context of meaningful choice within which individuals choose how to live their lives, and thus must be protected by the liberal state. Ashcroft will argue elsewhere that

Kymlicka's theory makes unsustainable assumptions regarding the effects of culture on meaning and identity, and thereby also cannot avoid essentialism and reification, and that these weaknesses can be traced to his overarching luck-egalitarian framework, which requires that any given individual is located within a single culture to act as an unchosen context of meaningful choice.

11. See Mark Bevir, *The Logic of the History of Ideas* (Cambridge: Cambridge University Press, 1999), chap. 2, for our underlying account of meaning and for a detailed examination of the issue of cultural limits.

12. In *Multicultural Citizenship,* Kymlicka suggests that some groups may have claims to self-rule based directly in historical agreements with the state, and also that some multicultural rights may grounded in the value of cultural diversity. Nevertheless, if the claim that we are located in a single societal culture as our context of meaningful choice is not tenable on the terms in which it is stated, Kymlicka has lost the central plank of his core "equality" argument based in individual autonomy and self-respect. Although his distinction between immigrants and national minorities turns largely on the decision of the former to immigrate rather than the role of culture per se, any attempt to keep groups cultural groups separate is fraught with empirical and philosophical problems. Kymlicka's modification of his original typology in his later work, such as *Multicultural Odysseys*, might appear to mitigate this problem, and thereby side-step our critique of multicultural political theory. The central thesis of *Multicultural Odysseys* is that the spread of multiculturalism across the globe requires tailoring multiculturalism to local conditions more carefully. Kymlicka's primary recommendation is to increase policies and laws that "target" specific types of group, thereby refining the Western-centric typology by adding new categories of rights and groups (pp. 8–9, and 24–25). Yet multiplying the number of groups and rights makes marking the boundaries between them harder, not easier. There are still no natural kinds to identify, and no stable criteria for choosing one boundary over another, or a particular version of the typology over an even more detailed one. Kymlicka's gloss on the typology in *Multicultural Odysseys* thus seems more like a concession to the "cosmopolitan critique" than a defense against it, and Ashcroft argues elsewhere that it fails to mitigate the theoretical and empirical problems with the typology, and his theory more broadly.

13. Australian policy-makers imported the idea of "multiculturalism" as a framework for managing cultural diversity from Canada, although—as in the UK and New Zealand—it is expressed primarily through policy rather than constitutional law. Unlike both Canada and New Zealand, however, Australian multiculturalism ostensibly applies to indigenous peoples and thereby also draws on international law, even as indigenous leaders reject their inclusion within "multiculturalism," and the dominant *public* understanding continues to be in terms of nonwhite immigration.

14. Here we refer to both standard policy approaches to multiculturalism and the more wide-ranging scope of political theory. Both of these seem to assume the existence of a cultural or national "core" that must subsequently learn to accommodate cultural diversity through integration and/or substate political autonomy. This assumption has little traction in the New Commonwealth, save in Malaysia, where the Malay are given preferential treatment in some respects, forming something like a "core" to the nation, albeit within an overall consociational model. As discussed at note 12 above, although the later Kymlicka acknowledges the problems with the typology and the need for more contextualized forms of multiculturalism, the underlying difficulties with separating groups/rights in both theory and practice seem more profound and pervasive than he realizes, and the traction of the cosmopolitan critique more enduring that he acknowledges (see Kymlicka, "Essentialist Critique" note 22 for more detail).

15. This is arguably also at work in Nigeria, Singapore, and Malaysia.

16. Stuart James Ward, *Australia and the British Embrace: The Demise of the Imperial Ideal* (Melbourne: Melbourne University Press, 2001); Ward, "The 'New Nationalism' in Australia, Canada and New Zealand: Civic Culture in the Wake of the British World," in Kate Darian-Smith, Patricia Grimshaw, and Stuart Macintyre, eds., *Britishness Abroad: Transnational Movements and Imperial Culture* (Melbourne: Melbourne University Press 2007), 231–63; and Ward, "Imperial Identities Abroad" in Sarah Stockwell, ed., *The British Empire: Themes and Perspectives* (Oxford: Blackwell 2007) 219–43. See

also the work of Jatinder Mann, such as *The Search for a New National Identity: The Rise of Multicultur-alism in Canada and Australia, 1890s–1970s* (New York: Peter Lang, 2016).

17. Here we are distinguishing between the demise of British "race patriotism" in favor of more local attachments and the broader British cultural currents out of which the new nationalisms were built.

18. For primary source material on different articulations of the relevant nations, see Jatinder Mann, "The Introduction of Multiculturalism in Canada and Australia, 1960s–1970s," in *Nations and Nationalism* 18, no. 3 (2012): 483–503, in particular 493–94 re Australia. This claim has less traction on Canada, but a prominent claim was that Canada was a compact between two nations (French and British) not five (English/Scots/Welsh/Irish/French), albeit that discourses of multiculturalism may have arisen in part to destabilize the dual compact account, e.g., by foregrounding the role of Ukrainians in settling the prairie provinces.

19. See, e.g., the work of Gurminder K. Bhambra, in particular *Rethinking Modernity: Postcolonialism and the Sociological Imagination* (New York: Palgrave Macmillan, 2007), Ward cited in n. 16 above, and Catherine Hall, "British Cultural Identities and the Legacy of Empire" in David Morley and Kevin Robins, eds., *British Cultural Studies: Geography, Nationality and Identity* (Oxford: Oxford University Press, 2001), 27–39.

20. In what follows, we generally use the term "polycentric" to refer to structures/institutions, and "pluralist" to refer to both practices of governance and orientations that embrace diversity and social experimentation more broadly.

21. E.g., religious groups and the Scheduled Castes in India, the three dominant groups in independence-era Nigeria, and the ethno-cultural groupings in Malaysia, Singapore, and Trinidad and Tobago.

22. Charges of essentialism are often leveled at Kymlicka's dominant theory of multiculturalism, although he rejects these, arguing they misdiagnose the issues and conflate theoretical and practical argument; see Will Kymlicka, "The Essentialist Critique of Multiculturalism: Theories, Policies, Ethos," in Varun Uberoi and Tariq Modood, eds., *Multiculturalism Rethought: Interpretations, Dilemmas, New Directions* (Edinburgh: Edinburgh University Press, 2015), 209–49, at 212. Kymlicka's organizing vocabulary is different from ours, revolving around the distinction between philosophical approaches, actual policies, and real-world outcomes, and utilizing his typology of indigenous peoples, national minorities, and immigrants (see the notes to chapter 1 for a fuller discussion). Our position would qualify as "post-multiculturalist" in Kymlicka's sense. Ashcroft will analyze the essentialist critique of liberal multiculturalism at greater length elsewhere, responding directly to Kymlicka's arguments, and so here we simply note the key differences between our position and "post-multiculturalism" as Kymlicka articulates it. Firstly, our critique of liberal multiculturalism does not turn purely on a rejection of "culturalist aspirations," which we accept as a social reality—albeit one we think has problematic effects, particularly at the level of the cultural nation—and try to accommodate through polycentricity. Secondly, our critique does not leave "all real-world practices of [liberal multiculturalism] untouched," but rather engages with the effects of "siloing" multicultural issues/groups in both theory and practice, and points toward a radical remaking of the state and liberal-democratic norms/practices far beyond that typically envisaged by liberal multiculturalists. Thirdly, we identify interconnected forms of essentialism in political theory, policy/law, *and* public discourse. We trace these back to the real-world entanglement of liberal and colonial governance, overly narrow policy approaches and resulting public discourse, and philosophical flaws in dominant forms of multicultural theory. Our holistic diagnosis of the problem, and our radical solution to it, addresses all three of Kymlicka's "levels" simultaneously, unlike the post-multiculturalists (ibid., 221–33). And lastly, our approach addresses the shortcomings Kymlicka identifies relating to temporary migrants, nationalism, and non–geographically concentrated religious groups (ibid., 239–44). For the broader political theory debates regarding essentialism, see Andrew Mason, "Multiculturalism and the Critique of Essentialism," in Anthony Simon Laden and David Owen, eds., *Multiculturalism and Political Theory* (Cambridge: Cambridge University Press, 2007), 221–43, and Sarah Song, "Multiculturalism," in *The Stanford Encyclopedia of Philosophy*, ed.

Edward N. Zalta, accessed November 19, 2018, https://plato.stanford.edu/archives/spr2017/entries/multiculturalism.

23. See, e.g., Jeremy Waldron, "Minority Cultures and the Cosmopolitan Alternative," *University of Michigan Journal of Law Reform* 25 (1991): 751–94.

24. Andrew Mason, "The Critique of Multiculturalism in Britain: Integration, Separation and Shared Identification," *Critical Review of International Social and Political Philosophy* 21, no. 1 (2018): 22–45.

25. Ashcroft and Bevir, "Pluralism, Nationality and Citizenship."

26. Supporting particular minority cultures via legal rights may require ascribing essential features to them, which might imbue them with a false naturalness that hampers reform. Public discourse or social practice might also embody underlying presumptions about the nature and worth of other cultures and thereby construct both minority and majority groups as social realities. For a discussion of effects that flow from interactions between and within minority and majority cultures, see Sarah Song, *Justice, Gender and the Politics of Multiculturalism* (Cambridge: Cambridge University Press, 2007).

27. Focusing on structures that can accommodate a wide variety of overlapping and constantly changing identities, rather than legislating on the basis of the nature of individual groups at a specific point in time, reduces the risk of "freezing" cultures in place. Kymlicka rejects this accusation in "The Essentialist Critique," but Ashcroft will argue in detail elsewhere that essentialism and reification are inevitable in Kymlicka's theory if he is to maintain its basic luck-egalitarian premises. Likewise, we reject Kymlicka's defense of minority rights as a response to majority nation-building on the basis that he only grants political autonomy to certain groups, a limit we see as unwarranted.

28. Seyla Benhabib, *The Claims of Culture: Equality and Diversity in the Global Era* (Princeton, NJ: Princeton University Press, 2002), and Song, *Justice, Gender and the Politics of Multiculturalism*.

29. There is therefore substantial overlap between our "constructivist" account of culture and that set out by Song, *Justice, Gender and the Politics of Multiculturalism*, particularly in relation to the importance of understanding local historical factors, the mutually conditioning nature of majority and minority cultures, and a bias toward deliberation as a way of resolving particular issues. Her commitment to substantive equality is stronger than ours, however, in part because she focuses on multiculturalism within individual liberal democracies, in particular, the United States. Also, our arguments suggest that the intertwined legacy of colonialism and liberalism calls undermines basic presumptions regarding liberal democracy and nation-state that Song perhaps takes for granted, or at least does not address directly. Finally, our focus on the mutually constructing nature of theory and practice foregrounds the importance of expressing different forms of life in practice, not just through deliberation and negotiation.

30. Arash Abizadeh, "Does Collective Identity Presuppose an Other? On the Alleged Incoherence of Global Solidarity," *American Political Science Review* 99, no. 1 (2005): 45–60, and Miller, *On Nationality*. See also Mark Bevir, "Postfoundationalism and Social Democracy," *Danish Yearbook of Philosophy* 35 (2001): 7–26, and Song, "Multiculturalism."

31. Michael Walzer, *Interpretation and Social Criticism* (Cambridge, MA: Harvard University Press, 1987), 14–15, and Walzer, *On Toleration* (New Haven, CT: Yale University Press, 1997).

32. See Kukathas, *Liberal Archipelago*. Ashcroft develops elsewhere a postfoundational critique of Kukathas's theory based on his account of conscience.

BIBLIOGRAPHY

Abbott, Tony. "A Conservative Case for Multiculturalism." *Quadrant* 50 (2006): 40–43.

———. "Vote of Thanks at the Inaugural Australian Multicultural Council Lecture." Speech, Parliament House, Canberra, September 19, 2012.

Abizadeh, Arash. "Does Collective Identity Presuppose an Other? On the Alleged Incoherence of Global Solidarity." *American Political Science Review* 99, no. 1 (2005): 45–60.

———. "Does Liberal Democracy Presuppose a Cultural Nation? Four Arguments." *American Political Science Review* 96, no. 3 (2002): 495–509.

Abu-Laban, Yasmeen, and Christina Gabriel. *Selling Diversity: Immigration, Multiculturalism, Employment Equity, and Globalization.* Toronto: University of Toronto Press, 2002.

Adebanwi, Wale. *Nation as Grand Narrative: The Nigerian Press and the Politics of Meaning.* Rochester, NY: University of Rochester Press, 2016.

———. *Yoruba Elites and Ethnic Politics in Nigeria: Obafemi Awolowo and Corporate Agency.* New York: Cambridge University Press, 2014.

Allen, Chris. "Opposing Islamification or Promoting Islamophobia? Understanding the English Defence League." *Patterns of Prejudice* 45, no. 4 (2011).

Alibhai-Brown, Yasmin. *After Multiculturalism.* London: Foreign Policy Centre, 2000.

———. "After Multiculturalism." *Political Quarterly* 72, no. 1 (2001): 47–56.

Anderson, Elizabeth. "Integration, Affirmative Action and Strict Scrutiny." *New York University Law Review* 77 (2002): 1195–1271.

Ansari, Iqbal. "Minorities and the Politics of Constitution Making in India." In *Minority Identities and the Nation State,* edited by D. L. Sheth and G. Mahajan, 113–37. Delhi: Oxford University Press, 1999.

Anthony, Andrew. *The Fallout: How a Guilty Liberal Lost His Innocence.* London: Jonathan Cape, 2007.

Appiah, Kwame Anthony. *The Ethics of Identity.* Princeton, NJ: Princeton University Press, 2005.

Arifalo, S. O. *The Egbe Omo Oduduwa: A Study in Ethnic and Cultural Nationalism, 1945–1965.* Akure, Nigeria: Stebak Books, 2001.

Ashcroft, Lord. "How the United Kingdom Voted on Thursday . . . and Why." Accessed November 9, 2018. http://lordashcroftpolls.com/2016/06/how-the-united-kingdom-voted-and-why.

Ashcroft, Richard T., and Mark Bevir. "Liberal Democracy, Nationalism and Culture: Multiculturalism and Scottish Independence." *Critical Review of International Social and Political Philosophy* 21, no. 1 (2018): 65–86.

———. "Pluralism, National Identity and Citizenship: Britain after Brexit." *Political Quarterly* 87 (2016): 355–59.

Aston, Heath. "Few Back Change to Race Laws." *Sydney Morning Herald.* August 1, 2014.

———. "Tony Abbott Dumps Controversial Changes to 18C Racial Discrimination Laws." *Sydney Morning Herald.* August 5, 2014.

Austin, Granville. *The Indian Constitution: Cornerstone of a Nation.* Oxford: Clarendon Press, 1966. 1st Indian ed.. with new preface, Bombay: Oxford University Press, 1972.

Australia. Bureau of Statistics. *Australian Demographic Statistics, June 2013.* Accessed November 9, 2018. www.abs.gov.au/AUSSTATS/abs@.nsf/Lookup/3101.0Main+Features1Jun%202013?OpenDocument.

———. Bureau of Statistics. *Cultural Diversity in Australia: Reflecting a Nation. Stories from the 2011 Census, 2012–2013.* Accessed November 9, 2018. www.abs.gov.au/ausstats/abs@.nsf/lookup/2071.0main+features902012-2013.

———. Citizenship Council. *Australian Citizenship for a New Century.* Canberra: Australian Government Publishing Service, 2000.

———. Council on Population and Ethnic Affairs. *Multiculturalism for All Australians: Our Developing Nationhood.* Canberra: Australian Government Publishing Service, 1982.

———. Department of Immigration and Multicultural Affairs. *New Agenda for Multicultural Australia.* Canberra: Australian Government Publishing Service, 1999.

———. Department of Immigration and Citizenship. *The People of Australia: Australia's Multicultural Policy.* Canberra: Department of Immigration and Citizenship, 2011.

———. Department of Immigration and Multicultural and Indigenous Affairs. *Multicultural Australia, United in Diversity. Updating the 1999 New Agenda for Multicultural Australia: Strategic Directions for 2003–2006.* Canberra: Australian Government Publishing Service, 2003.

———. Department of Social Services. *Multicultural Australia: United, Strong, Successful.* Canberra: Department of Social Services, 2017.

———. Department of Social Services. *Settlement and Multicultural Affairs: A Better Australia, 2014.* Page discontinued, on file.

———. Ethnic Affairs Council. *Australia as a Multicultural Society.* Canberra: Australian Government Publishing Service, 1978.

———. Federal Court. *Eatock v Bolt. FCA 1103.* September 28, 2011.

———. Human Rights Commission. *Leading for Change: A Blueprint for Cultural Diversity and Inclusive Leadership Revisited.* Sydney: AHRC, 2018.

———. Migrant Services and Programs. *Report of the Review of Post-Arrival Programs and Services for Migrants.* Frank Galbally (chair) et al. Canberra: Australian Government Publishing Service, 1978.

————. Multicultural Advisory Council. *The People of Australia: The Australian Multicultural Advisory Council's Statement on Cultural Diversity and Recommendations to Government.* Canberra: Australian Multicultural Advisory Council, 2010.

————. National Multicultural Advisory Council. *Australian Multiculturalism for a New Century: Towards Inclusiveness.* Canberra: Australian Government Publishing Service, 1999.

————. Office of Multicultural Affairs. *National Agenda for a Multicultural Australia.* Canberra: Australian Government Publishing Service, 1989.

Awolowo, Obafemi. *Awo: The Autobiography of Chief Obafemi Awolowo.* Cambridge: Cambridge University Press, 1960.

————. *Path to Nigerian Freedom.* London: Faber & Faber, 1946.

Azikiwe, Nnamdi. *Zik: A Selection from the Speeches of Nnamdi Azikiwe.* Cambridge: Cambridge University Press, 1961.

BBC News. "Merkel Says German Multicultural Society Has Failed." October 17, 2010.

————. "Shared Values Unite UK People, Says PM in Easter Message." April 16, 2017.

————. "State Multiculturalism Has Failed, Says David Cameron." February 5, 2011.

Bajpai, Rochana. "Beyond Identity? UPA Rhetoric on Social Justice and Affirmative Action." In *New Dimensions of Politics in India: The United Progressive Alliance in Power,* edited by Lawrence Saez and Gurharpal Singh. London: Routledge, 2012.

————. "The Conceptual Vocabularies of Secularism and Minority Rights in India." *Journal of Political Ideologies* 7, no. 2 (2002): 179–97.

————. "Constituent Assembly Debates and Minority Rights." *Economic and Political Weekly* 35, nos. 21–22 (2000): 1837–45.

————. *Debating Difference: Group Rights and Liberal Democracy in India.* Delhi: Oxford University Press, 2011.

————. "Secularism and Multiculturalism in India: Some Reflections." In *The Problem of Religious Diversity: European Challenges, Asian Approaches,* edited by Anna Triandafyllidou and Tariq Modood, 204–27. Edinburgh: Edinburgh University Press, 2017.

Balagangadhara, S. N., and Jakob de Roover. "The Secular State and Religious Conflict: Liberal Neutrality and the Indian Case of Pluralism." *Journal of Political Philosophy* 15, no. 1 (2007): 73–74.

Bannerji, Himani. *The Dark Side of Nation: Essays on Multiculturalism, Nationalism and Gender.* Toronto: Canadian Scholars' Press, 2000.

Banting, Keith, and Will Kymlicka. "Canadian Multiculturalism: Global Anxieties and Local Debates." *British Journal of Canadian Studies* 23, no. 1 (2010): 43–72.

————, eds. *Multiculturalism and the Welfare State: Recognition and Redistribution in Contemporary Democracies.* Oxford: Oxford University Press, 2007.

Barry, Brian. *Culture and Equality: An Egalitarian Critique of Multiculturalism.* Cambridge: Polity Press, 2001.

Barsh, Russell, and James Youngblood Henderson. "The Supreme Court's Van der Peet Trilogy: Naïve Imperialism and the Robes of Sand." *McGill Law Review* 42, no. 4 (1997): 993–1009.

Bartlett, Jamie, and Jonathan Birdwell. *From Suspects to Citizens: Preventing Violent Extremism in the Big Society.* London: Demos, 2010.

Basu, Amrita. "More Than Meets the Eye: Sub Rosa Violence in Hindu Nationalist India." Institute for Religion, Culture and Public Life (IRCPL) Conference on Democracy and Religious Pluralism, Columbia University, New York, February 12–13, 2016.

Bayat, Asef. *Life as Politics: How Ordinary People Change the Middle East.* Stanford, CA: Stanford University Press, 2009.

Bekker, Simon, and Anne Leidé. "Is Multiculturalism a Workable Policy in South Africa?" *International Journal on Multicultural Societies* 5, no. 2 (2003): 121–36.

Bello, Ahmadu. *My Life.* Cambridge: Cambridge University Press, 1962.

Bengio, Ofra, and Gabriel Ben-Dor, eds. *Minorities and the State in the Arab World.* Boulder, CO: Lynne Reiner, 1999.

Benhabib, Seyla. *The Claims of Culture: Equality and Diversity in the Global Era.* Princeton, NJ: Princeton University Press, 2002.

Betts, Katharine, and Robert Birrell, "Making Australian Citizenship Mean More." *People and Place* 15, no. 1 (2007): 45–61.

Bevir, Mark. *The Logic of the History of Ideas.* Cambridge: Cambridge University Press, 1999.

———. *New Labour: A Critique.* London: Routledge, 2005.

———. "Political Science after Foucault." *History of the Human Sciences* 24, no. 4 (2011).

———. "Postfoundationalism and Social Democracy." *Danish Yearbook of Philosophy* 35 (2001): 7–26.

———. *A Theory of Governance.* Oakland: University of California Press, 2013.

———, ed. *Historicism and the Human Sciences in Victorian Britain.* Cambridge: Cambridge University Press, 2017.

———, ed. *Modern Pluralism.* Cambridge: Cambridge University Press, 2012.

Bhambra, Gurminder K. *Rethinking Modernity: Postcolonialism and the Sociological Imagination.* New York: Palgrave Macmillan, 2007.

Bhargava, Rajeev. "Democratic Vision of a New Republic: India, 1950." In *Transforming India: Social and Political Dynamics of Democracy,* edited by Francine Frankel, Zoya Hasan, Rajeev Bhargava, and Balveer Arora, 26–59. Delhi: Oxford University Press, 2000.

———. "Indian Secularism: An Alternative, Trans-cultural Ideal." In *Political Ideas in Modern India: Thematic Explorations,* edited by V. R. Mehta and Thomas Pantham. New Delhi: Sage Publications, 2006.

———. *The Promise of India's Secular Democracy.* New Delhi: Oxford University Press, 2010.

Bilgrami, Akeel. "Gandhi the Philosopher." *Economic and Political Weekly* 38, no. 9 (September 27, 2003).

Birrell, Robert. *A Nation of Our Own: Citizenship and Nation-building in Federation Australia.* Melbourne: Longman, 1995.

Bissoondath, Neil. *Selling Illusions: The Cult of Multiculturalism in Canada.* Toronto: Penguin, 1994.

Bist, Umrao Singh. *Jaina Theories of Reality and Knowledge.* Delhi: Eastern Book Linkers, 1984.

Bloemraad, Irene. *Becoming a Citizen: Incorporating Immigrants and Refugees in the United States and Canada.* Berkeley: University of California Press, 2006.

Bolland, Nigel. *Creolization and Creole Societies: A Cultural Nationalist View of Caribbean Social History.* Vol. 1 of *Intellectuals in the Twentieth Century Caribbean: Spectre of the New Class: The Commonwealth Caribbean,* edited by A. Hennessy, 51–79. London: Macmillan, 1992.

Bolt, Andrew. "The Foreign Invasion." *Daily Telegraph.* 2 August 2018.

Borrows, John. "Frozen Rights in Canada: Constitutional Interpretation and the Trickster." *American Indian Law Review* 22, no. 1 (1997–98): 37–64.

Bouchard, Gérard. "What Is Interculturalism?" *McGill Law Journal* 56, no. 2 (2011): 435–68.

Bouchard, Gérard, and Charles Taylor. *Report of the Commission on Accommodation Practices Related to Cultural Difference.* Quebec: Government of Quebec, 2008.

Bowen, Chris. "The Genius of Australian Multiculturalism." Speech, Sydney Institute, February 17, 2011.

Braithwaite, Lloyd. "The Problem of Cultural Integration in Trinidad." *Social and Economic Studies* 3, no. 1 (1954): 82–96.

Brash, Don. "Nationhood." Speech, Orewa Rotary Club, January 27, 2004. Accessed December 1, 2018. www.scoop.co.nz/stories/PA0401/S00220.htm.

Brawley, Sean. "Mrs O'Keefe and the Battle for White Australia." *Memento,* no. 33 (Winter 2007): 6–8. Accessed December 1, 2018. www.naa.gov.au/naaresources/publications/memento/pdf/memento33.pdf.

Brocklehurst, Helen, and Robert Philips, eds. *History, Nationhood and the Question of Britain.* New York: Palgrave Macmillan, 2004.

Brown, Gordon. "Managed Migration and Earned Citizenship." Speech, Camden Centre, London, February 20, 2008. www.number10.gov.uk/output/Page14624.asp.

Brown, Judith. *Modern India: The Origins of an Asian Democracy.* Oxford: Oxford University Press, 1990.

Brown, Wendy. *States of Injury: Power and Freedom in Late Modernity.* Princeton, NJ: Princeton University Press, 1995.

Brubaker, Rogers. "The Return of Assimilation? Changing Perspectives on Immigration and Its Sequels in France, Germany, and the United States." *Ethnic and Racial Studies* 24 (2001): 531–48.

Burayidi, Michael A., ed. *Multiculturalism in a Cross-National Perspective.* Lanham, MD: University Press of America, 1996.

Burke, Hon. Kerry. *Review of Immigration Policy, Appendices to the Journal of the House of Representatives G42.* Wellington: Government Printer, 1986.

Burman, J. J. Roy. "Hindu-Muslim Syncretism in India." *Economic and Political Weekly* 31, no. 20 (May 18, 1996).

Burton, Antoinette, ed. *After the Imperial Turn: Thinking with and through the Nation.* Durham, NC: Duke University Press, 2003.

Cairns, Alan C. *Charter versus Federalism: The Dilemmas of Constitutional Reform.* Montreal and Kingston, ON: McGill–Queen's University Press, 1992.

———. *First Nations and the Canadian State: In Search of Coexistence.* Kingston, ON: Institute of Intergovernmental Relations, Queen's University, 2005.

Cameron, David. Speech, Handsworth Mosque, Birmingham, January 30, 2007.

———. Speech, Munich Security Conference, February 5, 2011. Accessed February 25, 2019. www.gov.uk/government/speeches/pms-speech-at-munich-security-conference.

Campbell-Hunt, Colin, John Brocklesby, Sylvie Chetty, Lawrence Corbett, Sally Davenport, Deborah Jones, and Pat Walsh. *World Famous in New Zealand: How New Zealand's*

Leading Firms Became World-Class Competitors. Auckland: Auckland University Press, 2001.

Castles, Stephen. "Multiculturalism in Australia." In *The Australian People: An Encyclopedia of the Nation, Its People and Their Origins,* edited by James Jupp. Cambridge: Cambridge University Press, 2001.

Castles, Stephen, Mary Kalantzis, Bill Cope, and Michael Morrissey, eds. *Mistaken Identity: Multiculturalism and the Demise of Nationalism in Australia.* Sydney: Pluto Press, 1988.

Chandhoke, Neera. *Beyond Secularism: The Rights of Religious Minorities.* New Delhi: Oxford, 1999.

———. "Negotiating Linguistic Diversity: A Comparative Study of India and the United States." In *Democracy and Diversity: India and the American Experience,* edited by K. Shankar Bajpai. New Delhi: Oxford University Press, 2007.

Chandler, J. A. *Explaining Local Government: Local Government in Britain since 1800.* Manchester: Manchester University Press 2007.

Chandra, Sudhir. *Continuing Dilemmas: Understanding Social Consciousness.* New Delhi: Tulika Books, 2002.

Chang, James. "Maori Views on Immigration: Implications for Maori/Chinese Interactions." In *The Dragon and the Taniwha: Maori and Chinese in New Zealand,* edited by Manying Ip. Auckland: Auckland University Press, 2009.

Chatterjee, Margaret. *Gandhi's Religious Thought.* Notre Dame, IN: University of Notre Dame Press, 1983.

Chatterjee, Partha. *Nationalist Thought and the Colonial World: A Derivative Discourse?* London: Zed Books, 1986.

———. *The Nation and Its Fragments: Colonial and Postcolonial Histories.* Delhi: Oxford University Press, 1995.

———. "Religious Minorities and the Secular State: Reflections on an Indian Impasse." *Public Culture* 8 (1995).

———. "Secularism and Tolerance." *Economic and Political Weekly* 29, no. 28 (July 9, 1994).

———. "Secularism and Tolerance." In *Secularism and Its Critics,* edited by R. Bhargava, 345–79. Delhi: Oxford University Press, 1998.

Chatterji, Probhat Chandra. *Secular Values for Secular India.* Delhi: South Asia Books, 1984.

Choudhury, Tufyal. "Evolving Models of Multiculturalism in the United Kingdom." In *Interculturalism: Europe and Its Muslims in Search of Sound Societal Models,* edited by Michael Emerson. Brussels: Centre for European Policy Studies, 2011.

Christie, Gordon 1998. "Aboriginal Rights, Aboriginal Culture and Protection." *Osgoode Hall Law Journal* 36, no. 3: 447–84.

Citizenship and Immigration Canada. *Evaluations of the Multiculturalism Program.* 2012. Accessed February 25, 2019. www.cic.gc.ca/english/pdf/research-stats/multiculturalism.pdf.

Claerhout, Sarah. "Gandhi, Conversion, and the Equality of Religions: More Experiments with Truth." *Numen—International Review For the History of Religions* 61, no. 1 (2014).

Cockburn, Harry. "Amber Rudd Speech Likened to Hitler's Mein Kampf." *The Independent.* October 5, 2016

Cohen, Nick. *What's Left? How Liberals Lost Their Way.* London: HarperPerennial, 2007.

Cole, Douglas. "'The Crimson Thread of Kinship': Ethnic Ideas in Australia, 1870–1914." *Historical Studies* 14 (1971): 511–25.

Coleman, James S. *Nigeria: Background to Nationalism*. Berkeley: University of California Press, 1958.

Colley, Linda. *Britons: Forging the Nation, 1707–1837*. New Haven: Yale University Press, 1992.

Collins, Hugh. "Political Ideology in Australia: The Distinctiveness of a Benthamite Society." *Dædalus* 114, no. 1, *Australia: Terra Incognita?* (Winter 1985): 147–69.

Corbridge, Stuart, and John Harriss. *Reinventing India: Liberalization, Hindu Nationalism and Popular Democracy*. Cambridge: Polity, 2000.

Commission on the Future of Multi-Ethnic Britain. *The Future of Multi-Ethnic Britain: The Parekh Report* . London: Profile Books, 2000.

Constituent Assembly Debates [India]: Official Report, 12 volumes. New Delhi: Lok Sabha Secretariat, 1946–1950.

Coulthard, Glen Sean. *Red Skins, White Masks: Rejecting the Colonial Politics of Recognition.* Minneapolis: University of Minnesota Press, 2014.

Crawford, James. *The Rights of Peoples.* Oxford: Clarendon Press, 1988.

Croucher, Shane. "British Jobs for British Workers: How a Far-Right Meme Went Mainstream." *International Business Times.* October 6, 2016.

Crowder, George. *Theories of Multiculturalism: An Introduction.* Cambridge: Polity Press, 2013.

Crowley, Daniel. "Plural and Differential Acculturation in Trinidad." *American Anthropologist* 59, no. 5 (1957): 817–24.

Crowe, David. "Scott Morrison Vows to Change Laws on Religious Freedom but Won't Be a 'culture warrior' PM." *Sydney Morning Herald*, September 7, 2018.

Cudjoe, Selwyn. "Multiculturalism and Its Challenges in Trinidad and Tobago." *Global Society* 48 (2011): 330–41.

Curchin, Katherine. "Pakeha Women and Maori Protocol: The Politics of Criticising Other Cultures." *Australian Journal of Political Science* 46, no. 3 (2011).

Curran, James, and Stuart Ward. *The Unknown Nation: Australia after Empire.* Melbourne: Melbourne University Publishing, 2010.

Dasgupta, Jyotirindra. "India's Federal Design and Multicultural National Construction." In *The Success of India's Democracy,* edited by Atul Kohli. Cambridge: Cambridge University Press, 2001.

Davidson, Alastair. *From Subject to Citizen: Australian Citizenship in the Twentieth Century.* Cambridge: Cambridge University Press, 1997.

Davison, Andrew. *Secularism and Revivalism in Turkey: A Hermeneutic Reconsideration.* New Haven, CT: Yale University Press, 1998.

Day, Shelagh, and Gwen Brodsky. "The Duty to Accommodate: Who Will Benefit?" *Canadian Bar Review* 75, no. 3 (1996): 433–73.

De Roover, Jakob. "Is Secularism the Solution to Communal Conflict in India?" *Indian Realist.* http://indianrealist.wordpress.com/2010/05/16/is-secularism-the-solution-to-communal-conflict-in-india; page discontinued.

———. "The Vacuity of Secularism: On the Indian Debate and Its Western Origins." *Economic and Political Weekly* 37, no. 39 (September 28, 2002).

De Roover, Jakob, and S. N. Balagangadhara, "The Dark Hour of Secularism: Hindu Fundamentalism and Colonial Liberalism in India." In *Making Sense of the Secular: Critical Perspectives from Europe to Asia,* edited by Ranjan Ghosh. New York: Routledge, 2013.

De Roover, Jakob, Sarah Claerhout, and S. N. Balagangadhara. "Liberal Political Theory and the Cultural Migration of Ideas: The Case of Secularism in India." *Political Theory* 39, no. 5 (2011).

De Schutter, Helder. "The Liberal Linguistic Turn: Kymlicka's Freedom Account Revisited." *Dve domovini/Two Homelands,* no. 44 (2016): 51–65.

DeHanas, Daniel, Therese O'Toole, Tariq Modood, and Nasar Meer. *Muslim Participation in Contemporary Governance: Literature Review Summary,* 2009. Accessed February 17, 2019. www.bristol.ac.uk/medialibrary/sites/ethnicity/migrated/documents/mpcg report.pdf.

Dominiczak, Peter, and Rosa Prince. "David Cameron to Fast-Track Tough Anti-Terror Laws." *Daily Telegraph,* May 13, 2015.

Drabble, John H. *An Economic History of Malaysia, c. 1800–1990: The Transition to Modern Economic Growth.* New York: St. Martin's Press, 2000.

Drummond, Lee. "The Cultural Continuum: A Theory of Intersystems." *Man* 15 (1980): 352–74.

Dudley, B. J. "Federalism and the Balance of Political Power in Nigeria." *Journal of Commonwealth Political Studies* 4, no. 1 (1966): 16–29.

Durie, Mason. *Te Mana, Te Kawanatanga: The Politics of Maori Self-Determination.* Auckland: Oxford University Press, 1998.

Eisenberg, Avigail. "Domestic and International Norms for Assessing Indigenous Identity." In *Identity Politics in the Public Realm,* edited by Avigail Eisenberg and Will Kymlicka, 137–62. Vancouver: University of British Columbia Press, 2011.

Eisenberg, Avigail, and Jeff Spinner-Halev. *Minorities within Minorities: Equality, Rights and Diversity.* Cambridge: Cambridge University Press, 2001.

Elder, Catriona. *Being Australian: Narratives of National Identity.* Sydney: Allen & Unwin, 2007.

Elshtain, Jean. *Democracy on Trial.* New York: Basic Books, 1995.

Engineer, Asghar Ali. *Communal Challenge and Secular Response.* Delhi: Shipra Publications, 2003.

Evans, J. M. "Immigration Act 1971." *Modern Law Review* 35, no. 5 (1972): 508–24.

Faaland, Just, J. R. Parkinson, and Rais Saniman. *Growth and Ethnic Inequality: Malaysia's New Economic Policy.* London: Hurst, 1990.

Faas, Daniel. *Negotiating Political Identities: Multiethnic Schools and Youth in Europe.* Farnham, Surrey, UK: Ashgate, 2010.

Favell, Adrian. *Philosophies of Integration: Immigration and the Idea of Citizenship in France and Britain.* London: Macmillan, 1998.

Fekete, Liz. "Anti-Muslim Racism and the European Security State." *Race and Class* 46, no. 1 (2004): 4–29.

Finn, Mike. "Dunkirk, Bond and All That: The Brexit Myth of British Exceptionalism." LSE politics blog, August 23, 2016

Fitzsimons, Patrick. "Neoliberalism and 'Social Capital': Reinventing Community." Paper presented at the AREA Symposium "Neo-liberalism, Welfare and Education: The New Zealand Experiment," New Orleans, 2000.

Fleras, Augie. *The Politics of Multiculturalism: Multicultural Governance in Comparative Perspective.* New York: Palgrave Macmillan, 2009.

Fleras, Augie, and Jean Leonard Elliott. *The Nations Within: Aboriginal-State Relations in Canada, the United States and New Zealand.* Auckland: Oxford University Press, 1998.

Fleras, Augie, and Paul Spoonley. *Recalling Aotearoa: Indigenous Politics and Ethnic Relations in New Zealand.* Oxford: Oxford University Press, 1999.

Fournier, Pascale. "The Ghettoization of Difference in Canada: 'Rape by Culture' or the Danger of a Cultural Defense in Criminal Law Trials." *Manitoba Law Journal* 29 (2002): 81–113.

Fozdar, Farida, and Brian Spittles. "The Australian Citizenship Test: Process and Rhetoric." *Australian Journal of Politics and History* 55 (2009): 496–512.

Fraser, Nancy. "From Redistribution to Recognition? Dilemmas of Justice in a 'Post-Socialist' Age." *New Left Review* 1, no. 212 (July–August 1995).

Furniss, Tom. "Cementing the Nation: Burke's *Reflections* on Nationalism and National Identity." In *Edmund Burke's Reflections on the Revolution in France: New Interdisciplinary Essays,* edited by John Whale, 115–44. Manchester: Manchester University Press, 2000.

Furnivall, John S. *Colonial Policy and Practice: A Comparative Study of Burma and Netherlands India.* Cambridge: Cambridge University Press, 1948.

Gagnon, Alain G., and Raffaele Iacovino. *Federalism, Citizenship and Quebec: Debating Multinationalism.* Toronto: University of Toronto Press, 2007.

Galanter, Marc. *Competing Equalities, Law and the Backward Classes in India.* Delhi: Oxford University Press, 1984.

"Galaxy Poll Shows Most Australians Think Multiculturalism Works Well." News Limited Network, January 24, 2013.

Galligan, Brian and Winsome Roberts. *Australian Citizenship.* Melbourne: Melbourne University Press, 2004.

Gandhi, Mohandas K. *An Autobiography: The Story of My Experiments with Truth.* Boston: Beacon Press, 1993.

———. *The Collected Works of Mahatma Gandhi.* 100 vols. Delhi: Government of India, Ministry of Information and Broadcasting, Publication Division, 1958–94.

———. *Gandhi on Christianity.* Edited by Robert Ellsberg. Maryknoll, NY: Orbis Books, 1991.

———. *The Moral and Political Writings of Mahatma Gandhi.* Edited by Raghavan N. Iyer. 2 vols. Oxford: Clarendon Press, 1986.

Godrej, Farah. "Ascetics, Warriors and a Gandhian Ecological Citizenship." *Political Theory* 40, no. 4 (2012).

———. *Cosmopolitan Political Thought: Method, Practice, Discipline.* Oxford: Oxford University Press, 2011.

———. "Nonviolence and Gandhi's Truth: A Method for Moral and Political Arbitration." *Review of Politics* 68, no. 2 (2006).

———. "Towards a Cosmopolitan Political Thought: the Hermeneutics of Interpreting the Other." *Polity* 41, no. 2 (2009).

Goh, Daniel P. S. "From Colonial Pluralism to Postcolonial Multiculturalism: Race, State Formation and the Question of Cultural Diversity in Malaysia and Singapore." *Sociology Compass* 2, no. 1 (2008): 232–52.

———. "The Plural Society and Multiculturalism in Malaysia and Singapore." In *Multicultural Challenges and Redefining Identity in East Asia,* edited by Nam-Kook Kim, 211–32. Farnham, Surrey, Engand: Ashgate, 2014.

Goh, Keng Swee. *The Economics of Modernization.* 1972. Singapore: Federal Publications, 1995.

———. *The Practice of Economic Growth.* 1977. Singapore: Federal Publications, 1995.

Goldberg, David Theo. "Introduction." In *Multiculturalism: A Critical Reader,* edited by David Theo Goldberg. Malden, MA: Blackwell, 1994.

Gomez, Edmund Terence. "The Politics and Policies of Corporate Development: Race, Rents and Redistribution in Malaysia." In *Malaysia's Development Challenges: Graduating from the Middle,* edited by Hal Hill, Tham Siew Yean, and Ragayah Haji Mat Zin, 63–82. London: Routledge, 2012.

Gomez, Edmund Terence, and K. S. Jomo. *Malaysia's Political Economy: Politics, Patronage and Profits.* Cambridge: Cambridge University Press, 1999.

Goodhart, David. *The British Dream: Successes and Failures of Post-war Immigration.* London: Atlantic Books, 2014.

———. *Progressive Nationalism: Citizenship and the Left.* London: Demos, 2006.

Goot, Murray, and Ian Watson. "Immigration, Multiculturalism, and National Identity." In *Australian Social Attitudes: The First Report,* edited by Shaun Wilson, Gabrielle Meagher, Rachel Gibson, David Denemark, and Mark Western, 182–203. Sydney: University of New South Wales Press, 2005.

Goulbourne, Harry. *Race Relations in Britain since 1945.* London: Macmillan, 1998.

Gove, Michael. "All Pupils Will Learn Our Island Story." Speech, October 5, 2010.

———. *Celsius 7/7.* London: Weidenfeld & Nicolson, 2006.

———. "1688 and All That." In *Being British: The Search for the Values That Bind the Nation,* edited by Matthew d'Ancona and Gordon Brown, 197–207. Edinburgh: Mainstream, 2009.

———. "What Do Britons Have in Common?" Paper presented at Quilliam Foundation Conference, April 23, 2009.

Grassby, A. J. *A Multi-cultural Society for the Future.* Canberra: Australian Government Publishing Service, 1973.

Green, Damian. "Making Immigration Work." Speech, Policy Exchange, February 2, 2012. Accessed November 16, 2018. www.homeoffice.gov.uk/media-centre/speeches/making-immigration-work.

Gunew, Sneja. *Haunted Nations: The Colonial Dimensions of Multiculturalism.* London: Routledge, 2004.

Gutmann, Amy. *Identity in Democracy.* Princeton, NJ: Princeton University Press, 2003.

———. "Introduction." In *Multiculturalism: Examining the Politics of Recognition,* edited by Amy Gutman. Princeton, NJ: Princeton University Press, 1994.

———. "The Challenge of Multiculturalism in Political Ethics." *Philosophy & Public Affairs* 22, no. 3 (1993): 171–206.

Haebich, Anna. *Spinning the Dream: Assimilation in Australia, 1950–1970.* North Fremantle, Western Australia: FremantlePress, 2008.

Hage, Ghassan. *White Nation: Fantasies of White Supremacy in a Multicultural Society.* Sydney: Pluto Press, 1998.

Hale, Charles R. "Does Multiculturalism Menace? Governance, Cultural Rights and the Politics of Identity in Guatemala." *Journal of Latin American Studies* 34 (2002): 485–524.

Hall, Catherine. "British Cultural Identities and the Legacy of Empire." In *British Cultural Studies: Geography, Nationality and Identity,* edited by David Morley and Kevin Robins. 27–39. Oxford: Oxford University Press, 2001.

Halstead, J. Mark. *Education, Justice and Cultural Diversity: An Examination of the Honeyford Affair, 1984–85.* London: Falmer Press, 1988.

Hampshire, James. *Citizenship and Belonging.* New York: Palgrave Macmillan, 2005.

Hansen, Randall. *Citizenship and Immigration in Post-War Britain.* Oxford: Oxford University Press, 2000.

Hanson, Allan. "The Making of the Maori: Culture Invention and Its Logic." *American Anthropologist* 91, no. 4 (1989): 890–902.

Harper, T.N. *The End of Empire and the Making of Malaya.* Cambridge: Cambridge University Press, 1999.

Harris, Michelle, Martin Nakata, and Bronwyn Carlson, eds. *The Politics of Identity: Emerging Indigeneity.* Broadway, NSW: UTS ePress, 2013.

Hartmann, Douglas, and Joseph Gerteis. "Dealing with Diversity: Mapping Multiculturalism in Sociological Terms." *Sociological Theory* 23, no. 2 (2005): 218–40.

Hartwich, Oliver Marc. *Selection, Migration and Integration: Why Multiculturalism Works in Australia (and Fails in Europe).* St Leonards: Centre for Independent Studies, 2011.

Havemann, Paul. *Indigenous Peoples' Rights in Australia, Canada & New Zealand.* Oxford: Oxford University Press, 1999.

Hayes, Carlton. *The Historical Evolution of Modern Nationalism.* New York: Macmillan, 1931.

Heath, Anthony, and Neli Demireva. "Has Multiculturalism Failed in Britain?" *Ethnic and Racial Studies* 37, no. 1 (2014): 161–80.

Hewer, Chris. "Schools for Muslims." *Oxford Review of Education* 27, no. 4 (2001): 515–27.

Hirschman, Charles. "The Making of Race in Colonial Malaya: Political Economy and Racial Ideology." *Sociological Forum* 1, no. 2 (1986): 330–61.

———. "The Meaning and Measurement of Ethnicity in Malaysia: An Analysis of Census Classifications." *Journal of Asian Studies* 46, no. 3 (1987): 555–82.

Hodge, Merle. "The Peoples of Trinidad and Tobago." In *David Frost Introduces Trinidad and Tobago,* edited by Michael Anthony and Andrew Carr. London: André Deutsch, 1975.

Horne, Donald. *The Avenue of the Fair Go: A Group Tour of Australian Political Thought.* Sydney: Harper Collins, 1997.

Horowitz, Donald L. *A Democratic South Africa? Constitutional Engineering in a Divided Society.* Berkeley: University of California Press, 1991.

———. *Ethnic Groups in Conflict.* Berkeley: University of California Press, 1985.

Howe, R. Brian, and David Johnson. *Restraining Equality: Human Rights Commissions in Canada.* Toronto: University of Toronto Press, 2000.

Humpage, Louise. "Radical Change or More of the Same? Public Attitudes towards Social Citizenship in New Zealand since Neoliberal Reform." *Australian Journal of Social Issues* 43, no. 2 (2008).

———. "What Do New Zealanders Think about Welfare?" *Policy Quarterly* 7, no. 2 (2011): 8–13.

India. *Constituent Assembly Debates: Official Report.* 12 vols. New Delhi: Lok Sabha Secretariat, 1946–50.

Inglis, Christine. *Multiculturalism: New Policy Responses to Diversity.* Paris: UNESCO, 1996.

Ip, Manying, ed. *The Dragon and the Taniwha: Maori and Chinese in New Zealand.* Auckland: Auckland University Press, 2009.

Iyer, Raghavan N. *The Moral and Political Thought of Mahatma Gandhi.* Santa Barbara, CA: Concord Grove Press, 1983.

Jaffrelot, Christophe. "The Hindu Nationalists and Power." In *The Oxford Companion to Politics in India,* edited by Niraja Gopal Jayal and Pratap Bhanu Mehta. Delhi: Oxford University Press, 2011.

James, Carl. ed. *Possibilities and Limitations: Multicultural Policies and Programs in Canada.* Halifax, NS: Fernwood, 2005.

Jayal, Niraja Gopal. *Democracy and the State, Welfare, Secularism, and Development in India.* Delhi: Oxford University Press, 1999.

Jayasuriya, Laksiri. "Australian Multiculturalism and the Politics of a New Pluralism." *Dialogue* 24 (2005): 75–84.

Jenkins, Roy. *Essays and Speeches.* London: Collins, 1967.

Jesudason, James V. *Ethnicity and the Economy: The State, Chinese Business, and Multinationals in Malaysia.* Singapore: Oxford University Press, 1989.

"Jews Silenced at Canberra Talkfest." *Australian Jewish News,* March 6, 2008.

Johnson, Carol. "Howard's Values and Australian Identity." *Australian Journal of Political Science* 2 (2007): 195–210.

Jomo, K. S. *Growth and Structural Change in the Malaysian Economy.* London: Macmillan, 1990.

Joppke, Christian. *Citizenship and Immigration.* Cambridge: Polity Press, 2010.

———. "Immigration and the Identity of Citizenship: The Paradox of Universalism." *Citizenship Studies* 12, no. 6 (2008).

———. *Immigration and the Nation-State: The United States, Germany, and Great Britain.* New York: Oxford University Press, 1999.

———. "The Retreat of Multiculturalism in the Liberal State: Theory and Policy." *British Journal of Sociology* 55 (2004): 237–57.

Jordens, Ann-Mari. *Alien to Citizen: Settling Migrants in Australia, 1945–1975.* Sydney: Allen & Unwin, 1997.

Jupp, James. "A Pragmatic Solution to a Novel Situation: Australian Multiculturalism." In *Political Theory and Australian Multiculturalism,* edited by Geoffrey Brahm Levey, 225–41. New York: Berghahn Books, 2008.

Kalantzis, Mary. "Multicultural Citizenship." In *Rethinking Australian Citizenship,* edited by Wayne Hudson and John Kane. Cambridge: Cambridge University Press, 2000.

Karatani, Rieko. *Defining British Citizenship: Empire, Commonwealth, and Modern Britain.* London: Frank Cass, 2003.

Kaviraj, Sudipta. "Languages of Secularity," *Economic and Political Weekly* 48, no. 50 (December 14, 2013).

Kelly, Paul. "The Curse of the M-word." *Weekend Australian.* August 30–31, 1997.

———. "Weighed Down by the M-word." *Australian.* February 23, 2011.

Kelly, Ruth. Speech by Communities Secretary Ruth Kelly to Muslims on Working Together to Tackle Extremism, Local Government House, London, October 11, 2006.

Kelsey, Jane. *A Question of Honour: Labour and the Treaty, 1984–1989.* Wellington: Allen & Unwin, 1990.

Khilnani, Sunil. *The Idea of India.* London: Hamish Hamilton, 1997.

Kirk-Greene, Anthony Hamilton Millard. *Lugard and the Amalgamation of Nigeria: A Documentary Record.* London: Frank Cass, 1969.

Kivisto, Peter. "We Really Are All Multiculturalists Now." *Sociological Quarterly* 53, no. 1 (2012): 1–24.

Kivisto, Peter, and Thomas Faist. *Citizenship: Discourse, Theory, and Transnational Prospects.* London: Blackwell, 2007.

Kiwan, Dina. "Citizenship Education at the Cross-Roads: Four Models of Citizenship and Their Implications for Ethnic and Religious Diversity." *Oxford Review of Education* 34, no. 1 (2008), 39–58.

Kohn, Hans. *The Idea of Nationalism: A Study in Its Origins and Background.* New York: Macmillan, 1944.

Koller, John M. "Why Is Anekantavada Important?" In "*Syadvada* as the Epistemological Key to the Jaina Middle Way Metaphysics of Anekantavada," edited by Tara Sethia, *Philosophy East and West* 50, no. 3 (2000).

Kukathas, Chandran. *The Liberal Archipelago: A Theory of Diversity and Freedom.* Oxford: Oxford University Press, 2003.

Kymlicka, Will. "Ethnocultural Diversity in a Liberal State: Making Sense of the Canadian Model(s)." In *Belonging? Diversity, Recognition and Shared Citizenship in Canada,* edited by Keith Banting, Thomas J. Courchene, and F. Leslie Seidle, 39–87. Montreal: Institute for Research in Public Policy, 2007.

———. "The Essentialist Critique of Multiculturalism: Theories, Policies, Ethos." In *Multiculturalism Rethought: Interpretations, Dilemmas, New Directions,* edited by Varun Uberoi and Tariq Modood. 209–49. Edinburgh: Edinburgh University Press, 2015.

———. *Finding Our Way: Rethinking Ethnocultural Relations in Canada.* Oxford: Oxford University Press, 1998.

———. *Liberalism, Community, and Culture.* Oxford: Oxford University Press, 1989.

———. *Multicultural Citizenship: A Liberal Theory of Minority Rights.* Oxford: Clarendon Press, 1995.

———. *Multicultural Odysseys: Navigating the New International Politics of Diversity.* Oxford: Oxford University Press, 2007.

———. *Multiculturalism: Success, Failure, and the Future.* Washington, DC: Migration Policy Institute, 2012.

———. *Politics in the Vernacular: Nationalism, Multiculturalism, and Citizenship.* Oxford: Oxford University Press, 2001.

———. "The Rise and Fall of Multiculturalism? New Debates on Inclusion and Accommodation in Diverse Societies." *International Social Science Journal* 61 (2010): 97–112.

Kymlicka, Will, and Baogang He, eds. *Multiculturalism in Asia.* Oxford: Oxford University Press, 2005.

Kymlicka, Will, and Wayne Norman, eds. *Citizenship in Diverse Societies.* Oxford: Oxford University Press, 2000.

Laden, Anthony Simon. "Negotiation, Deliberation, and the Claims of Politics." In *Multiculturalism and Political Theory,* edited by Anthony Simon Laden and David Owen. 198–217. Cambridge: Cambridge University Press, 2007.

Laden, Anthony Simon, and David Owen, eds. *Multiculturalism and Political Theory.* Cambridge: Cambridge University Press, 2007.

Lal, Vinay. "The Gandhi Everyone Loves to Hate." *Economic and Political Weekly* 43, no. 40 (October 4, 2008).

Lambert, Robert. "Empowering Salafis and Islamists against Al-Qaeda: A London Counter-Terrorism Case Study." *PS: Political Science & Politics* 41, no. 1 (2008): 31–35.

Latham, Mark. "A Big Country: Australia's National Identity." Speech, Sydney, April 20, 2004.

Leach, Robert. *British Political Ideologies.* 1991. 2nd ed. London: Prentice Hall Europe, 1996.

Lee, Soo Ann. *Economic Growth and the Public Sector in Malaya and Singapore, 1948–1960.* Singapore: Oxford University Press, 1974.

Lester, Anthony. "Nailing the Lie and Promoting Equality—The Jim Rose Lecture." Speech, Runnymede Trust, October 15, 2003.

Levey, Geoffrey Brahm. "The Australian Multiculturalism Debate Today." In State of the Nation: Essays for Robert Manne, edited by Gwenda Tavan, 176–88. Melbourne: Black, 2013.

———. "Diversity, Duality and Time." In *Multiculturalism and Interculturalism: Debating the Dividing Lines,* edited by Meer, Modood, and Zappata-Barrero. 201–224. Edinburgh: Edinburgh University Press, 2016.

———. "Inclusion: A Missing Principle in Australian Multiculturalism." In *Liberal Multiculturalism and the Fair Terms of Integration,* edited by Peter J. Balint and Sophie Guérard de Latour, 109–25. New York: Palgrave Macmillan, 2013.

———. "Liberal Nationalism and the Australian Citizenship Tests." *Citizenship Studies* 18 (2014): 175–89.

———. "Multiculturalism on the Move: An Australian Perspective." In *Multicultural Governance in a Mobile World,* edited by Anna Triandafyllidou. Edinburgh: Edinburgh University Press, 2017.

———. "The Turnbull Government's Multicultural Policy: Towards a New Post-Multiculturalism." Unpublished paper. University of New South Wales, Sydney, 2018.

Levy, Jacob T. "Contextualism, Constitutionalism, and *Modus Vivendi* Approaches." In *Multiculturalism and Political Theory,* edited by Anthony Simon Laden and David Owen, 173–97. Cambridge: Cambridge University Press, 2007.

———. *The Multiculturalism of Fear.* Oxford: Oxford University Press, 2000.

Lijphart, Arend. *Democracy in Plural Societies: A Comparative Exploration.* New Haven, CT: Yale University Press, 1977.

Lim, Chong-Yah. *Economic Development of Modern Malaya.* Kuala Lumpur: Oxford University Press, 1967.

Look Lai, Walton. *Indentured Labor, Caribbean Sugar: Chinese and Indian Migrants to the British West Indies, 1838–1918.* Baltimore: Johns Hopkins University Press, 1993.

Lopez, Mark. *The Origins of Multiculturalism in Australian Politics, 1945–1975.* Melbourne: Melbourne University Press, 2000.

Lugard, Frederick D. *Dual Mandate in British Tropical Africa.* Edinburgh: William Blackwood & Sons, 1922.

Macdonald, David B. "Aboriginal Peoples and Multicultural Reform in Canada: Prospects for a New Binational Society." *Canadian Journal of Sociology* 39, no. 1 (2014): 65–86.

MacLeod, Celeste Lipow. *Multiethnic Australia: Its History and Future.* Jefferson, NC: McFarland, 2006.

Madan, T. N. *Modern Myths, Locked Minds: Secularism and Fundamentalism in India.* Delhi: Oxford University Press, 1997.

———. "Secularism in Its Place." *Journal of Asian Studies* 46, no. 4 (1987).

MacKenzie, John. "Empire and Metropolitan Cultures." In *The Oxford History of the British Empire,* vol. 3, edited by Andrew Porter, 270–93. Oxford: Oxford University Press, 1999.

Mackintosh, John P. "Federalism in Nigeria." *Political Studies* 10, no. 3 (1962): 223–47.

Macklem, Patrick. *Indigenous Difference and the Constitution of Canada.* Toronto: University of Toronto Press, 2001,

Maddox, Marion. "Secularism and Religious Politics: An Australian Exception?" Paper presented at *Secularism and Beyond—Comparative Perspectives,* University of Copenhagen, May 29–June 1, 2007.

Mahajan, Gurpreet. *Identities and Rights: Aspects of Liberal Democracy in India.* Delhi: Oxford University Press, 1998.

———. "Indian Exceptionalism or Indian Model: Negotiating Cultural Diversity and Minority Rights in a Democratic Nation-State." In *Multiculturalism in Asia,* edited by Will Kymlicka and Baogang He, 288–313. Oxford: Oxford University Press, 2005.

Mahaprajna, Acharya. *The Quest for Truth in the Context of Anekanta.* Ladnun, India: Jain Vishva Bharati Institute, 2003.

Mamdani, Mahmood. *Citizen and Subject: Contemporary Africa and the Legacy of Late Colonialism.* Princeton, NJ: Princeton University Press, 1996.

Mann, Jatinder. "The Introduction of Multiculturalism in Canada and Australia, 1960s–1970s." *Nations and Nationalism* 18, no. 3 (2012): 483–503.

———. *The Search for a New National Identity: The Rise of Multiculturalism in Canada and Australia, 1890s–1970s.* New York: Peter Lang, 2016.

Mansbridge, Jane. "What Does a Representative Do? Descriptive Representation in Communicative Settings of Distrust, Uncrystallized Interests, and Historically Denigrated Status." In *Citizenship in Diverse Societies,* edited by Will Kymlicka and Wayne Norman, 99–123. Oxford: Oxford University Press, 2000.

Mansouri, Fethi, ed. *Cultural, Religious and Political Contestations: The Multicultural Challenge.* Cham, Zug, Switzerland: Springer, 2015.

Mansouri, Fethi, and Boulou Ébanda de B'béri, eds. *Global Perspectives on the Politics of Multiculturalism in the 21st Century: A Case Study Analysis.* London: Routledge, 2014.

Mansouri, Fethi, and Juliet Pietsch. "Local Governance and the Challenge of Religious Pluralism in Liberal Democracies: An Australian Perspective." *Journal of Intercultural Studies* 32 (2011): 279–92.

Mantena, Karuna. "Another Realism: The Politics of Gandhian Nonviolence." *American Political Science Review* 106, no. 2 (2012).

Markus, Andrew. "Attitudes to Multiculturalism and Cultural Diversity." In *Multiculturalism and Integration: A Harmonious Relationship*, edited by James Jupp and Michael Clyne. Canberra: ANU Press, 2011.

Marotta, Vince. "The Ambivalence of Borders: The Bicultural and the Multicultural." In *Race, Colour and Identity in Australia and New Zealand*, edited by John Docker and Gerhard Fischer. Sydney: University of New South Wales Press, 2000.

Marquand, David. "After Whig Imperialism: Can There Be a New British Identity?" *Journal of Ethnic and Migration Studies* 21, no. 2 (1995): 183–93.

Marshall, P. J. "No Fatal Impact? The Elusive History of Imperial Britain." *Times Literary Supplement,* March 12, 1993, 8–10.

Marshall, T. H. *Citizenship and Social Class.* Cambridge: Cambridge University Press, 1950.

Mason, Andrew. "Multiculturalism and the Critique of Essentialism." In *Multiculturalism and Political Theory*, edited by Anthony Simon Laden and David Owen, 221–43. Cambridge: Cambridge University Press, 2007.

Mason, Andrew. "The Critique of Multiculturalism in Britain: Integration, Separation and Shared Identification." In *Critical Review of International Social and Political Philosophy* 21, no. 1 (2018): 22–45.

Mathew, Shaj. "Brexit Exposes Britain's Massive Inferiority Complex." *New Republic,* June 22, 2016.

Matilal, Bimal Krishna. *The Central Philosophy of Jainism (Anekanta-vada).* Ahmedabad, India: Lalbhai Dalpathbhai Institute of Indology, 1981.

McAndrew, Marie. "Quebec's Interculturalism Policy: An Alternative Vision." In *Belonging? Diversity, Recognition and Shared Citizenship in Canada*, edited by Keith Banting, Thomas J. Courchene, and F. Leslie Seidle, 143–54. Montreal: Institute for Research in Public Policy, 2007.

McGhee, Derek. *The End of Multiculturalism? Terrorism, Integration & Human Rights.* Maidenhead, England: Open University Press & McGraw-Hill Education, 2008.

———. "The Paths to Citizenship: A Critical Examination of Immigration Policy in Britain Since 2001." *Patterns of Prejudice* 43, no. 1 (2009): 41–64.

McLaughlin, Eugene, and Sarah Neal. "Misrepresenting the Multicultural Nation, the Policy-Making Process, News Media Management and the Parekh Report." *Policy Studies* 25, no. 3 (2004): 155–74.

Meer, Nasar. *Citizenship, Identity and the Politics of Multiculturalism: The Rise of Muslim Consciousness.* New York: Palgrave Macmillan, 2010, 2015.

Meer, Nasar, and Tariq Modood. "How Does Interculturalism Contrast with Multiculturalism?" *Journal of Intercultural Studies* 33, no. 2 (2012): 175–96.

———. "The Multicultural State We're In: Muslims, 'Multiculture' and the 'Civic Re-Balancing' of British Multiculturalism." *Political Studies* 57, no. 3 (2009): 473–97.

Mehta, Pratap Bhanu. "Reason, Tradition and Authority: Religion and the Indian State." In *Toleration on Trial*, ed. Ingrid Creppell, Russell Hardin, and Stephen Macedo, 193–214. Lanham, MD: Lexington Books, 2008.

Mehta, Uday S. "Gandhi on Democracy, Politics and the Ethics of Everyday Life." *Modern Intellectual History* 7, no. 2 (2010).

———. "Gujarat—Hindu Rashtra Laboratory." In *Religion, Power and Violence: Expression of Politics in Contemporary Times*, ed. Ram Puniyani. Thousand Oaks, CA: Sage, 2005.

Mikaere, Annie. "Maori Women: Caught in the Contradictions of a Colonized Reality." *Waikato Law Review* 2 (1994).

Mill, John Stuart. *Considerations on Representative Government*. London: Parker, Son, & Bourn, 1861.

Miller, David. *On Nationality*. Oxford: Oxford University Press, 1995.

Millette, James. *Society and Politics in Colonial Trinidad*. Trinidad: Zed Books, 1985.

Missen, G. "Wage Labour and the Political Economy in West Malaysia." In *Industrialisation and Labour Force Processes: A Case Study of Peninsular Malaysia*, edited by T. G. McGee et al. Canberra: Australian National University, 1986.

Modood, Tariq. *Multiculturalism*. Cambridge: Polity Press, 2007.

———. *Multicultural Politics: Racism, Ethnicity and Muslims in Britain*. Edinburgh: Edinburgh University Press, 2005.

Mookerjee, Satkari. *The Jaina Philosophy of Non-Absolutism: A Critical Study of Anekanta-vada*. Delhi: Motilal Banarsidass, 1978.

Moran, Anthony. "White Australia, Settler Nationalism and Aboriginal Assimilation." *Australian Journal of Politics and History* 51 (2005): 168–93.

Morrison, Scott. "Australia: The Land of Our Adoption." Speech, Menzies Centre for Australian Studies, January 24, 2013.

"Most Still Enjoy a Culture Cocktail." *Australian*, December 22, 2005.

Mulgan, Richard. *Maori, Pakeha and Democracy*. Auckland: Oxford University Press, 1989.

Munasinghe, Viranjini. *Callaloo or Tossed Salad? East Indians and the Cultural Politics of Identity in Trinidad*. Ithaca, NY: Cornell University Press, 2001.

———. "Creating Impurity Out of Purity: Nationalism in Hybrid Spaces." *American Ethnologist* 29, no. 3 (2002): 663–92.

———. "Culture Creators and Culture Bearers: The Interface between Race and Ethnicity in Trinidad." *Transforming Anthropology* 6, nos. 1–2 (1997): 72–86.

Myers, Samuel L., and Bruce P. Corrie, eds. *Racial and Ethnic Economic Inequality: An International Perspective*. New York: Peter Lang, 2006.

Naipaul, V. S. *The Mimic Men: A Novel*. London: André Deutsch, 1967.

Nandy, Ashis. "An Anti-Secularist Manifesto." *Seminar* 314 (1985).

———. "Gandhi after Gandhi: The Fate of Dissent in Our Times." *Little Magazine* 1, no. 1 (May 2000).

———. "The Politics of Secularism and the Recovery of Religious Tolerance." *Alternatives: Global, Local, Political* 13, no. 2 (1988).

———. "The Twilight of Certitude: Secularism, Hindu Nationalism, and Other Masks of Deculturation." *Alternatives: Global, Local, Political* 22, no. 2 (1997).

Nanda, Meera. *Breaking the Spell of Dharma and Other Essays*. New Delhi: Manohar Publishers, 2003.

———. *Prophets Facing Backward: Postmodern Critiques of Science and Hindu Nationalism in India*. New Brunswick, NJ: Rutgers University Press, 2003.

Needham, Anuradha Dingwaney, and Rajeswari Sunder Rajan, eds. *The Crisis of Secularism in India*. Durham, NC: Duke University Press, 2007.

Neville-Jones, Pauline, et al. *An Unquiet World: Submission to the Shadow Cabinet*. London: National and International Security Policy Group, 2007. Accessed November 30, 2018. http://image.guardian.co.uk/sys-files/Politics/documents/2007/07/26/securityreport.pdf.

New Zealand. Labour and Immigration Research Centre. *Migration Trends 2015/2016*. Wellington: Ministry of Business, Innovation and Employment, 2016.

———. Ministerial Advisory Committee on a Maori Perspective and John Te Rangi-Aniwaniwa Rangihau. *Puao-te-ata-tu = Day Break: The Report of the Ministerial Advisory Committee on a Maori Perspective for the Department of Social Welfare.*Wellington: Department of Social Welfare, 1986.

———. Ministry of Business, Immigration and Employment. *Community Perceptions of Migrants and Immigration: 2015 Community Survey*. Wellington: Ministry of Business, Immigration and Employment, 2015.

———. Ministry of Social Development. *Connecting Diverse Communities*. Accessed February 25, 2019. www.msd.govt.nz/documents/about-msd-and-our-work/publications-resources/research/connecting-diverse-communities/cdc-public-engagement-2007.pdf.

———. Ministry of Social Development. *The Social Report 2016*. Wellington: Ministry of Social Development, 2016.

———. Office of the Prime Minister. *Growing an Innovative New Zealand*. Wellington: Government Printer, 2002.

Nigam, Aditya. *The Insurrection of Little Selves: The Crisis of Secular-Nationalism in India*. New Delhi: Oxford University Press, 2006.

Nor, Wan Asna Wan Mohd. "Political and Economic Accommodation in Peninsular Malaysia." In *Political Economy of Development in Malaysia,* edited by B. N. Ghosh and Muhammad Syukri Salleh, 21–44. Kuala Lumpur: Utusan Publications, 1999.

Nussbaum, Martha. "Affirmative Action and the Goals of Higher Education." Paper presented at Conference on Affirmative Action in Higher Education in India, the United States and South Africa, New Delhi, March 19–21, 2008.

Okin, Susan Moller. "Is Multiculturalism Bad for Women?" In *Is Multiculturalism Bad for Women?* edited by Joshua Cohen, Matthew Howard, and Martha C. Nussbaum. Princeton, NJ: Princeton University Press, 1994.

Olssen, Mark. "From the Crick Report to the Parekh Report: Multiculturalism, Cultural Difference, and Democracy—The Re-Visioning of Citizenship Education." *British Journal of Sociology of Education* 25, no. 2 (2004): 179–92.

Omi, Michael, and Howard Winant. *Racial Formation in the United States: From the 1960s to the 1990s,* 2nd ed. New York: Routledge, 1994.

Ooi, Keat Gin. "The Japanese Occupation and the Peoples of Sarawak." In *Southeast Asian Minorities in the Wartime Japanese Empire,* edited by Paul H. Kratoska, 133–52. London: RoutledgeCurzon, 2002.

O'Reilly, Tom, and David Wood. "Biculturalism and the Public Sector." In *Reshaping the State: New Zealand's Bureaucratic Revolution,* edited by Jonathan Boston, John Martin, June Pallot, and Pat Walsh. Auckland: Oxford University Press, 1991.

Osaghae, Eghosa E. "Ethnic Minorities and Federalism in Nigeria." *African Affairs* 90 no. 359 (1991): 237–258.

———. "Federalism, Local Politics and Ethnicity in Nigeria: Do Ethnic Minorities Still Exist in Nigeria?" *Journal of Commonwealth & Comparative Politics* 24, no. 2 (1986): 151–68.

———. "Managing Multiple Minority Problems in a Divided Society: The Nigerian Experience." *Journal of Modern African Studies* 36, no. 1 (1998): 1–24.

O'Sullivan, Dominic. *Beyond Biculturalism: The Politics of an Indigenous Minority.* Wellington: Huia, 2007.

Organisation for Economic Co-operation and Development. "Foreign-Born and Foreign Populations." *OECD Factbook 2015–2016.* Paris: OECD, 2016.

———. *International Migration Outlook 2016.* Paris: OECD, 2016.

McKay, Daniel. "Uluru Statement: A Quick Guide." Research Paper Series, 2016–17, Law and Bills Digest Section. Canberra: Parliamentary Library, 2017. Accessed November 19, 2018. http://parlinfo.aph.gov.au/parlInfo/download/library/prspub/5345708/upload_binary/5345708.pdf.

Paden, John N. *Ahmadu Bello, Sardauna of Sokoto: Values and Leadership in Nigeria.* London: Hodder & Stoughton, 1986.

Padmarajiah, Y.J. *A Comparative Study of the Jaina Theories of Reality and Knowledge.* Delhi: Motilal Banarsidass, 1963.

Panayi, Panikos. *An Immigration History of Great Britain: Multicultural Racism since 1800.* New York: Pearson Longman, 2010.

Pantham, Thomas. "Thinking with Mahatma Gandhi: Beyond Liberal Democracy." *Political Theory* 11, no. 2 (1983).

Parashar, Archana. *Women and Family Law Reform in India.* New Delhi: Sage, 1992.

Parekh, Bhikhu. *Colonialism, Tradition and Reform: An Analysis of Gandhi's Political Discourse.* Thousand Oaks, CA: Sage Publications, 2003.

———. *Gandhi's Political Philosophy: A Critical Examination.* Notre Dame, IN: University of Notre Dame Press, 1989.

———. *Rethinking Multiculturalism: Cultural Diversity and Political Theory.* Cambridge, MA: Harvard University Press, 2002.

Parekh, Bhikhu (chair), et al., and Runnymede Trust. *The Future of Multi-Ethnic Britain: Report of the Commission on the Future of Multi-Ethnic Britain.* London: Profile Books, 2000.

Parel, Anthony. "Introduction." In *Gandhi, Freedom, and Self-Rule,* edited by Anthony J. Parel. Lanham, MD: Lexington Books, 2000.

Pateman, Carole. *Participation and Democratic Theory.* Cambridge: Cambridge University Press, 1970.

Pathak, Pathik. *The Future of Multicultural Britain: Confronting the Progressive Dilemma.* Edinburgh: Edinburgh University Press, 2008.

Paul, Kathleen. *Whitewashing Britain: Race and Citizenship in the Postwar Era.* Ithaca, NY: Cornell University Press, 1997.

Pearson, David. "Biculturalism and Multiculturalism in Comparative Perspective." In *Nga Take: Ethnic Relations and Racism in Aotearoa/New Zealand,* edited by Paul Spoonley, David Pearson, and Cluny MacPherson. Palmerston North, NZ: Dunmore Press, 1991.

———. "The Ties That Unwind: Civic and Ethnic Imaginings in New Zealand." *Nations and Nationalism* 6, no. 1 (2000).

Perham, Margery. "Foreword." In *Path to Nigerian Freedom,* edited by Obafemi Awolowo. London: Faber & Faber, 1947.

Peters, Winston. "The End of Tolerance." Speech, Far North Community Centre, Kaitaia, July 28, 2005. Accessed November 19, 2018. www.scoop.co.nz/stories/PA0507/S00649.htm.

Phillips, Anne. *Multiculturalism without Culture.* Princeton, NJ: Princeton University Press, 2007.

Phillips, Melanie. *Londonistan: How Britain Created a Terror State Within.* London: Gibson Square Books, 2006.

Pitcher, Ben. *The Politics of Multiculturalism: Race and Racism in Contemporary Britain.* New York: Palgrave Macmillan, 2009.

Porter, Bernard. *Absent-Minded Imperialists: Empire, Society and Culture in Britain.* Oxford: Oxford University Press, 2006.

Povinelli, Elizabeth. *The Cunning of Recognition: Indigenous Alterities and the Making of Australian Multiculturalism.* Durham, NC: Duke University Press, 2002.

Qualifications and Curriculum Authority (Great Britain). *Education for Citizenship and the Teaching of Democracy in Schools: Report of the Advisory Group on Citizenship.* Edited by Bernard R. Crick et al. London: Qualifications and Curriculum Authority, 1998.

"Query over Future of Multiculturalism." SBS News (Australia), December 3, 2013. Accessed November 19, 2018. www.sbs.com.au/news/query-over-future-of-multiculturalism.

Rahim, Lily Zubaidah. *The Singapore Dilemma: The Political and Educational Marginality of the Malay Community.* Singapore: Oxford University Press, 1999.

Rajaratnam, S. "Our Cultural Heritage." In *S. Rajaratnam on Singapore: From Ideas to Reality,* edited by Kwa Chong Guan. 1960. Singapore: World Scientific Publishing, 2006.

Rao, B. Shiva. *The Framing of India's Constitution: Select Documents.* 4 vols. Delhi: Indian Institute of Public Administration, 1967.

Raz, Joseph. *Ethics in the Public Domain: Essays in the Morality of Law and Politics.* Oxford: Clarendon Press, 1994.

Renteln, Alison Dundes. *The Cultural Defense.* Oxford: Oxford University Press, 2004.

Retzlaff, Ralph. "The Problem of Communal Minorities in the Drafting of the Indian Constitution." In *Constitutionalism in Asia,* edited by R. N. Spann, 55–73. Bombay: Asia Publishing House, 1963.

Rhodes, R. A. W. "The Hollowing Out of the State: The Changing Nature of the Public Service In Britain." *Political Quarterly* 65, no. 2 (1994): 138–51.

Rich, Paul B. *Race and Empire in British Politics.* Cambridge: Cambridge University Press, 1996.

Robb, Andrew. "The Importance of a Shared National Identity." Speech, Transformations Conference, Australian National University, Canberra, November 27, 2006.

Rodan, Garry. *The Political Economy of Singapore's Industrialization: National State and International Capital.* London: Macmillan, 1989.

Rodriguez-Garcia, Dan. "Beyond Assimilation and Multiculturalism: A Critical Review of the Debate on Managing Diversity." *Journal of International Migration and Integration* 11, no. 3 (2010): 251–71.

Ruggiu, Ilenia. *Il guidice antropologo: Costituzione e tecniche di composizione dei conflitti multiculturali*. Milan: Franco Angeli, 2012.

Rudd, Amber. Speech at the Conservative Party conference. October 4, 2016. Accessed November 19, 2018. https://blogs.spectator.co.uk/2016/10/full-text-amber-rudds-conference-speech.

Ryder, Bruce. "The Canadian Conception of Equal Religious Citizenship." In *Law and Religious Pluralism in Canada,* edited by Richard Moon, 87–109. Vancouver: University of British Columbia Press, 2008.

Safa, Helen. "Popular Culture, National Identity, and Race in the Caribbean." *New West Indian Guide* 61, nos. 3–4 (1987): 115–26.

Sageman, Marc. *Leaderless Jihad: Terror Networks in the 21st Century*. Philadelphia: University of Pennsylvania Press, 2008.

Salée, Daniel. "The Quebec State and the Management of Ethnocultural Diversity: Perspectives on an Ambiguous Record." In *Belonging? Diversity, Recognition and Shared Citizenship in Canada,* edited by Keith Banting, Thomas J. Courchene, and F. Leslie Seidle, 105–42. Montreal: The Institute for Research in Public Policy, 2007.

Salmond, Alex. "Alex Salmond: We Must Leave UK but Maintain Our Other Unions." *Herald,* July 12, 2013.

"Sarkozy Joins Allies Burying Multiculturalism." Reuters, February 11, 2011.

Schmidgen, Wolfram. *Exquisite Mixture: The Virtues of Impurity in Early Modern England*. Philadelphia: University of Pennsylvania Press, 2012.

Scott, Evelyn. "The Importance of Reconciliation for Multiculturalism." Speech, Multicultural Extravaganza Dinner, Logan Diggers Club, October 7, 2000. Indigenous Law Resources Reconciliation and Social Justice Library. Accessed November 19, 2018. www.austlii.edu.au/au/other/IndigLRes/car/2000/0710.html.

Scotland's Future. Edinburgh: Scottish Government, 2013. Accessed November 19, 2018. www2.gov.scot/Publications/2013/11/9348/0.

Segal, Daniel. "Living Ancestors: Nationalism and the Past in Postcolonial Trinidad and Tobago." In *Trinidad Ethnicity,* edited by Kevin Yelvington, 221–39. Knoxville: University of Tennessee Press, 1994.

Sen, Amartya. "Secularism and Its Discontents." In *Unravelling the Nation: Sectarian Conflict in India,* edited by Kaushik Basu and Sanjay Subrahmanyam. Delhi: Penguin, 1996.

Sethia Tara, ed. *Ahimsa, Anekanta and Jainism*. Delhi: Motilal Banarsidass, 2004.

Shachar, Ayelet. "Group Identity and Women's Rights in Family Law: The Perils of Multicultural Accommodation." *Journal of Political Philosophy* 6, no. 3 (1998): 285–305.

Sharp, Andrew. *Justice and the Māori: Māori Claims in New Zealand Political Argument in the 1980s*. Oxford: Oxford University Press, 1990.

Shatzmiller, Marya, ed. *Nationalism and Minority Identities in Islamic Societies*. Montreal and Kingston, ON: McGill–Queen's University Press, 2005.

Shue, Henry. *Basic Rights: Subsistence, Affluence, and U.S. Foreign Policy*. Princeton, NJ: Princeton University Press, 1980.

Sides, John, and Jack Citrin. "European Opinion about Immigration: The Role of Identities, Interests and Information." *British Journal of Political Science* 37 (2007): 477–504.

Sieder, Rachel, ed. *Multiculturalism in Latin America: Indigenous Rights, Diversity and Democracy.* New York: Palgrave Macmillan, 2002.

Singh, Pritam. "Hindu Bias in India's 'Secular' Constitution: Probing Flaws in the Instruments of Governance." *Third World Quarterly* 26, no. 6 (2006): 909–26.

Skaria, Ajay. "Gandhi's Politics: Liberalism and the Question of the Ashram." *South Atlantic Quarterly* 101, no. 4 (2002).

Skilling, Peter. "National Identity in a Diverse Society." In *New Zealand Government and Politics,* edited by Raymond Miller. Melbourne: Oxford University Press, 2010.

Sklar, Richard L. *Nigerian Political Parties: Power in an Emergent African Nation.* Princeton, NJ: Princeton University Press, 1963.

Smith, Katherine. "Research, Policy and Funding: Academic Treadmills and the Squeeze on Intellectual Spaces." *British Journal Of Sociology* 61, no. 1 (2010): 176–95.

Smits, Katherine. "Justifying Multiculturalism: Social Justice, Diversity and National Identity in Australia and New Zealand." *Australian Journal of Political Science* 46, no. 1 (2011).

———. "Multicultural Identity in a Bicultural Context." In *New Zealand Government and Politics,* edited by Raymond Miller. Melbourne: Oxford University Press, 2006.

———. "The Neoliberal State and the Uses of Indigenous Culture," *Nationalism and Ethnic Politics* 20, no. 1 (2014).

Smits, Katherine, and Alix Jansen. "Staging the Nation at Expos and World's Fairs." *National Identities* 14, no. 2 (2012).

Sniderman, Paul M., and Louk Hagendoorn. *When Ways of Life Collide: Multiculturalism and Its Discontents in the Netherlands.* Princeton, NJ: Princeton University Press, 2007.

Song, Sarah. *Justice, Gender and the Politics of Multiculturalism.* Cambridge: Cambridge University Press, 2007.

———. "Multiculturalism." In *The Stanford Encyclopedia of Philosophy,* ed. Edward N. Zalta. Accessed November 19, 2018. https://plato.stanford.edu/archives/spr2017/entries/multiculturalism.

Soudien, Crain. "Dealing with Race: Laying Down Patterns for Multiculturalism in South Africa." *Interchange* 25, no. 3 (1994): 281–94.

Soutphommasane, Thinethavone. *Reclaiming Patriotism.* Cambridge: Cambridge University Press, 2009.

Spalek, Basia, and Alia Imoual. "Muslim Communities and Counter-Terror Responses: 'Hard' Approaches to Community Engagement in the UK and Australia." *Journal of Muslim Minority Affairs* 27, no. 2 (2007): 185–202.

Spencer, Ian R. G. *British Immigration Policy since 1939: The Making of Multiracial Britain.* New York: Routledge, 1997.

Spinner-Halev, Jeff. "Feminism, Multicultural Oppression, and the State." *Ethics* 112, no. 1 (2001): 84–113.

Srinivasan, T. N. ed. *The Future of Secularism.* New Delhi: Oxford University Press, 2007.

Stapleton, Julia. *Public Intellectuals and Public Identities in Britain since 1850.* Manchester: Manchester University Press, 2001.

Stears, Marc. "Guild Socialism." In *Modern Pluralism: Anglo-American Debates since 1880,* edited by Mark Bevir, 40–59. Cambridge: Cambridge University Press, 2012.

Stockwell, Sarah, ed. *The British Empire: Themes and Perspectives.* Oxford: Blackwell, 2007.

Stuempfle, Stephen. *The Steelband Movement: The Forging of National Art in Trinidad and Tobago.* Philadelphia: University of Pennsylvania Press, 1996.

Suberu, Rotimi. *Federalism and Ethnic Conflict in Nigeria.* Washington, DC: United States Institute of Peace Press, 2001.

———. "Federalism in Africa: The Nigerian Experience in Comparative Perspective." *Ethnopolitics* 8, no. 1 (2009): 67–86.

Tajuddin, Azlan. *Malaysia in the World Economy (1824–2011): Capitalism, Ethnic Divisions, and "Managed" Democracy.* Lanham, MD: Lexington Books, 2012.

Tambaiah Stanley J. *Sri Lanka: Ethnic Fratricide and the Dismantling of Democracy.* London: I. B. Tauris, 1986.

Tamir, Yael. *Liberal Nationalism.* Princeton, NJ: Princeton University Press, 1993.

Tate, John. "John Howard's 'Nation' and Citizenship Test: Multiculturalism, Citizenship, and Identity." *Australian Journal of Politics and History* 55 (2009): 97–120.

Tatia, Nathmal. *Studies in Jaina Philosophy.* Banaras: Jain Cultural Research Society, 1951.

Tavan, Gwenda. *The Long, Slow Death of White Australia.* Melbourne: Scribe, 2005.

Taylor, Charles. "Deep Diversity and the Future of Canada." In *Can Canada Survive? Under What Terms and Conditions?* edited by David M. Hayne. Toronto: University of Toronto Press, 1997.

———. "Interculturalism or Multiculturalism?" *Philosophy and Social Criticism* 38 (2012): 413–23.

———. "The Politics of Recognition." In *Multiculturalism: Examining the Politics of Recognition,* edited by Amy Gutmann. Princeton, NJ: Princeton University Press, 1994.

Taylor, Kenwyn. "Multiculturalism and the Political Process in Trinidad: A Case Study." *Journal of the Department of Behavioural Sciences* [University of the West Indies, St Augustine Campus, Trinidad and Tobago] 1, no. 1 (March 2012): 99–117.

Taylor-Gooby, Peter, and Edmunde Waite. "Toward a More Pragmatic Multiculturalism? How the UK Policy Community Sees the Future of Ethnic Diversity Policies." *Governance* 27, no. 2 (2014): 267–89.

Tejani, Shabnum. *Indian Secularism: A Social and Intellectual History, 1890–1950.* Bloomington: Indiana University Press, 2008.

Thakur, Ramesh. "In Defence of Multiculturalism." In *Immigration and National Identity in New Zealand,* edited by Stuart Greif. Palmerston North, NZ: Dunmore Press, 1995.

Thomas, Paul. *Youth, Multiculturalism and Community Cohesion.* New York: Palgrave Macmillan, 2011.

Tillin, Louise. "United in Diversity? Asymmetry in Indian Federalism." *Publius: The Journal of Federalism* 37, no. 1 (2007): 45–67.

Trinidad and Tobago. Ministry of the Arts and Multiculturalism. "Rationale for Policy Framework for Multiculturalism" (2011). Accessed November 28, 2018. www.culture.gov.tt/wp-content/uploads/2015/07/2012-02-National-Multiculturalism-Policy-Framework-Rationale.pdf.

———. Ministry of Planning. *Housing and Population Census Demographic Report.* Port of Spain: Central Statistical Office, 2011.

Trouillot, Michel-Rolph. *Haiti: State against Nation: The Origins and Legacy of Duvalierism.* New York: Monthly Review Press, 1990.

True, Jacqui, and Charlie Gao. "National Identity in a Global Political Economy." In *New Zealand Government and Politics,* edited by Raymond Miller. Melbourne: Oxford University Press, 2010.

Tully, James. *Strange Multiplicity: Constitutionalism in the Age of Diversity.* Cambridge: Cambridge University Press, 1995.

———. "The Struggles of Indigenous Peoples for and of Freedom." *In Political Theory and the Rights of Indigenous Peoples,* edited by Duncan Ivison, Paul Patton, and Will Sanders. Cambridge: Cambridge University Press, 2000.

Uberoi, Varun and Tariq Modood. "Inclusive Britishness: A Multiculturalist Advance." *Political Studies* 61, no. 1 (2013): 23–41.

———, eds. *Multiculturalism Rethought: Interpretations, Dilemmas, New Directions.* Edinburgh: Edinburgh University Press, 2015.

Van de Putte, André. "Nationalism and Nation." *Ethical Perspectives* 1 (1994): 104–23.

United Kingdom. Commission on Integration & Cohesion. *Our Shared Future: Themes, Messages and Challenges: A Final Analysis of the Key Themes from the Commission on Integration and Cohesion Consultation.* London: Home Office, 2007. Accessed November 30, 2018. http://image.guardian.co.uk/sys-files/Education/documents/2007/06/14/oursharedfuture.pdf.

———. Department for Communities and Local Government. *Creating the Conditions for Integration.* London: Home Office, 2012. Accessed November 16, 2018. https://assets.publishing.service.gov.uk/government/uploads/system/uploads/attachment_data/file/7504/2092103.pdf.

———. Home Office. *Life in the United Kingdom: A Guide for New Residents.* 3rd ed. London: Home Office, 2013.

———. Home Office. *Life in the United Kingdom: A Journey to Citizenship.* London: Home Office, 2004.

———. Home Office. Office for Security & Counter-Terrorism. *Preventing Violent Extremism: A Strategy for Delivery.* London: Home Office, 2008.

———. Home Office. *Prevent Strategy.* London: Home Office, 2011.

———. Home Office. *Secure Borders, Safe Haven.* London: Home Office, 2002.

———. Home Office. *Statement of Intent: Changes to Tier 1, Tier 2 and Tier 5 of the Points Based System; Overseas Domestic Workers; and Visitors.* London: Home Office, 2012.

———. Home Office. *Strength in Diversity: Towards a Community Cohesion and Race Equality Strategy.* London: Home Office, 2004.

———. Ministry of Housing. Communities & Local Government. "Multi-faith Communities to Benefit from New £3 Million Grant," February 27, 2014. Accessed November 30, 2018. www.gov.uk/government/news/multi-faith-communities-to-benefit-from-new-3-million-grant.

———. Records of the Colonial Office. Federated Malay States Sessional Papers. Legislative Council Proceedings and Papers, Labour Commission, 1891, CO275/44,66; Federal Council Proceedings and Papers, July 9, 1913, CO576/8, B23; Legislative Council Proceedings and Papers, April 14, 1924, CO 275/111, 1924, 35; Legislative Council Proceedings and Papers, February 12, 1934, CO273/135, 18. Public Records Office, National Archives, Kew, London.

Van Koningsbruggen, Peter. *Trinidad Carnival: A Quest for National Identity.* London: Macmillan Education, 1997.

Varshney, Ashutosh. "Contested Meanings: India's National Identity, Hindu Nationalism, and the Politics of Anxiety." *Dædalus* 122, no. 3, *Reconstructing Nations and States* (Summer 1993): 227–61.

Vaughan, Olufemi. "Ethno-Regionalism and the Origins of Federalism in Nigeria." In *Democracy and Prebendalism in Nigeria: Critical Interpretations,* edited by Wale Adebanwi and Ebenezer Obadare. New York: Palgrave Macmillan, 2013.

Verma, H. S. "Secularism: Reflections on Meaning, Substance and Contemporary Practice." In *Secularism and Indian Polity,* edited by Bidyut Chakrabarty. New Delhi: Segment Books, 1990.

Vickers, Michael. *A Nation Betrayed: Nigeria and the Minorities Commission of 1957.* Trenton, NJ: Africa World Press, 2010.

Volpp, Leti. "'Obnoxious to Their Very Nature': Asian Americans and Constitutional Citizenship." *Citizenship Studies* 5, no. 1 (2001): 57–71.

Von Vorys, Karl. *Democracy without Consensus: Communalism and Political Stability in Malaysia.* Princeton, NJ: Princeton University Press, 1975.

Waitangi Tribunal. *Ko Aotearoa Tenei: A Report into Claims Concerning New Zealand Law and Policy Affecting Māori Culture and Identity.* Wellington: Legislation Direct, 2011.

Waldron, Jeremy. "Minority Cultures and the Cosmopolitan Alternative." *University of Michigan Journal of Law Reform* 25 (1991): 751–94.

Walker, Ranginui. "Immigration Policy and the Political Economy of New Zealand." In *Immigration and National Identity in New Zealand: One People, Two Peoples, Many Peoples?* edited by Stuart Greif. Palmerston North, NZ: Dunmore Press, 1995.

Walzer, Michael. *Interpretation and Social Criticism.* Cambridge, MA: Harvard University Press, 1987.

———. *On Toleration.* New Haven, CT: Yale University Press, 1997.

Ward, Stuart James. *Australia and the British Embrace: The Demise of the Imperial Ideal.* Melbourne: Melbourne University Press, 2001.

———. "Imperial Identities Abroad." In *The British Empire: Themes and Perspectives* edited by Sarah Stockwell, 219–43. Oxford: Blackwell, 2007.

———. "A Matter of Preference: The EEC and the Erosion of the 'Old Commonwealth' Relationship." In *Britain, the Commonwealth and Europe,* edited by Alex May, 156–80. New York: Palgrave Macmillan, 2001.

———. "The 'New Nationalism' in Australia, Canada and New Zealand: Civic Culture in the Wake of the British World." In *Britishness Abroad: Transnational Movements and Imperial Culture,* edited by Kate Darian-Smith, Patricia Grimshaw, and Stuart Macintyre, 231–63. Melbourne: Melbourne University Press, 2007.

———, ed. *British Culture and the End of Empire.* Manchester: Manchester University Press, 2001.

Webber, Jeremy. *Reimagining Canada: Language, Culture, Community and the Canadian Constitution.* Montreal and Kingston, ON: McGill–Queen's University Press, 1994.

Weinstock, Daniel. "Interculturalism and Multiculturalism in Canada: Situating the Debate." In *Liberal Multiculturalism and the Fair Terms of Integration,* edited by Peter J. Balint and Sophie Guérard de Latour, 91–108. New York: Palgrave Macmillan, 2013.

Weldon, Steven. "The Institutional Context of Tolerance for Ethnic Minorities: A Comparative, Multilevel Analysis of Western Europe." *American Journal of Political Science* 50, no. 2 (2006): 331–49.

Wheare, K. C. *Federal Government*. Oxford: Oxford University Press, 1963.

Whitaker, C. S., Jr. *The Politics of Tradition: Continuity and Change in Northern Nigeria, 1946–1966*. Princeton, NJ: Princeton University Press, 1970.

Whitlam, Gough. Speech, Launch of the Office of the Commissioner for Community Relations, 1975.

Williams, Melissa. *Voice, Trust and Memory: Marginalised Groups and the Failings of Liberal Representation*. Princeton, NJ: Princeton University Press, 1998.

Windschuttle, K. *The White Australia Policy*. Sydney: Macleay Press, 2004.

Wong, Sook Ching, K. S. Jomo, and Kok Fay Chin. *Malaysian "Bail Outs"? Capital Controls, Restructuring and Recovery*. Singapore: Singapore University Press Press, 2005.

Wright, Matthew, and Irene Bloemraad. "Is There a Trade-off between Multiculturalism and Socio-Political Integration? Policy Regimes and Immigrant Incorporation in Comparative Perspective." *Perspectives on Politics* 10, no. 1 (2012).

Wright, Jessica. "George Brandis to Repeal 'Bolt laws' on Racial Discrimination." *Sydney Morning Herald*. November 8, 2013.

Young, Crawford. *Ethnic Diversity and Public Policy: A Comparative Inquiry*. London: Macmillan, 1998.

Young, Iris. *Justice and the Politics of Difference*. Princeton, NJ: Princeton University Press, 1990.

Young, Robert. *Colonial Desire: Hybridity in Theory, Culture, and Race*. London: Routledge, 1995.

Zubrzycki, Jerzy. "The Evolution of the Policy of Multiculturalism in Australia." In *1995 Global Cultural Diversity Conference Proceedings*. Canberra: Department of Immigration and Citizenship, 1995.

CONTRIBUTORS

WALE ADEBANWI is a Fellow of St Antony's College, Rhodes Professor of Race Relations, and director of the African Studies Centre, School of Global and Area Studies, at Oxford University. Previously, he was a professor in the Department of African American and African Studies, University of California, Davis, and lecturer in political science at the University of Ibadan, Nigeria. He is the author of *Nation as Grand Narrative: The Nigerian Press and the Politics of Meaning* (University of Rochester Press, 2016), *Yoruba Elites and Ethnic Politics in Nigeria: Obafemi Awolowo and Corporate Agency* (Cambridge University Press, 2014), and *Authority Stealing: Anti-Corruption War and Democratic Politics in Post-Military Nigeria* (Carolina Academic Press, 2012) and the editor or co-editor of seven books, including *The Political Economy of Everyday Life in Africa: Beyond the Margins* (James Currey 2017). He a co-editor of *AFRICA: Journal of the International African Institute*.

RICHARD T. ASHCROFT is a Lecturer in the Department of Political Science at the University of California, Berkeley. Previously, he practiced as a solicitor in the Senior Courts of England and Wales. His publications include *Pluralism, National Identity and Citizenship: Britain after Brexit* and *Liberal Democracy, Nationalism and Culture: Multiculturalism and Scottish Independence*, both co-authored with Mark Bevir. He is also the co-editor with Mark Bevir of *Multiculturalism in Contemporary Britain: Policy, Law and Theory*, a special edition of the *Critical Review of International Social and Political Philosophy*, a revised and extended version of which has been published by Routledge.

ROCHANA BAJPAI is a senior lecturer in politics at SOAS, University of London. She is a founding member of the SOAS Centre for Comparative Political Thought and a co-convener of the London Comparative Political Thought Group. Prior to joining SOAS, Rochana was a junior Research Fellow in politics at Balliol College, Oxford, and the Centre for Political Ideologies. She has also held fellowships at St. Anne's College (Anna Biegun Warburg) and Wolfson College, University of Oxford. Her publications include *Debating Difference: Group Rights and Liberal Democracy in India* (Oxford University Press, 2011),

"Non-extremist Outbidding: Muslim Leadership in Majoritarian India," *Nationalism and Ethnic Politics* 24, no. 3 (2018, with Adnan Farooqui), and "Rhetoric as Argument: Social Justice and Affirmative Action in India, 1990," *Modern Asian Studies* 44, no. 4 (July 2010).

MARK BEVIR is professor of political science and director of the Center for British Studies at the University of California, Berkeley; professor in the Graduate School of Governance, United Nations University (MERIT); and distinguished research professor in the College of Arts and Humanities, Swansea University. His publications include *The Logic of the History of Ideas* (Cambridge University Press, 1999), *The Making of British Socialism* (Princeton University Press, 2011), and *A Theory of Governance* (University of California Press, 2013).

AVIGAIL EISENBERG is a professor in the Department of Political Science at the University of Victoria. In 2013–18, she was chair of the department. She has published two monographs—*Reasons of Identity: A Normative Guide to the Political and Legal Assessment of Identity Claims* (Oxford University Press, 2009) and *Reconstructing Political Pluralism* (State University of New York Press, 1995)—both of which focus on different forms of group-based politics. She has convened numerous conferences and workshops, which have resulted in several collections of research papers, the most recent of these being *Accommodation and the Crisis of Multiculturalism*, co-edited with Patti Lenard, a special issue of *Law and Ethics of Human Rights* 10, no. 2 (2016), and *Recognition versus Self-determination: Dilemmas of Emancipatory Politics* (University of British Columbia Press, 2014), co-edited with Jeremy Webber, Glen Coulthard, and Andrée Boiselle. She co-founded the Victoria Colloquium on Legal and Political Thought and the Consortium on Democratic Constitutionalism, based at the University of Victoria.

FARAH GODREJ is associate professor of political science at the University of California, Riverside. Her areas of research and teaching include Indian political thought, Gandhi's political thought, cosmopolitanism, globalization, comparative political theory, and environmental political thought. Her research has appeared in journals such as *Political Theory, Review of Politics,* and *Polity,* and she is the author of *Cosmopolitan Political Thought: Method, Practice, Discipline* (Oxford University Press, 2011). Her new work explores the intersection between politics and materiality, focusing on the role of the body in ancient and contemporary Indian traditions of thought. She was the recipient of the 2013–14 University of California President's Research Faculty Fellowship in the Humanities.

DANIEL P. S. GOH is associate professor of sociology at the National University of Singapore. He specializes in comparative historical sociology and studies state formation, race and multiculturalism, urban politics, and religion. His most recent publications include the edited volumes *Worlding Multiculturalisms: The Politics of Inter-Asian Dwelling* (Routledge, 2015), *Precarious Belongings: Affect and Nationalism in Asia* (Rowman & Littlefield, 2017), and *Urban Asias: Essays on Futurity: Past and Present* (Jovis, 2018).

GEOFFREY BRAHM LEVEY is associate professor of political science at the University of New South Wales, Sydney. He is the editor of *Authenticity, Autonomy and Multiculturalism* (Routledge, 2015, 2017); *Political Theory and Australian Multiculturalism* (Berghahn Books, 2008, 2012); *The Politics of Citizenship in Immigrant Democracies: The Experience of the United States, Canada and Australia* (Routledge, 2015, 2017), with Ayelet Shachar; and *Secularism, Religion and Multicultural Citizenship* (Cambridge University Press, 2008), with Tariq Modood.

NASAR MEER is professor of race, identity and citizenship in the School of Social and Political Sciences at the University of Edinburgh. He is the author of *Citizenship, Identity, and the Politics of Multiculturalism: The Rise of Muslim Consciousness* (Palgrave Macmillan, 2010, 2015) and *Key Concepts in Race and Ethnicity* (Sage, 2014) and the editor or co-editor of *European Multiculturalisms: Cultural, Religious and Ethnic Challenges* (Edinburgh University Press, 2012), *Racialization and Religion* (Routledge, 2014), *Multiculturalism and Interculturalism: Debating the Dividing Lines* (Edinburgh University Press, 2016), and *Islam and Modernity: Critical Concepts in Sociology* (Routledge, 2017). In 2016, he was awarded the Royal Society of Edinburgh's Thomas Reid Medal for excellence in the social sciences, and in 2017, he was elected a Fellow of the Academy of Social Sciences.

TARIQ MODOOD is professor of sociology, politics and public policy and director of the Centre for the Study of Ethnicity and Citizenship at the University of Bristol and a Fellow of the British Academy. His latest books include *Multiculturalism: A Civic Idea* (Wiley, 2007, 2013), *Still Not Easy Being British: Struggles for a Multicultural Citizenship* (Trentham Books, 2010), and as co-editor *The Problem of Religious Diversity: European Challenges, Asian Approaches* (Edinburgh University Press, 2017).

VIRANJINI MUNASINGHE is associate professor of anthropology and Asian American studies at Cornell University. She received her B.A. in social anthropology (1985) from Sussex University, England, and Ph.D. (1994) in cultural anthropology from Johns Hopkins University. She is an historical anthropologist working in the Caribbean (Trinidad) and on the Asian diaspora in the Americas. Her academic interests include nations and empire, sovereignty and citizenship, comparison, ethnic studies, and postcolonial theory. Her publications include *Callaloo or Tossed Salad? East Indians and the Cultural Politics of Identity in Trinidad* (Cornell University Press, 2001); "Redefining the Nation: The East Indian Struggle in Trinidad," *Journal of Asian American Studies* 4, no. 1 (2001): 1–34; "Nationalism in Hybrid Spaces: The Production of Impurity out of Purity," *American Ethnologist* 29, no. 3 (2002: 663–92; "Theorizing World Culture through the New World: East Indians and Creolization," *American Ethnologist* 33, no. 4 (2006): 549–62; and "Dougla Logics and Nation Building in Trinidad," *South Asian Review* 27, no. 1 (2007):182–204. She is currently working on a book entitled *Nation, Time and the Caribbean Exception,* which reconsiders the founding logics of historic nations through the lens of Caribbean historicity.

KATHERINE SMITS is associate professor in politics and international relations at the University of Auckland, New Zealand. She specializes in political theory and is the author of numerous books, articles, and chapters on liberalism (historical and contemporary), multiculturalism, identity politics, and nationalism. She is currently working on a comparative study of multiculturalism policy and discourse in Britain, Australia, and New Zealand.

Abbott, Tony, 93–94, 96

Abbott government (Australia), 87, 93–96

Abizadeh, Arash, 247

Aboriginal people: in Australia, 83–86; racial exclusion of, 84

aboriginal rights, in Canada, 68, 75, 79nn4,7–8

Abrahamic religions, 15, 155, 161–62, 165n34, 238

Absolute Truth, 153–55, 163–64nn16,19

accommodations, minority: overview, 229; based on culture, 20n19; in Canada, 13, 68, 72–75, 78; in India, 128, 136–37, 144; in New Zealand, 114; in Nigeria, 170; in Quebec, 72

Action Group (AG) (Nigeria), 171, 179–81, 186

active citizenship, 52–58

Adebanwi, Wale, 15, 167–90

Adivasis, 131, 135

affirmative action: in India, 127, 129, 135, 139, 141; Kymlicka on, 147n40; in New Zealand, 114; Race Relations Acts and, 43n38

affirmative multiculturalism, 88

Afghanistan: overview, 6; war in, 34

Africa: comparisons to, 128, 144, 217; federalism in, 172; issues in postcolonial Africa, 15; political instability in, 167. *See also* Kenya; Nigeria

African people: in Britain, 47; in New Zealand, 107; as slaves, 237; in Trinidad and Tobago, 16, 21n28, 217, 225–26n2, 234. *See also* Afro-Trinidadians

Afro-Creoles, 16, 223–24, 234, 237, 240

Afro-Trinidadians, 16, 21n28, 213, 223–26, 225n1, 232, 248n4

AG (Action Group) (Nigeria), 179–81, 186

Alberta Human Rights Act, 80n19

Alibhai-Brown, Yasmin, 47, 50

AMAC (Australian Multicultural Advisory Council), 87, 91

Ambedkar, Bhimrao (Babasaheb), 130–31, 136, 148n69

An American Dilemma (Myrdal), 43n38

anekantavāda (many-sidedness), 15, 152, 155, 161–62

Anglo-Australian identity/culture, 13, 84–88, 90–93

Anglo Indians, 129

anti-discrimination, legislation, 34, 85

anti-extremism, legislation, 35

anti-immigration: in New Zealand, 114; Thatcher and, 32–33

anti-Muslim sentiments, 48, 78

anti-racism: in Britain, 31, 33, 36, 46–47; in postwar Britain, 28–29

anti-terrorism: citizenship strategies and, 55–59; legislation, 35; war on terror, 6

Anwar Ibrahim, 207

Aotearoa. *See* New Zealand

apartheid, in South Africa and Zimbabwe, 21n27

Ashcroft, Richard T., 1–45, 229–52, 249n10, 250n12, 251n22, 252n27

Asia, comparisons to, 128, 144, 217

Mosques and Imams National Advisory Board (MINAB), 56

Mulani v Commission scolaire Marguerite-Bourgeoys, 71–74

"A Multi-cultural Society for the Future" (Grassby) (speech), 85

Multicultural Australia: United, Strong, Successful (national policy statement), 86, 96–97

Multicultural Australia: United in Diversity (national policy statement), 90

Multicultural Citizenship (Kymlicka), 250n12

multiculturalism: overview, 16–17, 38–39, 229–30; arrested multiculturalisms, 191–208; bifurcated approach to, 29, 33–34, 36, 38, 43–44n53, 174; British Commonwealth and, 7–11, 240–42; constitutional protections and, 78; contesting of, 167–90; critiques of, 20n19, 48–49, 91, 121n18; definitions of, 2–3, 146n2, 168–69, 229; liberalism, colonialism and, 236–40; in political practice, 230–33; in political theory, 233–36, 249n6, 250n14; term usage, 50; as theory and practice, 3–6, 242–48. *See also* British multiculturalism; Canadian multiculturalism; Caribbean multiculturalism; Indian multiculturalism; Malaysian federalism; Nigerian multiculturalism; Singaporean multiculturalism

Multiculturalism Act of 1988 (Canada), 69–70

multicultural literature: aspects of, 10–11; British Commonwealth and, 12–13; descriptive case studies, 8–10; normative issues, 8–11; political theory and, 8–11; on South Africa, 168

Multicultural Odysseys (Kymlicka), 250n12

"The Multicultural State We're In" (Meer and Modood), 48, 54

multinationalism, 132

multiracialism: overview, 200–201; divergence of, 192, 208; in Malaysia, 15–16, 201–3; in Singapore, 15–16, 203–5

Munasinghe, Viranjini, 16, 21n28, 212–28, 248n4

Munshi group, 183

muscular liberalism, 20n20, 35, 92, 239

Muslims: accommodations for, 54, 76; in Australia, 90, 93; in Europe, 90; extremism and, 49; in India, 127, 129, 131–34, 136, 140–44, 148nn68–69, 157–58; in New Zealand, 107, 109, 115; in Nigeria, 187n21; PET (Prevent) strategy, 56–59; reasonable accommodation and, 78

Myrdal, Gunnar, 43n38

Naipaul, V. S., 219

Nandy, Ashis, 159–60, 163n9, 164n29

National Agenda for a Multicultural Australia (national policy statement), 85–86

National Anti-Racism Strategy (Australia), 93

national cohesion, 52–54, 214

National Conference (Nigeria), 169

National Council of Nigerian Citizens (NCNC), 171–72, 178–81, 183, 186

National Front (Barisan Nasional), 202, 206–7

national identity: overview, 4, 18n7, 20n20, 25–26, 38–39, 40n4; in African states, 167; in Australia, 13, 83–84, 86–90, 92; Brexit and, 37, 231; British, 26, 40n5, 40n7, 40n8, 231, 235; British Multiculturalism after Empire and, 25–45; Cameron government, 35; in Canada, 41n12, 78; citizenship and, 52; deviations from, 61n20; in Dominions, 41n12; inclusiveness, 47; in India, 132–33, 142; in Ireland, 41n12; legislation, 28; in New Zealand, 14, 104, 106–18, 234; in Nigeria, 167; in Trinidad and Tobago, 16, 219, 222–23, 240

nationalism: Brexit and, 37; in India, 131–33, 137, 148n85; Jacobin nationalism, 178–80; liberal nationalist multiculturalism, 83–106; in Malaysia and Singapore, 15–16, 196; minority nationalism in Canada, 71; models of, 132–33; in New Zealand, 116; in Nigeria, 170; of Quebec, 71–72, 80n23; in Trinidad and Tobago, 214, 218–19, 222–23

Nationality, Immigration and Asylum Act of 2002, 52

national minorities: overview, 8, 38, 229, 231–33; in New Zealand, 109, 231; in theory and practice, 19n14. *See also* indigenous peoples; Maori people; Québécois

National Operations Council (Malaysia), 201

National Party (New Zealand), 115, 121n28

Native Authority System, 173

naturalization laws, 41n11, 52, 55

natural multiculturalism, 213

NCNC (National Council of Nigerian Citizens), 171–72, 178–81, 183, 186

Near Neighbors strategy, 59

Nehru, Jawaharlal, 134, 142–43, 158

Nehruvians, 158

Neo-Burkean nationalism, 181–84

neo-Gandhians, 159–60

neoliberalism: in Britain, 33–34; in New Zealand, 14, 106, 115, 118–19, 231

NESBs (non-English-speaking backgrounds), 85

Netherlands, 49, 83, 90

religious diversity: overview, 12; in New Zealand, 107

religious dress: *Charte des Valuers* legislation, 71, 74; *Mulani v Commission scolaire Marguerite-Bourgeoys*, 71–74; in New Zealand, 117

religious family law, in India, 127–28, 130–31, 136–37, 140, 143, 146n20, 147n43

religious freedom: in Australia, 96–97; Gandhian secularism as, 151; in India, 128, 131, 136–37, 161; protections for, 72

religious hatred, in Britain, 50

religious laws, in India, 127–28, 130–31

religious minorities: in Britain, 31, 50, 57; in India, 128–29, 134, 140–42

religious protections, in Canada, 68

reparations, 3

Report on Education of 1985, 33

resistance, 112, 170

Resource Management Act (New Zealand), 111

restricted multicultural appoach, 136–37

restricted multicultural approach, 128, 136–37

Rhodes, R. A. W., 44n58

Rhodesia, 42n22, 172. *See also* Zimbabwe

Richard Constitution, 179

Richards, Arthur, 177

riots: race riots, 29, 34–35, 192, 200–201, 209; religious riots, 158; urban riots, 48

Rose Report of 1969, 43n38

Royal Commission on the Electoral System, 111

RSS (Rashtriya Swayamsevak Sangh), 142

Rudd, Kevin, 90–91

Rudd government (Australia), 87, 90–91

Runnymede Trust, 51–52

R. v. N.S., 2012 SCC 72, 76

Sabah, 198, 207

Samoan people, 107

Saniman, Rais, 201–3

Sarawak, 198, 207

Sarkozy, Nicolas, 91, 121n18

Savarkar, V. D., 142

SBS (Special Broadcasting Service), 88

Scheduled Castes (SC), 131–33, 135, 138, 141, 148n69, 231. *See also* caste minorities

Scheduled Tribes (ST), 131–33, 135–36, 138, 141, 148n69

Schmidgen, Wolfram, 216

Scotland: Brexit and, 37; devolution in, 51; differences, 234; independence for, 26, 37–39, 40n5, 48

Scruton, Roger, 20n19, 61n20

secondary immigration, 30

secularism: in India, 128, 132–34, 136–37, 142, 144–45, 150–66; Nandy on, 164n29; understandings of, 14–15, 151, 157; Western liberal secularism, 150, 230, 238

secularism, Indian: overview, 150–51, 161–62; Gandhi's influence on, 157–61; in Gandhi's thought, 14–15, 150; Gandhi's views on, 157–61; interpreting Gandhi's writings and, 151–52; in post-independence India, 157–61, 165n48; religion as doctrinal truth (R2), 154–57; religion as truth-seeking (R1), 152–54; as religious neutrality, 158

security issues, 37, 55–56

Segal, Daniel, 218

self-governance: in India, 139; for indigenous groups, 20n19, 249n6; Kymlicka on, 250n12; minority groups and, 20n19, 249n6; in New Zealand, 109; in Nigeria, 176; rights of, 79n10, 229; in South Africa and Zimbabwe, 21n27

Semitic model of religion, 160–61, 165n35, 238

separationist multiculturalism, 88, 91

settlement processes: overview, 12; anti-terrorism and, 48; in Australia, 85; in Canada, 69; in Caribbean, 213; in New Zealand, 105–6; in Trinidad and Tobago, 217

settler colonies, white-dominated, 11, 217, 226n9

settler-Maori relations, 104–6, 109

7/7 bombings, 34, 48, 56–57

Shah Bano debate, 141

Sharples, Pita, 113

Sikhs, 107, 132, 136, 142, 148n69, 148n77

siloing of issues, 16, 230, 232, 251n22

Singapore: overview, 15–16, 191, 230, 233; corporatist multiracialism, 203–5; decolonization, 197–98; economy of, 15–16, 198; globalizing capital in, 205–8; industrialization of, 198, 203–5; race riots, 192; racial conflicts, 198–201; racial formation, 193–95; state formation in, 15–16, 191–211; state-led industrialization, 203–5

Singapore Alliance Party, 198–200, 202

Singaporean multiculturalism: overview, 191–93, 208–9; arrested multiculturalisms, 205–8; capitalist development, 200–205; colonial racial formation contradictions, 193–95; decolonization, 197–98; globalization, 205–8; multiracialisms, 200–205; political economy of racial conflict, 198–200

Skaria, Ajay, 160

Smith, Jacqui, 55

Smith, M. G., 219, 227n30

Smits, Katherine, 14, 107–26

9 780520 299320